Project Management Offices: A Practice Guide

Project Management Institute

Library of Congress Cataloging-in-Publication Data

Names: Project Management Institute issuing body
Title: Project management offices : a practice guide / Project Management Institute.
Description: Newtown Square, Pennsylvania : Project Management Institute, Inc, [2025] | Includes index. | Summary: "The Project Management Institute has created this Project Management Offices: A Practice Guide with an ambitious vision: to reshape PMOs worldwide. This comprehensive guide transcends traditional good practices, offering a forward-looking roadmap distilled from the collective wisdom of hundreds of seasoned PMO professionals across the globe. These experts, ranging from leaders of world-class PMOs in renowned organizations to esteemed consultants, bring diverse backgrounds and extensive experience in establishing, operating, and evolving PMOs. We extend our heartfelt thanks to all of these volunteers who generously contributed their time, expertise, and insights to the development and review of this guide. Their dedication and commitment have been invaluable in shaping this comprehensive resource"-- Provided by publisher.
Identifiers: LCCN 2025001772 | ISBN 9781628258226 trade paperback | ISBN 9781628258233 epub
Subjects: LCSH: Project management
Classification: LCC HD69.P75 P761684 2025 | DDC 658.4/04--dc23/eng/20250524
LC record available at https://lccn.loc.gov/2025001772

ISBN: 978-1-62825-823-3 (ebook)
ISBN: 978-1-62825-822-6 (paperback)

Published by:
Project Management Institute, Inc.
18 Campus Blvd., Ste. 150
Newtown Square, Pennsylvania 19073-3299 USA
Phone: +1 610 356 4600
PMI.org
Online Support: www.pmi.org/about/contact

The paper used in this book complies with the Permanent Paper Standard issued by the National Information Standards Organization (Z39.48—1992).

This publication has been designed with sustainability in mind, using practices that minimize paper usage and reduce environmental impact.

10 9 8 7 6 5 4 3 2 1

Preface

The Project Management Institute has created *Project Management Offices: A Practice Guide* with an ambitious vision: to reshape PMOs worldwide.

This comprehensive guide transcends traditional good practices, offering a forward-looking roadmap distilled from the collective wisdom of hundreds of seasoned PMO professionals across the globe. These experts, ranging from leaders of world-class PMOs in renowned organizations to esteemed consultants, bring diverse backgrounds and extensive experience in establishing, operating, and evolving PMOs. We extend our heartfelt thanks to all of these volunteers who generously contributed their time, expertise, and insights to the development and review of this guide. Their dedication and commitment have been invaluable in shaping this comprehensive resource.

The genesis of this guide dates back to the early 2010s, culminating in significant milestones such as the founding of the PMO Global Alliance (PMOGA) and the release of the PMO Value Ring™ methodology in 2017. PMOGA's rapid growth led to its acquisition by the Project Management Institute (PMI) in late 2023, solidifying its position as the world's largest and most respected PMO community.

As the PMI global PMO community, PMOGA continued to refine and expand the methodology through extensive feedback and innovative ideas from its members. This iterative process resulted in the new PMO Value Ring™ framework, which forms the core of this practice guide. It combines an innovative, customer-centric approach with an unwavering focus on value generation, enabling PMO professionals to tailor their approaches to specific organizational contexts.

The development of this guide began with a comprehensive literature review, encompassing diverse academic research and expert-authored books. This exploration identified key themes, challenges, and gaps in current PMO knowledge, providing a solid theoretical foundation and inspiring new concepts to address these areas. What sets this guide apart, however, is its deep roots in practical experience. Through numerous discussions, surveys, interviews, case studies, and collaborative sessions with seasoned professionals worldwide, we have gathered insights that reflect the true complexity and diversity of PMO practices.

This blend of theory and practice has resulted in a guide that is both comprehensive and immediately applicable. It challenges conventional thinking while offering tested solutions to common PMO challenges, contributing fresh, innovative insights to the field of PMO management.

Structured for accessibility, this guide ensures value for PMO professionals at all levels. Whether you are establishing a new PMO, optimizing an existing one, or evolving your PMO into a strategic powerhouse, you will find immediately applicable strategies and frameworks.

We invite you to approach this guide with the same intellectual curiosity that drove its development. Explore it thoroughly, but also consider how the insights align with or challenge your own experiences. By engaging critically and creatively with this material, you can be equipped to adapt these concepts to your unique context, furthering the evolution of PMO practices in your organization and the broader community.

Remember, the journey of PMO excellence is ongoing, and this guide is your companion. Let it inspire you to question, innovate, and elevate your PMO practices beyond the conventional. And always keep in mind: At their core, PMOs are about people—those who run them, those who benefit from them, and those whose lives are impacted by the projects they oversee.

Embark on the future of PMOs, where value creation and customer focus light the path. Your journey starts now!

Americo Pinto
PMO Global Alliance (PMOGA) Managing Director
Project Management Institute

Table of Contents

List of Figures and Tables

Figures

Tables

1

Introduction

In an era where organizational success increasingly hinges on effective project management, the role of the project management office (PMO) has never been more critical. *Project Management Offices: A Practice Guide* is designed not only to bridge the gap between theoretical knowledge and practical application but also to shape the future of PMOs.

Drawing from the collective wisdom of the global PMO community, this guide offers insights that are both innovative and deeply rooted in real-world experience. The guide addresses key challenges facing modern PMOs, such as demonstrating value; aligning with organizational vision, mission, and strategy; and fostering continuous improvement.

The objective of *Project Management Offices: A Practice Guide* is to equip PMO professionals with adaptable strategies that can be tailored to their unique organizational contexts, enabling them to transform their PMOs into strategic assets that drive measurable results and deliver effective value for their organizations. As readers journey through these pages, they will uncover a wealth of practical approaches designed to elevate their PMO's impact and navigate the intricate complexities of today's organizational landscape.

This guide equips PMO professionals with forward-thinking strategies to anticipate and prepare for the challenges and opportunities that lie ahead. By blending time-tested practices with innovative concepts, the guide provides a comprehensive roadmap for PMO excellence that not only addresses current needs but also positions PMOs as catalysts for future organizational success. This dynamic approach ensures that readers are not just solving today's problems but are also proactively shaping the strategic role of PMOs in an ever-evolving business environment.

The Target Audience for This Guide

Project Management Offices: A Practice Guide is designed to serve a diverse audience of professionals involved in or aspiring to work in PMOs. This comprehensive resource caters to individuals at various career stages and with different levels of PMO experience, ensuring that it provides value to a broad spectrum of practitioners in the field:

- **PMO leaders**, including directors, managers, and senior professionals responsible for establishing, running, or transforming PMOs may benefit from this guide. These individuals may find strategic insights and practical frameworks to enhance their PMO's effectiveness, align it with organizational goals, and drive measurable value. The guide offers them advanced strategies for navigating complex organizational dynamics, optimizing PMO performance, and positioning their PMO as a strategic asset within their organization.

- **PMO consultants** form another key audience for this guide. These professionals, who advise organizations on PMO good practices and implementation strategies, may find a wealth of information to support their consulting engagements. In addition to offering a comprehensive, up-to-date framework and tools, this guide provides a forward-looking vision for PMOs. It equips PMO consultants with cutting-edge insights that may improve their recommendations and enable them to deliver greater value to their clients.
- **Executives overseeing PMOs** may also benefit from this guide. The guide offers them a strategic perspective on how PMOs can drive organizational success, providing insights into leveraging PMOs for strategic alignment and value creation. This high-level view can help executives make informed decisions about PMO investments and strategic direction.
- **PMO team members**—the support staff working within PMOs—are another crucial target audience. The guide provides a comprehensive understanding of PMO practices and emerging trends. This knowledge enables them to contribute more effectively to their PMO's success and advance their careers within the field.
- **Project management practitioners** aspiring to transition into PMO roles may also benefit from this guide. Whether they are project managers looking to move into PMO leadership positions or professionals from other disciplines interested in PMO careers, this guide offers a thorough grounding in PMO principles and practices. The guide provides a clear roadmap for developing the skills and knowledge necessary to succeed in PMO roles.
- **PMO customers** and other professionals may also benefit from this guide, which offers detailed information to assist anyone who wants to understand how they can benefit from having a PMO that can work with and for them, as well as how they can work with and support a PMO.

By catering to this diverse audience, *Project Management Offices: A Practice Guide* aims to elevate PMOs and develop PMO professionals worldwide. It serves as a comprehensive resource that PMO professionals can return to throughout their careers, finding relevant insights and strategies as they progress and take on new challenges in the dynamic field of PMOs and PMO leadership.

The Source of the Knowledge in This Guide

The knowledge encapsulated in *Project Management Offices: A Practice Guide* comes from a rich tapestry of sources, blending innovative research with time-tested practical experience. This comprehensive approach ensures that the guide offers both theoretical depth and real-world applicability, making it an invaluable resource for PMO professionals at all levels.

This guide is the product of a rigorous and comprehensive methodology that combines extensive research, practical experience, and collaborative input from hundreds of seasoned PMO practitioners and experts from dozens of countries. These contributors have been part of the global PMO community for more than a decade, playing a vital role in developing this material.

Project Management Offices: A Practice Guide is founded on a robust foundation of academic and business research, underpinned by a comprehensive literature review, to ensure that the concepts presented are anchored in solid theoretical frameworks. The bibliography section offers readers an extensive compilation of books and academic articles related to the topics discussed in this guide, providing additional resources for deeper study and understanding of certain aspects that are presented more concisely in the following sections.

To complement this foundation, hundreds of experienced PMO professionals participated in surveys and interviews, including PMO leaders, consultants, team members, and executives across the globe. Bringing together their multiple perspectives on current practices, challenges, and future trends, the guide addresses the most pressing concerns of today's PMO professionals.

An expert panel of thought leaders from project management and adjacent fields engaged in insightful debates and discussions, challenging assumptions and refining concepts to incorporate perspectives from areas that are traditionally outside of project management, such as customer experience, which is central to the framework proposed in this guide. Exploring the intersection of these diverse fields through collaborative discussions helped to develop a holistic approach that rethinks the PMO's role in driving organizational success while ensuring that these recommendations are both innovative and grounded in real-world applicability.

To further strengthen the guide's foundation, an in-depth analysis was conducted of dozens of PMOs that excelled in recent annual PMO Global Awards—the largest and most prestigious awards program recognizing PMO excellence worldwide, originally created by the PMO Global Alliance and now part of the Project Management Institute. By examining these high-performing PMOs alongside those facing significant challenges, the guide distills key lessons and practices that form the core of this area, capturing emerging trends and future directions.

Dozens of workshops with PMO professionals were conducted over a period of 6 years to test, validate, and refine the ideas that form the frameworks presented in this guide. This hands-on approach ensures that recommendations are not only theoretically sound but also practically implementable. In fact, many aspects of the framework have been utilized by PMOs around the world long before the publication of this guide.

Finally, this guide was reviewed by an extensive group of experienced PMO professionals from various countries and industries. This process allowed thousands of professionals from the global project management community to provide valuable feedback.

By employing this multifaceted methodology, *Project Management Offices: A Practice Guide*, a resource deeply rooted in practical experience and collaborative engagement, has been developed. This guide is much more than just a compilation of existing knowledge; it is a trusted, up-to-date, and future-oriented resource that provides PMO professionals at all levels with insights and strategies that can be immediately applied to enhance PMO performance and drive organizational success.

The Innovative Edge of This Guide

Project Management Offices: A Practice Guide represents a significant leap forward in PMO management practices, offering a fresh, innovative approach that sets it apart from traditional approaches. Its relevance and unique contributions make it an indispensable tool for PMO professionals navigating the complexities of modern organizational environments.

Firstly, this guide introduces a paradigm shift in how PMOs are conceptualized and operated. Moving beyond the traditional view of PMOs as mere administrative entities, it presents a dynamic, value-driven model that positions PMOs as strategic partners in organizational success. This shift is crucial in today's fast-paced business environment, where PMOs must continually demonstrate their value and adaptability.

A key innovation of this guide is its customer-centric approach to PMO management. Unlike many existing resources that focus primarily on functions, services, processes, and methodologies, this guide emphasizes understanding and meeting the needs of PMO customers within the organization. It provides frameworks for identifying customer needs, tailoring PMO services, and measuring customer satisfaction, enabling PMOs to become more responsive and valuable to their organizations.

The guide introduces a sophisticated maturity model specifically designed for PMO services. This model goes beyond simple, stage-based progressions, offering a multidimensional framework that allows PMOs to assess and develop their capabilities across various services. This nuanced approach to maturity enables PMOs to evolve in a more targeted and effective manner.

Another unique aspect is the guide's integration of agile principles into PMO operations. While many resources treat traditional and agile approaches as mutually exclusive, this guide offers an innovative approach for creating an agility-driven PMO that can support both predictive and adaptive project environments. This flexibility is crucial for PMOs operating in diverse organizational contexts.

The guide also breaks new ground in its approach to measuring and communicating PMO value. It introduces the concept of "perception of value" for PMOs—advanced metrics and valuation techniques that go beyond traditional project success measures—helping PMOs articulate their contributions to strategic organizational goals. This is particularly relevant in an era where PMOs are increasingly expected to justify their existence and demonstrate tangible business impact, becoming a strategic investment for the future and not just a "cost center."

The guide stands out in its visionary perspective. It not only addresses current challenges but also prepares PMO professionals for emerging trends and future scenarios. It provides strategies for creating flexible PMO structures that can quickly pivot in response to changing organizational needs or external pressures. This adaptability is crucial in today's volatile business environment.

Project Management Offices: A Practice Guide is highly relevant to today's PMO professionals because it addresses the evolving challenges they face while providing innovative solutions and forward-looking strategies. By embracing the concepts and strategies presented in this guide, PMO professionals can transform their PMOs into dynamic, value-driven entities that are indispensable to their organizations' success.

2

How to Read This Guide

Project Management Offices: A Practice Guide has been designed to provide a comprehensive and interconnected understanding of modern PMO management. Each section builds upon the previous sections and sets the stage for those that follow, creating a cohesive narrative and an integrated knowledge structure.

While each section of this guide focuses on specific aspects of PMO management, reading the entire guide from beginning to end is strongly recommended to fully grasp the logical progression of concepts, understand the interconnections among different elements, and appreciate the overarching mindset underpinning the recommended practices, thereby offering maximum benefit.

The indications listed in this section can be used as a quick reference guide, allowing professionals to revisit specific sections as needed in practice. This approach can help professionals apply concepts effectively and understand how each element contributes to a high-performance PMO.

PMO professionals should consider the broader context when applying information from any specific section. Success in implementing and managing PMOs depends on a holistic approach that integrates all aspects discussed in this guide.

The purpose of each section is summarized as follows.

Part 1—Building a New PMO Mindset

- **Section 3—Understanding the PMO.** This section provides a foundational understanding of PMOs, essential for newcomers and those seeking to refresh their knowledge on their evolving role in modern organizations. The section offers a historical perspective on PMO evolution, an updated definition, and a comprehensive overview of traditional PMO types, which the guide challenges with a more flexible and adaptive approach.

  Key insights:

  - PMOs are organizational entities that centralize portfolio, program, and project management activities.
  - PMOs have evolved from administrative support to strategic partners in organizational success.
  - The role and structure of PMOs may vary based on organizational needs and maturity.

- **Section 4—Navigating Organizational Landscapes.** This section offers insights into various organizational contextual scenarios where PMOs can exist. It is valuable for PMO professionals aiming to identify their organization's current contextual scenario and understand associated challenges and opportunities when designing, establishing, or operating PMOs. The section also explores how PMOs transition between scenarios and how to recognize signs of impending changes.

  Key insights:

  - Eight organizational contextual scenarios are identified: potential, kickoff, growing, thriving, crisis, decline, collapse, and resurgence.
  - Each scenario requires different PMO strategies and approaches.
  - PMOs should adapt to changing organizational contexts to remain effective.

- **Section 5—The PMO as a Value-Driven Service Provider.** This section introduces a transformative PMO mindset that combines service orientation, agility, and a strong focus on value. The section redefines PMOs as adaptive service providers, integrates agility principles to enhance responsiveness, and addresses the challenge of demonstrating the PMO's value.

  Key insights:

  - The shift from a process-centric to a customer-centric, value-driven approach is highlighted.
  - A focus on delivering tangible benefits to the organization is critical.
  - Agility-driven PMO concept: The PMO should be able to adapt to changing needs and environments.

- **Section 6—Embracing PMO Customer Centricity.** This section delves into the core of a customer-centric PMO. From understanding PMO customer types to identifying desired outcomes, the section provides crucial insights for PMO success, offering strategies for customer segmentation and prioritization and exploring the 30 most common PMO outcomes.

  Key insights:

  - Identify and prioritize PMO customers and their needs.
  - Details for the 30 most common potential outcomes (benefits) from a PMO are provided.
  - PMOs should tailor services to meet specific customer expectations.
  - PMOs should continuously gather and act on customer feedback.

- **Section 7—PMO Services and PMO Maturity.** This section presents a comprehensive list of the 26 most common strategic, tactical, and operational PMO services across portfolio, program, and project domains. The section introduces flexible service approaches that adapt to varying needs and challenges traditional PMO maturity concepts, offering a more nuanced understanding based on service efficiency and alignment with evolving customer needs.

  Key insights:

  - The 26 most common PMO services across strategic, tactical, and operational levels are provided.

- PMO service approaches are detailed: consultative, supportive, facilitation, directive, controlling, and managed.
- PMO maturity focuses on improving service sophistication and effectiveness.

- **Section 8—PMO Competence Model.** This section explores the 30 core competencies that PMO professionals should have to excel in their roles and how they can be applied to different PMO competency domains (design, operation, and improvement). The section provides guidance on assessing current competency levels, identifying gaps, and developing targeted improvement plans. This information is particularly valuable for PMO leaders aiming to build high-performing teams and ensure their PMO remains a strategic asset to the organization.

  Key insights:

  - The 30 core competencies for PMO professionals are explained.
  - PMO professionals should align competencies with PMO services and organizational needs.
  - Tips for developing strategies for ongoing PMO team skill enhancement are provided.

Part 2—The PMO Value Ring™ Framework

- **Section 9—Framework Overview.** This section provides an overview of the PMO Value Ring™ framework, a new PMI model for creating and operating value-driven, customer-centric PMOs. The section presents a future-proof, holistic approach to PMO management that emphasizes continuous value delivery and alignment with organizational needs, which is crucial for transforming PMO operations into strategic assets.

  Key insights:

  - A customer-centric approach to PMO design and operation is outlined.
  - Five key elements are detailed: PMO customer, organizational baseline elements, PMO structural components, PMO customer experience cycle, and the value-generating PMO flywheel.
  - An emphasis on continuous value delivery and alignment with organizational needs is essential.

- **Section 10—The Organizational Baseline Elements.** Building on the PMO Value Ring™ framework, this section explores the foundational elements influencing PMO design and operation. The section examines how organizational strategy, structure, culture, and industry context impact PMO effectiveness and offers strategies to align PMO practices with these baseline elements.

  Key insights:

  - Organizational strategy guides PMO alignment with business objectives.
  - Organizational structure influences PMO positioning and authority.
  - Organizational culture and maturity affect the PMO approach and acceptance.
  - An industry-specific profile shapes PMO practices based on industry characteristics.

- **Section 11—The PMO Structural Components.** This section delves into the PMO structural components, the essential building blocks of an effective PMO within the PMO Value Ring™ framework. The section guides professionals in developing clear mandates, robust strategies, and effective governance frameworks, establishing a solid foundation for PMOs and setting the stage for effective service delivery and value creation.

  Key insights:

  - The PMO mandate defines the purpose, responsibilities, and authority of the PMO.
  - PMO governance establishes decision-making processes and accountability.
  - PMO strategy outlines how the PMO will deliver value over time.

- **Section 12—The PMO Customer Experience Cycle.** This section introduces a new approach to PMO management, placing the customer at the center. The section presents the five stages of the PMO customer experience cycle within the PMO Value Ring™ framework: exploration, design, deployment, enhancement, and realization, which are crucial for creating customer-centric, value-driven PMOs.

  Key insights:

  - The five stages of the PMO customer experience cycle are outlined: exploration, design, deployment, enhancement, and realization.
  - An iterative process focused on continuous improvement and value delivery is critical.
  - An emphasis on ongoing customer engagement and feedback is essential.

Part 3—Diving Into the Value-Generating PMO Flywheel

- **Section 13—Flywheel Overview.** This section introduces a dynamic model to operationalize the PMO customer experience cycle, forming the heart of the PMO Value Ring™ framework. The section explains the value-generating PMO flywheel model and how its steps interact to enable continuous value creation for PMO customers. Strategies to implement the model and overcome common obstacles are offered.

  Key insights:

  - The value-generating PMO flywheel is a 10-step model for operationalizing the PMO customer experience cycle.
  - The value-generating PMO flywheel builds momentum for continuous value creation.
  - An emphasis on the interconnectedness of PMO activities is essential.

- **Section 14—Step 1: Awareness Building.** This section explores the first step of the value-generating PMO flywheel, focusing on educating and developing the maturity of PMO customers. The section offers strategies for creating awareness about the PMO's role, capabilities, and value, enhancing understanding of the PMO's potential within the organization.

  Key insights:

  - Educating stakeholders about PMO capabilities and value is critical.
  - Establishing regular communication channels is a key to PMO success.
  - Creating a PMO brand within the organization enhances effectiveness.

- **Section 15—Step 2: Needs Assessment.** This section covers the second flywheel step and provides techniques for conducting practical needs assessments. The section offers strategies to uncover underlying challenges and opportunities beyond the stated needs, creating a solid foundation for effective service delivery and value creation in PMOs.

  Key insights:

  - Identifying customer pain points and expectations leads to enhanced PMO effectiveness.
  - Using outcome-based language to understand the true needs of customers is essential.
  - Prioritizing needs based on organizational impact is a critical success factor.

- **Section 16—Step 3: Value Proposition.** This section details the third flywheel step, guiding professionals in articulating clear, compelling statements of PMO value. The section explores key elements of effective PMO value propositions, which are crucial for driving engagement with PMO services and positioning the PMO as a strategic organizational partner.

  Key insights:

  - Guidance for articulating how the PMO will address identified needs is provided.
  - Aligning PMO services with customer expectations is a key success factor.
  - Developing a compelling narrative and proposal of PMO value helps to gain overall support for the PMO.

- **Section 17—Step 4: Service Development.** Focusing on the fourth flywheel step, this section explains how to create, refine, and evolve value-driven PMO services. The section covers key stages of the service development process, offering strategies for customer involvement and ensuring flexibility in service design.

  Key insights:

  - Creating or refining PMO services based on identified needs is essential.
  - Guidance on establishing service delivery approaches and performance indicators is provided.
  - Aligning resources and competencies with service requirements is a key success factor.

- **Section 18—Step 5: Service Onboarding.** This section, covering the fifth flywheel step, provides insights on effectively introducing new or improved PMO services. The section offers strategies for change management and measuring onboarding success, ensuring smooth adoption and early value realization of new PMO services.

  Key insights:

  - Guidance for introducing new or improved services to PMO customers is provided.
  - Providing training and support for PMO service adoption is essential.
  - Managing changes associated with new PMO service implementation is a key element for success.

- **Section 19—Step 6: Service Operation.** Detailing the sixth flywheel step, this section focuses on effective practices for managing day-to-day PMO service delivery. The section covers vital aspects of successful service operations, emphasizing consistent, high-quality execution in realizing the PMO's value proposition. The section also highlights the importance of integrating feedback, maintaining operational efficiency, and leveraging technology to enhance service reliability and customer satisfaction.

  Key insights:

  - Guidance on the day-to-day management of PMO services is provided.
  - Executing service-level agreements (SLAs) is a key to PMO success.
  - Managing resources and workload effectively is essential.

- **Section 20—Step 7: Service Monitoring.** This section explores the seventh flywheel step, discussing effective tracking, measurement, and analysis of PMO service performance. The section covers key elements of successful PMO service monitoring and strategies for defining key performance indicators (KPIs) to measure service efficiency in delivering agreed-upon service levels.

  Key insights:

  - Recommendations for tracking PMO service performance against established metrics are provided.
  - Guidance for ensuring compliance with SLAs is detailed.
  - Gathering data for continuous improvement contributes to PMO success.

- **Section 21—Step 8: Service Improvement.** Covering the eighth flywheel step, this section focuses on enhancing PMO services by improving their maturity and sophistication to increase the chances of delivering the promised value to PMO customers. The content is essential for PMO professionals who want to understand the key aspects of effective service improvement. The section is particularly valuable for professionals seeking strategies for analyzing and monitoring data, identifying improvement opportunities, and measuring the impact of improvements. These skills are crucial for those aiming to maintain PMO relevance and value through ongoing service maturity enhancement.

Key insights:

- Enhancing PMO service maturity and effectiveness is critical to a PMO's success.
- Implementing changes based on performance data and PMO customer feedback is an effective improvement strategy.
- Continuously aligning PMO services with evolving customer and organizational needs contributes to a PMO's overall effectiveness.

- **Section 22—Step 9: Value Delivery.** This section explores the ninth flywheel step, focusing on realizing and demonstrating tangible PMO benefits. The section covers key elements of successful value delivery and effective strategies for communicating PMO value, which are crucial for justifying the PMO's existence and securing ongoing organizational support.

  Key insights:

  - Realizing and demonstrating tangible benefits of PMO services is essential.
  - The importance of quantifying the PMO's impact on organizational success is discussed.
  - Recommendations for communicating value to stakeholders effectively and implementing changes based on performance data and PMO customer input are provided.

- **Section 23—Step 10: Value Recognition.** Covering the final value-generating PMO flywheel step, this section ensures that delivered PMO value is acknowledged and leveraged. It explores key aspects of successful value recognition, offering strategies for building awareness of PMO contributions, facilitating customer acknowledgment, enhancing PMO credibility, and creating a positive feedback loop.

  Key insights:

  - Guidance on ensuring customers acknowledge and appreciate the PMO's value is provided.
  - Recommendations for developing strategies to enhance value perception are detailed.
  - Creating a positive feedback loop for ongoing PMO support is essential for PMO success.

- **Section 24—Conclusion**

Part 4—Appendices

- **Appendix X1—Contributors and Reviewers**
- **Appendix X2—PMO Customer Expectation Assessment.** This section provides a comprehensive assessment for systematically evaluating and understanding PMO customer needs and expectations regarding the outcomes generated by the PMO. The section includes recommendations from the global PMO community on how to translate customer expectations into effective, actionable services, ensuring that the PMO remains aligned with the evolving needs of its customers and the organization.

Key insights:

- Systematically evaluating customer needs and expectations is key.
- Using standardized assessments to gather PMO customers' expectations regarding the outcomes that should be generated by the PMO is essential.
- Aligning PMO services with identified customer priorities helps ensure PMO success.

- **Appendix X3—PMO Service Maturity Assessment.** This section provides a comprehensive assessment to evaluate PMO service maturity. The section introduces a detailed maturity model with five levels that allow PMOs to assess their current capabilities across the 26 most common PMO services. The content covers key aspects of conducting the PMO maturity assessment, interpreting results, and using these insights to drive targeted improvements.

  Key insights:

  - Using standardized assessments to evaluate PMO service maturity helps to ensure the PMO is performing as planned.
  - Using the maturity model to guide PMO service improvement is a key success factor.
  - Recommendations for establishing action plans to evolve PMO service maturity are provided.

- **Appendix X4—Critical Competency Profiles for PMO Service Delivery.** This section provides an in-depth analysis of the most critical competencies—selected from 30 core competencies—that are essential for the effective delivery of each of the 26 most common PMO services. Based on the collective experience and insights of the global PMO community, this list highlights the competencies deemed most crucial for effectively delivering each service.

  Key insights:

  - Focusing on key competencies enhances performance where it matters most, improving service outcomes.
  - Aligning skill development with services equips professionals to meet demands, significantly improving results.
  - Using this competency profile as a practical guide enables PMO professionals to focus their skill development on areas that will most enhance their service delivery.

Part 1

Building a New PMO Mindset

3

Understanding the PMO

Why This Section Matters to PMO Professionals

For PMO professionals, a deep understanding of the PMO's nature, evolution, and diversity is not just academic knowledge—it is a critical foundation for success. This section is essential because it provides the context necessary to navigate the complex and ever-changing landscape of PMOs in modern organizations.

Firstly, this section provides a historical context that helps to appreciate how PMOs have transformed from their inception to their current form. This knowledge allows PMO professionals to better understand the core functions and roles that PMOs have played over the decades and how these have been influenced by changing business needs and technological advancements.

Secondly, recognizing the diverse paths of PMO development highlights the importance of adaptability and customization. By studying these variations, PMO professionals can gain insights into how PMOs can be tailored to meet specific organizational requirements and cultural contexts.

Lastly, this section provides a rich repository of ideas and practices that professionals can draw from. It highlights the benefits and limitations of various approaches and encourages a more flexible, hybrid approach tailored to the specific needs of the organization. This flexibility is key to maintaining relevance and effectiveness in rapidly changing business environments.

Defining the PMO

In recent years, the PMO has become a significant aspect of leading organizations across the globe. As businesses face increasingly complex challenges and a rapidly changing global economic environment, PMOs have emerged as crucial for ensuring project success and driving organizational strategy.

For at least four decades, PMOs have been defined as management entities that standardize the project-related governance processes and facilitate the sharing of resources, methodologies, tools, and techniques to maximize the return on project investments.[1] However, the role of PMOs has

[1] Project Management Institute (PMI). (2024). *PMI Lexicon of Project Management Terms—Version 4.0.* PMI.

evolved far beyond this basic definition. Modern PMOs are increasingly becoming dynamic and adaptable entities that are crucial in aligning project outcomes with organizational objectives, fostering innovation, and driving business value.

The significance of PMOs in today's business environment is immense. As organizations increasingly rely on projects to implement strategy and drive change, PMOs serve as the crucial link between executive vision and operational execution. They can operate at strategic, tactical, or operational levels, becoming invaluable partners to their customers and empowering leaders to achieve success.

However, it is important to note that PMOs are not one-size-fits-all entities. Their structure, function, and focus vary significantly based on organizational needs, industry context, and maturity levels. In the vast landscape of project management literature, the PMO emerges as a concept with myriad interpretations. While consensus exists on its fundamental nature—a centralized team or department within an organization—the specifics of its functions and scope vary widely.

A common confusion occurs when people refer to the PMO leader as "the PMO," which is conceptually incorrect unless they are referring to a "project management officer," a title that is not commonly used for professionals leading PMOs. Typically, these leaders are referred to as managers, coordinators, or directors, depending on the PMO's characteristics. Referring to the PMO as a single individual minimizes the significant impact it has on organizational performance. The PMO as an entity ensures that projects are managed effectively and aligned with business objectives, while the PMO leader is just one part of this larger system. It is crucial to differentiate between the PMO as an organizational entity and the PMO leader as the individual who manages and leads its functions.

Some definitions emphasize the PMO's role in standardizing processes and methods, while others highlight its function in supporting projects and project managers. More strategic interpretations position the PMO as a key player in portfolio management. Occasionally, though less commonly, the PMO is described as the central hub for project management despite project managers often being dispersed across various business units.

Amid this diversity of perspectives, one common thread persists: The PMO is invariably a formal organizational entity dedicated to managing portfolios, programs, and projects. However, its precise purpose, scope, and responsibilities can differ significantly from one organization to another.

Rather than attempting to craft an all-encompassing definition, it is more pragmatic to acknowledge this inherent diversity. Thus, we propose a simple yet flexible PMO definition:

> *PMOs are organizational entities, typically established as departments or teams, primarily tasked with centralizing activities related to the management of portfolios, programs, and/or projects. The nature of these activities can vary according to the unique needs of each organization.*

While not always called project management offices, some organizational units serve the same purpose under different names. These entities align with the core PMO definition by performing common PMO functions and sharing similar objectives.

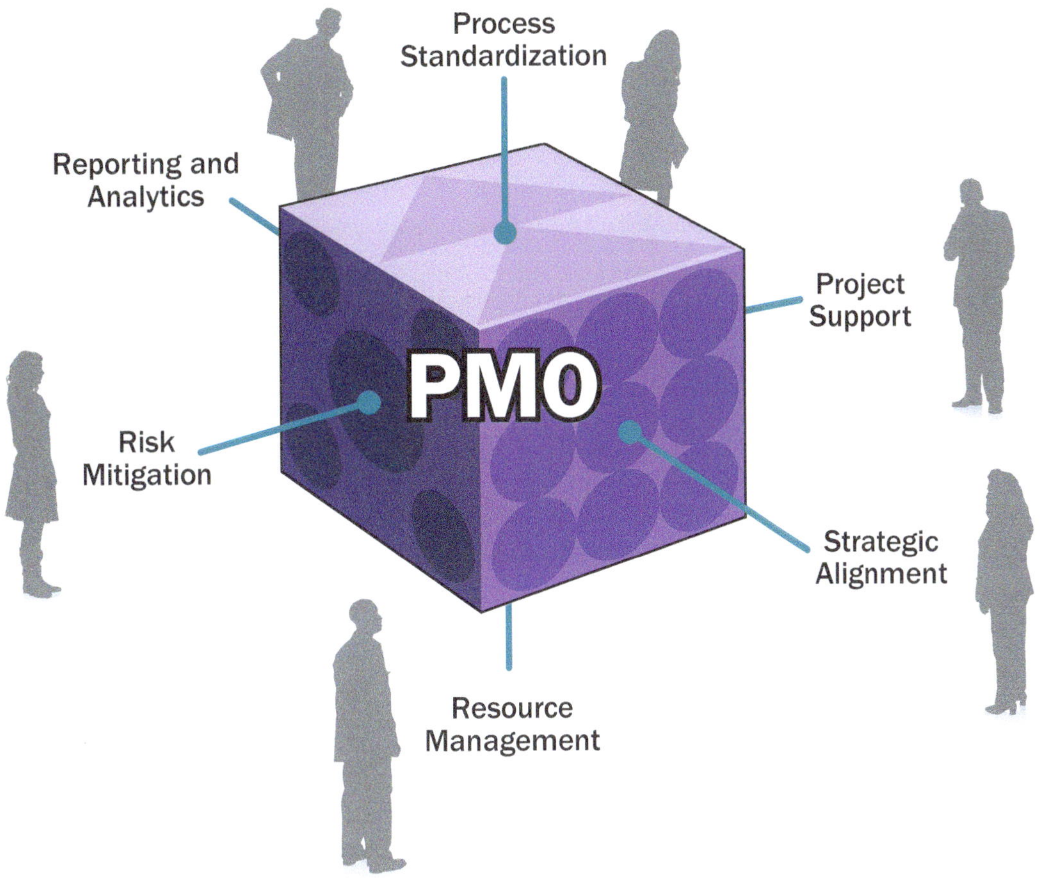

Figure 3-1. Different PMO Viewpoints

To illustrate the multifaceted nature of PMOs, consider a cube with each of its six sides presenting one component of a concept. When combined, the six concepts form a fuller picture of the cube and what it represents. If there are six people, each one looking at only one side of the cube, they will each have a limited perception of what the full cube represents. But when combining their knowledge, they gain a better picture of the cube as a whole (see Figure 3-1).

This example serves as an apt metaphor for understanding PMOs. As each individual's perception of the cube is correct yet incomplete, so are the various perspectives on PMOs. Each viewpoint captures a valid aspect of what a PMO can be, but none encapsulates its full potential.

PMO professionals, like those viewing only one side of the cube, often focus on specific aspects of PMO functionality based on their experiences and areas of expertise. Some may emphasize process standardization, others project support, and others strategic alignment. While each perspective is valid, it represents only a part of the PMO's potential scope.

Organizations are not static entities. They move, evolve, grow, and face new challenges. A PMO that remains rigidly focused on one aspect of its potential functionality risks becoming less effective over time.

For instance, a PMO initially established to enforce project management standards may need to pivot toward portfolio management and strategic alignment as the organization matures. Recognizing and adapting to these changing needs is paramount for PMO success.

The example of the cube underscores the importance of recognizing and integrating diverse perspectives in understanding PMOs. It highlights that PMOs can and should be different, adapting to their organization's specific needs and contexts.

PMO professionals should remain aware that their current perspective, while valuable, is part of a larger, dynamic whole. As the organizational context shifts, so must the PMO's approach, ensuring it continues delivering value and supporting strategic objectives effectively.

In essence, the key to PMO success lies in embracing this diversity and maintaining the flexibility to adapt. By doing so, PMOs can remain relevant, effective, and valuable assets in the ever-changing landscape of modern organizations.

This guide explores the multifaceted nature of PMOs; their evolving role in modern organizations; and good practices for establishing, operating, and improving effective PMOs. By understanding the critical role of PMOs in today's business context, PMO professionals can better position themselves to drive organizational success and navigate the complexities of modern project management.

Understanding PMO Challenges

The evolving landscape of project management presents numerous challenges for PMOs in today's organizations. These challenges are diverse and complex, ranging from strategic alignment issues to technological disruptions, and addressing them is crucial for PMOs to remain relevant and valuable in the modern business environment.

One of the primary challenges that PMOs face is demonstrating tangible value to the organization. In an era of lean operations and budget scrutiny, PMOs are under increasing pressure to justify their existence by showing how they contribute to the bottom line. This challenge is compounded by the difficulty in quantifying the often-intangible benefits of effective project management, such as improved decision-making and risk mitigation.

Another significant challenge is adapting to the rapid pace of technological change. As new technologies emerge, such as artificial intelligence (AI), PMOs should continuously evolve to incorporate these innovations while ensuring consistency across the organization. This balancing act between innovation and stability is a constant struggle for many PMOs.

Strategic alignment also remains a persistent challenge. PMOs should ensure that programs and projects are executed efficiently and contribute meaningfully to organizational goals. This effort requires a deep understanding of business strategy and translating it into actionable project portfolios.

A 2023 research-based thought leadership report from the Project Management Institute suggested that PMOs with increasingly strategic roles can generate more value for their organizations.[2] However, securing a seat on the executive board and gaining the trust of senior management remains a significant challenge for many PMOs, which are still often viewed by executives as tactical and operational areas rather than strategic assets.

This challenge persists not only because PMOs may need to position themselves adequately within their organizations but also because, in many cases, low organizational maturity in project management prevents executives from fully recognizing the potential value offered by the PMO. This lack of value recognition creates a complex dynamic where PMOs struggle to elevate their status and influence within the organization despite their potential to drive significant strategic value.

PMOs face the dual challenge of demonstrating their strategic value while simultaneously educating and influencing organizational leaders about the broader impact of effective project management. This effort requires PMOs to develop sophisticated communication strategies that can articulate their value proposition in terms that resonate with executive leadership, often translating project management outcomes into business impacts and strategic advantages.

Moreover, PMOs should navigate the delicate balance of providing immediate, tangible benefits while also working toward long-term strategic alignment and organizational maturity. Obtaining this balance often involves a gradual process of building credibility through consistent value delivery, coupled with ongoing efforts to raise awareness about project management's strategic potential.

Decoding the PMO: From Origins to Modern Adaptability

The PMO has a rich history of continuous evolution, reflecting the ever-changing needs of businesses and the increasing significance of project management. Over time, these organizational units have evolved from merely providing technical support to becoming key strategic players in today's business environment.

It should be noted that the evolution of PMOs globally has not followed a uniform path. Their development has differed significantly across different regions and industries due to influences such as local organizational cultures and maturity levels. Whereas some areas now boast widespread PMO sophistication in their business landscape, others are still at the early stages of this journey, with much room for growth and refinement in their PMO practices.

---

[2] Project Management Institute (PMI). (2023, March). *The Evolution of PMOs: Delivering Value Through xMOs*. PMI.

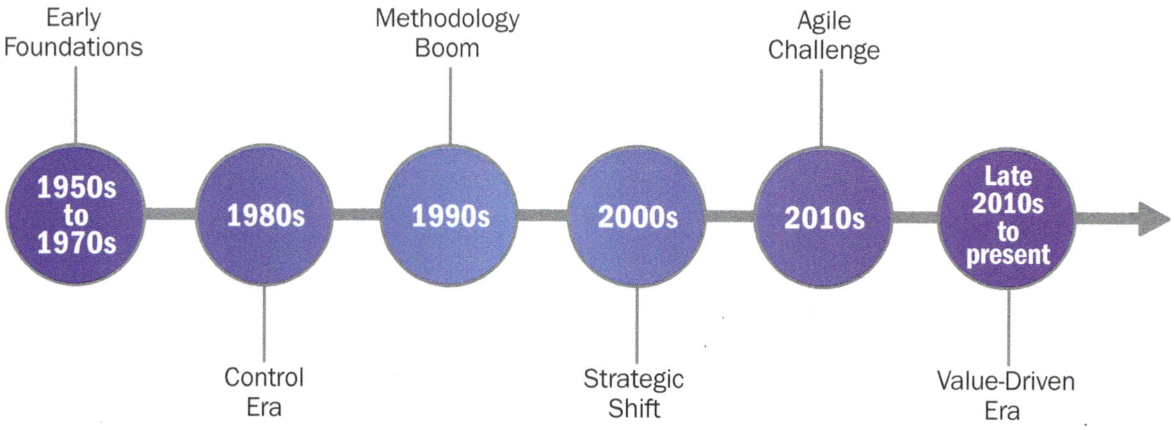

Figure 3-2. PMO Timeline

Here is a detailed look at the key stages in the development of PMOs over the decades (see Figure 3-2):

- **Early Foundations (1950s to 1970s).** What we recognize today as PMOs can be traced back to the mid-20th century. To implement large-scale government and military projects, centralized project management functions were established during the 1950s and 1960s. For instance, the U.S. Department of Defense set up PMOs to manage complex defense projects during the Cold War era, and this approach is still successfully used today. Similarly, NASA used a centralized approach for managing projects in coordination with the Apollo space mission, which was considered an ambitious undertaking during the 1960s. These early versions of PMOs were geared toward managing large-scale, elaborate projects that called for detailed coordination as well as oversight. Their role was mostly about processes—mainly schedule control, resource allocation, and cost control.
- **The Control Era (1980s).** PMOs began appearing in corporate settings through operational perspectives focused on control and auditing around the 1980s. During this period, PMOs acted like watchdogs that ensured adherence to predetermined schedules, budgets, or specifications within any given project context. Performing in this capacity meant maintaining tight control over execution, often through stringent reporting processes coupled with robust monitoring systems. Though it kept projects disciplined, this control-centric approach sometimes made PMOs appear bureaucratic, hence stalling progress in those projects. However, this approach laid the foundation for future sophistication of project management practices.
- **The Methodology Boom (1990s).** The focus of PMOs changed significantly in the 1990s. As a distinct discipline of its own, project management became a unit of interest to the PMOs, which then created standardized project management methodologies, tools, and other tactical aspects associated with projects. During this time, formalized project management methodologies were introduced, and Project Management Institute's *A Guide to the Project Management Body of Knowledge (PMBOK® Guide)* was widely adopted. In this role, PMOs were the custodians of

methodology, responsible for training project managers, developing standard templates and processes, and ensuring consistency in executing projects throughout their organizations. In addition, during this period, project management software played an important role in expanding PMO capabilities. Such technological advancement helped improve an organization's ability to keep track of projects, allocate resources, and report on their progress, making them more valuable.

- **The Strategic Shift (2000s).** PMOs started taking a more strategic shape upon moving into the new millennium. Portfolio management became a buzzword, and most PMOs aligned projects with organizational strategy. This alignment resulted in enterprise project management offices (EPMOs), which signified a change in company-wide project oversight toward strategic alignment with corporate objectives. New technologies also made more integrated and accessible project management tools possible. However, the benefits of these advancements were often limited by the need for more organizational maturity in project management practices. PMOs were tasked with managing projects and driving organizational change toward improving overall project management maturity.
- **The Agile Challenge (2010s).** In the 2010s, there was a rapid rise in agile methodologies that presented both a challenge and an opportunity to PMOs. Traditional, control-oriented PMOs were questioned; some even claimed they were incompatible with the "new agile world." This situation forced PMOs to review their role and value proposition. PMO professionals began to think about how they would be able to generate value for their organizations from the top down rather than continue focusing purely on technical aspects like most PMOs. Therefore, this change was essential in ensuring the continued relevance and necessity of PMOs amid the changing landscape of project management. PMOs started injecting hybrid project environments—borrowing from both traditional and agile mindsets. They dropped their focus on rigid methods to enable agility across organizations.
- **The Value-Driven Era (Late 2010s to present).** More recently, PMOs increasingly realize that it is through this generation of organizational value that they can survive and become indispensable partners for stakeholders, especially top management. This insight has been driven by more proficient leaders within its ranks, who are aided by simplified processes and highly automated and integrated tools. Modern-day PMOs bridge gaps between actualities, needs, constraints, and challenges faced by the organizations they work for, which allows for improved perception or recognition of values associated with them. This improvement represents a significant shift in organizational management, where control-centric entities turn into value-driven strategic partners. Today's PMOs are no longer about managing projects; instead, they focus on using them to facilitate organizational strategy, make innovation realizable, and enhance tangible value creation. Given this complex environment combined with the increasing rate of change, PMOs are becoming more critical strategic partners to organizations.

It is clear that the evolution of PMOs is still far from over. The most successful will be those that can guess and respond to what organizations require at any particular time, take advantage of emergent technologies, and continually illustrate such value in contributing to organizational objectives.

Exploring PMO Types and Models: A Spectrum of Approaches

PMO professionals often turn to established models when implementing or redesigning PMOs. However, the abundance of available models presents a conundrum: Which one is truly the "best" or "right" choice? This dilemma often leads to a problematic assumption that one model is ideal, rendering all others obsolete or irrelevant.

This traditional approach—seeking a perfect PMO model as a panacea for all organizational challenges—needs to be revised because it encourages organizations to adopt a perceived "ideal" model and, if unsuccessful, await the next trend to try again. Such a strategy critically overlooks one of the most salient characteristics of PMOs—their inherent uniqueness.

PMOs represent a complex phenomenon that defies universal consensus, unlike the relatively standardized practices for portfolio, program, and project management. The truth is that there are no empirically proven, universally ideal, or consistently effective PMO models. While various models proposed by different authors offer valuable insights, they should not be viewed as mutually exclusive paths. Instead, these models should be seen as a palette of options that can potentially be combined to meet specific organizational needs.

Figure 3-3 illustrates some of the different PMO types that can be implemented. The most relevant literature on PMOs helps to provide a more comprehensive list that includes:

- **Agile PMO.** An agile PMO is specifically designed to support agile project management methodologies, such as Scrum, Kanban, or Extreme Programming (XP). This type of PMO focuses on fostering agile practices, principles, and values, promoting continuous improvement and providing guidance on agile tools and techniques.
- **Control tower PMO.** The control tower PMO has a more active role in project management, ensuring that projects comply with established policies, processes, and methodologies. This type of PMO oversees project management practices, monitors project performance, and audits projects to ensure consistent organizational execution. The control tower PMO is more focused on maintaining quality and control over projects.
- **Consultative PMO.** A consultative PMO focuses on providing expert advice, guidance, and support to project teams within an organization. This type of PMO is similar to the supportive PMO, as it offers a range of services to help project teams improve their project management practices and achieve project success. The primary difference is the emphasis on a more proactive advisory role in the consultative PMO.
- **Controlling PMO.** The controlling PMO has a moderate-to-high level of control within the organization; it enforces compliance with established project management policies, methodologies, and frameworks. This PMO type focuses on managing risks, issues, and change requests; overseeing project management practices; and ensuring that projects consistently follow organizational processes and standards to maintain quality and control.
- **Departmental PMO.** The departmental PMO is specific to a particular department or business unit within the organization, providing project management support and guidance tailored to that department's needs.

Figure 3-3. PMO Types

- **Directive PMO.** The directive PMO has a high level of control, actively managing and directing projects within the organization. It is suitable for organizations with higher project management maturity and a need for centralized control and consistency. This PMO type ensures projects are effectively managed and deliver expected results, often having authority over project managers and teams and being deeply involved in project management decision-making processes.
- **Delivery PMO.** The delivery PMO is responsible for managing and delivering projects within the organization, providing the necessary tools, processes, and resources. With a moderate level of control, it focuses on ensuring that projects are delivered on time, within budget, and to the expected quality standards. A delivery PMO supports project teams in executing their projects, monitoring progress, and reporting on project performance, and is primarily concerned with the day-to-day management and successful completion of projects.
- **Enterprise PMO (EPMO).** An EPMO is a high-level PMO with a broad scope and authority within the organization. The EPMO is responsible for overseeing and coordinating all PMO activities, ensuring alignment with the organization's strategic objectives and providing a consistent approach to project management across the organization.

- **Functional PMO.** The functional PMO is responsible for the management of projects within a specific functional area or domain, such as IT, human resources, or finance. The functional PMO supports that department by providing project management guidance, resources, and tools tailored to the specific needs of that domain.
- **Hybrid PMO.** A hybrid PMO combines elements of different PMO types based on the specific needs and context of the organization. A hybrid PMO can be tailored to the organization's requirements, offering a more flexible approach to project management.
- **Innovation PMO.** The innovation PMO focuses on driving experimentation within an organization by providing support for projects and initiatives aimed at fostering innovation, creativity, and new product development. The innovation PMO may work closely with research and development (R&D) teams as well as cross-functional project teams.
- **Operational PMO.** An operational PMO focuses on supporting individual projects and project teams within an organization. The operational PMO provides project management guidance, tools, and resources to ensure the successful execution and delivery of projects. The operational PMO has a more tactical role, addressing the day-to-day needs of project teams, and is closely aligned with project execution and delivery.
- **Portfolio management office.** The portfolio management office (Pf-PMO) is responsible for managing the organization's entire portfolio of programs, projects, and other work. The Pf-PMO oversees the portfolio to ensure alignment with the organization's strategy, prioritize investments, and optimize resource allocation. With the highest level of authority and strategic focus, the Pf-PMO plays a crucial role in portfolio management and delivery, ensuring that all initiatives support the overall organizational goals.
- **Program management office.** The program management office (Pg-PMO) is responsible for managing and coordinating multiple related projects that are part of a larger program. This type of PMO focuses on ensuring that the program's objectives and benefits are achieved, managing interdependencies among projects, and providing program-level governance. With a strategic role within the organization, the Pg-PMO is closely aligned with program management and delivery, ensuring that all projects within the program contribute to the overall program goals.
- **Project-specific PMO.** Sometimes called a project controls office (PCO), a project-specific PMO is established to support a single, large-scale, or high-risk project. This type of PMO provides dedicated project management support and resources to help ensure the project's successful delivery.
- **Project support office.** A project support office (PSO) provides administrative support and coordination for individual projects and project teams within an organization. The PSO ensures that project managers have the necessary resources, tools, and guidance to successfully manage their projects. A PSO handles activities such as project tracking, reporting, and documentation, focusing on the day-to-day needs of project teams. With a more tactical role, the PSO is closely aligned with project execution and delivery.
- **Project management center of excellence.** A project management center of excellence (PMCoE) is a specialized type of PMO dedicated to promoting and enhancing an organization's

project management capabilities. The PMCoE serves as a central hub for project management knowledge, skills, resources, and accepted practices, aiming to improve the organization's overall project management maturity and effectiveness.

- **Supportive PMO.** The supportive PMO focuses on providing support to project teams through the provision of tools, templates, accepted practices, and training. The supportive PMO typically has a low level of control within the organization and primarily aims to improve project management practices by sharing knowledge and resources. The supportive PMO helps project teams with day-to-day project management tasks and offers guidance when needed.
- **Strategic PMO.** The strategic PMO focuses on aligning the organization's portfolios, programs, and projects with its strategic objectives and ensuring that they deliver value. The strategic PMO involves project prioritization, resource allocation, benefits realization, and governance. A strategic PMO typically has a high level of authority within the organization and works closely with senior management to ensure that the organization's project portfolio is effectively managed.
- **Tactical PMO.** The tactical PMO is responsible for managing and coordinating multiple related projects, ensuring that the organization's project management processes are followed consistently and that good practices are shared. This type of PMO focuses on improving the organization's project management capabilities and serves as a central repository for project management knowledge, skills, and resources.
- **Transformation management office.** The transformation management office (TMO) drives and manages large-scale organizational change initiatives. The TMO oversees and coordinates programs and projects that are critical to achieving strategic goals, ensuring alignment with the organization's vision and strategy.
- **Value management office.** A value management office (VMO) is responsible for ensuring that projects deliver maximum value to the organization. The VMO focuses on evaluation, prioritization, tracking of project benefits, and return on investment (ROI), ensuring that projects align with the organization's strategic objectives and contribute to its success.
- **xMO.** This concept is centered around the idea that the PMO's traditional focus on portfolios, programs, and projects can be extended to other areas of the organization, where management support and expertise can add value. By embracing this broader scope, the xMO can better support the organization's strategic objectives, facilitate cross-functional collaboration, and enhance organizational agility. An example of an xMO is the change management office (CMO), which focuses on managing organizational change, ensuring that the organization can adapt to new strategies, technologies, or business models.

The literature on PMOs presents a rich tapestry of types, each offering unique perspectives on how these entities can function within organizations. This diversity reflects the complex and multifaceted nature of PMOs and the varied needs of the organizations they serve.

In analyzing the types of PMOs described in this section, each one approaches the subject from one of the following perspectives:

- **Scope of coverage.** The type of PMO is defined by its scope of influence, which can range from overseeing the entire organization to a specific department or division, or even a single program or project. Each type of PMO addresses unique needs and operates within different scopes, emphasizing the importance of context-specific structures in project management. The main types include departmental PMOs, EPMOs, project-specific PMOs, Pg-PMOs, and functional PMOs.
- **Service approach.** The type of PMO is determined by its operational approach, which can be consultative, controlling, or directive. The primary types include the control tower PMO, consultative PMO, supportive PMO, directive PMO, and PSO. Each PMO type adapts its service approach to best meet the organization's needs, balancing guidance, support, and control.
- **Type of functions.** The type of PMO is determined by the set of functions it provides, which can be operational, tactical, strategic, or any other specific combination of predetermined functions. The primary types include the agile PMO, delivery PMO, innovation PMO, operational PMO, Pf-PMO, PMCoE, strategic PMO, tactical PMO, and VMO.
- **Flexible models.** More recently, new approaches emphasizing greater flexibility have emerged. While still categorized as specific types, these approaches gradually break away from rigid classifications, proposing a more adaptable approach grounded in each organization's unique needs. The primary types include hybrid PMOs and xMOs.

Each approach offers valuable insights into how PMOs can be structured and operated. However, it is crucial to understand that no single type should be considered a universal solution. Instead, these models should inspire PMO professionals to develop tailored solutions that address their organization's unique needs.

The Limitations of Traditional PMO Types

While the various PMO types outlined in the literature provide valuable insights, they also present several limitations when applied rigidly:

- **Oversimplification.** Predefined models often fail to capture the full complexity of an organization's needs.
- **Static nature.** These models may not account for the dynamic, ever-changing nature of business environments.
- **One-size-fits-all mentality.** These models can lead to a cookie-cutter approach that does not address unique organizational challenges.
- **Focus on structure over value.** There is a risk of prioritizing adherence to a model over delivering tangible benefits.

Rigidly adhering to one of these models often forces an organization to conform to a perspective that does not align with its unique context.

Reimagining PMO Models: Beyond One-Size-Fits-All Solutions

The evolution of PMOs reflects a growing understanding that flexibility and customization are key to their success. Empirical evidence consistently shows that the most-valued PMOs craft bespoke structures tailored to their unique organizational context rather than rigidly adhering to a single, predefined model.

While the project management literature offers a rich array of PMO models, each with valuable insights, treating these as universal solutions can be counterproductive. Organizations are dynamic entities with ever-changing needs, and PMOs should mirror this adaptability to remain relevant and practical.

The danger lies in the temptation to seek a "perfect" PMO model or to jump from one trendy type to another. Such approaches often lead to misalignment between the PMO and the organization's actual needs, resulting in decreased value perception and effectiveness.

Instead of rigidly categorizing PMOs or adhering strictly to predefined types, successful PMOs often exhibit a blend of characteristics drawn from multiple types. This hybridization allows them to create a unique structure that best serves their context and stakeholder needs.

As organizations face new challenges and opportunities, new PMO types will inevitably emerge. However, the key to success lies not in adopting these new types wholesale, but in drawing inspiration from them to further refine and adapt existing PMO structures.

PMO professionals should focus on creating and continuously evolving tailored models based on their organization's specific needs. They should recognize that the label or category assigned to a PMO becomes far less important than its effectiveness and alignment with organizational goals.

The most successful PMOs of the future will transcend rigid categorizations and create genuinely customized structures. By embracing flexibility, focusing on stakeholder needs, and continually adapting to change, PMOs can position themselves as indispensable strategic partners in organizational success.

This evolution in PMO thinking represents not just a change in structure or function but a fundamental shift in how people perceive the role of project management within organizations. It is a move toward a more nuanced, context-specific approach that addresses each organization's unique challenges and opportunities.

In this new paradigm, the "best" PMO is not one that perfectly fits a predefined model but one that perfectly fits its organization—today, tomorrow, and into the future. By embracing this flexible, adaptive approach, PMOs can help ensure their continued relevance and value in an increasingly complex and fast-paced business world, driving organizational success through tailored, effective project management practices.

Looking Ahead to the Next Section

Having established a solid foundation for understanding PMO fundamentals, it is essential to recognize that PMOs do not operate in isolation. PMOs function within intricate organizational environments influencing their structure, performance, and overall success.

The following section will explore these organizational contexts and how different scenarios affect PMO operations. This knowledge equips PMO professionals to adjust their strategies to address their organizations' unique needs and challenges.

By mastering these environments, PMOs can establish themselves as crucial assets that drive project success, no matter the organizational setting. The next section explores the diverse landscapes where PMOs must operate and excel.

4

Navigating Organizational Landscapes

Why This Section Matters to PMO Professionals

The Organizational Context Scenarios framework outlined in this section is crucial for PMO professionals. The scenarios provide valuable insights into how PMO professionals can identify the current context in their organization, enabling them to develop and apply contextually relevant strategies. By understanding these scenarios, PMO professionals can tailor their approaches to fit the unique challenges and opportunities within their organizations, enhancing their ability to deliver effective solutions.

Ultimately, this section equips PMO professionals with the knowledge and tools to navigate the complexities of PMO management across various types of organizational scenarios. Whether working in low-maturity environments, launching a new PMO, maximizing the success of existing PMOs, preventing PMO decline, or even reintroducing a PMO after a previous failure, PMO professionals face a range of challenges that require strategic insight and adaptability. By understanding these diverse scenarios, professionals can implement targeted strategies that address specific organizational needs and drive sustainable success.

The Organizational Contextual Scenarios Dynamics

PMOs are not static; they evolve, adapt, and sometimes encounter difficulties as they progress through different contextual scenarios. The Organizational Contextual Scenarios framework offers a detailed framework to understand these dynamics, providing valuable insights into the various challenges and opportunities that PMOs may face at different points in their journey.

To fully appreciate the significance of this framework, it is essential to consider its place within the broader context of organizational theory and project management practice. The framework aligns with systems thinking principles, recognizing that PMOs do not exist in isolation but are part of a complex organizational ecosystem. Each scenario in the framework reflects the internal PMO state, its interactions with various stakeholders, and its response to external environmental factors.

The framework also touches upon aspects of organizational behavior, culture, and maturity. The initial scenarios highlight the importance of cultural readiness and executive buy-in for PMO success. The framework's recognition of potential decline and collapse scenarios, even if they are not the inevitable destiny for every PMO, serves as a reminder that PMOs should consistently articulate and demonstrate their value proposition.

Finally, the inclusion of a resurgence scenario in the framework is particularly noteworthy, as it acknowledges the potential for organizational learning and renewal. This concept aligns with theories of organizational resilience and adaptive capacity, suggesting that even after significant setbacks, PMOs can evolve and reestablish their value proposition.

As organizations grapple with increasing complexity and uncertainty in their project environments, the Organizational Contextual Scenarios framework offers a valuable compass for navigating these challenges and achieving potential opportunities. The framework encourages a dynamic and adaptive approach to PMO management, recognizing that the PMO's role and focus may need to adapt in response to changing organizational needs and external pressures.

With a closer look at each of the eight scenarios, it becomes evident that this framework is not just a theoretical construct but a practical tool for guiding PMO strategies and operations. The framework offers a roadmap for navigating the complex journey of PMO development, adaptation, and renewal, providing insights that can help organizations maximize the value they derive from their PMOs.

Understanding the Eight Organizational Contextual Scenarios

Experience shows that organizations may go through distinct contextual scenarios that significantly impact their PMO initiatives. Eight scenarios that typically influence PMO initiatives have been identified, and each one presents its own unique challenges and opportunities. Recognizing the current organizational context can significantly shape the PMO strategy.

Understanding these scenarios is crucial for tailoring the PMO strategy. Each scenario requires a different approach, and recognizing the current organizational context is the first step in aligning the PMO with organizational needs. PMOs that understand and adapt to these scenarios thrive in the long run.

There is no assumption of linear progression through these scenarios. In reality, PMOs may not always transition through stages in a predictable sequence. Some PMOs may skip certain scenarios or experience them in a different order, and various parts of the PMO may mature at different rates or exist in different stages simultaneously, depending on the unique strategic needs and circumstances of the organization. This nonlinear and dynamic nature emphasizes the importance of flexibility when applying this model.

Figure 4-1 illustrates the eight organizational contextual scenarios, each representing a distinct state in the organization's journey, highlighting the unique characteristics, challenges, and opportunities faced by PMO professionals at each stage.

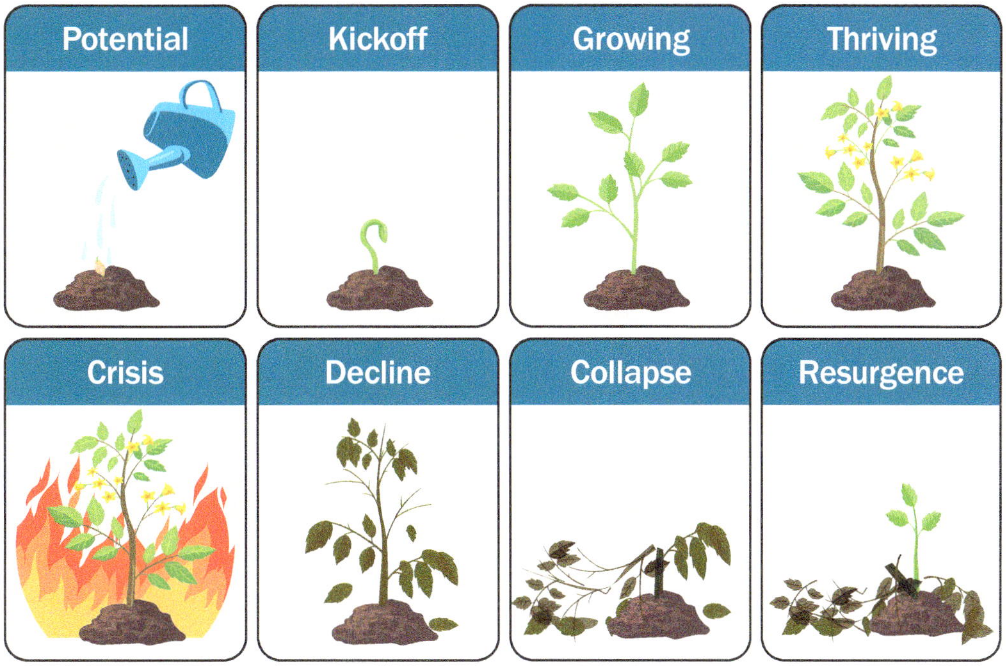

Figure 4-1. Organizational Contextual Scenarios

Potential Scenario

This first scenario represents the earliest state of a PMO initiative. The organization recognizes the potential benefits of a PMO but lacks the necessary cultural foundation or maturity to implement one effectively. Although the organization is not ready for a PMO, the potential exists. It is necessary to focus on changing the organizational culture before considering setting up a PMO.

Though experts see the potential for a beautiful tree in a few years, they also know the current scenario is akin to fertile ground awaiting cultivation. The soil has potential fertility but requires adequate preparation to become suitable for planting. Proper preparation, including tilling and enriching the soil, is essential to transform this potential into a robust and flourishing tree.

This scenario is characterized by:

- **High-potential environment.** The organization has recognized the benefits of a PMO but is not yet prepared for implementation.
- **Absence of formal project management structures or processes.** There are no established frameworks or methodologies in place.

- **Initial discussions and planning around PMO concepts.** Conversations about the PMO's potential roles, benefits, and structures are beginning but no formal action has been taken.
- **Organizational culture and maturity.** A significant need for cultural change and maturity development has been identified.

Key Focus Areas for Development

Addressing the following focus areas can help the organization prepare the "soil" for the PMO, ensuring a successful future implementation.

- **Cultural change.** Prioritize creating a culture that values project management and understands the role of a PMO.
- **Education and advocacy.** Inform key stakeholders about the benefits and functions of a PMO.
- **Foundation building.** Begin laying the groundwork for future PMO implementation, including basic training and initial process development.

Kickoff Scenario

In this scenario, the organization has achieved a baseline level of cultural readiness and maturity. Executive leadership demonstrates sufficient awareness of the potential contributions of a PMO, enabling initial buy-in and a basic understanding of its value. A minimal level of project management culture and maturity has been established, allowing for the initial implementation of a PMO.

This scenario is analogous to a fertile piece of land being ready for planting after careful preparation. The soil has been tilled and enriched, creating the ideal conditions for seeds to thrive. The land is poised to support robust growth and a bountiful harvest.

This scenario is characterized by:

- **Introduction of basic project management frameworks and methodologies.** Implement foundational project management practices to guide initial projects.
- **Setup of early-stage projects and processes.** Establish preliminary processes and start the initial projects to demonstrate PMO capabilities.
- **Executive buy-in and initial support for the PMO concept.** Gain the necessary executive sponsorship and support to initiate the PMO.
- **Formation of initial PMO team requirements and role definitions.** Define the roles and responsibilities of the initial PMO team members.

Key Focus Areas for Development

By addressing the following focus areas, the organization can help ensure the successful establishment and growth of the PMO, setting a strong foundation for future stages.

- **Cultural reinforcement.** Continue fostering a project management culture and reinforce the importance of the PMO.
- **Stakeholder engagement.** Actively engage with stakeholders to maintain and build upon initial support and buy-in.
- **Process optimization.** Refine and optimize early-stage processes based on feedback and initial project outcomes.
- **Capability building.** Develop the skills and capabilities of the PMO team to handle increasing responsibilities and complexities.

Growing Scenario

This scenario marks a significant period of expansion and maturity for the organization in terms of project management. The PMO begins to scale its operations and refine its processes while delivering initial customer benefits. As the PMO scales up operations, results are measured and the promised benefits begin to materialize. The key here is to keep the momentum going and consistently demonstrate value.

This scenario is like a young tree entering a growth spurt, extending its branches and leaves and delivering its first fruits. The tree's rapid expansion symbolizes newfound potential and energy. With each new leaf and fruit, it demonstrates its capacity for growth and productivity. This phase is marked by vigor and promise, showing early signs of the abundant harvests to come and illustrating the benefits of a supportive environment and careful nurturing.

This scenario is characterized by:

- **Increasing portfolio of projects managed by the PMO.** The PMO handles a growing number of projects, showcasing its expanding influence.
- **Enhancement of processes and methodologies.** Refine and optimize processes to improve efficiency and effectiveness.
- **Growth in PMO team size and resources.** Expand the team and acquire additional resources to support increased operations.
- **Expanding stakeholder engagement and support.** Strengthen relationships with stakeholders and secure broader organizational support.

Key Focus Areas for Development

By concentrating on the following focus areas, the organization can help ensure the PMO's successful expansion and maturation, creating a robust framework for future advancements.

- **Sustaining momentum.** Ensure that the PMO continues to demonstrate value and maintain its growth trajectory.
- **Performance measurement.** Regularly assess project outcomes and PMO performance to identify areas for improvement.
- **Capacity building.** Enhance the skills and capabilities of the PMO team to handle more complex projects.
- **Stakeholder communication.** Keep stakeholders informed and engaged with the PMO's progress and achievements.

Thriving Scenario

This scenario represents the peak of organizational project management performance and PMO recognition. The PMO reaches its zenith, generating substantial value for customers and the organization and gaining widespread acknowledgment for its relevance, importance, and contributions to project success and organizational goals.

This scenario is like a mature tree in full bloom, producing abundant fruit and being recognized for its strength, beauty, and the life it supports. Its branches are laden with fruit, providing nourishment and shelter to many. The tree stands as a symbol of resilience and vitality, admired for its contributions to the ecosystem. This flourishing state showcases the pinnacle of growth and the rewards of sustained care and nurturing.

This scenario is characterized by:

- **High levels of efficiency and effectiveness in project delivery.** Projects are delivered on time, within scope and budget, and consistently meet or exceed expectations.
- **Strong governance and adherence to established processes.** Robust governance frameworks ensure compliance and high-quality standards.
- **High stakeholder satisfaction and engagement.** Stakeholders are highly satisfied and actively engaged with the PMO, recognizing its value.
- **Continuous delivery of successful projects.** The PMO consistently delivers successful projects that drive organizational success.

Key Focus Areas for Development

By focusing on the following areas, the organization can maintain and enhance the PMO's peak performance, helping to ensure it continues to deliver substantial value and support the achievement of strategic goals.

- **Sustaining excellence.** Maintain high standards of project management and continuously seek opportunities for improvement.
- **Innovation.** Encourage innovation and adopt new methodologies and technologies to stay ahead.
- **Stakeholder relationship management.** Strengthen and maintain strong relationships with stakeholders to help ensure ongoing support and engagement.
- **Recognition and reward.** Recognize and reward the contributions of the PMO team to sustain motivation and high performance.

Crisis Scenario

This scenario marks a turning point where the organization faces challenges that impact the PMO's value proposition. Stakeholders may struggle to perceive the PMO's value, and executive support begins to wane.

This scenario is like a once-vibrant plant starting to wilt. Deprived of nutrients, it declines in vitality and impact unless intervention revives its strength. The plant's leaves begin to yellow and fall, symbolizing its struggle to survive. Without timely care and the restoration of essential resources, the tree faces an inevitable decline, highlighting the urgent need for immediate action to restore its health and vitality.

This scenario is characterized by the following:

- **Processes, systems, and artifacts are not used.** If the PMO has developed processes, systems, and artifacts that are not being used, it is a sign that the PMO is not meeting their customer's needs or delivering the expected benefits.
- **Constant complaints about the PMO performance.** If customers constantly complain about the PMO's performance, it is a sign that the PMO is not delivering the expected benefits or meeting their needs.
- **Reduction of PMO autonomy.** If the PMO's autonomy is being reduced, it is a sign that the organization may not be committed to the PMO or that the PMO is not delivering the expected benefits.
- **PMO customers complain about bureaucracy.** If stakeholders complain that the PMO is adding unnecessary bureaucracy and slowing down the project delivery process, it is a sign that the PMO may not be effectively balancing the need for governance with the need for agility.

- **Resistance to the PMO does not subside over time.** If customers continue to resist the PMO's efforts, even after it has been in operation for some time, it is a sign that the PMO is not meeting their needs or delivering the expected benefits.
- **The PMO is not invited to attend important meetings.** If the PMO is not being invited to attend important meetings, it is a sign that it is not seen as a strategic partner within the organization.
- **Decreasing efficiency and effectiveness in project delivery.** Projects are increasingly delayed, over budget, or failing to meet quality standards.

Key Focus Areas for Development

Addressing the following focus areas can stabilize the PMO, mitigate immediate challenges, and lay the groundwork for recovery and renewed growth.

- **Diagnostic assessment.** Conduct a thorough evaluation to identify the root causes of the crisis.
- **Stakeholder reengagement.** Actively communicate with stakeholders to rebuild trust and demonstrate the PMO's value.
- **Resource reallocation.** Ensure the PMO has the necessary resources to overcome challenges.
- **Process improvement.** Identify and implement improvements to enhance efficiency and effectiveness.
- **Leadership intervention.** Strong leadership is crucial to guide the PMO through the crisis and ensure timely corrective actions.

Decline Scenario

If the organizational crisis is not effectively managed, this scenario emerges. The PMO is losing support rapidly and struggling to demonstrate or deliver on its expected value. Resistance to PMO activities intensifies, and its necessity comes into question. Even drastic measures may prove insufficient to halt the downward trajectory, as reversing the decline requires a herculean effort.

This scenario is like a tree suffering from severe neglect, with its leaves dying and falling off. The neglected plant's survival is in doubt as it struggles to maintain any vitality. Attempts to stop its decline might fail because its roots are weak and its branches are brittle. Without immediate and comprehensive intervention, the plant faces an almost certain demise, highlighting the critical need for timely care and resources to potentially revive and restore its health.

Key characteristics of this scenario include:

- **Loss of executive-level support.** When executives begin to question the PMO's value, it is a clear sign that the PMO may not be delivering what it should.
- **Eroding PMO customer support and engagement.** PMO customers are disengaging and losing faith in the PMO's ability to add value.

- **Constant changes in PMO leadership.** A high turnover rate within the PMO leadership team is a sign that the organization may not be committed to the PMO or that the PMO is not delivering the expected benefits.
- **High turnover in the PMO team.** Similarly, a high turnover rate within the PMO team is a sign that the team may not be functioning effectively or that there are deeper issues at play.
- **Cost-cutting in the PMO.** If the PMO is subject to cost-cutting measures, it is a sign that the organization may not see it as a strategic partner or that it is not delivering the expected benefits.
- **The PMO's performance is often sabotaged.** If customers actively work to sabotage the PMO's efforts, it is a sign that a deeper issue is at play, and the PMO urgently needs to reassess its approach.
- **PMO customers hide information from the PMO.** If customers withhold information from the PMO, it is a sign that they do not trust the PMO or do not believe it is providing value.

Key Focus Areas for Development

Addressing the following focus areas can help the organization attempt to halt the PMO's downward trajectory, stabilize its operations, and create opportunities for potential recovery and revitalization.

- **Immediate intervention.** Act quickly to stabilize the PMO by addressing the most critical issues first.
- **Rebuild trust.** Engage with stakeholders to rebuild trust and demonstrate a commitment to reversing the decline.
- **Resource allocation.** Ensure that adequate resources are allocated to support the PMO's recovery efforts.
- **Process reevaluation.** Review and improve current processes to enhance efficiency and effectiveness.
- **Leadership and guidance.** Strong leadership is crucial to guide the PMO through this challenging period and restore its credibility and value.

Collapse Scenario

In this scenario, the organizational context is such that the PMO ceases to function effectively or becomes obsolete. Lacking executive backing, autonomy, resources, and influence, the PMO fails to deliver minimal value, rendering it dispensable to the organization. This scenario is undesirable but sometimes necessary for a fresh start. It represents the potential end of the PMO's life cycle within the current organizational context.

This scenario is like a plant that has withered beyond recovery. Deprived of sunlight, water, and nutrients, it no longer grows or blooms, becoming lifeless. The plant, lacking necessary support and resources, fails to sustain even minimal vitality, which sometimes signifies the end of its life cycle. This inevitable decline reflects the consequences of prolonged neglect and insufficient intervention, emphasizing the critical need for consistent care and resources to sustain life.

Characteristics of this scenario include:

- **Complete breakdown of PMO processes and governance.** The PMO can no longer maintain any of its established processes or governance structures.
- **Total loss of stakeholder confidence and support.** Stakeholders no longer believe in the PMO's ability to add value, resulting in a complete withdrawal of support.
- **Inability to manage projects effectively.** Projects suffer due to the lack of effective management, leading to frequent failures.
- **Consideration of disbanding the PMO.** The organization seriously considers dissolving the PMO as it no longer serves its purpose.

Key Focus Areas for Development

Addressing the following focus areas can help the organization determine the best course of action, whether it involves attempting to revive the PMO or deciding to disband it and start a new one.

- **Root cause analysis.** Conduct a thorough analysis to understand the underlying reasons for the PMO's collapse.
- **Stakeholder communication.** Communicate openly with stakeholders about the challenges and potential solutions.
- **Strategic decision-making.** Decide whether to attempt a PMO revival or to disband and start fresh.
- **Resource reallocation.** If revival is chosen, allocate the necessary resources to address deficiencies.
- **Leadership and vision.** Strong leadership is essential to either guide the revival process or manage the transition to a new structure.

Resurgence Scenario

In this scenario, the organizational context allows for the PMO idea to be reborn. This reemergence can be complex and risky, potentially complicated by organizational trauma from past experiences. While challenging, this scenario can lead to an even more robust PMO if managed correctly. It represents a potential rebirth of the PMO concept, often rising from the ashes of previous failures.

This scenario is like a dormant seed sprouting anew after a wildfire. Like a seedling facing the remnants of a forest fire, with the right care and procedures, the new plant can grow stronger than before. This process involves overcoming significant challenges, but if managed correctly, it can result in a more robust and resilient tree. The rebirth from the ashes symbolizes renewal and the potential for greater strength, demonstrating the power of effective management and nurturing.

This scenario is characterized by:

- **Renewed focus on rebuilding and improving the PMO.** Concentrate efforts on reconstructing the PMO with improved strategies.
- **Reestablishment of governance and processes.** Implement robust governance frameworks and refined processes.
- **Reengagement of stakeholders with a refreshed strategy.** Reconnect with stakeholders through a newly devised strategy to gain their support.
- **Early signs of recovery and improvement.** Look for initial indicators of positive changes and enhanced performance.
- **Learning from previous failure.** Apply lessons learned from past setbacks to avoid repeating mistakes and help strengthen the PMO.

Key Focus Areas for Development

By focusing on these areas, the organization can successfully navigate the complexities of reestablishing the PMO, leading to a more resilient and effective project management office that supports organizational goals.

- **Customer-centric and value-driven practices.** Implement the new PMO based on established practices that focus on customer needs and delivering value.
- **Change management.** Effectively manage the transition and address any organizational resistance.
- **Stakeholder communication.** Ensure transparent communication to rebuild trust and demonstrate renewed value.
- **Continuous improvement.** Implement mechanisms for ongoing assessment and enhancement of PMO practices.
- **Resource optimization.** Ensure the optimal use of resources to support the resurgence efforts.
- **Leadership and vision.** Apply strong leadership to guide the resurgence and inspire confidence among stakeholders.

Signs of Transition Between Scenarios

The transition between these organizational contextual scenarios is rarely a sudden event but rather a gradual process marked by several key indicators. Recognizing these signals is crucial for proactive PMO management and timely intervention. While specific indicators may vary depending on the organization and its context, several common signs often herald a shift from one state to another.

Here are some examples:

- **Stakeholder perception and support.** As a PMO moves from a growing to a thriving state, there is typically an increase in positive feedback from stakeholders, greater engagement in PMO initiatives, and more frequent requests for PMO services. Conversely, a shift toward the crisis state might be signaled by growing skepticism about the PMO's value, reduced stakeholder participation (particularly at the executive level), and increased resistance to PMO-led initiatives.
- **Executive support.** A transition to a more positive state is often accompanied by increased executive backing, manifesting as greater resource allocation, more frequent inclusion in strategic discussions, or expanded PMO authority. On the other hand, waning executive support, such as budget cuts or reduced access to leadership, can signal a move toward less favorable states.
- **Performance metrics.** A PMO moving toward a thriving state typically shows consistent improvement in KPIs such as on-time delivery, budget adherence, and stakeholder satisfaction. Conversely, declining project success rates or increasing numbers of troubled projects might indicate a shift toward crisis or decline states.
- **PMO's ability to adapt and innovate.** A PMO moving toward more positive states often demonstrates increasing agility, regularly introducing new methodologies or tools to improve project delivery. Stagnation in processes or resistance to change, on the other hand, might indicate a move toward less favorable states.
- **Organizational alignment.** As a PMO moves toward more positive states, there is typically increasing alignment between PMO activities and organizational strategic objectives. A disconnect between PMO focus and organizational priorities might signal a shift toward crisis or decline states.
- **Quality and quantity of PMO outputs.** A move toward more positive states is often marked by an increase in the volume and quality of PMO deliverables such as reports, training sessions, or process improvements. A decline in these outputs, or a decrease in their perceived value, might signal a transition to less favorable states.
- **Team morale and turnover within the PMO.** A PMO moving toward more positive states often experiences improved team morale, lower turnover rates, and an ability to attract top talent. Increasing turnover, difficulty in recruiting, or low team morale might signal a transition toward less favorable states.
- **PMO's influence on organizational culture.** As a PMO moves toward more positive states, there is typically a growing project management culture across the organization, with increased adoption of PMO-recommended practices. A decline in this cultural influence might signal a shift toward less favorable states.
- **PMO's role in decision-making processes.** A transition to more positive states is often accompanied by the PMO playing an increasingly strategic role, being consulted on major decisions that impact portfolio and project management. A reduction in this decision-making influence might signal a move toward less favorable states.

- **Organizational changes.** Changes within the organization can also trigger transitions between states. Structural shifts, leadership changes, or shifts in strategic direction can all impact the PMO's state.

It is important to note that these indicators should not be considered in isolation but rather as part of a holistic assessment of the PMO's health. A combination of these indicators often signals the transition between states, and the significance of each may vary depending on the specific organizational context.

Regular monitoring of these indicators can help PMO professionals and organizational executives to identify state transitions early, allowing for timely and appropriate strategic responses.

Strategies for Different Organizational Contextual Scenarios

Each organizational contextual scenario presents unique challenges and opportunities. Recognizing these states allows organizations to implement targeted strategies that are most appropriate for their status quo. These strategies are not one-size-fits-all solutions but rather tailored approaches designed to maximize success.

For PMO professionals, having a toolkit of strategies for each scenario is invaluable. Having different strategies at hand can enable PMO professionals to proactively address challenges and exploit opportunities for growth and improvement. These strategies serve as a starting point for developing tailored approaches that consider the unique context and needs of each organization.

Detailed and extensive strategies for each organizational contextual scenario are outlined in Table 4-1.

In each of these scenarios, it is crucial for PMO professionals to remain adaptable, maintain open communication with stakeholders, and continuously align the PMO's efforts with organizational needs and strategic objectives. By applying these strategies, PMO professionals can effectively navigate the challenges and opportunities presented at each stage of the PMO life cycle, ensuring the PMO's relevance and value to the organization.

The Organizational Contextual Scenarios framework provides valuable insights into the dynamics of PMOs, offering a structured approach to understanding their most common states. This framework serves as a powerful tool for PMO professionals, guiding their strategies and decision-making processes.

The framework's key strength lies in its structured understanding of organizational scenarios, categorizing them into eight distinct states. This categorization provides clarity and a common language, enabling PMO professionals to communicate more effectively about their organization's current state and future direction and helping them to tailor their approaches to specific organizational contexts.

Despite these benefits, the framework has limitations that warrant consideration. One primary concern is the risk of oversimplification. The eight distinct scenarios may not fully capture the complex and fluid nature of real-world PMOs, which often exhibit characteristics of multiple states simultaneously. This complexity can make it challenging to neatly categorize a PMO into a single scenario.

Table 4-1. Strategies for Organizational Contextual Scenarios

Scenario	Strategies
Potential	• Conduct an organizational readiness assessment. • Evaluate the current project management maturity level. • Foster a project-centric culture. • Build executive support.
Kickoff	• Create a compelling PMO proposal. • Obtain buy-in from executive leadership and key stakeholders. • Define the PMO's mandate, governance structure, and strategy. • Identify PMO customers and their needs. • Develop a value proposition for the PMO and outline its services. • Develop PMO services, processes, and performance indicators. • Form and prepare the PMO team. • Establish clear roles and responsibilities within the PMO. • Onboard PMO customers and launch PMO operations. • Measure initial results and make necessary adjustments.
Growing	• Complete onboarding and transition to regular operations. • Enhance customer engagement. • Prioritize reporting and analytics. • Concentrate on building capabilities. • Focus on achieving quick wins. • Measure value delivery. • Identify and fill potential gaps.
Thriving	• Refine the PMO value proposition. • Expand the customer base. • Refine and expand the PMO's service offerings. • Align closely with organizational strategy. • Develop tailored approaches. • Optimize resource utilization. • Enhance PMO maturity. • Focus on continuous improvement. • Measure value recognition.
Crisis	• Conduct a PMO health assessment. • Develop a crisis management plan. • Reengage PMO customers. • Realign with organizational needs. • Align PMO strategy closely with current organizational priorities. • Develop a revised value proposition for the PMO. • Reassess and adjust service offerings.
Decline	• Perform a comprehensive PMO audit. • Develop a turnaround strategy for the PMO. • Create a roadmap for rebuilding PMO capabilities. • Reassess and potentially redesign the PMO's organizational structure. • Evaluate and address skill gaps within the PMO team. • Reestablish executive support. • Implement stringent performance management. • Consider bringing in new leadership to drive the turnaround.

Table 4-1. Strategies for Organizational Contextual Scenarios (Continued)

Scenario	Strategies
Collapse	• Plan for an orderly shutdown. • Support staff transition. • Capture lessons learned. • Manage stakeholder communication. • Investigate potential for decentralized functions. • Consider outsourcing the PMO. • Explore possibilities for a future PMO resurgence.
Resurgence	• Ensure the use of an appropriate framework for the PMO. • Develop a compelling new vision. • Secure strong executive sponsorship. • Rebuild trust through transparency. • Focus on cultural change.

Another limitation is the assumption of linear progression. In reality, PMOs may not always progress through states in a predictable sequence. Some may skip certain states or experience them in a different order, reflecting the unique strategic needs and circumstances of each organization. This nonlinear nature emphasizes the need for flexibility in applying the framework.

The framework's effectiveness can also be limited by contextual variations. What constitutes success for one PMO might differ significantly for another, underscoring the importance of customization in its application. PMO professionals should adapt the framework to their specific organizational culture, goals, and challenges.

The treatment of the resurgence scenario, while valuable, presents another area for consideration. While it offers one path forward after a PMO's collapse, it is important to recognize that organizations have multiple options. Some organizations may choose to reimagine their project management approach entirely rather than resurrect a previous model. Acknowledging this range of possibilities makes the framework more comprehensive and practical.

To maximize the benefits of the framework while mitigating its limitations, PMO professionals should adopt a flexible approach to its application. This approach involves recognizing that PMOs may exhibit characteristics of multiple scenarios simultaneously and adapting strategies accordingly. Continuous assessment is crucial, regularly evaluating the PMO's state and adjusting approaches as needed, rather than rigidly adhering to predefined paths.

Customization is key to effective implementation. The framework should be tailored to specific organizational contexts, acknowledging that success metrics may vary across different PMOs. It is also important to view the framework as part of a broader toolkit for PMO management, integrating it with other relevant models and practices for a more holistic approach.

In conclusion, the Organizational Contextual Scenarios framework provides a valuable foundation for understanding and managing different scenarios encountered within organizations. By recognizing its limitations and embracing its flexibility, PMO professionals can apply the framework more effectively to their unique situations.

Looking Ahead to the Next Section

As PMOs continue to navigate diverse organizational landscapes, a significant shift in thinking has emerged: the move toward a value-driven service provider model. This evolution marks a profound change in how PMOs function and contribute to organizations. By adopting a service-oriented mindset, PMOs can transition from rigid, process-centric entities to dynamic, customer-focused partners, committed to improving project outcomes and driving overall organizational success. This shift naturally complements the adaptability required in various organizational scenarios.

In the next section, the specifics of this value-driven approach and how it empowers PMOs to remain agile, responsive, and invaluable across different contexts are explored, as well as how PMOs can leverage this new mindset to maximize their effectiveness and impact.

5

The PMO as a Value-Driven Service Provider

Why This Section Matters to PMO Professionals

This section is vital for PMO professionals, offering insights into service-oriented PMOs and agility principles. The information in this section equips PMO professionals with tools to adapt practices, enhance responsiveness to changing business needs, and foster continuous improvement.

The section also addresses the challenge of justifying a PMO's existence, emphasizing customer perceptions in value recognition. Details are provided to help empower professionals to shift from process enforcement to value creation and perception management, positioning the PMO as an indispensable strategic asset.

By embracing a service provider model and agile mindset, PMOs can align with organizational goals, boost stakeholder satisfaction, and demonstrate measurable value. This approach is crucial in today's dynamic environment, where adaptability and value delivery are paramount.

Reimagining the PMO as a Service Provider

A service provider is an entity—whether an individual, team, or organization—that offers specialized services to meet the specific needs of its customers. These providers possess unique expertise, resources, and capabilities in particular fields, delivering value through intangible benefits rather than physical products.

Service providers are characterized by their intense focus on understanding and fulfilling customer needs. They operate under defined service agreements, continuously adapting their offerings to meet evolving demands. This adaptability and customer-centric approach have made the service-provider model increasingly relevant in our dynamic business environment.

PMOs stand at a critical juncture in their evolution. Traditionally viewed as administrative bodies focused on enforcing standards and processes, PMOs now have the opportunity to reimagine their role within organizations.

By adopting a service-provider mindset, PMOs can transform from rigid, process-focused entities into dynamic, customer-oriented partners dedicated to enhancing project success and driving organizational performance.

This shift represents a fundamental transformation in how PMOs operate and deliver value. At its core, the service-provider mindset places the needs and satisfaction of the PMO's "customers"—project managers, executives, team members, and other stakeholders—at the forefront of all operations. This perspective transforms the PMO from an administrative or control-focused unit into a valuable, strategic asset that actively contributes to the organization's success.

Adopting a service-provider approach allows PMOs to:

- Align more closely with organizational goals and strategies.
- Enhance their responsiveness to changing project and business needs.
- Improve stakeholder satisfaction and engagement.
- Demonstrate clear, measurable value to the organization.
- Foster a culture of continuous improvement and innovation in project management practices.

This section will explore the key characteristics of service-oriented PMOs, compare them with traditional PMO structures, and examine the benefits and implementation challenges of this approach.

By understanding and embracing the service-provider mindset, PMOs can position themselves as indispensable partners in organizational success, driving project excellence and strategic achievement in an increasingly complex business world.

The transformation of a PMO into a service-oriented entity involves adopting several key characteristics that distinguish it from traditional PMO models. These characteristics reflect a fundamental shift in focus, priorities, and operational approach. By embracing these traits, PMOs can position themselves as valuable, customer-centric service providers within their organizations. The core characteristics that define a service-oriented PMO and how each trait contributes to a more dynamic, responsive, and value-driven approach to project management are outlined in Table 5-1.

The key attributes of the approaches not only differentiate service-oriented PMOs from their traditional counterparts but also enable them to adapt more effectively to the ever-changing needs of modern organizations and their diverse project portfolios.

Adopting a Service-Provider Mindset

The service-provider mindset represents a powerful evolution in how PMOs operate and deliver value. By focusing on customer needs, offering flexible and tailored services, proactively engaging with stakeholders, and continuously improving based on feedback, PMOs can position themselves as indispensable partners in achieving project success and driving organizational strategy.

Table 5-1. Traditional, Process-Focused PMO Versus a Modern, Service-Oriented PMO

Process-Focused PMOs	Service-Oriented PMOs
Standards enforcement: Only enforces standards, processes, and methodologies across the organization	**Value delivery:** Prioritizes delivering value to customers within the organization
Process-centric: Emphasizes adherence to established project management processes	**Customer-centric:** Puts the needs of its customers at the forefront
Uniform practices: Strong emphasis on creating and maintaining uniform practices across all projects	**Flexible adaptation:** Maintains necessary standards while flexibly adapting practices to meet specific project needs
Reactive approach: Often responds to issues as they arise rather than proactively addressing potential challenges	**Proactive approach:** Actively engages with projects and departments, offering support and guidance before issues arise
Output-focused: Often focuses heavily on generating and distributing reports on project status and metrics	**Outcome-focused:** Offers a clear set of services to generate the customers' expected outcomes
One-size-fits-all approach: Tends to apply the same approaches across all projects regardless of specific needs	**Tailored approaches:** Recognizes that different projects and departments may require different approaches and tailors services accordingly
Rigid structure: Tends to be more rigid and slower to adapt to changing organizational needs	**Agile adaptation:** More agile and can quickly adapt to changing organizational needs
Process compliance: Measures success by compliance with processes	**Value for the customer:** Measures efficacy, customer satisfaction, and value delivered

The most important characteristics of a PMO established with a service-provider mindset include:

- **Customer focus.** Prioritize understanding and meeting the needs of internal customers. Place customer needs and satisfaction at the forefront of all operations. Proactively engage with customers to understand their individual needs and offer solutions.
- **Value delivery.** The primary goal is to deliver value to the organization. Success is measured by customer satisfaction and value delivered, not just project outcomes or process adherence.
- **Specialized expertise.** PMOs offer specialized knowledge in project management. This expertise is a service provided to various departments and teams within the organization.
- **Service offerings.** Like external service providers, PMOs should have a clear catalog of services they offer to their internal customers.
- **Scalability.** PMOs can often scale their services based on organizational needs, offering more intensive support for high-priority projects or scaling back for departments with high project management maturity.

- **Proactive engagement.** PMOs proactively engage with customers to understand their needs and offer solutions, rather than simply reacting to requests.
- **Relationship management.** PMOs focus on building and maintaining strong relationships with their customers, a key characteristic of successful service providers.
- **Performance metrics.** Like other service providers, PMOs should measure and report on their performance, demonstrating their value to the organization.
- **Continuous improvement.** PMOs regularly refine and adapt their services based on feedback and changing organizational needs, much like external service providers evolve to meet market demands.

This approach not only enhances the perceived value of the PMO but also contributes to better project outcomes, improved stakeholder satisfaction, and ultimately, greater organizational success.

The future of PMOs lies not just in methodologies and processes but in the ability to understand, anticipate, and meet the evolving needs of organizational customers. As organizations continue to face complex challenges in rapidly changing environments, PMOs that embrace this service-oriented approach will be well positioned to adapt, thrive, and drive meaningful value.

By viewing the PMO through the lens of a service provider, organizations can leverage their capabilities more effectively, leading to improved project outcomes, better resource utilization, and stronger alignment between project execution and organizational strategy.

The Agility Foundation for PMO Practice

The journey toward an agility-driven PMO begins with a deep understanding of the *Manifesto for Agile Software Development* and its principles. Created in 2001 by a group of software developers, the *Agile Manifesto* was a response to the limitations of traditional, plan-driven approaches to software development. While initially focused on software, the principles outlined in the manifesto contain universal truths that can be powerfully applied to PMO operations and organizational management at large.

The concept of agility has transcended its origins in software development to become a crucial paradigm for PMOs. As organizations face increasingly complex challenges and dynamic environments, traditional PMO approaches often fall short of delivering the responsiveness and value required for success.

The *Agile Manifesto* contains values and principles that can be powerfully applied to PMOs. By adapting them to the PMO context, a framework for more flexible, value-driven, and customer-centric PMOs can be created.

This adaptation is not merely about adopting agile approaches and methodologies for project execution. Instead, it represents a fundamental shift in how PMOs operate, interact with customers, and deliver value to the organization. It requires rethinking the PMO through the lens of agility, emphasizing continuous delivery, embracing change, fostering collaboration, and prioritizing value over rigid processes.

The *Agile Manifesto*'s four core values offer a transformative perspective on how PMOs can operate more effectively in today's dynamic business environment. By reinterpreting and applying these values in the context of PMO operations, organizations can emphasize the importance of human interactions over rigid processes, the delivery of valuable services over extensive planning, close customer engagement over strict service-level agreements, and flexibility and adaptability over rigid adherence to plans.

Each of these four values can be reinterpreted and applied in the context of PMO operations:

1. **People and relationships over rigid processes.** This principle emphasizes the importance of human interactions and team dynamics in achieving success. For PMOs, this means shifting focus from enforcing rigid processes to fostering effective collaboration and communication. In practice, this might include implementing more flexible work structures, encouraging cross-functional collaboration, and prioritizing team-building activities.
2. **Delivering valuable services over extensive planning.** Just as agile software development prioritizes working software over comprehensive documentation, an agility-driven PMO should focus on delivering tangible value to its customers rather than getting delayed with excessive planning or documentation. This does not mean abandoning planning altogether but rather adopting a more iterative approach, where plans are regularly revisited and adjusted based on feedback and changing circumstances. PMOs should strive to deliver services and support in incremental, valuable chunks rather than waiting for large, comprehensive rollouts.
3. **Close customer engagement over strict service-level agreements.** This principle underscores the importance of ongoing collaboration and communication with customers. For PMOs, this means moving beyond rigid service-level agreements to foster genuine partnerships with their internal customers. The engagement effort involves actively seeking feedback, cocreating solutions, and maintaining an ongoing dialogue to ensure PMO services remain aligned with evolving organizational needs.
4. **Flexibility and adaptability over rigid adherence to plans.** A PMO's ability to respond quickly to change is crucial. This means developing the PMO's capacity to pivot quickly when circumstances change rather than stubbornly adhering to outdated plans or processes. In practice, this might involve implementing more flexible services or developing rapid response capabilities to address emerging customer needs.

Beyond these four values, the *Agile Manifesto* also outlined 12 principles that can be adapted to the PMO context, providing a roadmap for PMOs seeking to enhance their agility, relevance, and impact within their organizations. These principles offer a guiding framework for PMOs to evolve from process-centric entities to strategic, value-driven partners in organizational success.

The 12 principles of the *Agile Manifesto* adapted to a PMO context are:

1. The highest priority is to satisfy the organization through early and continuous delivery of valuable and adaptable PMO services.
2. Embrace changing organizational priorities and the needs of PMO customers even late in PMO initiative development. The PMO should leverage change to enhance its value, the organization's competitive advantage, and its strategic flexibility.
3. Deliver valuable PMO services and improvements incrementally, from weekly updates to monthly enhancements, prioritizing shorter delivery cycles to enable rapid feedback and adaptation.
4. Foster daily collaboration between the PMO team and PMO customers throughout the PMO initiatives. Break down silos and encourage cross-functional engagement.
5. Build PMO services and initiatives around motivated, cross-functional teams. Provide the teams with the necessary resources, autonomy, and support, trusting them to deliver value and drive continuous improvement.
6. Prioritize direct, real-time communication within the PMO and with PMO customers. While documentation is valuable, effective communication (face to face or virtual) is the most effective way of sharing information, aligning expectations, and resolving issues.
7. Measure PMO success primarily through the tangible value delivered to the PMO's customers and the organization. Focus on outcome-based metrics that demonstrate the PMO's impact on business objectives and customer satisfaction.
8. Promote sustainable operations through a balanced workload, continuous learning, and adaptable processes. The PMO should set a pace that allows for consistent value delivery while avoiding burnout and maintaining long-term effectiveness.
9. Continuously enhance PMO services through technical excellence, process optimization, and innovative solutions. Regularly assess and upgrade the PMO's services, tools, methodologies, and competencies to stay aligned with evolving organizational needs.
10. Embrace simplicity in PMO operations by focusing on high-value services and eliminating unnecessary complexity. Continuously refine processes, streamline governance, and prioritize efforts that directly contribute to organizational success.
11. Empower self-organizing teams within the PMO to design and evolve service offerings, methodologies, and practices. The most effective PMO structures, processes, and solutions emerge from teams that have the autonomy to innovate and adapt to changing organizational needs.
12. At regular intervals, the PMO conducts thorough self-assessments to evaluate its effectiveness, relevance, alignment with organizational goals, and overall value for its customers and the organization. Based on these reflections, the PMO continuously refines its strategies, services, and practices to enhance its value proposition and agility.

These adopted principles emphasize the PMO's focus on delivering value, embracing change, fostering collaboration, and continuously improving its practices to better serve the organization.

Embracing these agile values and principles represents a significant shift for many PMOs. The shift requires moving away from a control-oriented mindset toward one that prioritizes flexibility, collaboration, and continuous value delivery. This move can be challenging, as it often involves unlearning deeply ingrained practices and ways of thinking. However, the potential benefits of this transformation are substantial. By adopting an agile mindset, PMOs can become more responsive to organizational needs, better equipped to handle uncertainty and change, and more effective in driving real business value. The PMO can move from being perceived as bureaucratic overhead to becoming a true strategic partner in organizational success.

It is important to note that embracing agility does not mean abandoning all structure or governance. Rather, it involves finding a balance between flexibility and control, and between responsiveness and consistency. The goal is to create a PMO that can provide the necessary structure and support while remaining adaptable and value-focused.

PMOs That Adapt and Thrive

Contrary to popular belief, agility in PMOs is not merely about adopting agile methodologies or tools. At its core, agility represents a profound shift in behavior and mindset. This distinction is crucial for understanding the true nature of what we might call an agility-driven PMO.

An agility-driven PMO is not defined by the services it offers but by how the PMO operates and adapts to the needs of its customers and the organization as a whole. It is entirely possible, and in many cases desirable, for a PMO to offer no services that involve traditional agile methodologies or tools. Services are simply the means to meet customer needs, and true agility lies in the ability to flexibly choose and adapt these means in a responsive manner.

Consider, for instance, an energy company with a portfolio of large capital projects. In this context, a predictive approach might be more suitable than an adaptive one. Conversely, in a technology company, more adaptive methods may be preferable. The key lies in the PMO's ability to assess the context and choose the most appropriate approach, whether it is labeled "agile" or "traditional."

One more example, now using an approach that categorizes problems based on their complexity and uncertainty: Consider a tech company with well-established, off-the-shelf products. Despite being in the IT sector, their projects might have low uncertainty, making a predictive approach more suitable. Conversely, large investment projects with uncertain outcomes, such as developing new energy solutions, might benefit from a hybrid approach. The PMO should assess the uncertainty level and choose the appropriate method, blending agile and traditional approaches as needed.

In many environments, a hybrid approach will make the most sense. This situation is particularly true for PMOs serving a variety of customers from different departments (e.g., IT and engineering) with specific needs and challenges. True agility manifests in the ability to navigate this spectrum of approaches, selecting and combining elements as needed to deliver maximum value.

In practice, this might mean a PMO in a large manufacturing company using traditional, predictive methods for plant construction projects while simultaneously employing an agile approach for IT initiatives and a hybrid approach for product development. The agility lies not in the methods used but in the PMO's ability to select, adapt, and switch between these approaches as needed, always with an eye on delivering maximum value to the organization.

The essence of agility in PMOs, therefore, lies in how the PMO behaves—striving to adhere to agile values and principles regardless of the specific solutions it uses to serve its customers. In other words, agility in PMOs is not about what the PMO does but how it does it and how it responds to the needs of its customers and the organization. True agility manifests in the ability to adapt and navigate across this spectrum of approaches, selecting and combining elements as needed to deliver maximum value.

This transformation allows PMOs to become more responsive to organizational needs, better equipped to handle uncertainty and change, and more effective in driving real business value. This shift enables PMOs to move from being perceived as bureaucratic overhead to becoming agile enablers of organizational success.

Implementing Agility in PMO Practice

Implementing agility in PMO practice involves several key steps and considerations to ensure a successful transformation. This process begins with developing an adaptive mindset that embraces change, values flexibility, and prioritizes continuous improvement.

Creating a responsive structure and implementing customer-centric practices are crucial for agility. The PMO should offer flexible services that adapt to changing organizational needs and leverage data for informed decision-making.

Leadership plays a vital role in driving and sustaining agility, while transparent communication and collaboration enhance the process. Lastly, fostering innovation and maintaining a focus on delivering value will help the PMO become a true agility-driven entity.

The key steps and considerations for implementing agility in PMO practice include the following:

- **Develop an adaptive mindset.** The foundation of an agility-driven PMO is a mindset that embraces change, values flexibility, and prioritizes continuous improvement.
- **Create a responsive structure.** The organizational structure of the PMO should support agility and quick decision-making.
- **Implement customer-centric practices.** Putting the PMO customer at the center of PMO operations is crucial for agility.
- **Develop flexible service offerings.** An agility-driven PMO should be able to quickly adapt its services to meet changing organizational needs.
- **Embrace data-driven decision-making.** Leveraging data is crucial for making informed, agile decisions.

- **Promote decentralized management.** An agility-driven PMO promotes shared management with project and product teams. This approach empowers teams to make decisions and adapt quickly to changes.
- **Evaluate and navigate complexity.** Continuously assess and manage project complexity to ensure that approaches and plans enable teams to successfully navigate the project life cycle.
- **Foster adaptive leadership.** PMO leaders play a crucial role in driving and sustaining agility.
- **Enhance transparent communication.** Open and clear communication is essential for an agility-driven PMO.
- **Enhance collaboration and knowledge sharing.** Agility thrives on effective collaboration and rapid knowledge dissemination.
- **Foster innovation.** An agility-driven PMO should be a catalyst for innovation.

Implementing these practices requires patience, persistence, and a willingness to learn and adapt. It is important to remember that becoming an agility-driven PMO is a journey, not a destination. Regular reflection, continuous improvement, and a relentless focus on delivering value should be at the heart of this transformation.

Agility in PMOs is an ongoing commitment to adaptation, improvement, and value delivery. This commitment requires not just new skills and practices but a fundamental shift in how the PMO views itself and its position within the organization.

This journey toward becoming an agility-driven PMO is about cultivating a mindset of flexibility, customer centricity, and continuous improvement. The shift toward agility is about being responsive to change, focused on value delivery, and committed to enabling organizational success.

Navigating the Challenges of Demonstrating PMO Value

Quantifying the value of a PMO is a multifaceted challenge. Unlike straightforward financial metrics, the value generated by a PMO often encompasses a range of intangible benefits that, while critical to organizational success, are difficult to measure and express in purely monetary terms.

Empirical attempts to demonstrate the monetary value of a PMO to an organization's business have been ongoing. While academic initiatives have provided valuable insights into the PMO phenomenon, they have often presented inconclusive results when attempting to demonstrate the expected impact of a PMO on an organization's business.

Research has shown that finding a universal model is challenging due to the many variables that can influence how a PMO generates an impact on the business. These variables include the organization's culture, project management maturity, executive sponsorship, and, most importantly, the specific needs of each organization and how the PMO was set up to meet those needs.

On the other hand, the recent experience of some of the most prominent and successful PMOs globally has shown that PMOs that do not consistently generate perceived value for their customers—no matter how well they excel at the technical quality of their work—are constantly challenged and questioned.

These PMOs face a constant risk of being discontinued. Just like a service provider that does not deliver the expected benefits, PMOs that cannot make customers realize the value they generate for the organization are at risk of becoming obsolete.

Value Is in the Eye of the Beholder

As beauty, value is in the eye of the beholder. This phrase underscores a fundamental truth about PMO value: Success is not defined solely by the objective delivery of value but also by how this value is perceived by the PMO's customers.

A PMO might implement the most efficient processes and deliver projects on time and within budget, but if stakeholders do not recognize and value these efforts, the PMO's contributions may go unappreciated.

Each customer's perception of value will differ based on their individual pain points and needs. Therefore, mapping these pains and needs is essential for the PMO to design solutions that effectively meet customer expectations.

The Journey of Value Generation

Value generation is a journey where each customer's expectations evolve as their maturity increases. This dynamic process allows the PMO to construct a value journey for each customer, enabling continuous value delivery that meets evolving expectations and needs. PMO professionals should understand the importance of adapting and evolving alongside customers, ensuring that the PMO remains relevant and valuable over time.

A delivered value can be tangible or intangible, and both forms can be measured. Tangible values include cost savings, revenue increases, and efficiency gains. On the other hand, intangible values encompass improved communication, stakeholder satisfaction, and enhanced collaboration. Both types of value are critical and need to be recognized and measured to demonstrate the PMO's impact effectively.

The Concept of Customer Perception of Value

The concept of "customer perception of value" refers to the customer's evaluation of the benefits they receive from a product or service in relation to the costs or sacrifices they make. This evaluation is subjective and varies based on individual preferences, experiences, and expectations. Based on extensive knowledge from other knowledge areas, the general concept of "value perception" has been adapted to the reality of PMOs.

The perception of value is a subjective feeling that reflects whether customer expectations have been met. While technical indicators are essential, they cannot fully reflect an organization's perception of a PMO's relevance to the business. However, it is possible to manage and measure how a PMO generates value perception for its customers, and the experiences of world-class PMOs indicate that a PMO's ability to generate value perception is critical for its survival and continuity.

PMOs should focus on generating value perception and ensuring that customers recognize the value they bring to the organization to justify their existence and enable them to thrive. By focusing on delivering services and support that PMO customers perceive as valuable, a PMO can more effectively demonstrate its worth and contribute to the success of its customers and the organization.

The Influence of Maturity on Value Perception

The customer's maturity significantly influences the perception of value in project management. Even when a PMO delivers substantial value, it may not be recognized by customers who lack the maturity to understand the importance of the outcomes generated.

To better understand this concept, consider the analogy of an adult and a child being offered a real Ferrari—the highly coveted car—or a remote-controlled Ferrari toy. With a mature understanding, the adult would choose the real Ferrari for its undeniable value. In contrast, the child might choose the toy as it meets their expectation of benefits and aligns with their limited understanding of the real Ferrari's value.

In the real world, this situation might manifest in a scenario where high-level executives, despite being highly experienced and competent in their business areas, focus on tactical and operational aspects of project management rather than strategic ones. Their lower project management maturity may prevent the executives from fully appreciating the strategic value provided by the PMO.

Looking Ahead to the Next Section

With the PMO positioned as a value-driven service provider, it is clear how this approach can elevate PMOs into strategic assets for their organizations. Yet, to truly thrive in this capacity, PMOs should do more than offer services—they should adopt a customer-centric mindset. Shifting the focus from processes to people is the next pivotal step in the evolution of PMOs.

In the following section, the concept of PMO customer centricity and exploring how it can further boost the PMO's ability to deliver value and contribute to organizational success will be explored. The strategies for understanding customer needs, customizing services, and fostering strong stakeholder relationships will also be explained. This customer-centric approach builds on the value-driven model, pushing PMO effectiveness to new levels.

6

Embracing PMO Customer Centricity

Why This Section Matters to PMO Professionals

This section is critical for PMO professionals as it represents a paradigm shift in how PMOs operate and deliver value. The customer-centric approach transforms PMOs from process-oriented entities to strategic partners focused on meeting customer needs and expectations. This section provides the framework for this transformation, offering practical insights into understanding customer expectations, tailoring services, and measuring customer satisfaction.

The section also includes a list of 30 common, expected PMO outcomes drawn from extensive global research. With this customer-focused approach, PMO professionals can prioritize efforts, tailor services, and create tangible value, ultimately increasing the PMO's impact and proving its worth to the organization.

Defining PMO Customers

At the heart of a modern PMO lies a clear understanding of who exactly qualifies as a PMO customer. In essence, PMO customers are stakeholders within an organization that directly receive, use, or benefit from the services provided by the PMO.

While the terms "customers" and "stakeholders" are sometimes used interchangeably in the context of PMOs, they represent distinct concepts that are crucial to understand.

- **PMO customers.** This grouping includes those stakeholders who directly receive and use PMO services. They have specific needs that the PMO aims to meet and can provide direct feedback on the value and quality of PMO offerings. The relationship is transactional and service oriented.
- **Other PMO stakeholders.** PMO stakeholders encompass a broader group, including anyone who has an interest in or is affected by the PMO's activities, whether they directly use its services or not.

All PMO customers are stakeholders, but not all stakeholders are customers. For example, at a large retail chain undergoing a digital transformation, IT team leaders often utilize the PMO's mentoring services, making them both direct customers and stakeholders of the PMO. In contrast, store managers across the country, while not direct customers since they don't receive services from the PMO, are still stakeholders because the transformation will significantly impact their store operations, making them indirectly affected by the outcomes of the PMO's work.

The most frequent PMO customers can be broadly categorized into several groups (see Figure 6-1).

The common groups of PMO customers include:

- **Project managers.** Often the primary customers, project managers rely on the PMO for methodologies, tools, templates, and support in managing their projects.
- **Program managers.** Program managers depend on the PMO for program-level support, including resource allocation, interproject dependencies, and strategic alignment.

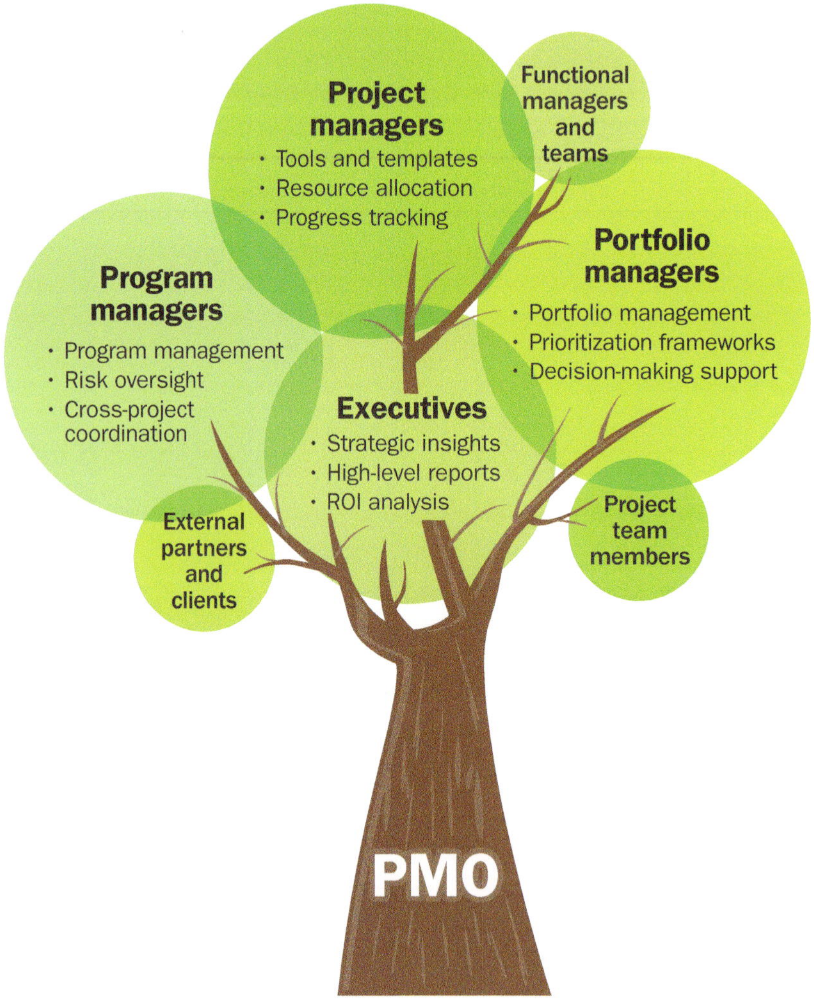

Figure 6-1. Common PMO Customer Groups

- **Portfolio managers.** These customers look to the PMO for portfolio-level insights, prioritization frameworks, and strategic decision-making support.
- **Executives and senior management.** Senior and executive-level management are customers who receive the PMO's strategic insights, performance reports, and decision-support services.
- **Project team members.** Project professionals across the team use PMO-provided tools and processes in their day-to-day project work.
- **Functional managers and teams.** Other managers and team members in the organization rely on the PMO for coordination across different departments, resource management, and aligning project outcomes with functional objectives.
- **External partners or clients.** In some cases, external entities may be PMO customers if they directly benefit from or interact with PMO services.

To qualify as a PMO customer, an individual should have a direct interaction with or dependency on the PMO's offerings. The key factor is that these customers have specific needs that the PMO aims to fulfill through its services.

Different customers have varying requirements—a project manager might need hands-on support with risk management practices, while the CEO might require high-level, strategic insights for decision-making.

By understanding these groups and their unique demands, PMOs can enhance their service delivery, providing tailored, value-added support that drives organizational success and delivers meaningful value.

Building a Customer-Centric PMO

The concept of customer centricity is very much in tune with the ethos of service providers such as a PMO because it recognizes that putting the customer at the center of operations is of paramount importance. This shift to customer centricity represents a fundamental change in how PMOs approach their strategies, processes, and overall performance. PMOs should now consider evolving customer needs and expectations; it is no longer possible to justify the PMO's existence by focusing solely on methods, tools, or any other technical outputs it generates.

Customer centricity as a critical differentiator enables PMOs to create stronger relationships, foster commitment, and achieve sustainable growth. This positioning acknowledges that customers have substantial power in an age of abundant choices and information. Customers not only require quality services but also want exceptional experiences and meaningful interactions at every touchpoint with the PMO.

Being customer centric is particularly important for PMOs. As internal service providers, PMOs should align their value proposition with the needs of their organizational customers, thus ensuring that project management practices deliver business value directly. By adopting a customer-centric approach, PMOs can cease being mere administrative entities and turn into strategic partners, pushing for organizational success.

Customer centricity refers to being strategic in approaching businesses' decisions, operations, and interactions, placing customers at their core. This philosophy prioritizes understanding, anticipating, and fulfilling customer needs to create long-term value and satisfaction.

At the heart of customer centricity is an understanding that the PMO's role is to serve its customers—the various persons who depend on PMO services. This change in perspective turns the usual idea of a PMO as a process-oriented, administrative entity into one that contributes value and becomes a partner in organizational success.

Principles of a Customer-Centric PMO

Adopting a customer-centric approach within a PMO requires adherence to several key principles that ensure the PMO remains focused on delivering value and meeting the needs of its customers. The fundamental principles of a customer-centric PMO are illustrated in Figure 6-2.

The principles of customer-centric PMOs include the following:

- **Customer-first mindset.** All decisions, processes, and services should be assessed based on how they meet the customers' needs. This mentality helps ensure that every action taken by the PMO is aligned with the goal of enhancing customer satisfaction and delivering tangible benefits. By prioritizing customer needs, the PMO can build trust and foster long-term relationships.
- **Value delivery.** The focus should be on delivering value to PMO customers rather than just enforcing procedures or methodologies. Value delivery involves understanding what constitutes value for different customers and ensuring that PMO activities contribute to achieving the most relevant outcomes, whether they are strategic, tactical, or operational.

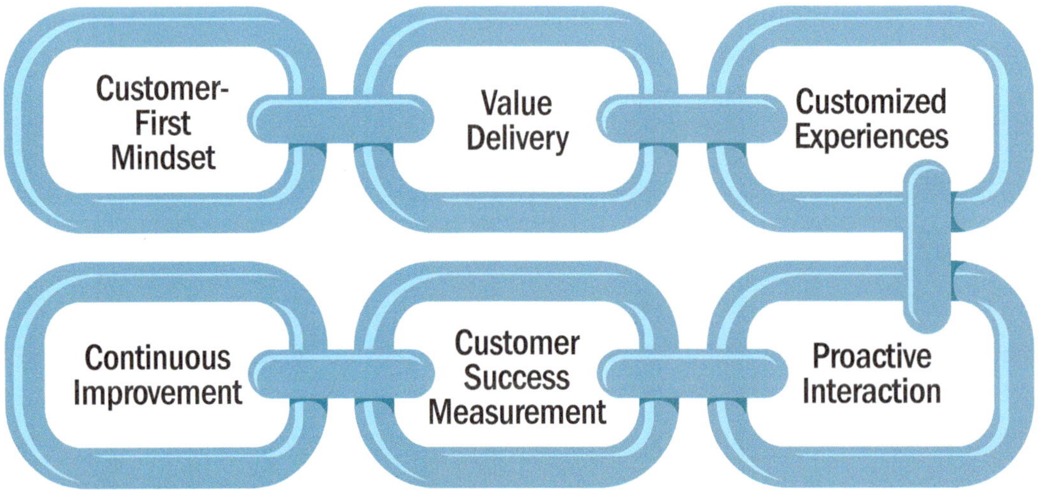

Figure 6-2. Key Principles of a Customer-Centric PMO

- **Customized experiences.** Services and interactions should be adapted according to PMO customers' needs, culture, and maturity level. This customization requires a deep understanding of the customer landscape, including their specific challenges, preferences, and expectations. By providing personalized services, the PMO can enhance its effectiveness and relevance.
- **Proactive interaction.** The PMO should actively seek out customer concerns rather than waiting for them to be raised, helping to ensure satisfactory results. Proactive interaction involves regularly engaging with customers to identify potential issues early and address them promptly. This approach helps build a responsive and agile PMO that can quickly adapt to changing customer needs.
- **Customer success and satisfaction measurement.** Define and track metrics that reflect PMO customer success, satisfaction, commitment, and advocacy. These metrics provide valuable insights into how well the PMO meets customer expectations and where improvements are needed. Regular measurement and analysis of these metrics can help in maintaining a customer-centric focus and driving continuous improvement.
- **Constant feedback loops and continuous improvement.** Regularly gather feedback from PMO customers to improve customer touchpoints and service outcomes continuously. Feedback is a critical component of a customer-centric approach as it provides direct input from the customers about their experiences and needs. By establishing a continuous feedback loop, the PMO can ensure that it remains aligned with customer expectations and adapts its services accordingly.

Identifying PMO Customers' Expectations

Understanding PMO customers' expectations is paramount to a PMO's success and relevance. These expectations represent the potential outcomes that customers anticipate from the PMO and its offered services. By gaining deep insight into these needs, the PMO can tailor its strategies and services to align closely with what truly matters to its customers.

PMO customers should articulate their needs to the PMO in terms of benefits and outcomes rather than technical functions, services, or outputs. Their primary concern is achieving effective results that address practical challenges in their daily work. By focusing on desired outcomes, customers enable the PMO to better understand the actual value they seek, allowing for more targeted and impactful solutions.

This outcome-oriented communication fosters a more substantial alignment between the PMO's offerings and the customers' actual needs, ultimately leading to higher satisfaction and more meaningful contributions to organizational success.

For instance, an executive is primarily interested in having reliable, comprehensive information readily available for decision-making—an outcome that enhances their ability to lead effectively. This desired result is more important to them than the processes, specific reports, or data analysis tools the PMO might use to deliver this information. Similarly, a project manager's primary concern is not the project management methodology but rather the results it enables—more efficient, cost-effective, and predictable projects.

By proactively seeking to understand and address these outcome-focused expectations, the PMO can tailor its services to truly align with customer needs and add meaningful value to its work. This customer-centric approach enables the PMO to anticipate requirements, offer relevant solutions, and consistently deliver impactful results that resonate with its customers' objectives.

To illustrate this concept, consider the analogy of a physician treating patients with various types of pain. Patients expect the doctor to alleviate their pain and cure them. If these expectations are met, the value of the physician's work is recognized. Just as different types of pain require specific treatments, different PMO customers have distinct needs that should be addressed with tailored services.

In the PMO world, every "pain" requires a specific "medicine," meaning that each challenge or desired outcome aligns with a tailored PMO service. Just as a doctor prescribes treatment to address a patient's symptoms, the PMO offers services designed to tackle specific organizational needs. For example, when there is a "pain" of lacking strategic alignment, the "medicine" might be portfolio management support to better connect the projects with strategic goals. In another case, if the challenge is inconsistent information for decision-making, the PMO could implement integrated systems and project status reporting to deliver reliable insights. Similarly, if the aim is to increase team motivation, the PMO might "prescribe" training or mentoring services. This approach ensures that every customer and organizational need is matched with a targeted solution.

When collecting PMO customers' expectations initially, it might seem logical to present customers with a "menu" of potential PMO services and ask them to select their preferences. However, this approach is fundamentally flawed. The crux of the issue lies in the disparity between the technical language of PMO services and the outcome-oriented language of PMO customers.

Asking PMO customers to choose from a list of services is akin to a doctor asking patients to select their preferred medicines. Customers, like patients, are typically not experts in the matter and cannot make informed decisions about which services best meet their needs. The solution lies in communicating with PMO customers using outcome-oriented language.

By asking each customer to select and prioritize the outcomes they value most, the PMO can identify the priorities it should focus on delivering. For instance, if a priority outcome is "more availability of resources with skills in project management," it becomes evident that "provide training and project competency development" is more likely to generate this outcome than "monitoring and controlling programs or projects." Assessing how well each service can generate each outcome allows the PMO to identify the most critical services to deliver the expected results.

Understanding and meeting PMO customer expectations is fundamental to creating a PMO that consistently generates value. By focusing on benefits and communicating in a customer-centric language, PMOs can align their services with customer needs, fostering engagement, continuous improvement, and strategic alignment. This approach enhances the PMO's impact and ensures its long-term relevance and success within the organization.

The 30 Potential PMO Outcomes

Building on the customer-centric approach, this section presents a powerful resource for PMO professionals: a curated list of 30 potential PMO outcomes. This comprehensive list has emerged from extensive research within the global PMO community, encompassing PMOs from diverse regions and industries. The insights gathered represent a broad spectrum of experiences, challenges, and good practices observed across various organizational contexts.

The outcomes listed have been distilled from interactions with PMO leaders, project managers, and stakeholders from multinational corporations, government agencies, nonprofit organizations, and small- to medium-sized enterprises. This diverse sample ensures that the list captures a wide range of potential needs and pain points that PMOs might encounter, regardless of their specific industry or geographical location. The 30 potential outcomes of a PMO are detailed in Table 6-1.

The PMO Customer Expectation Assessment, found in Appendix X2 of this guide, is a valuable tool for PMO professionals. For each of the 30 outcomes, it features "Evidence of Need," which highlights signs that a customer may face challenges in a specific area; "How to Question the Customer," which offers conversation starters to explore needs and expectations; and "Recommended Services," which lists common PMO services that could address the specific outcome. This assessment helps PMOs to determine needs systematically, prioritize services based on customer requirements, make informed decisions about resource allocation, and create a strategic, customer-centric approach to PMO operations.

Benefits of a Customer-Centric PMO

Transforming a traditional PMO into a customer-centric one can significantly enhance its relevance and effectiveness within an organization. Some typical advantages associated with this transformation include:

- **Added value creation.** When PMO services align with customers' needs, then value-chain activities become more visible on both sides. This alignment helps ensure that the PMO contributes directly to the achievement of organizational goals and delivers outcomes that are meaningful to its customers. As a result, the PMO is seen as a valuable partner in the organization's success.

    Example: At a global manufacturing company, executives struggled to see the connection between strategies and projects. The PMO introduced a comprehensive portfolio management process that visually mapped projects to strategic objectives. This initiative allowed executives to clearly perceive the value of ongoing projects, leading to more informed decision-making and a 25% increase in strategically aligned projects within 6 months.

Table 6-1. Potential Outcomes of a PMO

	Outcome	Description
1	**Better availability of skilled resources**	**Ensuring that the organization has access to highly skilled project and program managers to lead these initiatives effectively** This outcome is typically perceived in the medium to long term, as developing skilled resources requires consistent effort and time for training and experience to yield results.
2	**Better organizational change management**	**Implementing structured organizational change management practices to ensure smooth transitions and minimize disruptions** This outcome is typically perceived in the medium to long term, as seeing the benefits of recommended services related to organizational change management takes time to fully materialize.
3	**Better control over project teams**	**Establishing clear reporting structures and accountability measures to effectively manage project teams** This outcome is typically perceived in the short to medium term. While some improvements in team control can be seen quickly with the implementation of recommended services, fully optimized team management may take several months to achieve.
4	**Better definition of roles and responsibilities**	**Clearly defining roles and responsibilities to ensure that all project team members understand their duties and contributions** This outcome is typically perceived in the short to medium term. While initial role definitions can be established quickly, fully embedding and optimizing these roles across the organization may take several months.
5	**Better project prioritization**	**Prioritizing projects based on their strategic value and impact to ensure optimal resource allocation and focus** This outcome is typically perceived in the medium term. While initial prioritization can be established relatively quickly, the full benefits of optimized project selection often become apparent over several months as projects progress.
6	**Better quality of project results**	**Ensuring that projects deliver high-quality results that meet or exceed stakeholder expectations** This outcome is typically perceived in the medium to long term. While some quality improvements may be noticeable in the short term, consistently delivering high-quality results across multiple projects often takes time and becomes more apparent over a longer period.

Table 6-1. Potential Outcomes of a PMO (Continued)

	Outcome	Description
7	**Better talent management**	**Developing and implementing strategies to attract, retain, and develop top talent in project management** This outcome is typically perceived in the medium to long term. The full benefits of attracting, developing, and retaining top talent often become apparent over a longer period.
8	**Effective knowledge transfer**	**Facilitating the transfer of knowledge and good project management practices within the organization to maintain consistency and expertise** This outcome is typically perceived in the medium term. While some knowledge transfer occurs immediately through some services provided by the PMO, the full benefits of organization-wide knowledge-sharing and application usually become apparent over several months.
9	**Enhanced decision-making**	**Providing accurate, timely information to support better decision-making processes, leading to more successful portfolio, program, or project outcomes** This outcome is typically perceived in the short to medium term. While some improvements in decision-making can be seen quickly with better data and processes, the full impact on project outcomes may take several months to become apparent.
10	**Enhanced project customer experience**	**Delivering projects that consistently meet or exceed project customer expectations, leading to higher satisfaction and loyalty** This outcome is typically perceived in the medium term. While some improvements in project customer experience may be noticeable quickly, consistently delivering enhanced experiences across multiple projects often takes several months to achieve and become apparent.
11	**Enhanced resource management**	**Optimizing the allocation and use of resources to ensure that projects are adequately staffed and supported** This outcome is typically perceived in the medium term. While initial improvements in resource allocation can be seen quickly, the full benefits of optimized resource management across multiple projects often become apparent over several months as projects progress.
12	**Greater alignment with strategic objectives**	**Ensuring that all programs and projects support the organization's strategic goals, maximizing their impact and value** This outcome is typically perceived in the medium to long term. While initial alignment can be established quickly, the full benefits of strategically aligned programs and projects often become apparent over a longer period as they deliver results that contribute to organizational objectives.

(Continued)

Table 6-1. Potential Outcomes of a PMO (Continued)

Outcome		Description
13	Greater integration among organizational areas	**Promoting collaboration and integration among different departments to ensure cohesive and efficient project execution** This outcome is typically perceived in the medium to long term. While initial steps toward integration can be implemented quickly, achieving meaningful and lasting integration among different organizational areas often requires time to overcome silos and establish new collaborative practices.
14	Higher return on investment (ROI)	**Maximizing the financial return on portfolios, programs, and projects by ensuring they deliver significant value and align with strategic goals** This outcome is typically perceived in the long term. While some improvements in project selection and execution can be seen earlier, the full financial impact and higher ROI often become apparent only after projects are completed and benefits are realized, which can take a year or more.
15	Improved availability of information	**Providing timely and accurate portfolio, program, and project information to support decision-making processes** This outcome is typically perceived in the short to medium term. While some improvements in information availability can be seen quickly with the implementation of new systems and processes, fully optimizing information flow and utilization may take several months to achieve.
16	Improved collaboration and communication	**Enhancing communication channels and fostering collaboration to ensure all project team members and stakeholders are aligned and informed** This outcome is typically perceived in the short to medium term. While some improvements in collaboration and communication can be seen quickly with new practices and tools, fully embedding a collaborative culture across the organization may take several months to achieve.
17	Improved organizational commitment to results	**Cultivating a culture of accountability and focusing on achieving portfolio, program, and project results that align with organizational goals** This outcome is typically perceived in the medium to long term. While initial steps toward improving commitment can be implemented quickly, fully embedding a results-focused culture across the organization often requires time to change mindsets and establish new practices.
18	Improved project budget management	**Ensuring strict budget controls and financial oversight to keep projects within budget** This outcome is typically perceived in the short to medium term. While improvements in budget tracking and control can be seen quickly, the full benefits of consistently keeping projects within budget often become apparent over several months as multiple projects are completed.

Table 6-1. Potential Outcomes of a PMO (Continued)

Outcome		Description
19	Improved project customer relationships	**Building and maintaining strong relationships with project customers through effective communication and meeting expectations** This outcome is typically perceived in the medium term. While some improvements in project customer relationships can be seen quickly with better communication practices, building strong relationships often takes a history of consistent performance and engagement across multiple project touchpoints.
20	Improved performance management	**Monitoring and managing portfolio, program, and project performance to identify issues early and ensure successful delivery** This outcome is typically perceived in the short to medium term. While some improvements in performance tracking can be seen quickly, the full benefits of enhanced performance management across multiple projects often become apparent over several months as the system matures.
21	Improved success rates	**Ensuring that programs and projects are completed on time and within budget while meeting their objectives, which enhances overall organizational success** This outcome is typically perceived in the medium to long term. While some improvements in project execution can be seen quickly, consistently higher success rates across multiple projects and programs often take time to achieve and become apparent, usually over a period of 6 months to a year or more.
22	Improved reliability of information provided	**Ensuring that all portfolio, program, and project information is reliable, up to date, and accurate to support informed decision-making** This outcome is typically perceived in the short to medium term. While initial improvements in data quality can be seen quickly with new systems and processes, fully establishing a culture of reliable information across all projects may take several months to achieve and validate.
23	Improved stakeholder engagement	**Engaging stakeholders throughout program or project life cycles to ensure their needs are met and expectations managed** This outcome is typically perceived in the short to medium term. While some improvements in stakeholder engagement can be seen quickly with new practices, building strong, consistent engagement across all stakeholder groups often takes several months to fully establish and demonstrate results.
24	Increased organizational learning	**Fostering a culture of learning and continuous improvement by capturing and sharing lessons learned** This outcome is typically perceived in the medium to long term. While initial steps toward capturing and sharing lessons can be implemented quickly, building a true culture of organizational learning and seeing its impact on project performance often takes a year or more to fully realize.

(Continued)

Table 6-1. Potential Outcomes of a PMO (Continued)

Outcome		Description
25	Increased productivity on projects	**Implementing good practices and tools to boost the productivity and efficiency of project teams** This outcome is typically perceived in the short to medium term. While some productivity improvements can be seen quickly with new tools and processes, fully optimizing team productivity across multiple projects often takes several months as teams adapt to and master new practices.
26	Increased visibility of project progress	**Providing clear and regular updates on project progress to ensure all stakeholders are informed and aligned** This outcome is typically perceived in the short term. Improvements in project progress visibility can often be seen quickly with the implementation of new reporting processes and tools, usually within the first few weeks or months of implementation.
27	More accurate project forecasting	**Using reliable data and methodologies to provide accurate project forecasts and better planning** This outcome is typically perceived in the medium term. While initial improvements in forecasting can be seen relatively quickly, developing truly accurate and reliable forecasting capabilities often takes several months as historical data accumulates and forecasting models are refined based on actual project outcomes.
28	Reduction of risk exposure	**Implementing comprehensive risk management strategies to identify, assess, and mitigate risks** This outcome is typically perceived in the medium term. While initial risk identification and mitigation strategies can be implemented quickly, the full benefits of reduced risk exposure on portfolios, programs, and projects often become apparent over several months as programs and projects progress and potential risks are successfully managed or avoided.
29	Stronger governance and compliance	**Establishing and maintaining strong governance frameworks to ensure compliance with all relevant regulations and policies** This outcome is typically perceived in the medium to long term. While initial portfolio, program, and project governance structures can be established quickly, fully embedding strong governance practices and demonstrating consistent compliance across the organization often takes several months to a year to achieve and validate.
30	Reduction of project life cycle	**Streamlining project processes to reduce the time required to complete projects and deliver results faster** This outcome is typically perceived in the medium term. While some improvements in project efficiency can be seen quickly, consistently reducing project life cycles across multiple projects often takes several months to achieve as new methodologies and practices are fully adopted and refined.

- **Enhanced PMO customer relationships.** Emphasizing customer success and satisfaction leads to closer, more positive ties across the entire organization. Strong customer relationships are built on trust, communication, and a shared commitment to achieving project goals. By focusing on customer needs, the PMO can build stronger, more collaborative relationships with stakeholders.

  Example: A technology firm's PMO established a mentorship program for inexperienced project managers. By providing one-on-one guidance, regular check-ins, and tailored advice, the PMO developed strong, trust-based relationships with the project managers. As a result, project success rates improved by 40% over a year, and the PMO became known as a trusted partner in professional development.

- **Flexible responses.** Ongoing feedback from PMO customers allows the PMO to respond quickly to changing specific contexts. Flexibility is crucial in a dynamic business environment where customer needs and project requirements can evolve quickly. A customer-centric PMO is better equipped to adapt to these changes and provide timely, effective support.

  Example: A diversified conglomerate's PMO noticed that its IT and construction divisions had vastly different project management needs. In response, they developed two distinct methodologies: an agile-based approach for the fast-paced IT division and a more traditional waterfall method for the construction unit. This tailored approach led to a 60% increase in methodology adoption rates across both divisions within 3 months.

- **Better strategic fit.** The PMO understands customer needs so that its services can effectively align with general organizational strategy. Aligning PMO services with organizational strategy helps ensure that the PMO contributes to the achievement of strategic objectives and provides value that supports the overall direction of the organization.

  Example: Anticipating the organization's impending digital transformation efforts, a retail company's PMO proactively launched an extensive project management competency development program. When the transformation initiative was officially announced 6 months later, the organization already had a pool of more than 100 trained professionals ready to lead critical projects.

- **Increased PMO relevance.** To help ensure that such a unit is needed and accountable in the organization, the PMO should take a customer-focused standpoint. A customer-centric PMO demonstrates its value through its ability to meet customer needs, solve problems, and deliver successful project outcomes. This relevance helps secure the PMO's position within the organization and justify its existence.

  Example: A financial services firm's PMO conducted a comprehensive review of its services and tools. The PMO identified several practices and tools that were no longer justified by their customers' actual needs. The PMO sunsetted these outdated services and tools and redirected efforts to develop new services to address emerging customer needs. This proactive approach not only saved the company US$500,000 annually but also positioned the PMO as an innovative, forward-thinking unit essential to the organization's future success.

In short, a customer-centric PMO represents an evolution of PMO practices. Integrating operations with an organization's actual needs significantly improves value. By doing this, PMOs can create more value, deliver better project results, and position themselves as critical to their organization's success.

Looking Ahead to the Next Section

Having explored the concept of PMO customer centricity, it is clear how this approach can greatly enhance a PMO's effectiveness and add value to the organization. To fully unlock this potential, however, PMOs should have a deep understanding of the services they provide and how these offerings evolve over time.

The following section explores PMO services and maturity, covering a wide range of services—from strategic guidance to operational support. The section describes how these services mature and adapt, enabling PMOs to consistently improve their value proposition. By mastering service delivery and maturity, PMO professionals can be better equipped to implement customer-centric strategies that meet and exceed expectations at every stage.

7

PMO Services and PMO Maturity

Why This Section Matters to PMO Professionals

This section provides PMO professionals with a comprehensive list of the 26 most common PMO services, based on research from the global PMO community. The section offers a detailed overview of strategic, tactical, and operational services widely implemented across various organizations.

Additionally, it introduces a valuable model that highlights different approaches for delivering these services to PMO customers, moving beyond the traditional, one-size-fits-all categorization. This flexible framework enables more nuanced and adaptable service delivery. The section also clarifies what PMO maturity truly means and presents a model for evaluating the maturity of PMO services.

By exploring this range of services, delivery methods, and the concept of service maturity, PMO professionals can gain insights into how to tailor their offerings to meet the unique needs of their organization.

From PMO Functions to PMO Services

PMOs should evolve from functional units into strategic service providers within their organizations. This shift reflects a deeper understanding of how PMOs can drive value and contribute to organizational success in today's complex business landscape.

At their core, PMOs serve as central hubs for portfolio, program, and project management expertise. A PMO offers a comprehensive suite of services designed to enhance capabilities and drive organizational success. These offerings are not static; they evolve as the organization's goals change, PMO customers' requirements arise, and the PMO itself matures.

The transition from viewing PMO activities as "functions" to "services" represents a fundamental change in organizational mindset. This customer-centric approach positions the PMO as a value provider, focusing on meeting its customers' needs. By framing their offerings as services, PMOs can more clearly articulate their value proposition and align with organizational needs.

This service-oriented approach offers several advantages. A focus on service allows for greater flexibility and adaptability, enabling PMOs to adjust their offerings based on changing organizational needs. Services are typically easier to define, measure, and evaluate, facilitating performance tracking and continuous improvement efforts.

Moreover, the service model encourages more active customer engagement, creating a two-way relationship rather than a top-down, functional approach. The service mindset fosters a value-driven mentality, where the PMO should clearly demonstrate its value to the organization. This perspective professionalizes the PMO role, positioning it as a strategic partner rather than just an administrative function.

The service approach also allows for customization, enabling PMOs to tailor their offerings to meet the diverse needs of different customers, departments, or business units. The approach often comes with clearer expectations and service-level agreements, increasing accountability and leading to improved service quality and stakeholder satisfaction.

By embracing this service-oriented mindset, PMOs can transform from static, process-oriented entities into proactive, value-generating partners in organizational success. This evolution positions the PMO to play a more strategic role, directly contributing to organizational agility, efficiency, and overall success.

In essence, PMO services are designed to enhance project management maturity, drive strategic alignment, and ultimately contribute to the achievement of organizational goals. Understanding and leveraging these diverse services is essential for both PMO professionals and organizational leaders seeking to maximize the value of their project management initiatives in an increasingly complex business environment.

Service Categories and Domains

PMO services encompass a wide range of functions designed to support and enhance portfolio, program, and project management within an organization. These services are integral to ensuring that projects are executed efficiently, strategically aligned with organizational goals, and deliver maximum value.

These PMO services can be classified into three main categories: strategic, tactical, and operational, as detailed in Table 7-1.

Additionally, these services can be applied across the three different domains. By tailoring PMO services to these domains, organizations can effectively address their distinct needs:

- **Portfolio.** This domain encompasses the strategic management of all programs and projects within an organization. PMO services in this domain include portfolio planning, prioritization, performance measurement, and alignment with organizational strategy. This ensures that the portfolio delivers maximum value and supports the organization's overall objectives.
- **Program.** This domain involves the coordinated management of multiple related projects that are aligned to achieve a common goal. PMO services here include program governance, resource allocation, risk management, and benefits realization, ensuring that all projects within the program deliver their intended benefits.
- **Project.** This domain focuses on the management of individual projects, ensuring that each project is completed on time, within budget, and to the required quality standards. PMO services in this domain include project planning, execution, monitoring, and closure.

Table 7-1. Features of Strategic, Tactical, and Operational PMOs

PMO Service Type	Features
Strategic	• Aligns directly with the organizational portfolio, strategy, and goals • Involves executive-level decision-making and oversight • Impacts the entire organization or multiple departments • Influences organizational culture and project management maturity
Tactical	• Serves multiple programs, projects, or customers simultaneously • Involves middle management and senior project professionals • Standardizes processes and methodologies • Manages shared resources and interdependencies • Facilitates communication and coordination across different initiatives
Operational	• Serves individual programs, projects, or customers • Involves project managers and team members directly • Provides day-to-day support and problem-solving • Focuses on specific project deliverables and milestones

Most Common PMO Services

The services provided by PMOs can vary significantly depending on the organization. However, there are several common services that world-class PMOs offer to drive organizational success. Table 7-2 provides a comprehensive overview of the 26 most common PMO services observed in the global PMO community, their categories (strategic, tactical, or operational), and applicable domains (portfolio, program, and project).

It is important to highlight that other services or variations of services presented in Table 7-2 can be observed, albeit less frequently, in PMOs around the world. Although these variations are not common and therefore not listed, this does not make them any less necessary or relevant. On the contrary, they are essential in tailoring PMOs to the specific needs of each organization, ensuring that unique particularities and demands are effectively addressed.

Table 7-2. Common PMO Services Observed in the PMO Community

	Service	Description
		Strategic Services
1	**Advice to executive level**	Providing strategic guidance and advice to senior executives on portfolio, program, and project management to ensure alignment with organizational goals and objectives **Domains:** portfolio/program/project
2	**Benefits realization management**	Managing and measuring the realization of benefits from an organization's portfolio of programs and projects to ensure they deliver the expected value to the organization **Domains:** portfolio/program
3	**Foster project culture**	Promoting project management culture within the organization to enhance project awareness, support, and collaboration **Domains:** portfolio/program/project
4	**Governance oversight**	Establishing and maintaining governance frameworks to ensure portfolios, programs, and projects are managed in accordance with organizational policies and standards **Domains:** portfolio/program/project
5	**Organizational change management**	Managing the impact of organizational changes on programs and projects to ensure smooth transitions and minimize disruption **Domains:** program/project
6	**Portfolio management**	Overseeing the selection, prioritization, monitoring, and overall management of programs and projects within the portfolio to ensure alignment with strategic objectives and optimal resource allocation **Domain:** portfolio
7	**Strategic planning support**	Providing support for strategic planning activities to ensure programs and projects align with long-term organizational goals **Domain:** portfolio
		Tactical Services
8	**Knowledge management**	Capturing, organizing, and sharing portfolio, program, and project management knowledge; lessons learned; and good practices to foster continuous improvement and organizational learning **Domains:** portfolio/program/project
9	**Methodologies and frameworks management**	Developing, implementing, and maintaining standardized methodologies and frameworks to ensure consistency and quality in portfolio, program, and project management **Domains:** portfolio/program/project

Table 7-2. Common PMO Services Observed in the PMO Community (Continued)

Service		Description
10	**Resource management**	Allocating and managing resources effectively across projects to ensure optimal utilization and minimize conflicts **Domain:** project
11	**Systems and tools management**	Managing and maintaining systems and tools to support effective portfolio, program, and project management **Domains:** portfolio/program/project
12	**Training and development**	Offering training and development programs to enhance the skills and competencies in portfolio, program, and project management within the organization **Domains:** portfolio/program/project
		Operational Services
13	**Audit assessments**	Conducting thorough audits and assessments of projects to ensure compliance with standards, identify issues, and recommend improvements **Domain:** project
14	**Change control management**	Overseeing the change control process to manage changes in programs and projects, ensuring minimal disruption and alignment with objectives **Domains:** program/project
15	**Customer relationship management**	Maintaining and enhancing relationships and interfaces with project customers to ensure their needs and expectations are met throughout the project life cycle **Domain:** project
16	**Data analytics and reporting**	Providing data analytics and reporting services to monitor project performance, identify trends, and support informed decision-making **Domain:** project
17	**Issue management**	Identifying, tracking, and managing issues that arise in projects to ensure they are resolved promptly and do not impact success **Domain:** project
18	**Mentoring and coaching**	Providing mentoring and coaching to project managers and teams to enhance their skills, knowledge, and performance **Domain:** project

(Continued)

Table 7-2. Common PMO Services Observed in the PMO Community (Continued)

Service		Description
19	**Performance management**	Monitoring and managing the performance of programs and projects to ensure they meet their objectives and deliver expected outputs and outcomes **Domains:** program/project
20	**Program management**	Managing and coordinating multiple related projects as a program to deliver benefits and achieve strategic goals **Domain:** program
21	**Project management**	Managing and coordinating a project to deliver specific objectives within scope, time, budget, and quality constraints **Domain:** project
22	**Project support services**	Offering comprehensive technical support to project managers, including assistance with project planning and task coordination, while working under the guidance of the project manager **Domain:** project
23	**Quality assurance**	Ensuring that project deliverables meet defined quality standards through systematic quality assurance processes **Domain:** project
24	**Risk management**	Identifying, assessing, and managing risks throughout the program and project life cycles to minimize their impacts on success **Domains:** program/project
25	**Specialized services**	Providing specialized services customized to meet the unique requirements of individual projects; PMO team members possess the expertise and resources necessary to support project managers in activities where they may lack specific technical or domain knowledge **Domain:** project
26	**Stakeholder engagement**	Identifying and managing stakeholder expectations and engagement to ensure their support and involvement in projects **Domain:** project

PMO Service Approaches

The concept of PMO service approaches represents a significant evolution in how PMOs operate and deliver value within organizations. This shift moves away from traditional, rigid service models toward a more dynamic and flexible approach that enables PMOs to better meet the evolving needs and expectations of their diverse customer base.

Traditionally, PMOs were often categorized into fixed types such as consultative, directive, supportive, or controlling, with the assumption that a PMO would operate uniformly regardless of its customers or the services provided. However, this one-size-fits-all approach has proven to inadequately represent the reality observed in PMOs across various organizations worldwide.

In fact, the reality within organizations is far more nuanced. Depending on the characteristics of the customers, such as their project management maturity level and the specific services being provided, different approaches can and should be utilized. This realization has led to the development of a more flexible, customer-centric model of PMO service delivery.

Tailoring Approaches to Customer Needs

A key insight in this new paradigm is that a PMO might offer the same service to two different customers using distinct approaches. For example, the PMO could adopt a consultative manner for one customer while taking a more controlling approach for another. This decision is typically influenced by the maturity level of each customer in terms of project management capabilities.

Consider a scenario where a PMO is providing services to both the IT and finance departments of an organization. The IT department, being more frequently involved in projects, is likely to have a higher project management maturity level. In contrast, the finance department, which is primarily process-oriented, might have a lower maturity level in project management. Consequently, the PMO might provide the same service to both departments but with different approaches, offering more autonomy to IT and less to finance.

This customer-centered approach recognizes that different departments or teams within an organization can have vastly different experiences with—and capabilities in—project management. By tailoring the approach to the specific needs and maturity levels of different customers, the PMO can provide the right balance of support and autonomy, enhancing its effectiveness and value to the organization. The different approaches allow PMOs to gradually increase the autonomy given to customers as their capabilities and maturity grow. The primary approaches a PMO might use for a specific service are shown in Figure 7-1.

The primary approaches include:

- **Consultative approach.** In this approach, the PMO acts as an advisor, providing expert advice and recommendations. The customers maintain full control over portfolios, programs, and projects, making their own decisions based on the guidance received. This approach is often suitable for mature customers with solid capabilities and maturity.

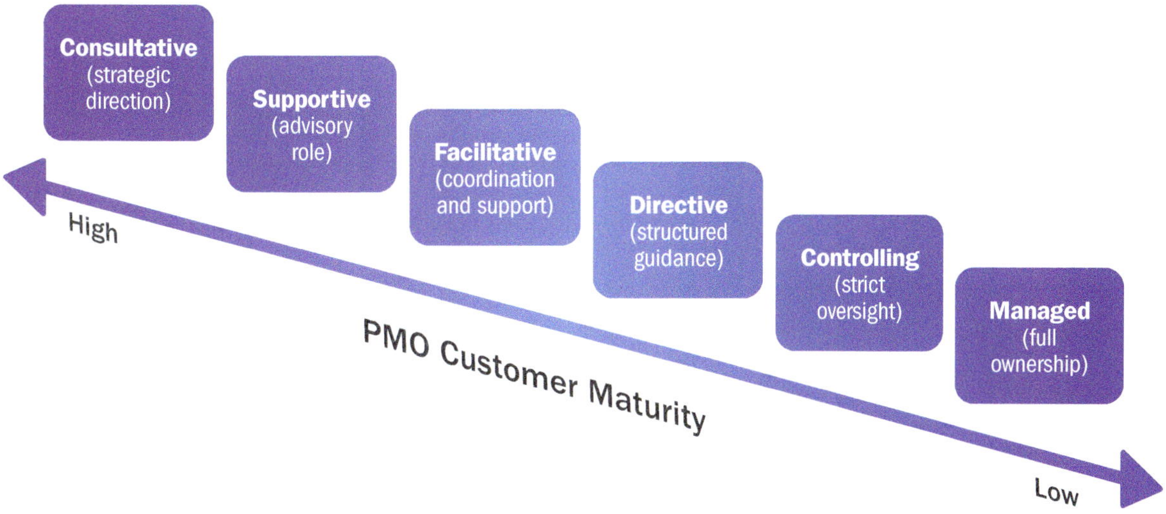

Figure 7-1. PMO Service Approaches

- **Supportive approach.** In this approach, the PMO offers practical assistance, tools, and resources to help customers execute their responsibilities more effectively. While the PMO facilitates and supports, the customers retain significant control and autonomy over portfolios, programs, and projects. This approach can be effective for customers with moderate capabilities and maturity.
- **Facilitative approach.** This approach involves the PMO facilitating activities with customers through collaborative sessions. Customers have a high level of involvement and ownership with the PMO, creating an environment conducive to achieving shared goals related to portfolios, programs, and projects. This approach can be particularly useful in cross-functional scenarios where customers have moderate capabilities and maturity.
- **Directive approach.** In this approach, the PMO implements standardized processes and provides clear guidelines for executing specific tasks. While customers follow the established processes, they have less control over how tasks are executed, as the PMO dictates the processes related to portfolios, programs, and projects. This approach might be necessary for customers with low capabilities and maturity.
- **Controlling approach.** In this approach, the PMO oversees and regulates processes under the customer's responsibility, maintaining control over portfolios, programs, and projects. The PMO has the authority to make decisions and implement actions, significantly reducing customer autonomy. This approach might be used in high-risk projects or with customers with very low capabilities and maturity.
- **Managed approach.** This is the most hands-on approach, where the PMO takes full responsibility for managing specific portfolio, program, or project activities for the organization or its customers. The PMO actively manages activities, leaving customers with minimal control over execution. This approach might be used for strategic, organization-wide initiatives or in cases where the customer lacks the capacity to manage the initiatives or activities effectively.

It is important to note that some PMO services may not encompass all of the approaches and may be restricted to only a few of them.

Choosing the Right Approach

The choice of service approach may depend on several factors, including the organization's culture, the level of the customer's project management maturity, available resources, and the nature of the projects being managed.

PMOs may also adopt a hybrid model, combining elements of different approaches to best meet the organization's needs. For example, an organization might use a managed approach for core strategic projects. Alternatively, a PMO might adopt a supportive approach for most projects but take on a directive role for high-priority initiatives requiring strict standards adherence.

Ultimately, the goal of these various approaches is to enhance project management effectiveness, align project outcomes with organizational objectives, and deliver value to the organization. The key to successful implementation lies in clarity and consistency in how the chosen approach is applied and understood within the organization.

By tailoring the approach to the organization's specific needs and context, PMOs can ensure they provide the most effective support for project success. Flexibility and adaptability are essential, allowing the PMO to evolve and adjust its strategies as organizational needs change over time.

This adaptive strategy allows PMOs to meet customers where they are in terms of project management maturity, providing the right level of support to drive continuous improvement and success.

Applying Service Approaches in Various PMO Services

Examples of how different services align with specific approaches include:

Example #1—Service: Advice to Executive Level

- **Consultative approach.** The PMO provides strategic guidance to executives based on accepted practices and industry standards.
- **Supportive approach.** The PMO offers tools and templates to help executives plan and manage strategic initiatives.
- **Facilitative approach.** The PMO organizes strategic planning workshops with executives to collaboratively define project priorities and goals.
- **Directive approach.** To ensure alignment with organizational goals, executives should establish strategic directives.

Example #2—Service: Benefits Realization Management

- **Consultative approach.** The PMO advises on the most appropriate methods and practices for benefits realization based on industry benchmarks.
- **Supportive approach.** The PMO provides frameworks and tools to help measure and manage benefits across portfolios and programs.
- **Directive approach.** The PMO mandates specific benefits realization processes and metrics that should be adhered to by program managers.
- **Managed approach.** The PMO takes full responsibility for tracking and reporting benefits realization metrics to help ensure alignment with strategic goals.

Example #3—Service: Methodologies and Frameworks Management

- **Consultative approach.** The PMO provides expert advice on selecting and tailoring methodologies to suit organizational needs.
- **Supportive approach.** The PMO offers training and resources to help teams understand and apply methodologies.

- **Facilitative approach.** The PMO leads collaborative sessions to develop or refine methodologies and frameworks with input from various stakeholders.
- **Directive approach.** The PMO implements standardized methodologies and frameworks that should be followed by all programs and projects.

Example #4—Service: Training and Development

- **Consultative approach.** The PMO provides personalized coaching and mentoring to project professionals to help them improve their capabilities.
- **Supportive approach.** The PMO offers training programs and resources to enhance project management skills across the organization.
- **Facilitative approach.** The PMO organizes workshops and peer-learning sessions to share knowledge and good practices.
- **Directive approach.** The PMO requires mandatory training for all project professionals to help ensure compliance with organizational standards.

Example #5—Service: Audit Assessments

- **Consultative approach.** The PMO advises project teams on accepted practices to meet audit requirements and improve project performance.
- **Supportive approach.** The PMO provides guidelines and tools to help project teams prepare for audits and address identified issues.
- **Directive approach.** The PMO conducts mandatory audits to help ensure compliance with project management standards and identify areas for improvement.
- **Managed approach.** The PMO takes responsibility for conducting thorough audits and implementing necessary corrective actions.

Example #6—Service: Customer Relationship Management

- **Consultative approach.** The PMO provides expert advice on improving project customer engagement and satisfaction.
- **Supportive approach.** The PMO offers tools and resources to help project teams manage project customer relationships effectively.
- **Facilitative approach.** The PMO organizes regular meetings and feedback sessions between project teams and project customers to foster collaboration.
- **Directive approach.** The PMO establishes clear guidelines and processes for managing project customer interactions and expectations.

Example #7—Service: Risk Management

- **Consultative approach.** The PMO advises on good practices and strategies for identifying and mitigating project risks.
- **Supportive approach.** The PMO provides risk management tools and resources to help project teams effectively manage risks.
- **Facilitative approach.** The PMO leads risk assessment workshops to collaboratively identify and address project risks.
- **Directive approach.** The PMO implements mandatory risk management processes and frameworks that should be followed by all projects.

Example #8—Service: Governance Oversight

- **Consultative approach.** The PMO advises program and project managers on good practices and compliance requirements, helping them align their activities with governance standards while maintaining some flexibility.
- **Supportive approach.** The PMO provides tools, templates, and resources to help program and project managers meet governance requirements, offering practical support without enforcing compliance.
- **Facilitative approach.** The PMO organizes workshops and training sessions to educate project teams on governance practices, encouraging collaborative learning and self-compliance among teams.
- **Controlling approach.** The PMO enforces strict governance policies and procedures that all programs and projects should adhere to. This approach involves regular audits, compliance checks, and the authority to halt or redirect projects that do not meet governance standards, ensuring that all activities align with organizational policies.

Example #9—Service: Resource Management

- **Consultative approach.** The PMO provides expert advice on resource management strategies, helping program and project managers to optimize resource allocation based on good practices and organizational goals.
- **Supportive approach.** The PMO offers tools and systems to track and manage resources, providing assistance to project teams in efficiently utilizing available resources while retaining control over their allocation.
- **Facilitative approach.** The PMO facilitates resource planning meetings, bringing together project managers and resource owners to collaboratively address resource allocation challenges and help ensure alignment with organizational priorities.

- **Controlling approach.** The PMO centrally controls the allocation and utilization of resources across all programs and projects. This approach includes approving resource requests, reallocating resources as needed, and monitoring resource usage to prevent overallocation or underutilization, ensuring optimal efficiency and adherence to strategic priorities.

Example #10—Service: Portfolio Management

- **Consultative approach.** The PMO advises on portfolio management good practices, helping executives make informed decisions about which projects to include in the portfolio and how to prioritize them.
- **Supportive approach.** The PMO provides tools and frameworks for portfolio analysis and reporting, assisting executives in tracking portfolio performance and making data-driven decisions.
- **Facilitative approach.** The PMO organizes portfolio review meetings, facilitating discussions among executives to assess portfolio performance, address challenges, and realign priorities as needed.
- **Controlling approach.** The PMO maintains strict oversight over portfolio selection, prioritization, and monitoring, ensuring that all programs and projects align with strategic objectives. The PMO has the authority to approve or reject projects based on strategic fit and resource availability.

By aligning these services with the most suitable approaches, the PMO can effectively meet each service's specific needs and challenges, ensuring maximum impact and relevance within the organization.

The service approaches presented in this section revolutionize our understanding of PMOs, definitively dispelling the outdated notion that PMOs can be rigidly classified into simplistic categories such as directive PMO, controlling PMO, or supportive PMO. This evolution in thinking is based on observations of successful PMOs worldwide, revealing that the reality is far more nuanced and complex than these rigid classifications suggest.

In practice, high-performing PMOs demonstrate a remarkable ability to adapt their approaches dynamically, often employing different strategies simultaneously across various services and customers within the same organization. This flexibility allows PMOs to tailor their support to the specific needs, maturity levels, and contexts of each customer, maximizing the value they deliver.

For instance, a PMO might adopt a consultative approach when working with a highly mature IT department on strategic planning, while taking a more directive stance with a less experienced marketing team on project execution. Simultaneously, it could provide supportive services to the finance department for resource management. This adaptability enables the PMO to meet each customer's unique needs effectively, fostering growth and success across the entire organization.

Moreover, this flexible approach allows PMOs to evolve their services over time, gradually shifting from more hands-on, controlling approaches to more consultative ones as their customers' capabilities mature. This evolution helps ensure that the PMO continues to add value, even as the organization's needs change.

In essence, the modern PMO is not defined by a single approach but by its ability to seamlessly transition among multiple approaches, always with the goal of delivering maximum value. This sophisticated understanding of PMO capabilities opens up new possibilities for how these entities can drive organizational success, foster innovation, and support strategic objectives across all levels of project management maturity.

As PMO professionals internalize this more nuanced perspective, they can develop more comprehensive, flexible, and impactful service offerings. This approach not only enhances the PMO's ability to meet current organizational needs but also positions it to adapt and thrive in the face of future challenges and opportunities.

Understanding PMO Service Maturity

Project management maturity has long been a focus for organizations aiming to enhance their project delivery capabilities. While organizational project management maturity is a well-established concept, there is growing recognition that PMO maturity is a distinct and equally crucial aspect.

PMO maturity refers to the sophistication and effectiveness with which a PMO delivers its services and contributes to organizational success. Unlike organizational project management maturity, which assesses an organization's overall portfolio, program, and project management capabilities, PMO maturity specifically examines the PMO's evolution and performance.

The *Cambridge Dictionary* defines *maturity* as "a very advanced or developed form or state." In the context of PMOs, this concept encompasses the progressive development of the PMO's practices, capabilities, and ability to deliver value to the organization.

Traditionally, many organizational maturity models have oversimplified PMO effectiveness by treating the mere existence of a PMO as a marker of maturity. This approach fails to account for the varying levels of development and effectiveness that PMOs can exhibit, creating a significant gap in understanding and assessing PMO performance.

Furthermore, the idea of a standardized "mature PMO" model is problematic. PMOs should be adaptable to meet their organizations' unique needs and expectations, making this standardization counterproductive. The key to PMO success lies in tailoring approaches and services to specific organizational contexts.

The concept of PMO service maturity represents a significant evolution in the understanding of how PMOs contribute to organizational success. By focusing on the sophistication of service delivery rather than adherence to a predefined model, this approach allows for a more nuanced and effective assessment of PMO performance.

The PMO service maturity model recognizes that two PMOs can provide the same service with vastly different levels of sophistication and potential value generation. The focus shifts from what services a PMO performs to how effectively it performs them.

This perspective challenges two common myths about PMO maturity:

- **A strategic PMO is a mature PMO.** This myth ignores that maturity is about service delivery effectiveness, not the type of services provided. Even a PMO offering only strategic services can have low maturity if it does not deliver those services effectively.
- **A PMO should evolve from an operational to a strategic approach.** A PMO's evolution does not necessarily follow this path. The PMO's approach should be defined by customer needs and expectations, not a predetermined evolutionary path.

A critical aspect of a PMO is aligning services with customer needs and expectations. Peter Drucker's famous quote, "There is nothing so useless as doing efficiently that which should not be done at all," perfectly encapsulates this critical aspect of PMO maturity. A PMO might excel in delivering a wide array of services with great efficiency, but if these services do not address the organization's actual needs, they add little value.

For a PMO, being strategic, tactical, or operational is not an objective in itself but a consequence of meeting customers' needs. A mature PMO not only performs its chosen services well but also selects services that deliver value in its specific organizational context.

The goal is not necessarily to reach the highest service maturity level in all dimensions—strategic, tactical, and operational. Instead, the focus should be on achieving the right level of service maturity to effectively support the organization's needs and strategic objectives.

Therefore, it is essential to understand that PMO service maturity alone does not equate to success. While a higher level of service sophistication can indeed increase the likelihood of delivering the desired outcomes, it is equally vital for the PMO to ensure that its services are genuinely aligned with the needs of its customers and the organization. In other words, a high level of maturity without proper alignment to real needs will fail to generate a perception of value, ultimately leading to a waste of resources, efforts, and funds. This misalignment will inevitably result in the decline of the PMO, even if it provides technically flawless services. Success is achieved not by maturity alone but by delivering value that resonates with and meets the PMO customers' and organization's true priorities.

Appendix X3 in this guide offers a PMO Service Maturity Assessment—a comprehensive model for evaluating the maturity of the 26 most common PMO services. This assessment provides:

- A structured approach to measure the current maturity level of PMO services;
- Identified strengths and areas for improvement in PMO services;
- Assistance in establishing benchmarks and goals for PMO development; and
- Guidance on enhancing PMO services.

Looking Ahead to the Next Section

This section detailed PMO services and maturity, examining the various roles a PMO can play and explaining how they can progress over time. However, delivering these services and successfully navigating maturity requires PMO professionals to possess a specific set of skills.

The next section explores the critical area of building PMO competencies. The essential skills, knowledge areas, and traits needed for PMO professionals to thrive will be presented. From strategic thinking and stakeholder engagement to technical expertise and leadership, the section guides PMO professionals on how to develop and strengthen these competencies. This emphasis on skills provides the groundwork for applying the service and maturity concepts discussed, helping to ensure that PMOs deliver maximum value to their organizations.

8

Developing Competencies for PMOs

Why This Section Matters to PMO Professionals

Understanding how to develop competencies is crucial for PMO professionals seeking to enhance their effectiveness and strategic value within their organizations. This section provides a comprehensive roadmap for continuous professional growth, emphasizing the importance of ongoing skill development in the dynamic field of portfolio, program, and project management.

This section empowers PMO professionals to take charge of their career progression by outlining a structured approach to competency development. The section offers a systematic method for self-assessment, gap analysis, and targeted improvement, enabling practitioners to align their skills with current job requirements and future career aspirations.

Ultimately, this comprehensive approach to competency development equips PMO professionals with the tools and mindset needed to excel in their roles, adapt to change, and position themselves as indispensable assets within their organizations. This approach reinforces the critical role of continuous learning in maintaining the PMO's strategic relevance and impact.

Core competencies are the foundation of PMO professionalism. These competencies encompass a range of skills, including communication, leadership, analytical thinking, and stakeholder engagement. Every PMO professional should excel in these areas to ensure overall PMO effectiveness. However, it is important to note that certain specialized competencies may be required depending on the specific services the PMO provides. These targeted competencies enable professionals to develop expertise in their roles and contribute meaningfully to the PMO's success.

The required proficiency levels for core competencies can vary significantly. Factors influencing this include the complexity of PMO services, organizational maturity, and, most importantly, the service-level agreements (SLAs) established with PMO customers. Higher expectations and goals often necessitate more advanced competencies to enable the PMO to deliver superior outcomes.

When PMO professionals lack the necessary skills and knowledge, it can lead to inefficiencies, errors, and missed opportunities. This impacts immediate deliverables and can erode the PMO's credibility within the organization.

To help ensure consistent value delivery, PMOs should prioritize their ongoing competency development. This effort involves regularly assessing PMO team competencies, identifying gaps, and implementing targeted training programs. This competency development work also requires fostering a culture of continuous learning, where PMO team members are encouraged to expand their skills and stay current with industry trends and good practices.

Core Competencies for PMO Professionals

At the core of an exceptional PMO are versatile professionals who possess wide-ranging skill sets and diverse competencies. These fundamental abilities are crucial for successfully navigating the intricate ecosystem of contemporary organizations, helping the PMO to not only meet but exceed expectations in delivering concrete value to both its customers and the broader organization.

Drawing from the experience of PMO leaders worldwide, 30 core competencies have been identified as essential for PMO professionals. These competencies cover a wide range of areas, from technical expertise to soft skills. By mastering these competencies, PMO professionals can be equipped to effectively demonstrate the PMO's value to customers at all levels. These 30 core competencies empower individuals to enhance the PMO's overall effectiveness and contribute to driving organizational success through a customer-focused, value-driven approach. The core competencies are:

1. **Accuracy.** Ensure correctness in PMO service outputs and verify details to maintain consistent quality and reliability that directly impact PMO customer satisfaction and value.
2. **Adaptability.** Swiftly adjust PMO strategies, services, and practices to accommodate changing customer needs, market conditions, and organizational priorities.
3. **Analytical skills.** Leverage data analysis to identify patterns, trends, and insights that drive value-based decision-making and enhance outcomes for PMO customers.
4. **Business acumen.** Understand the organization's business to align PMO activities with strategic objectives and maximize value delivery.
5. **Collaboration.** Foster cross-functional teamwork to achieve common goals, emphasizing customer-centric PMO outcomes and value creation across the organization.
6. **Communication.** Skillfully articulate and exchange information across diverse stakeholder groups, with the ability to tailor messages for different audiences.
7. **Conflict resolution.** Address disagreements or disputes with a focus on preserving customer relationships and maintaining value-driven outcomes.
8. **Continuous improvement.** Consistently enhance PMO services, processes, and practices to increase efficiency, effectiveness, and customer value delivery.
9. **Cultural awareness.** Recognize and respect cultural differences in the organization to better serve diverse customers and optimize value creation.
10. **Customer focus.** Prioritize customer needs and expectations in all PMO strategies, services, and activities, ensuring that PMO outcomes deliver tangible value.
11. **Decision-making.** Make timely, informed choices that balance customer needs, organizational goals, and value creation in the organizational context.

12. **Interpersonal intelligence.** Apply emotional intelligence and empathy to navigate complex stakeholder relationships.
13. **Integrity and ethics.** Uphold ethical standards in all PMO activities to build trust and support trust-based relationships with customers.
14. **Innovation.** Generate and implement creative solutions that enhance PMO services and deliver increased value to customers.
15. **Leadership.** Guide the PMO team, customers, and stakeholders to achieve value-driven goals.
16. **Negotiation.** Skillfully balance diverse interests to reach agreements that maximize value for customers and the organization.
17. **Objectivity.** Maintain an unbiased perspective to ensure fair and value-focused decision-making.
18. **Proactivity.** Anticipate customer needs and potential challenges, taking the initiative to address issues before they impact customer satisfaction and the PMO's value.
19. **Problem-solving.** Efficiently identify and resolve issues that threaten PMO outcomes and customer satisfaction, minimizing disruptions to value delivery.
20. **Process management.** Optimize PMO processes to enhance efficiency, quality, and value creation.
21. **Project management.** Apply good practices to manage projects, ensuring optimal value delivery.
22. **Relationship building.** Foster strong, collaborative partnerships with PMO customers to enhance trust, understanding, and effective recognition of PMO value.
23. **Resilience.** Maintain focus on value generation despite setbacks, adapting strategies to overcome obstacles while helping to ensure successful outcomes.
24. **Risk management.** Identify and mitigate risks that could impact customer satisfaction and service delivery while safeguarding expected outcomes and value generation.
25. **Stakeholder engagement.** Effectively engage with all stakeholders to help ensure alignment on customer-centric goals and value-driven PMO outcomes.
26. **Strategic influence.** Effectively persuade and educate customers about the PMO's strategic value and how its services drive organizational success.
27. **Strategic thinking.** Align PMO strategies, value propositions, and services with long-term organizational goals and customer needs, working to ensure sustained value creation.
28. **Teamwork.** Foster a collaborative environment where PMO team members work cohesively to deliver customer value and achieve PMO success.
29. **Time management.** Efficiently prioritize tasks to maximize value delivery within timelines and customer expectations.
30. **Training skills.** Design and implement effective learning strategies to enhance customers' competencies, including training, mentoring, and coaching.

Exploring PMO Competency Domains

PMO competency domains encompass the various areas of responsibility that PMO professionals engage in while working within a PMO. These domains categorize the specialized expertise required depending on the PMO professional's role, shaping their approach to delivering effective services aligned with organizational needs.

The three primary PMO competency domains are design, operation, and improvement. Each domain represents a fundamental aspect of PMO management, outlining the skills and responsibilities professionals should master to ensure effective service delivery and maximize value (see Figure 8-1).

The features of each competency domain are as follows:

- **Design.** This domain focuses on the design and development of PMO services. The domain is essential for establishing a solid foundation for service delivery, ensuring that services are strategically aligned and effectively meet stakeholder needs.
- **Operation.** This domain involves the day-to-day management and execution of PMO services. The domain focuses on delivering services according to the established plans, ensuring consistency, efficiency, quality, and value delivery.
- **Improvement.** This domain focuses on refining and optimizing PMO services to enhance their efficiency, effectiveness, and value delivery. The domain involves analyzing performance data, gathering feedback, and implementing actions to ensure continuous improvement.

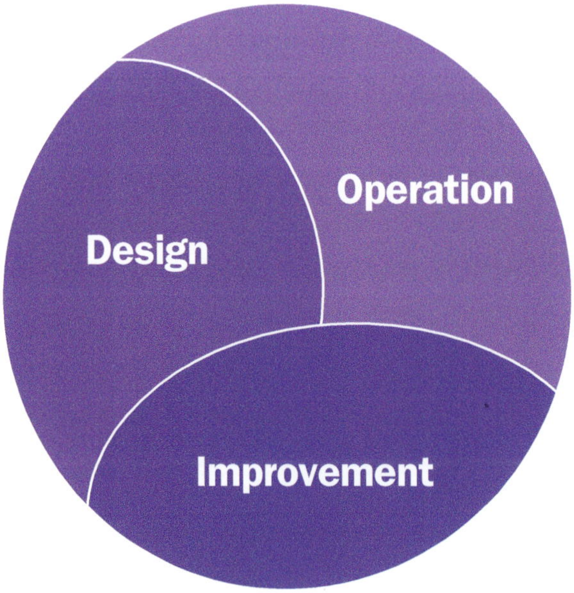

Figure 8-1. PMO Competency Domains

The PMO competency domains offer a structured approach to understanding and developing the diverse competencies required in a PMO. By categorizing expertise into design, operation, and improvement domains, this model provides PMO professionals with a clear path for skill development and career growth.

This three-domain structure allows PMO professionals to focus their skill development on specific areas of service expertise. The model also provides a framework for PMO leaders to ensure their teams possess a balanced mix of competencies, covering all aspects of service management from conception to optimization.

By embracing this approach, PMOs can ensure their services are well-designed, efficiently delivered, and continuously refined. This systematic development of competencies across all domains fosters an adaptable, effective PMO that is strategically aligned with organizational goals.

The PMO competency domains are a valuable tool for individual professional development and organizational capability building. The model empowers PMOs to deliver consistent value, drive strategic initiatives, and solidify their position as crucial contributors to organizational success.

The 30 core competencies for PMO professionals, along with real-world examples of their application in the three competency domains, are detailed in Table 8-1.

Aligning Core Competencies With PMO Services

The PMO's effectiveness is not solely a function of the services it provides but is deeply rooted in the competencies of its professionals. While possessing a diverse set of skills is advantageous, it is essential to recognize that certain competencies are more critical than others when it comes to delivering specific PMO services effectively. This nuanced understanding of competency importance enables PMO professionals to focus their development efforts on the skills that will most significantly enhance their performance and the value they deliver to the organization.

The alignment between core competencies and PMO services is a strategic approach that maximizes both individual and organizational effectiveness. By identifying which competencies are paramount for each service, PMO professionals can tailor their skill development to meet the precise demands of their roles.

For instance, strategic services such as providing advice to executive leadership or supporting strategic planning require competencies like business acumen, strategic thinking, and strategic influence. Professionals excelling in these areas can better understand the organization's vision, align projects and programs with long-term goals, and influence decision-making processes at the highest levels. Their ability to communicate effectively and lead with integrity further enhances their impact, ensuring that the PMO is seen as a valuable strategic partner within the organization.

Tactical services, including knowledge management and training and development, benefit significantly from competencies like collaboration, training skills, and continuous improvement. Professionals with strengths in these areas can effectively disseminate knowledge, foster a culture of learning, and enhance team capabilities, all of which contribute to the organization's adaptability and innovation.

Table 8-1. Core Competencies Applied to Different Domains

Competencies		Examples of Domain Application
1	**Accuracy**	• **Design**: Ensuring precise service definitions and requirements • **Operation**: Maintaining consistent quality in service delivery • **Improvement**: Analyzing data accurately to identify areas for enhancement
2	**Adaptability**	• **Design**: Creating flexible service models • **Operation**: Adjusting services to meet changing customer needs • **Improvement**: Implementing new approaches based on feedback and trends
3	**Analytical skills**	• **Design**: Using data to inform service-design decisions • **Operation**: Monitoring service performance metrics • **Improvement**: Identifying patterns and trends for service optimization
4	**Business acumen**	• **Design**: Aligning service design with organizational strategy • **Operation**: Ensuring services deliver business value • **Improvement**: Proposing enhancements that align with business goals
5	**Collaboration**	• **Design**: Working with customers to define service requirements • **Operation**: Coordinating with teams to deliver services effectively • **Improvement**: Engaging cross-functional teams for service enhancements
6	**Communication**	• **Design**: Articulating service concepts and plans clearly • **Operation**: Providing regular updates on service performance • **Improvement**: Presenting improvement proposals effectively
7	**Conflict resolution**	• **Design**: Addressing customer disagreements in service planning • **Operation**: Resolving issues that arise during service delivery • **Improvement**: Navigating differing opinions on service changes
8	**Continuous improvement**	• **Design**: Incorporating feedback loops into service design • **Operation**: Identifying opportunities for incremental improvements • **Improvement**: Increasing the PMO service maturity and measuring enhancement initiatives
9	**Cultural awareness**	• **Design**: Considering cultural factors in service design • **Operation**: Adapting service delivery to diverse cultural contexts • **Improvement**: Incorporating cultural insights into service enhancements

Table 8-1. Core Competencies Applied to Different Domains (Continued)

Competencies		Examples of Domain Application
10	**Customer focus**	• **Design**: Centering service design on customer needs • **Operation**: Ensuring responsive and satisfactory service delivery • **Improvement**: Using customer feedback to drive service enhancements
11	**Decision-making**	• **Design**: Making strategic choices in service design • **Operation**: Making timely decisions during service delivery • **Improvement**: Deciding on which enhancements to prioritize
12	**Interpersonal intelligence**	• **Design**: Understanding customer emotions and needs in service planning • **Operation**: Managing relationships during service delivery • **Improvement**: Navigating emotions during change processes
13	**Integrity and ethics**	• **Design**: Ensuring ethical considerations in service design • **Operation**: Maintaining ethical standards in service delivery • **Improvement**: Upholding integrity in improvement processes
14	**Innovation**	• **Design**: Developing novel service concepts • **Operation**: Implementing creative solutions in service delivery • **Improvement**: Generating innovative ideas for service enhancement
15	**Leadership**	• **Design**: Guiding the vision for new services • **Operation**: Inspiring the PMO team in service delivery • **Improvement**: Leading change initiatives for the PMO
16	**Negotiation**	• **Design**: Balancing customer interests in service planning • **Operation**: Negotiating resources for service delivery • **Improvement**: Gaining buy-in for service changes
17	**Objectivity**	• **Design**: Maintaining impartiality in service-design decisions • **Operation**: Evaluating service performance without bias • **Improvement**: Assessing improvement needs objectively
18	**Proactivity**	• **Design**: Anticipating future needs in service design • **Operation**: Addressing potential issues before they arise • **Improvement**: Initiating enhancement processes proactively

(Continued)

Table 8-1. Core Competencies Applied to Different Domains (Continued)

Competencies		Examples of Domain Application
19	**Problem-solving**	• **Design**: Addressing challenges in service conceptualization • **Operation**: Resolving issues in service delivery • **Improvement**: Tackling complex problems for service enhancement
20	**Process management**	• **Design**: Developing efficient PMO service processes • **Operation**: Ensuring smooth execution of PMO service processes • **Improvement**: Optimizing PMO processes for better service delivery
21	**Project management**	• **Design**: Planning the implementation of new PMO services • **Operation**: Offering project management service for customers • **Improvement**: Overseeing PMO-service-enhancement initiatives
22	**Relationship building**	• **Design**: Establishing connections with customers for service input • **Operation**: Maintaining strong relationships during service delivery • **Improvement**: Collaborating with customers for service enhancements
23	**Resilience**	• **Design**: Persisting through challenges in service development • **Operation**: Adapting to obstacles in service delivery • **Improvement**: Overcoming resistance to change in enhancement efforts
24	**Risk management**	• **Design**: Identifying potential risks in service design • **Operation**: Mitigating risks during service delivery • **Improvement**: Assessing risks associated with service changes
25	**Stakeholder engagement**	• **Design**: Engaging customers in service planning • **Operation**: Managing customers' expectations during delivery • **Improvement**: Involving customers in improvement initiatives
26	**Strategic influence**	• **Design**: Gaining support for new service concepts • **Operation**: Promoting the value of ongoing services • **Improvement**: Advocating for necessary service enhancements
27	**Strategic thinking**	• **Design**: Aligning service design with long-term goals • **Operation**: Ensuring service delivery supports strategic objectives • **Improvement**: Identifying strategic opportunities for PMO value proposition enhancement

Table 8-1. Core Competencies Applied to Different Domains (Continued)

Competencies		Examples of Domain Application
28	**Teamwork**	• **Design**: Collaborating on service design teams • **Operation**: Fostering teamwork in service delivery • **Improvement**: Working together on improvement initiatives
29	**Time management**	• **Design**: Meeting deadlines in service development • **Operation**: Ensuring timely service delivery • **Improvement**: Balancing improvement efforts with ongoing operations
30	**Training skills**	• **Design**: Developing training plans for service onbarding • **Operation**: Providing ongoing training for service delivery • **Improvement**: Training teams on new processes or enhancements

Conversely, operational services like audit assessments and quality assurance demand a different set of competencies, including attention to detail and objectivity. These competencies are crucial for delivering unbiased evaluations that can lead to process improvements and risk mitigation. Professionals who excel in these competencies help maintain the organization's credibility and operational excellence.

Understanding this alignment is not just about improving individual performance; it also has profound implications for team dynamics and resource allocation within the PMO. By mapping competencies to services, leaders can assemble teams where each member's strengths are optimally utilized, leading to more cohesive and high-performing units. This strategic deployment of human resources helps ensure that programs and projects receive the expertise they need, when they need it, thereby enhancing overall project success rates and value delivery.

The Critical Competency Profiles for PMO Service Delivery, which provides an in-depth analysis of essential competencies for effective PMO service delivery, can be found in Appendix X4. The profiles outline the competencies identified as critical for each of the 26 most common PMO services, along with explanations of their significance for successful execution.

How to Develop Competencies for PMO Professionals

Recognizing the critical importance of continuous professional development, forward-thinking PMO professionals understand that staying ahead of the curve is not just beneficial—it is essential. By cultivating a robust set of core competencies and specialized skills, PMO professionals can elevate their performance, enhance the PMO's value proposition, and ultimately contribute to the organization's strategic objectives.

This guide outlines a comprehensive approach to competency development for PMO professionals, offering a roadmap for self-assessment, targeted improvement, and ongoing growth. By following these steps, PMO professionals can embark on a journey of continuous learning and adaptation, ensuring they remain at the forefront of project management excellence.

For PMO professionals aiming to enhance their capabilities or develop their teams, consider the following comprehensive approach:

- **Conduct a thorough assessment of current competencies.** Evaluate skills against both core PMO requirements and service-specific needs. Use standardized assessment tools and seek input from peers and supervisors.
- **Identify competency gaps and prioritize areas for improvement.** Analyze assessment results to pinpoint competency deficiencies. Align improvement priorities with organizational goals and PMO strategic objectives.
- **Develop a personalized development plan.** Create a detailed development plan with specific, measurable, achievable, relevant, and time-bound (SMART) goals. Include both short-term and long-term objectives to ensure continuous progress.
- **Pursue diverse learning opportunities.** Engage in formal training programs and pursue relevant certifications. Seek hands-on experience through challenging assignments and cross-functional projects. Attend industry workshops and seminars to learn from experts and peers.
- **Continuously gather and act on feedback.** Implement a structured feedback system involving colleagues, customers, and mentors. Conduct regular self-reflection exercises to assess progress and adjust development plans. Use 360-degree feedback mechanisms to gain a comprehensive view of performance.

Consider implementing a formal PMO talent management program to maximize the impact of competency development efforts. This program should align individual growth plans with organizational objectives, provide resources for skill development, and create opportunities for knowledge sharing within the PMO community.

PMO professionals can significantly enhance their ability to deliver value by focusing on core and specialized competencies. This holistic approach ensures the achievement of promised outcomes and positions the PMO as a strategic asset capable of driving organizational success and meeting evolving customer needs.

Remember, competency development is an ongoing journey that requires dedication and adaptability. As the business landscape evolves, so should the skills of PMO professionals. By staying committed to continuous improvement and embracing a growth mindset, PMO professionals can help ensure they remain effective, relevant, and indispensable to their organizations.

Looking Ahead to the Next Section

Having explored the key PMO competencies, PMO professionals should now be aware of the knowledge and skills necessary to thrive in their roles. But to truly amplify their impact, PMO professionals should use a comprehensive framework that brings together all of the concepts covered.

The following section presents the PMO Value Ring™ framework, an innovative model that unites customer centricity, value delivery, service maturity, and competency development into a unified approach. This framework serves as a roadmap for PMO success, guiding professionals through every stage of development and operation. By embracing and applying this framework, PMO professionals can maximize their potential, helping to ensure that their PMOs consistently deliver value and contribute to organizational success. Part 2 explores this transformative model and how it can be used to revolutionize PMO practice.

Part 2

The PMO Value Ring™ Framework

9

Framework Overview

Why This Section Matters to PMO Professionals

This section introduces a comprehensive framework that transforms PMOs from tactical overseers to strategic partners driving organizational success. The framework sets the foundation for a new era of PMO management, where value creation and customer satisfaction are at the forefront, making it indispensable knowledge for any PMO professional aiming to stay relevant and impactful in today's dynamic business environment.

By mastering this framework, PMO professionals can elevate their role from project management enforcers to strategic value creators. The framework equips PMO professionals with the tools to design, implement, operate, and evolve PMOs that consistently deliver value and contribute directly to organizational success.

Introducing the New PMO Value Ring™ Framework

The PMO Value Ring™ framework represents a groundbreaking approach for PMO professionals, marking a significant paradigm shift in how PMOs function and deliver value within organizations. This innovative framework goes beyond traditional PMO models by emphasizing value creation and delivery, effectively transforming PMOs from being perceived as mere tactical and operational overseers into strategic partners that drive organizational success.

At the core of the PMO Value Ring™ framework lies the critical alignment between projects and strategic goals. This alignment ensures that every project, regardless of its size or scope, contributes meaningfully to the overarching objectives of the organization. By doing so, the framework elevates the role of the PMO, positioning it as an indispensable catalyst in achieving long-term organizational success. This strategic alignment is not just about mapping projects to goals; it is about creating a symbiotic relationship where project outcomes directly fuel strategic achievements.

The framework's strength lies in its flexible, transparent, and customer-centric approach that maximizes value creation. It encourages PMOs to adopt a more dynamic and proactive role, moving away from the traditional, reactive stance often associated with project management offices. By focusing on delivering measurable benefits and aligning their efforts with customers' needs and business priorities, PMOs can effectively demonstrate their value to their organizations.

Moreover, the PMO Value Ring™ framework promotes a culture of continuous improvement and adaptability. In an era characterized by rapid technological advancements and shifting market dynamics, the ability to adapt quickly is a critical success factor. The framework encourages PMOs to regularly assess and refine their processes, methodologies, and performance metrics. This ongoing evaluation ensures that PMOs stay aligned with the evolving needs of the organization and its customers. By embedding adaptability into their DNA, PMOs can become more resilient and better equipped to navigate the complexities of modern business landscapes.

The customer-centric aspect of the PMO Value Ring™ framework is particularly noteworthy and deserves special attention. By placing the needs and expectations of PMO customers at the forefront of their operations, PMOs can deliver more relevant and impactful services. This customer-first approach represents a significant departure from traditional PMO models that often prioritize processes over people.

By focusing on customer needs, PMOs can tailor their services to deliver maximum value, enhance customer satisfaction, and foster stronger relationships. This approach not only improves the perception of the PMO within the organization but also builds trust and credibility with PMO customers at all levels.

The PMO Value Ring™ framework represents a critical redefinition of the role of PMOs within organizations. Focusing on value creation, strategic alignment, and customer centricity enables PMOs to transition from being operational support units to becoming strategic enablers of organizational success. This transformation is not just beneficial; it is essential for PMOs to remain relevant and effective in an increasingly complex and competitive business landscape.

PMO professionals who master this framework elevate their role from mere enforcers of processes and tools to true creators of value. Equipped with the recommended practices outlined here, they gain the skills to design, implement, operate, and continuously improve PMOs that reliably deliver value and make a tangible impact on organizational success. By shifting their focus to strategic alignment and measurable outcomes, these professionals can build PMOs that not only support project execution but also drive business growth, enhance PMO customer satisfaction, and foster a culture of continuous improvement. In doing so, they position the PMO as a central player in achieving long-term organizational goals.

The primary goal for which the PMO Value Ring™ framework was designed is value generation. This goal goes beyond completing projects on time and within budget; it ensures that each PMO customer can achieve their project-related objectives, thus contributing directly to the organization's strategic goals.

The framework emphasizes generating valuable outcomes through strong customer orientation, a trend witnessed in successful PMOs across the globe. The following five key elements were incorporated into the present framework to ensure consistent delivery of such value by PMOs (see Figure 9-1):

- **PMO customer.** At the center is the PMO customer, who serves as the primary reference point for PMO professionals as they continuously shape PMO strategies, define objectives, and manage operations. By becoming a true partner to its key customers, the PMO can effectively generate value for them and for the organization as a whole.

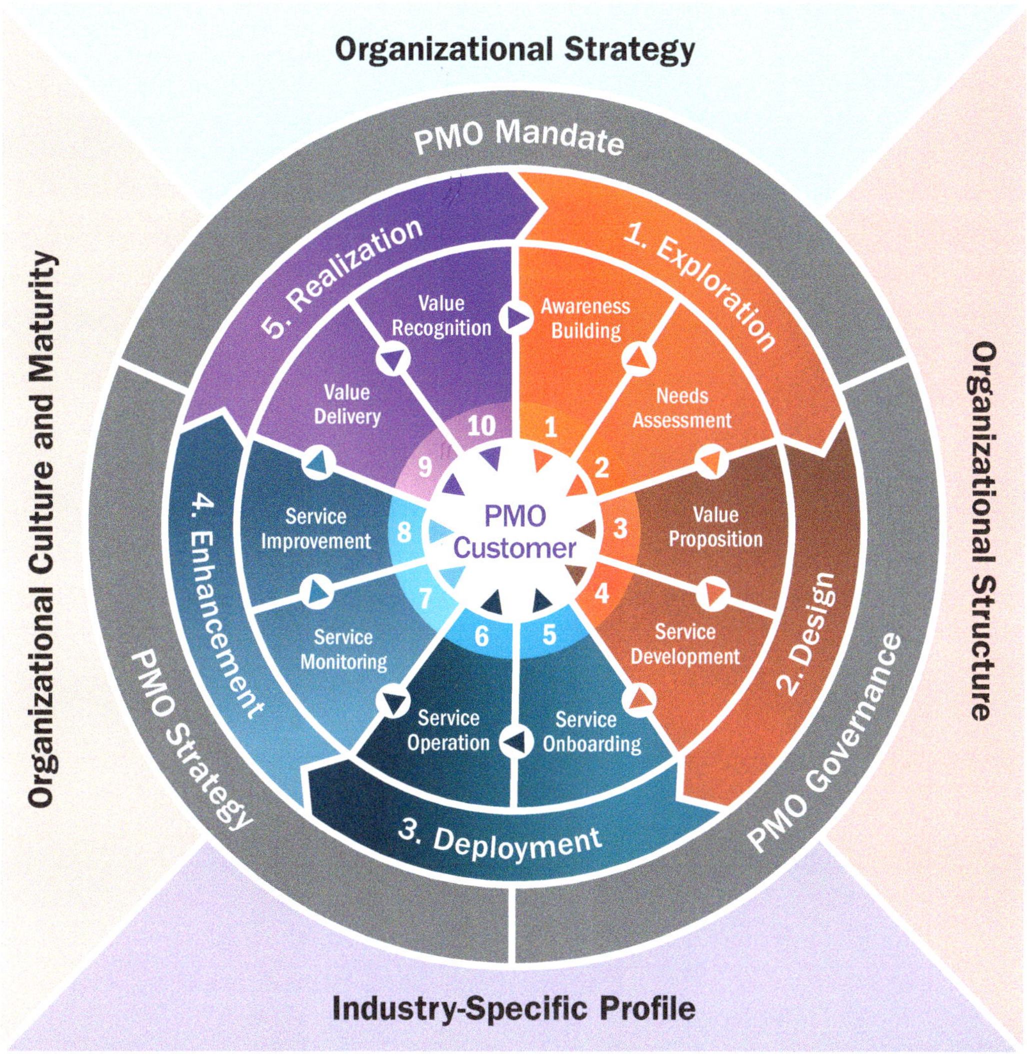

Figure 9-1. PMO Value Ring™ Framework

- **Organizational baseline elements.** These elements are foundational components in any application of the PMO Value Ring™ framework. The elements include organizational strategy, culture and maturity, structure, and industry-specific profile, forming the backdrop that enables customized approaches aligned with the unique needs of each scenario. Through this integration, PMOs become more deeply embedded within organizations, enhancing their ability to generate value.
- **PMO structural components.** These components form the pillars upon which successful PMOs are built. The pillars include the PMO mandate, PMO strategy, and PMO governance. These components define essential aspects of a PMO, establishing objectives, scope of operations, responsibilities, authority, and a clear vision for the PMO's evolutionary journey within the organization.

- **PMO customer experience cycle.** This stage consists of exploration, design, deployment, enhancement, and realization—all aimed at delivering effective value through positive and ever-changing experiences with PMO customers. This stage is an iterative cycle that responds continuously to evolving customers' needs, expectations, and feedback, hence playing the role of a binding agent between customers and PMOs, ensuring that the PMO becomes increasingly relevant and strategic within the organization.
- **Value-generating PMO flywheel.** At its core, the value-generating PMO flywheel breaks down the PMO customer experience cycle into actionable steps that highlight the continuous nature of value generation, with each successive cycle building momentum for future successes.

Moving Beyond One-Size-Fits-All PMO Models

A crucial aspect of the PMO Value Ring™ framework is that it sets itself apart from conventional approaches, which, while valuable sources of inspiration, do not adequately represent the diversity of PMOs in the real world. While many traditional models advocate for an "ideal PMO" as a universal benchmark, the PMO Value Ring™ framework takes a fundamentally different approach. This innovative framework recognizes that successful PMOs vary significantly across organizations and considers this variability a vital component of PMO success, rather than a deviation from a standardized model.

The PMO Value Ring™ framework emphasizes that each PMO should be uniquely tailored to meet the specific needs, goals, and cultural nuances of its organization. By focusing on a flexible and customer-centric approach, the framework empowers PMO leaders to adapt their strategies, prioritize relevant services, and align their efforts with the organization's unique objectives. This adaptability not only enhances the PMO's effectiveness but also strengthens its ability to deliver measurable value and support long-term business success, positioning the PMO as a dynamic contributor rather than a one-size-fits-all solution.

Experience shows that successful PMOs in diverse organizations worldwide exhibit unique characteristics, and this diversity is a critical success factor. Recognizing this, the PMO Value Ring™ framework does not impose a single, ideal model or PMO type as a universal standard for organizations to achieve. Instead, it acknowledges the value of the various perspectives offered in literature as sources of inspiration rather than ready-made solutions. These perspectives serve as adaptable ideas, providing PMO professionals with options to draw from while considering their organization's specific needs, strategic goals, and unique environment.

The PMO Value Ring™ framework serves as a "bridge" that empowers PMO professionals to design their own customized solutions, recognizing that each organization has unique needs, challenges, and cultural contexts shaping its ideal PMO structure. Rather than aiming to replace existing models, the framework acknowledges their validity and usefulness as sources of inspiration. Instead of prescribing what a PMO should be, the focus is instead on guiding how the PMO should be created and bridging diverse perspectives. This approach enables professionals to refine and adapt these perspectives into unique solutions that meet the specific requirements of each organizational context.

In practice, the application of the PMO Value Ring™ framework might result in vastly different PMO structures, even within the same industry. For instance, two technology companies might end up with distinctly different PMO models based on their specific growth stages, market positions, organizational cultures, and strategic priorities. This adaptability is particularly valuable in today's fast-paced business environment, where organizations need to be agile and responsive to change.

A PMO designed and managed using the PMO Value Ring™ framework is inherently more flexible and better positioned to evolve alongside the organization it serves. This approach demonstrates that successful PMOs differ significantly from one organization to another and acknowledges this variability as a critical factor in PMO success, rather than viewing it as a deviation from a standard model.

The following sections delve into each aspect of the PMO Value Ring™ framework, allowing PMO professionals to thoroughly understand its components.

Looking Ahead to the Next Section

The PMO Value Ring™ framework is a comprehensive model that can help PMO professionals to build value-driven, customer-centric PMOs. However, to apply the framework effectively, it is essential to understand the key elements that shape the PMO's design and management.

The following section explores the organizational baseline elements—factors like strategy, structure, culture, and industry profiles—that define the environment in which a PMO operates. By gaining a deeper understanding of these foundational elements, PMO professionals can better align their efforts with their organization's unique context, ensuring that their PMOs meet organizational needs and constraints.

10

The Organizational Baseline Elements

Why This Section Matters to PMO Professionals

Understanding the organizational baseline elements is crucial for PMO professionals, as they form the foundation of a successful PMO. This section explores four critical elements that are akin to an organization's DNA, shaping the environment in which a PMO operates and influencing its design, operation, and ultimate impact.

Comprehending these baseline elements is essential for PMO professionals to create a PMO that aligns seamlessly with the organization's goals and culture. This understanding enables PMO professionals to navigate complex organizational dynamics, adapt to changing environments, and position the PMO as an indispensable catalyst for organizational success.

This section provides PMO professionals with the knowledge and skills needed to analyze their organization's unique context, tailor their approach accordingly, and create sustainable PMO success.

Decoding the Organizational Context

The first component of the PMO Value Ring™ framework is the organizational baseline elements, which form the foundation for a successful PMO. See Figure 10-1.

A PMO does not exist in isolation or operate in a vacuum. It is a part of its organization's ecosystem. As the survival and prosperity of a living organism both depend on a proper fit with its surroundings, a successful PMO is contingent upon its capacity for aligning with and leveraging its foundation. Failure to consider these elements may lead to a PMO becoming alienated and a possible failure to demonstrate value and gain traction within the organization.

Four critical elements determine how a PMO should be designed and operated:

- **Organizational strategy.** Organizational strategy provides a clear direction and purpose for the PMO, acting as a guiding compass. Aligning closely with organizational strategy makes the PMO a powerful catalyst for strategic execution that translates top-level objectives into tangible PMO outcomes, thereby driving organizational success.

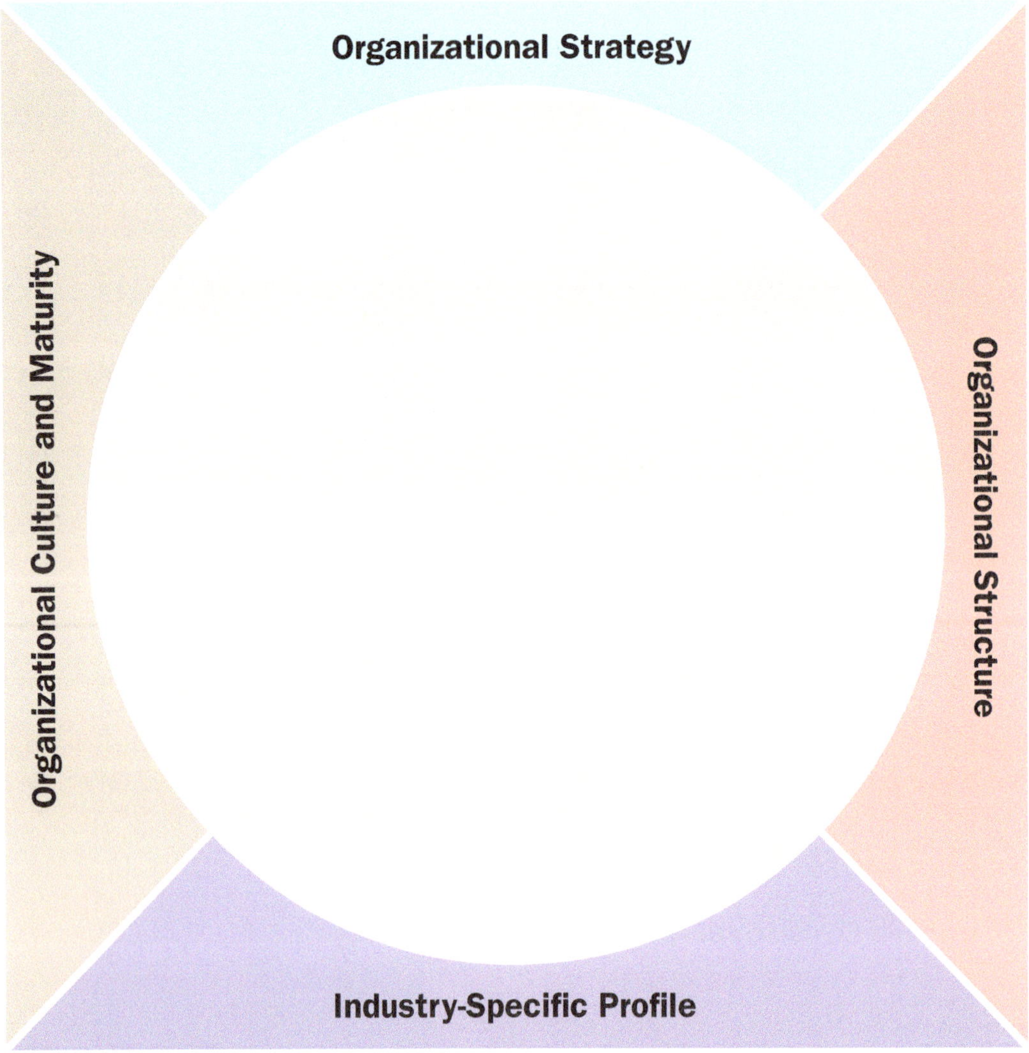

Figure 10-1. PMO Baseline Elements

- **Organizational structure.** PMOs operate within the organizational structure framework. The ability of any given PMO to perform well depends mainly on whether it can navigate around an organization's preexisting structure to develop supportive processes and methods that will blend smoothly with already established hierarchies and communication channels. It is important to understand the "true structure," as the real dependencies, power, and influence network often differ from what is shown on organizational charts.
- **Organizational culture and maturity.** Invisible forces such as organizational culture and maturity can propel some PMOs forward but hinder others' progress. Successful PMOs should consider such features while incrementally raising the overall level of project management maturity when dealing with projects based on cultural norms.

- **Industry-specific profile.** The industry-specific profile provides the broader context against which a PMO operates. This element implies that each industry has certain particularities in terms of regulations, practices, or challenges that may force any given PMO toward adjusting its strategies, methodologies, and areas of focus correspondingly.

Taken together, these elements form an organization's DNA—melding the environment within which a PMO functions while influencing its design, operation, and ultimate impact every step of the way. The concept of "organizational DNA" is more than just a metaphor; it represents every organization's unique characteristics. For PMOs, understanding this DNA is the first step toward establishing a mutually beneficial relationship between the PMO and the wider organization.

These four organizational baseline elements create an individual stamp for each organization, which requires different tailored approaches for PMO implementation and management. Each aspect has significance in its own right; however, it is their connection that really gives meaning to the PMO as presented under an operational context. One misalignment can cause chain reactions that may influence how effective and valuable a PMO can be. Therefore, comprehending these interactions is crucial for any PMO executive who wants to create sustainable value while driving organizational transformation.

These elements are also not static. They can change with market shifts, business growth, or new strategic challenges. Successful PMO professionals should consistently adjust their strategies to position their PMOs as indispensable catalysts for organizational success.

These elements are explained in greater detail next, examining their finer aspects and how they impact the PMO. This broader perspective can grant PMO professionals significant knowledge and skills to help navigate complex issues related to organizations, thereby enhancing the sustainability of PMO success.

Organizational Strategy: The Backbone of PMO Success

Organizational strategy is the foundational compass for a PMO, providing critical direction and purpose. Just as a ship in rough waters relies on a map and compass to steer it where desired, organizational strategy acts as the compass that guides the way through the intricate maze of project management.

The organizational strategy is like an organization's roadmap toward its vision. The strategy outlines where an organization wants to go and how it wants to get there, including setting goals, long-term objectives, and practical steps for achievement. For PMO professionals, understanding this strategy well is not optional but, rather, a necessary trait. Inattentive movement or a lack of a clear understanding by a PMO team about organizational strategy can lead to purposeless activities with no meaningful impact.

A company's strategic priorities and goals are stipulated in the organizational strategy. When there is a change in strategic priorities or goals, such as a shift in organizational strategy, the PMO should realign its focus accordingly. For example, if in the future an organization decides to pivot toward innovation, then it may have projects that foster innovation and could possibly develop new methodologies supporting these types of projects within the PMO team. Such alignment helps ensure that all efforts delivered by the PMO are relevant, enhancing its value toward achieving overall strategic objectives.

The influence of organizational strategy on PMO operations is both profound and multifaceted as seen in these areas:

- **Portfolio management.** Organizational strategy provides a critical filter for project selection and prioritization. The PMO evaluates potential projects through this lens, ensuring resources are directed at initiatives that truly contribute to organizational goals.
- **Methodology selection.** Strategic considerations often come into play when deciding among adaptive, predictive, or hybrid approaches. For example, strategies focused on rapid innovation may lean more toward an agile approach, while those targeting predictability would tend more toward a traditional approach.
- **Capability development.** PMOs that understand the direction of the organization and are forward-looking can cultivate the right team skills and competencies to prepare for future needs rather than just meeting today's demands.
- **Technology adoption.** Tools and technologies often accompany strategic priorities. For example, a strategy focused on data-driven decision-making may include investments in modern analytics platforms or the innovative potential of artificial intelligence.
- **Governance structure.** An organization's approach to risk and innovation influences a PMO's level of control and oversight. A more flexible governance structure may be required when rapid market expansion is emphasized.

Understanding the company's objectives alone is insufficient for effective strategic alignment; action is needed beyond this point to integrate these goals proactively into all aspects of PMO operations. PMOs that successfully align themselves with their organization's strategies frequently transform from simple project execution nodes to trusted strategic partners. These PMOs become instrumental in not only implementing strategy but also in informing and shaping it, providing valuable insights derived from their unique vantage point overseeing multiple projects and initiatives across the organization.

Aligning the PMO with organizational strategy should not be set up once; instead, it requires constant tuning over time, and an effective PMO should be able to adapt quickly when these changes occur. This dynamic alignment helps ensure that the PMO continues to deliver value and remains a critical driver of organizational success.

Organizational Culture and Maturity: The Invisible Forces Shaping the PMO

PMO success is significantly influenced by organizational culture and maturity, which are unseen forces. It is important for PMO professionals to comprehensively understand these inputs as they seek to establish a PMO that adds value and thrives within their organization's unique nature.

Organizational culture involves an organization's overall values, belief systems, attitudes, and practices. Organizational culture may be seen in the underlying rules of operation, rewarded behaviors, and dominant mindsets. In this case, maturity refers to how advanced organizations are with project management techniques at the portfolio, program, and project levels. Hence, these dynamics either become launching pads or obstacles to PMO success.

The dynamic between an organization's evolving culture and maturing project management practices has a significant impact on the PMO itself. For instance, a more mature organization may require more sophisticated project tracking and reporting mechanisms, which the PMO should implement. Similarly, a shift toward a more collaborative or innovative culture may necessitate changes in how the PMO fosters team dynamics and project execution.

Critical aspects of organizational culture and maturity that PMO professionals should consider include:

- **Values and norms.** Value and norms comprise the basic principles used when making choices within an organization.
- **Communication patterns.** These patterns influence how information flows through the organization, whether flat or hierarchical.
- **Risk tolerance.** Risk tolerance determines how well the organization handles uncertainty, including innovation.
- **Decision-making processes.** Decision-making processes help determine whether decisions are made by consensus or from the top down.
- **Collaborative dynamics.** The collaboration dynamics influence how different departments work together within the organization.
- **Change readiness and adaptability.** These factors influence the organization's ability to accept and absorb new ideas.
- **Organizational project management maturity.** This level of maturity influences an organization's level of knowledge, understanding, and application of portfolio, program, and project management practices.
- **Hidden interests and informal authority.** These factors include unofficial power structures, patterns, and interests that may influence decision-making and reporting within an organization.

The implementation and operation of a PMO are highly influenced by an organization's environment. PMO professionals should consider the organization's history with PMOs such as any past successes or failures.

The perceived value of the PMO and its ability to execute complex practices depend on organizational project management maturity and the acumen of PMO customers. In less mature environments, starting with simpler processes before introducing more advanced approaches is often necessary.

PMOs should not forget that organizational maturity and culture are dynamic; they change over time due to external pressures, transformational leadership, and strategic reorientation. Successful PMO professionals track such changes and adjust their approaches accordingly.

Organizational Structure: Integrating the PMO With the Organization

Organizational structure forms the foundational framework that shapes the effectiveness of a PMO. It serves as a blueprint, defining how various components of an organization interact and function together.

A deep understanding of the organizational structure is crucial for PMO professionals to create an influential and effective PMO that seamlessly integrates into the organizational fabric. The organizational structure encompasses several critical aspects that directly impact PMO design and operations, such as but not limited to:

- **Hierarchy levels.** The layers of management and reporting lines;
- **Decision-making authority.** The processes and locations of decision-making within the organization;
- **Departmental boundaries.** How responsibilities are divided across different units;
- **Communication channels.** Both formal and informal pathways for information flow;
- **Resource allocation.** The distribution of human and financial resources;
- **Governance models.** Frameworks for oversight and accountability; and
- **Cultural dynamics.** The interplay between structure and organizational culture.

It is crucial to recognize that organizational structures are not static; they evolve as organizations change and grow. PMOs should stay attuned to these structural shifts and be prepared to adapt accordingly.

Changes in the organizational structure can impact the PMO's role and how it interacts with other departments. For instance, if the organization undergoes a restructuring that affects reporting lines or departmental boundaries, the PMO may need to clarify its new role and responsibilities. This clarification can ensure that the PMO operates smoothly within the new organizational framework and maintains its effectiveness.

By profoundly understanding and skillfully navigating this structural landscape, PMO professionals can create a PMO that fits seamlessly into the organizational structure and becomes a driving force for efficiency, collaboration, and strategic success. This adaptive approach ensures that the PMO remains relevant and valuable as the organization evolves, positioning it as an indispensable asset in achieving organizational objectives.

Industry-Specific Profile: Tailoring the PMO to Different Realities

An organization's industry-specific profile can significantly shape the way its PMO operates. This profile encompasses the unique characteristics, challenges, and accepted practices of the organization's industry or economic sector. For PMO professionals, recognizing and adapting to these nuances is crucial for driving real value and ensuring organizational success.

Key factors that shape PMOs across different industries include:

- **Regulatory environment.** The regulatory environment varies across sectors and regions, influencing compliance requirements and operational frameworks.
- **Project types.** Project types can differ among industries, leading to methodology variations and unique management approaches.
- **Technology landscape.** Sectors and regions may differ in technological integration levels, affecting project execution and management.
- **Market dynamics.** Economic conditions, competition, and market trends may influence the priorities of projects' timelines.
- **Risk profile.** Every industry has its own risks, which may necessitate the development of risk management strategies tailored to each sector.
- **Stakeholder ecosystems.** The diversity and expectations of PMO customers may differ from industry to industry, affecting PMO strategies.
- **Industry standards and practices.** Project management methodologies may be influenced by each sector's applicable standards.
- **Cultural and maturity factors.** A PMO's effectiveness may depend on the maturity level of project management practices in its respective industry as well as the sector's cultural norms in a particular country.

To exemplify these differences, consider some industry examples showing how PMOs should align their approaches, methodologies, and focus areas with specific challenges, regulations, and good practices within sectors:

- **Construction.** This sector focuses on large-scale, long-term projects with a high emphasis on safety and environmental regulations and complex stakeholder engagement.
- **Energy.** The energy sector should consider regulatory compliance for its capital-intensive projects as well as rapid technology changes, particularly related to renewable energy.
- **Financial services.** The financial sector faces challenges with cybersecurity and regulatory compliance as well as the fast pace of technology adoption in the industry.
- **Government.** The government sector has unique considerations such as public accountability, complex stakeholder engagement, strict procurement laws, and long-term planning efforts.
- **Healthcare.** Healthcare organizations should consider patient safety, data privacy, regulatory compliance, and innovation that is balanced with efficiency.
- **Information technology.** The IT sector faces challenges with rapid project cycles, agile methodology considerations, innovation, continuous integration, and deployment practices.

To effectively meet these industry-specific requirements, PMO professionals should understand the importance of adjusting their approach to appropriately respond to their sector's specific demands.

This careful consideration of industry challenges has been demonstrated by successful PMOs, highlighting that flexibility is not just desirable but rather necessary for driving value in any project.

The fact that industry landscapes are dynamic is vital. PMO professionals should be ready to adjust strategies as sectors change, new regulations come into effect, and technology disrupts various industries.

An industry-specific profile is an essential determinant for all aspects of PMO operations. By blending project management principles and practices with sector-specific realities, PMO professionals can create customized approaches that help ensure their PMO's relevance, effectiveness, and value within distinctive contexts.

Looking Ahead to the Next Section

The organizational baseline elements set the foundation for understanding the contextual factors that can influence a PMO's operations. The upcoming section examines the PMO structural components—the PMO mandate, PMO strategy, and PMO governance. These components further build the foundation on which PMOs function, outlining their purpose, strategic direction, and operational framework. By mastering the development and implementation of these structural elements, PMO professionals can position their PMOs to deliver meaningful value within their specific organizational environments.

11

The PMO Structural Components

Why This Section Matters to PMO Professionals

For PMO professionals, understanding the structural components of a PMO is crucial, as these elements provide the foundation for a successful and impactful PMO. This section highlights three core components—PMO mandate, PMO governance, and PMO strategy—that go beyond theory; they serve as practical, actionable pillars that bring the PMO to life.

By delving into these components, PMO professionals can establish a solid PMO structure and help ensure their PMO operates effectively, aligns with organizational goals, and delivers tangible value. This section equips PMO professionals with the knowledge to establish a solid PMO structure, fostering a strategic and value-driven approach in their organizations.

Building the PMO Foundations

At the heart of every high-performing PMO stands the PMO structural components, which provide the foundation for PMOs to excel. While the organizational baseline elements discussed in the previous section set the stage, providing the contextual backdrop against which a PMO operates, the PMO structural components bring the PMO to life, giving it form, direction, and purpose.

The complex relationships among the PMO structural components and the organizational baseline elements are of paramount importance. Each structural component is deeply influenced by—and should align seamlessly with—the organization's strategy, structure, culture and maturity, and industry-specific profile. This symbiotic relationship can ensure that the PMO is not an isolated entity but an integral part of the organizational ecosystem, capable of effecting change and driving improvement from within the organization's very fabric. The three PMO structural components earn the designation of "structural" because they constitute the essential elements upon which the PMO is constructed. The components provide the necessary architecture for the PMO to operate effectively and efficiently.

A well-structured PMO is built on three fundamental pillars: mandate, strategy, and governance. See Figure 11-1.

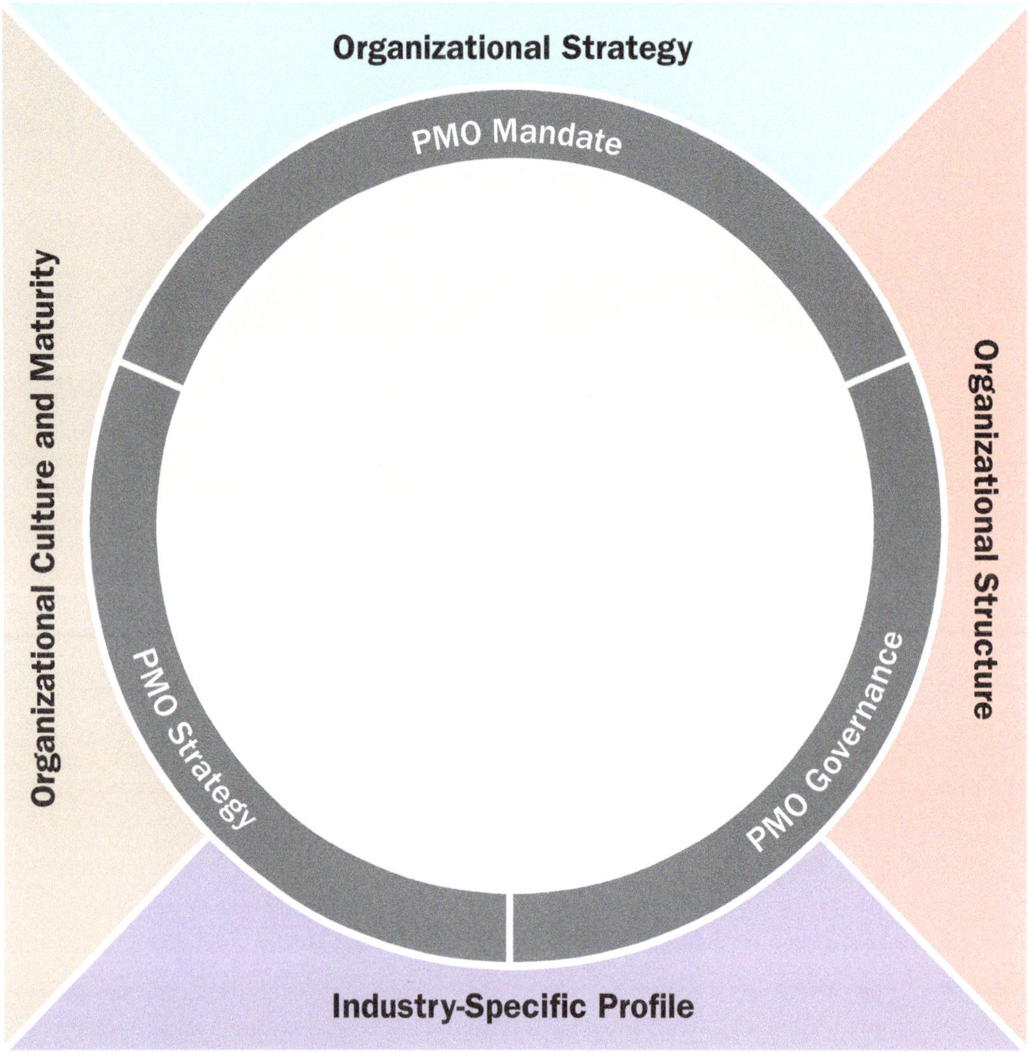

Figure 11-1. PMO Structural Components

These elements work in concert to define the PMO's purpose, approach, and operational framework:

- **PMO mandate.** This component defines the PMO's "why," articulating its purpose and justification within the organizational context. The mandate ensures that the PMO's activities align with the organization's strategic objectives, providing a clear rationale for its existence and operations.

- **PMO governance.** This component establishes the PMO's "who" and "when," setting forth the decision-making processes, roles, responsibilities, and accountability mechanisms. Governance guides PMO operations, maintaining consistency in its practices. PMO governance also defines the policies, procedures, and standards that govern the PMO's day-to-day activities.
- **PMO strategy.** This component outlines the PMO's "what" and "how," establishing the long-term plan that defines how the PMO will grow and evolve to continuously deliver value to the organization. PMO strategy focuses on the specific actions and improvements the PMO may undertake to enhance its impact over time.

These three components are far from theoretical ideas; they are practical, actionable elements that can bring a PMO to life, allowing it to navigate an organization's complexities with clear direction and accuracy. The components serve as a critical bridge, translating broad organizational imperatives into a value-driven PMO that is ideally attuned to organizational needs.

In essence, the PMO mandate sets the foundation, PMO strategy charts the path for future development, and PMO governance enforces accountability and control. Together, they ensure that the PMO not only delivers value but also continuously adapts and aligns with the organization's long-term vision and evolving maturity.

The interrelationships among the PMO mandate, PMO strategy, and PMO governance are crucial for ensuring the long-term coherence and effectiveness of the PMO. These three elements are mutually reinforcing: The mandate provides direction, strategy drives continuous improvement and adaptation, and governance ensures alignment and compliance. Together, they can ensure that the PMO is not only equipped to fulfill its current responsibilities but is also capable of evolving and improving over time.

In addition, understanding the intricate relationships among these organizational baseline elements and the PMO structural components (organizational strategy, organizational culture and maturity, organizational structure, and industry-specific profile) is crucial for PMO professionals. This understanding allows for proactive adjustments to the PMO structural components in response to organizational changes, ensuring that the PMO remains a relevant, effective, and value-driving entity within the organization. See Figure 11-2.

The three PMO structural components and their essential elements, implementation strategies, and good practices are presented in more granular detail in the next sections. Strategies to develop a clear and compelling PMO mandate, craft a PMO strategic plan that aligns seamlessly with organizational goals, and establish a PMO governance framework that ensures efficient, effective, and value-driven PMO operations are explained.

PMO Mandate: The Starting Point of a Successful PMO

The PMO mandate is the cornerstone of a successful PMO. It provides an all-encompassing declaration that defines the PMO's purpose, coverage scope, and responsibilities in the organizational context. A well-articulated mandate serves as a guide to steer the PMO's strategy and ensure it aligns with the organization's overall goals.

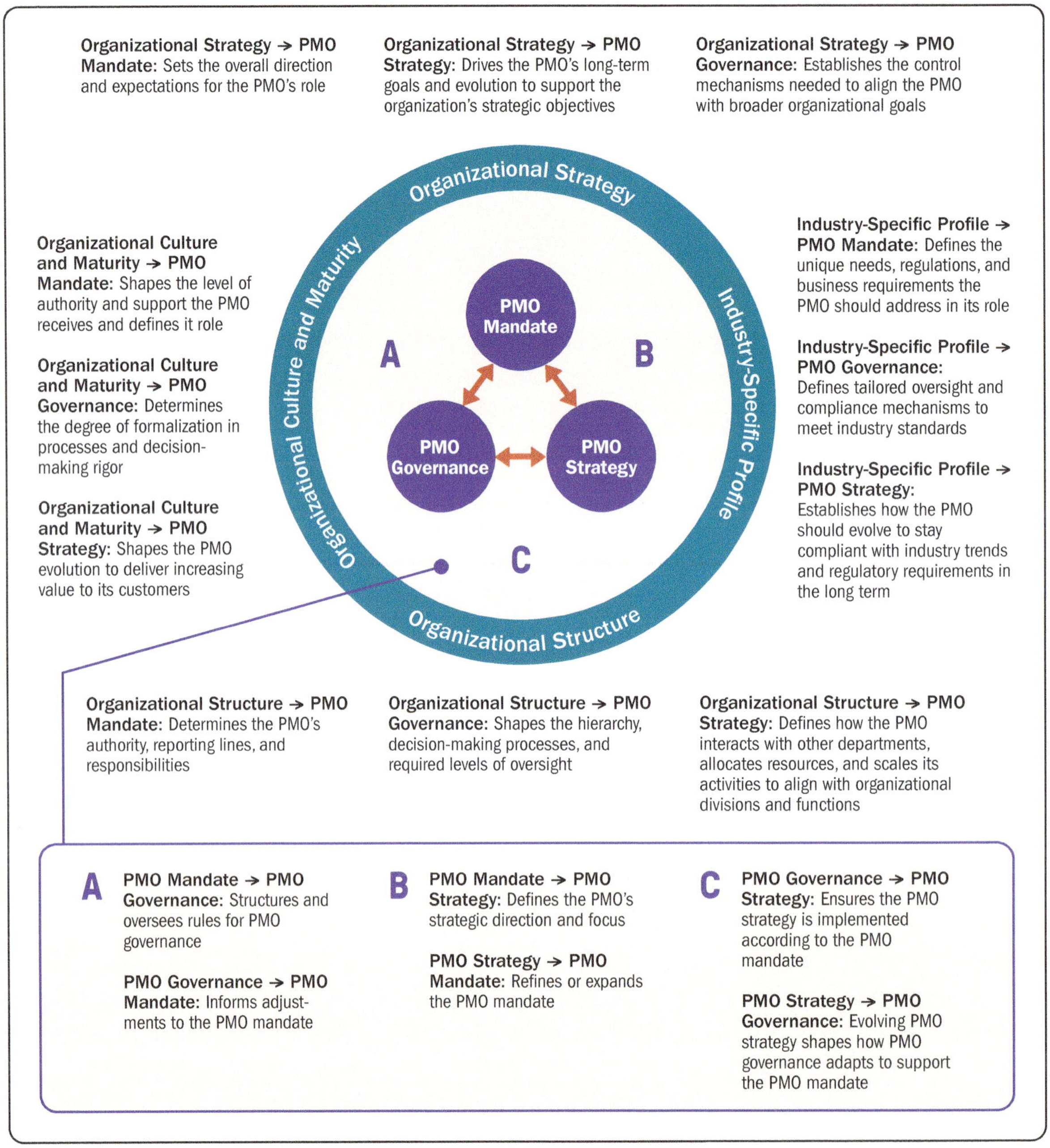

Figure 11-2. Fundamental Pillars of a PMO

The PMO mandate answers essential questions such as: Why does the PMO exist? What value is it expected to deliver? and Who are its primary customers? The closer the PMO mandate is linked to the organizational strategy, the more relevant and impactful its contributions can be.

The PMO mandate is involved in several crucial areas, including:

- **Clarity of purpose.** Clearly stated mandates are essential in minimizing confusion among stakeholders on who does what, leading to minimal conflicts.
- **Responsibility definitions.** To prevent underutilization or overreach, the PMO mandate determines limits on what the PMO can do.
- **Stakeholder alignment.** The PMO mandate can ensure that all stakeholders understand the PMO's purpose and value proposition.
- **Strategic alignment.** The mandate helps "align" or synchronize the PMO's activities with the organization's strategic objectives.
- **Performance benchmark.** The PMO mandate provides baseline metrics against which the PMO's performance can be measured and evaluated over time.

One significant factor defining the PMO mandate is the PMO coverage scope, which determines how far-reaching or influential a PMO can be. Typically, there are three levels as follows:

- **Enterprise PMO.** An enterprise PMO (EPMO) operates at the highest organizational level, aligning all portfolios and projects with strategic business objectives across the entire organization.
- **Departmental/divisional PMO.** The departmental or divisional PMO operates within a specific area, aligning projects within that area to the department or division goals. It has authority within the specified area.
- **Program-/project-specific PMO.** By definition, a temporary PMO operates in support of a specific program or large, complex project, aligning activities to the program or project and having authority over its scope.

The PMO mandate is greatly influenced by the coverage scope selection. The PMO coverage scope should be aligned with organizational needs and maturity levels.

The PMO charter formalizes the PMO mandate, clarifying in a preliminary perspective the PMO coverage scope, why it is needed, what it seeks to achieve, and where it fits within an organization's structure. The charter establishes the initial pillars for PMO success, thus ensuring alignment, clarity, and organizational support.

The following items should be included in the PMO charter, which is developed from a high-level perspective based on preliminary information collected. This information will be reviewed, validated, and detailed in the subsequent steps of this framework.

- **PMO purpose and mission.** This information details why the PMO exists within the organization.
- **PMO vision.** The PMO vision explains what the PMO wants to be in the medium and long term.
- **PMO coverage scope.** The coverage scope can determine the level of influence that the PMO may have such as enterprise level, departmental or divisional level, or program-/project-specific level. However, hybrid structures, such as an EPMO combined with divisional PMOs within key business areas relevant to the organization, are also common.
- **PMO objectives.** The objectives represent the initially identified needs that led to the decision to establish a PMO.
- **PMO stakeholders.** This information includes a preliminary identification of the key PMO customers and an initial understanding of their needs.
- **Basic resource needs.** This information includes a preliminary evaluation of the resource needs required for the effective establishment of the PMO.
- **Implementation roadmap.** A preliminary roadmap should be included as a phased plan for establishing or evolving the PMO.
- **PMO success criteria.** The success criteria includes preliminary KPIs and metrics that will be used to measure PMO success.
- **Review-and-update process.** The review-and-update process provides a mechanism for periodically reviewing and updating the PMO mandate.
- **PMO charter approval.** The charter approval comprises any formal sign-offs or approvals from key stakeholders and executive sponsors that may be required.

These are foundational PMO aspects; they establish a PMO's identity and purpose from a high-level strategic and tactical perspective. However, it is essential to note that while the PMO charter provides an overview, it does not include all of the operational details about the PMO, which will be detailed in the next steps of this framework.

PMO Governance: The Backbone of PMO Operations

Effective PMO operations hinge on robust governance, which is crucial for ensuring that the PMO functions smoothly and adds significant value to the organization.

PMO governance encompasses decision-making processes, levels of autonomy, roles and responsibilities, accountability measures, and the overall governance framework within which the PMO works. Efficient governance helps ensure that a PMO is aligned with the organization's objectives, operates transparently, and functions effectively.

It is important to note that PMO governance is different from portfolio, program, and project governance—all related concepts in project management. The key difference lies in their scope and focus as follows:

- **PMO governance.** PMO governance examines the policies, procedures, and standards that guide the operation/management of a PMO as an organizational entity. This governance includes a definition of reporting structures, decision-making authorities, accountability measures, and paths of escalation. The PMO governance framework also establishes roles and responsibilities within the PMO and delineates authority levels for different aspects of the PMO.
- **Portfolio governance.** Distinct from program and project management, portfolio governance oversees the entire portfolio life cycle to maintain strategic alignment. Portfolio governance focuses on the policies, procedures, and standards that govern the selection, prioritization, and management of an organization's collection of programs and projects, ensuring optimal resource allocation and alignment with overall business strategy.
- **Program governance.** Program governance focuses on the policies, procedures, and standards that oversee the coordination and management of related projects, ensuring the realization of collective benefits and strategic objectives that exceed those achievable through individual project management.
- **Project governance.** Project governance refers to the framework of policies, processes, and decision-making structures that guide the planning, execution, and control of a single project. Project governance establishes clear roles, responsibilities, and accountability measures to ensure a project aligns with organizational objectives, meets stakeholder expectations, and delivers intended outcomes within the defined constraints of scope, time, cost, and quality.

While the PMO often plays a role in portfolio, program, and project governance, PMO governance is about how the PMO itself is structured and managed to support these other governance functions effectively. The PMO might develop and enforce governance standards for portfolios, programs, and projects, but PMO governance ensures the PMO has the proper structure and authority to perform these functions effectively.

A PMO governance structure should include:

- **PMO roles and responsibilities.** Who does what within the PMO, and how do they interact with the rest of the organization?
- **PMO reporting lines.** Who does the PMO report to within the organization? What are the established channels and processes for the PMO to report its activities, progress, and issues?
- **PMO decision-making processes.** What decisions can be made at what level within the PMO? When and how should decisions be escalated to higher authorities? How are stakeholders involved in the decision-making process? How are decisions recorded and communicated?

- **PMO autonomy levels.** What is the PMO's level of autonomy and how are decisions made at various levels?
- **PMO accountability.** How are the PMO and its team members held accountable for their actions and decisions?
- **PMO performance metrics.** What are the KPIs established to measure the effectiveness and efficiency of the PMO?
- **PMO compliance.** How will the PMO's adherence to organizational policies, industry standards, and ethical guidelines be ensured?
- **Change management.** How are changes to the way activities are conducted within the PMO proposed? How should approved organizational changes be launched smoothly and effectively communicated?
- **Conflict resolution.** How will disputes between PMO customers and other stakeholders be resolved? How can these grievances be forwarded to higher authorities? How should third parties participate in solving these complicated matters?
- **PMO continuous improvement.** How will the feedback loops be captured and how will lessons learned be applied? How does PMO governance evolve as the PMO and organization mature?

Effective PMO governance is essential for the success and sustainability of a PMO. The governance process provides the structure and guidelines necessary for the PMO to operate efficiently, make decisions effectively, and deliver value to the organization. By clearly defining roles, responsibilities, decision-making processes, and accountability measures, PMO governance can ensure that the PMO can navigate complex organizational landscapes while aligning with strategic objectives.

Implementing robust PMO governance is an ongoing process that requires careful planning, stakeholder engagement, and a willingness to adapt. As the PMO and organization evolve, so too must the PMO governance framework. Regular reviews and refinement of governance measures can help ensure that the PMO remains practical, relevant, and valuable to the organization and its customers.

The PMO governance framework develops alongside the organization's journey through this framework. The governance framework begins as a simple proposal, built on the initial assumptions outlined in the PMO charter. At this early stage, the framework is deliberately kept straightforward, recognizing that much will be discovered and adjusted as the PMO grows and evolves.

As the PMO progresses, the framework naturally gains more clarity and detail. By engaging with customers and understanding their needs, the PMO refines its services and obtains more accurate information.

What starts as a basic outline gradually transforms into a comprehensive framework with clearly assigned roles, decision-making processes, and accountability structures. This gradual evolution ensures that the framework remains practical and aligned with the PMO's ongoing development.

Taking this step-by-step approach allows the PMO governance framework to stay flexible and responsive to the organization's changing needs. The PMO avoids the mistake of adding unnecessary complexity too soon and instead grows in a way that reflects its current state and its value contribution.

PMO Strategy: Charting the Course for Value Delivery

The PMO strategy is a comprehensive and dynamic plan that outlines how the PMO will deliver value to its stakeholders over the short, medium, and long term. This strategy is a crucial element that bridges the gap between the PMO mandate and its day-to-day operations, ensuring that the PMO remains aligned with organizational goals while consistently meeting the evolving needs of PMO customers.

Primarily, it is about creating a roadmap for value delivery. While this document provides information on "what" to do, it does not show "how" to do it. The following are some of the critical components of a typical PMO strategy:

- **PMO vision and mission alignment.** This alignment details how a broader, high-level vision and mission statement, as defined in the PMO charter, can be operationalized over different timeframes: short term, middle term, and long term. The vision and mission help PMO professionals understand their direction by transforming these aims into practical choices and measurable results. This effort links PMO performance objectives to the overall purpose, ensuring alignment in every aspect of PMO operations.
- **PMO alignment with organizational objectives.** The PMO strategy outlines how the PMO will continuously align its activities with broader organizational goals and strategies, ensuring that the PMO remains a valuable strategic asset in the organization. These activities include mechanisms for regularly reviewing and adjusting priorities based on shifting focus points within the organization or through showing a direct impact on primary business targets by projects through various means.
- **PMO maturity and evolution roadmap.** This component of the PMO strategy focuses on the internal development of the PMO and project management capabilities within the organization. The roadmap provides a step-by-step plan to improve organizational project management practices and competencies.
- **PMO value journey.** This aspect of the PMO strategy is externally focused, mapping out how the PMO's value proposition to its customers will evolve. This component details the progression of the PMO, outlining how it will continuously adapt its services to meet changing business and customer needs. The value journey includes strategies to communicate a PMO's value, emphasizing how the PMO will shape customer perceptions of its value and become indispensable to the organization's success.
- **PMO performance metrics and KPIs.** The PMO charter's high-level success metrics are elaborated in the PMO strategy, which establishes detailed KPIs and performance metrics to

measure progress toward achieving the vision and mission. This component includes both quantitative and qualitative measures of PMO effectiveness and value delivery, as well as a system for regular reviews and refinement of these metrics to ensure they remain relevant and aligned with organizational priorities.

- **PMO customer engagement plan.** The PMO strategy details how engagement with different PMO customers will evolve to support realizing the vision and mission. This plan includes strategies for managing expectations, building relationships, and ensuring continuous alignment with customer needs. The plan outlines tailored approaches for different customer groups and mechanisms for gathering and acting on customer feedback to drive continuous improvement.
- **PMO resource and capability development.** The PMO strategy specifies how resources (human, financial, technological) and capabilities will be developed and utilized to achieve the vision and fulfill the mission. This component includes training, hiring, technology adoption, process improvement plans, resource allocation, and building a culture of continuous learning and development within the PMO and across the organization.
- **PMO risk management.** The PMO strategy details how risks to achieving the PMO vision and mission will be identified, assessed, managed, and mitigated over time, encompassing internal PMO risks, broader organizational risks that could impact PMO effectiveness, and dangers related to PMO customers' perceptions of value. This effort includes developing strategies to proactively address potential misalignments between PMO services and stakeholder expectations and safeguarding the PMO's relevance and perceived value within the organization.
- **PMO service portfolio evolution.** The PMO strategy defines how the PMO's service offerings will evolve to meet changing organizational needs and drive increasing value. This effort includes developing a framework for regularly assessing the effectiveness of current services, identifying emerging needs, and developing new capabilities to ensure the PMO remains at the forefront of project management excellence.
- **PMO communication and change management.** The PMO strategy includes developing plans for effectively communicating the PMO's value proposition and managing the organizational changes necessary for PMO success. This effort encompasses a comprehensive approach to change management, including strategies for overcoming resistance, fostering buy-in at all levels of the organization, and ensuring the smooth adoption of new processes and practices introduced by the PMO.
- **PMO continuous improvement.** The PMO strategy establishes mechanisms for ongoing evaluation and improvement of PMO practices, ensuring that the PMO contributes value and remains relevant. This effort includes regular assessments of PMO performance, benchmarking against industry practices, and a structured approach to implementing improvements based on lessons learned and emerging practices in project management and organizational effectiveness.
- **Innovation and adaptation.** The PMO strategy outlines how the PMO will foster innovation in project management practices and adapt to emerging trends and technologies. This effort includes creating plans for staying abreast of industry developments, experimenting with new methodologies and tools, and cultivating a culture of innovation within the PMO.

By addressing these components, the PMO strategy translates the high-level aspirations of the PMO charter into concrete, measurable action plans, helping the PMO to remain aligned with its core objectives while navigating the complexities and changes of the organizational environment.

The PMO strategy should not be considered static; it requires frequent reviews and updates to stay relevant amid organizational and environmental changes. Keeping the strategy dynamic is essential for ensuring it continues to add value by aligning with the organization's evolving needs. These activities, usually conducted annually, allow proactive adjustments to be made, helping to ensure the PMO remains an important asset within the organization. Customer involvement should occur during these reviews, considering both internal and external factors affecting the PMO's performance.

The PMO strategy begins as a high-level outline based on initial assumptions and goals. As the PMO engages with its customers, the strategy gains depth and specificity. This approach helps ensure that the PMO strategy remains aligned with organizational objectives, responsive to PMO customers' needs, and focused on delivering increasing value over time.

Several critical situations warrant a thorough review and potential update of the PMO strategy:

- **PMO establishment and evolution.** This work is performed during the initial PMO setup, creating a foundational document. The document is then evolved upon reaching significant maturity milestones to reflect higher sophistication and set new goals.
- **Organizational changes.** This review is performed during major restructuring to align with new organizational designs. Reviews may also be performed when key customers change, particularly at the executive level, or following shifts in overall organizational strategy.
- **Project portfolio dynamics.** This review is performed after any significant adjustments to the project portfolio composition are made, as well as upon completion of any major programs or projects to incorporate lessons learned.
- **External environment shifts.** Reviews may occur in response to significant market changes, including industry trends and competitive pressures, and when facing new regulatory requirements or economic conditions.
- **Technological advancements.** These reviews may occur upon the adoption of new project management tools or methodologies or when implementing enterprise-wide systems or emerging technologies (e.g., AI, blockchain).
- **Customer feedback and performance reviews.** These reviews may be performed in response to substantial customer feedback about the PMO's performance or value delivery. Reviews may also be done as part of the annual strategic PMO planning cycle to ensure ongoing relevance and effectiveness.

In essence, a well-crafted and regularly updated PMO strategy serves as a living roadmap, guiding the PMO's evolution, aligning its activities with organizational objectives, and ensuring its continued relevance and value in the face of changing business landscapes and customer expectations.

Looking Ahead to the Next Section

Building upon the structural components, the next component of the PMO Value Ring™ framework shifts the focus toward customer experience. Delivering real value means prioritizing how PMOs engage with and serve their customers.

The next section introduces the PMO customer experience cycle—a model that places the customer at the heart of PMO activities. This cycle, from exploration to realization, offers a clear framework for consistently meeting and exceeding customer expectations. By adopting this approach, PMO professionals can help ensure their structural components are used effectively to create positive, value-driven experiences.

12

The PMO Customer Experience Cycle

Why This Section Matters to PMO Professionals

Understanding the PMO customer experience cycle is crucial for PMO professionals as it represents a comprehensive approach to transforming the PMO into a strategic asset.

This section introduces a customer-centric framework that shifts the PMO's focus from merely executing projects to delivering tangible value to customers and stakeholders. By adopting this cycle, PMO professionals can enhance their ability to meet evolving organizational needs, foster stronger stakeholder relationships, and drive continuous improvement.

This cycle provides practical insights into each stage of the customer experience cycle, highlighting how PMOs can adapt their services, measure success, and maintain strategic alignment. Embracing this approach allows PMO professionals to elevate their PMOs from tactical support roles to pivotal drivers of organizational success, ensuring they remain relevant, effective, and valued within their organizations.

From Concept to Value: The PMO Customer Experience Journey

The role of PMOs has transcended traditional boundaries, moving beyond mere oversight to become a strategic driver of organizational success. At the core of this transformation lies the PMO customer experience cycle, an approach that places the PMO's customers at the center of its operations (see Figure 12-1).

The PMO customer experience cycle embodies a customer-centric philosophy and represents a paradigm shift in the PMO landscape. The cycle recognizes that the factual accuracy of a PMO's success lies not just in the efficient execution of an organization's projects but in the tangible value it delivers to its customers.

This cycle comprises five stages, and each one is carefully crafted to ensure that the PMO remains attuned to the evolving needs of its customers, continuously adapts its services, and demonstrates measurable impact and value.

- **Exploration stage.** This stage marks the beginning of the cycle, where the PMO engages in profound discovery to understand the current landscape, customer needs, and potential opportunities. The stage is characterized by educating customers about the PMO's potential value and actively listening to their needs and expectations. This exploration sets the foundation for all subsequent stages by ensuring the PMO's efforts are grounded in a thorough understanding of its customers' realities.

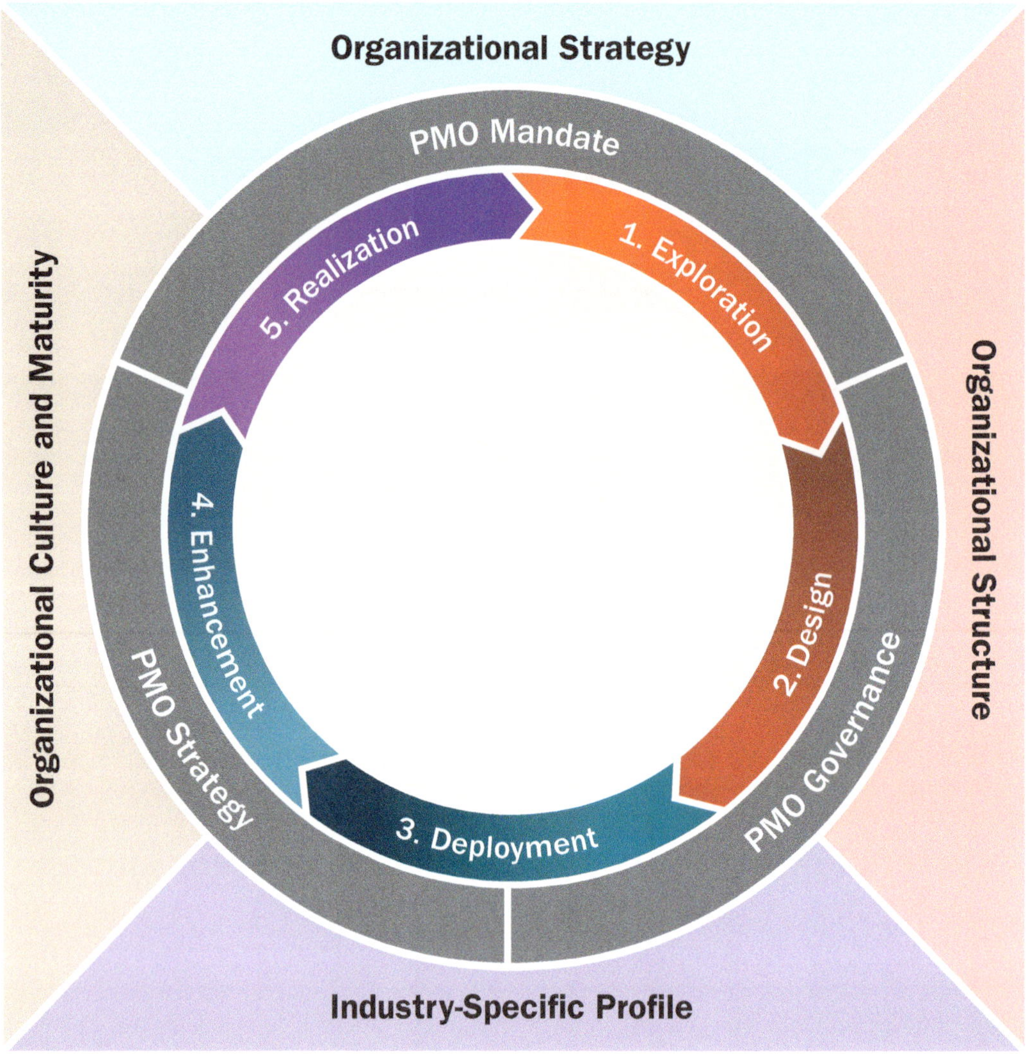

Figure 12-1. PMO Customer Experience Cycle

- **Design stage.** The PMO leverages the insights from the exploration stage to develop a tailored proposal that can deliver the expected outcomes. This creative stage involves collaborative problem-solving, innovative thinking, and service design, with the goal of developing offerings that meet current needs and anticipate future challenges and opportunities.
- **Deployment stage.** This stage brings the designed solutions to life. Deployment involves the day-to-day operations of the PMO, ensuring a smooth implementation of planned services and executing them in alignment with established service levels and goals. The PMO should navigate

operational complexities in this stage, integrating new services and processes effectively within the organization.

- **Enhancement stage.** This stage is about continuous improvement, driven by performance metrics, feedback loops, service maturity improvement, and agile adaptations. In this stage, the PMO works on increasing service maturity by consistently refining its offerings and learning from both successes and setbacks to enhance the value delivered.
- **Realization stage.** This stage focuses on measuring the outcomes of PMO services, demonstrating the PMO's value, and ensuring PMO customer expectations are met. This stage emphasizes the recognition and appreciation of the value generated by the PMO, validating its contributions to the organization.

The Iterative Power of the Cycle

What makes the PMO customer experience cycle powerful is its iterative nature. It is not a linear process with a definitive end but a continuous loop of improvement and value creation. Each revolution of the cycle builds upon the learnings and achievements of the previous one, driving a spiral of increasing value and organizational impact.

The cycle is a dynamic and fluid process that operates as a continuous, interconnected system rather than a rigid, linear sequence. This concept is fundamental to understanding the PMO customer experience cycle's effectiveness and its ability to drive ongoing value creation.

The PMO customer experience cycle is designed to be perpetually moving. While the stages—exploration, design, deployment, enhancement, and realization—follow a logical sequence, they do not operate in isolation or come to a complete halt before the next stage begins. Instead, they overlap and intertwine, creating a seamless activity and value-generation flow.

In essence, the dynamic nature of the PMO customer experience cycle transforms the PMO from a reactive support function into a proactive value creator. The cycle enables the PMO to simultaneously manage current needs, anticipate future requirements, and continuously evolve its offerings to maximize the value it delivers to the organization.

Each stage of the PMO customer experience cycle is detailed in this section, showing how PMO professionals can leverage it to elevate their PMO's strategic relevance, demonstrate tangible value, and become indispensable partners in driving organizational success.

The Exploration Stage: Laying the Foundation for Organization's Evolution

The exploration stage is the crucial first step in the PMO customer experience cycle, setting the foundation for all subsequent stages. This stage is characterized by a dual focus: understanding the present and preparing for the future, which involves thorough discovery, active engagement, and strategic preparation.

The exploration stage focuses on educating and nurturing PMO customers to recognize potential value that they may not yet be aware of due to varying levels of project management maturity. Exploration also involves identifying the current needs of PMO customers, setting the groundwork for developing a compelling value proposition for the PMO.

In this stage, the PMO takes on the roles of educator and investigator, fostering an environment where more advanced project management practices can be established while uncovering current customer needs. The objectives of the exploration stage include:

- **Understanding the current landscape.** Assess the organization's project management environment by analyzing existing processes, tools, methodologies, and data on project success rates, challenges, and inefficiencies.
- **Educating and nurturing customers.** Elevate the organization's project management literacy through workshops, seminars, and targeted communications, preparing customers to recognize and appreciate more sophisticated PMO offerings in the future.
- **Identifying customer needs.** Engage with PMO customers to understand their perspectives, challenges, and aspirations. Identify both explicit and implicit needs to inform future PMO offerings. Discover specific pain points and challenges that PMO customers face, providing a foundation for tailored solutions.
- **Building relationships and trust.** Establish strong relationships and build trust with PMO customers, from C-suite executives to project team members.
- **Sowing the seeds of value proposition.** Begin formulating the PMO's value proposition by identifying how it will add tangible value to the organization, guiding the development of PMO services and solutions in subsequent stages.

At its core, the exploration stage is about discovery. PMO professionals engage with PMO customers—from C-suite executives to project team members—to build relationships, establish trust, and understand their perspectives, challenges, and aspirations. These interactions are not just about gathering information but about laying the groundwork for future collaborations and demonstrating the PMO's commitment to adding value.

A unique and crucial aspect of the exploration stage is its educational component. Recognizing that the value of a PMO may not be immediately apparent to all customers, especially in organizations with lower project management maturity, this stage includes efforts to educate and nurture PMO customers. Through workshops, seminars, and targeted communications, the PMO begins to elevate the organization's project management maturity, preparing current or potential customers to recognize and appreciate more sophisticated PMO offerings in the future.

The exploration stage is also where the seeds of the PMO's value proposition are sown. By identifying pain points, understanding customer needs (both explicit and implicit), and aligning with organizational strategy, the PMO begins to formulate how it will add tangible value to the organization. This emerging value proposition will guide the development of PMO services and solutions in subsequent PMO customer experience cycle stages.

Notably, the exploration stage is not a one-time event but the beginning of an ongoing process. While this stage marks the start of the PMO customer experience cycle, the spirit of exploration—discovery and continuous learning—should persist throughout the cycle.

This stage is not just about gathering information; it is about building relationships, establishing credibility, and nurturing an environment where the PMO's value can be fully recognized and appreciated. The insights and connections made during this stage will inform all subsequent cycle phases, ensuring that the PMO's efforts are well aligned with organizational needs and poised to deliver maximum value.

The Design Stage: Crafting the PMO's Value Blueprint

Following the exploration stage of the PMO customer experience cycle is the crucial design stage. This pivotal stage transforms insights and understanding gleaned from exploration into a strategic blueprint for action. The design stage is where the PMO's potential value to the organization begins to take tangible form, setting the foundation for all subsequent implementation and operation stages.

The PMO's vision focuses on the design stage, laying the groundwork for transformative change in the organization's project management practices. Design is a stage of creativity, strategic thinking, and careful planning that will shape the PMO's impact for years.

This stage is characterized by its emphasis on strategic alignment. The PMO should ensure that its proposed value and services are not just addressing immediate customers' needs but are also closely aligned with the organization's overarching goals and strategic direction. This alignment is crucial for gaining executive support and ensuring the PMO's long-term relevance and success.

At its core, the design stage is about crafting a compelling value proposition, articulating how the PMO will drive meaningful change and deliver tangible benefits to its customers and the broader organization.

A key output of the design stage is the definition of the PMO's portfolio of services. Selecting the right mix of services is critical, as it will shape the PMO's ability to deliver on promises of outcomes and drive value generation for its customers.

The design stage also involves creating a roadmap for the implementation and evolution of the PMO. This roadmap provides a strategic view of how the PMO will roll out its services, build its capabilities, and gradually increase its impact on the organization over time. This stage considers the organization's current project management maturity, resource constraints, and the need to demonstrate early wins while planning for long-term, sustainable improvements.

Throughout this stage, customer engagement remains crucial. The design process should involve key customers to ensure the proposed PMO strategy and services resonate with their needs and expectations. This collaborative approach leads to better design outcomes and helps build buy-in and support for the PMO's future initiatives.

It is important to note that the design stage is not about creating a rigid, unchangeable PMO value proposition and portfolio of services. Instead, this stage is about developing a flexible proposal that can adapt to changing organizational needs and customer expectations. The PMO value proposition and service portfolio outlined in this stage should be viewed as living elements, subject to refinement and adjustment as the PMO gains experience and the organization's needs evolve.

The design stage incorporates several essential activities such as crafting a compelling PMO value proposition, developing a strategic service portfolio, and considering challenges the PMO may face during this crucial phase. The outcomes of this stage set the stage for successful implementation and value delivery in the subsequent stages of the PMO customer experience cycle. The design stage's objectives include:

- **Formulating the PMO value proposition.** Develop a clear, compelling PMO value proposition that addresses the evolving needs and value perceptions of customers, delivering measurable benefits such as enhanced efficiency, project alignment, and improved resource utilization.
- **Developing a portfolio of PMO services.** Outline a portfolio of services based on the value proposition, identifying types that address needs and support the value proposition without defining details.
- **Detailing PMO services.** Define all necessary details for the implementation of each service, establishing processes, responsibilities, involved resources, performance indicators, agreed-upon service levels with customers, and established goals.
- **Creating a high-level roadmap.** Conclude with a roadmap for implementing the PMO and its services, balancing quick wins with long-term improvements in project management practices, while also considering customer needs, value delivery, and value perception.

As the PMO moves from design to the next stage, it carries a clear vision of how it will add value to the organization, a strategic outline of the services it will offer to deliver on this vision, and a roadmap for bringing this vision to life. These elements provide the foundation for the next stages in the PMO customer experience cycle, where the focus will shift to operations and performance measurement.

The Deployment Stage: Bringing the PMO Vision to Life

Following the design stage is the dynamic and transformative deployment stage of the PMO customer experience cycle. This critical phase is where carefully crafted plans and value propositions materialize into tangible actions and services. The deployment stage is where the tangible work begins—where the PMO's potential value to the organization becomes a reality. This stage ensures that the PMO's services are available and effectively integrated into the organization's fabric, delivering tangible value from the outset.

In the deployment stage, the PMO's impact begins to be felt across the organization. Deployment is a stage of action, learning, and transformation that sets the tone for the PMO's long-term effectiveness and value delivery. Successfully navigating this stage is crucial for establishing the PMO as an indispensable asset in driving project management excellence and supporting organizational success. The deployment stage's objectives include:

- **Building infrastructure.** Establish the tools, technologies, and infrastructure to support PMO operations.
- **Allocating resources.** Effectively allocate and manage the resources required to deploy PMO services.
- **Implementing services.** Introduce the designed PMO services and processes across the organization.
- **Engaging PMO customers.** Maintain active communication and engagement with customers throughout the deployment process.
- **Onboarding customers.** Prepare and educate PMO customers about the newly introduced services and processes.
- **Mitigating risks.** Identify and address potential risks and challenges during the deployment phase.
- **Managing change.** Manage the transition and address resistance to new PMO practices and processes.
- **Planning scalability.** Prepare for scaling PMO services as adoption increases and organizational needs evolve.

Success in this stage sets the foundation for long-term PMO effectiveness and prepares the way for continuous improvement and value delivery in the subsequent stages of the PMO customer experience cycle.

The Enhancement Stage: Elevating PMO Performance and Maturity

Following the deployment stage of the PMO customer experience cycle is the critical enhancement stage. This phase represents a pivotal moment in the PMO's journey, when the focus shifts from implementation to optimization and growth.

The enhancement stage is where the PMO, based on its performance measurements, begins to refine its value proposition, advance its services, and establish itself as an essential asset to its customers. A key aspect of this stage is its cyclical nature—it is not a one-time event but an ongoing process of learning, adaptation, and growth. This continuous improvement approach helps ensure that the PMO remains agile and responsive to the organization's evolving needs.

The enhancement stage is characterized by a dual focus: measuring and improving the performance of PMO services and assessing and advancing the overall maturity of the PMO. This stage is crucial for continuously increasing the likelihood of delivering desired outcomes through ever-more-efficient services.

Insights gained from these measurement and assessment activities drive the development of targeted action plans for improvement. These plans go beyond addressing deficiencies; they strategically enhance the PMO's capabilities to deliver greater value to the organization. This enhancement may involve refining existing services, introducing new offerings, upgrading tools and technologies, or developing the skills of PMO staff.

The enhancement stage's objectives include:

- **Measuring service performance.** Establish and implement systems to measure the performance of PMO services.
- **Assessing service maturity.** Conduct comprehensive assessments of the PMO's maturity level. Identify gaps between current maturity and desired levels.
- **Planning improvement.** Develop targeted action plans to address identified gaps and enhance PMO capabilities.
- **Refining services.** Continuously refine and improve existing PMO services based on performance data and feedback.
- **Developing capabilities.** Enhance the skills and competencies of PMO staff and project managers.
- **Fostering innovation.** Encourage and implement innovative approaches to improve efficiency and generate value.

The enhancement stage is crucial for ensuring that the PMO remains relevant, effective, and aligned with organizational needs over time. The PMO can continuously improve its services by systematically measuring performance, assessing and developing maturity, and implementing targeted improvements. This stage transforms the PMO from a static entity into a dynamic, evolving force that drives ongoing project management excellence and organizational success.

The Realization Stage: Solidifying PMO Value and Preparing for Future Growth

The realization stage of the PMO customer experience cycle is a critical phase that demonstrates the PMO's current value and sets the stage for its future evolution. In this pivotal stage, the PMO's impact on the organization comes into sharp focus, deepening relationships with its customers and preparing the groundwork for a new cycle of increased value delivery.

Realization is dedicated to quantifying and demonstrating the tangible benefits that the PMO has delivered to the organization, ensuring value recognition by the PMO customers. This effort involves measuring the actual outcomes of PMO services against the PMO customer needs and expectations established in earlier stages. Additionally, this stage focuses on understanding and assessing how PMO customers and stakeholders perceive the value provided by the PMO.

The power of the realization stage is its creation of a comprehensive picture of PMO value and impact that combines tangible outcome measurements with customer perceptions. This stage is potent in deepening the PMO's customer relationship. As tangible benefits are demonstrated and positive perceptions reinforced, the PMO strengthens its position as a trusted partner in organizational success.

Moreover, the realization stage is a culmination and a springboard for future growth. This stage marks the beginning of a new cycle in the PMO's evolution, initiating an upward spiral of increasing value. The insights gained during this stage from measurable outcomes and customer feedback inform the PMO's future strategies, allowing it to refine its services, target new areas for improvement, and align even more closely with evolving customer needs.

This cyclical nature of the realization stage helps ensure that the PMO remains dynamic and responsive. Each cycle builds upon the last, with the PMO continuously enhancing its capabilities, expanding its influence, and delivering enhanced value to the organization. It transforms the PMO from a static entity into a learning organization, constantly adapting and growing in response to successes and challenges.

The realization phase assists PMOs in strengthening their strategic position, securing resources for future initiatives, and setting the stage for an even more significant impact in subsequent cycle iterations. The realization stage's objectives include:

- **Measuring value delivery.** Quantify and demonstrate the tangible outcomes and benefits delivered by the PMO.
- **Assessing customer perception.** Measure and analyze how PMO customers perceive the value of PMO services.
- **Documenting success stories.** Capture and communicate success stories and case studies demonstrating PMO value.
- **Reporting value performance.** Develop and deliver comprehensive reports on PMO value creation. Effectively communicate the PMO's value proposition and achievements to all levels of the organization.
- **Planning future value.** Identify opportunities for the PMO to deliver increased value in future cycles.
- **Deepening customer relationships.** Strengthen relationships with PMO customers based on demonstrated value.

The realization stage is where the PMO's journey comes full circle, demonstrating the tangible and perceived value it brings to its customers and the organization. By effectively measuring and communicating concrete outcomes and customer perceptions, the PMO can solidify its position as an invaluable partner for its customers.

This phase provides the evidence and narrative needed to secure ongoing support, resources, and strategic influence, ensuring that the PMO continues to play a pivotal role in driving organizational success. Ultimately, a well-executed realization stage transforms the PMO from a cost center into a recognized value driver within the organization.

Looking Ahead to the Next Section

The PMO customer experience cycle is a model that helps PMO professionals to create value-driven, customer-centric operations for their PMOs. To bring this cycle to life, a practical tool is needed to translate its stages into actionable steps.

The next section introduces the value-generating PMO flywheel, a dynamic model that operationalizes the PMO customer experience cycle. Borrowed from business philosophy, the flywheel demonstrates how sustained, incremental efforts can create a self-reinforcing loop of success for PMOs. By implementing this model, PMO professionals can ensure consistent value delivery and build momentum for continuous improvement. This powerful concept and how it can propel PMO success will be explained in Part 3.

Part 3

Exploring the Value-Generating PMO Flywheel

13

Flywheel Overview

Why This Section Matters to PMO Professionals

This section introduces an innovative model that shifts the PMO's role from a traditional, process-centric approach to a dynamic, customer-focused entity that drives continuous improvement and tangible value creation.

The value-generating PMO flywheel breaks down the PMO customer experience cycle into 10 actionable steps, providing a clear roadmap for PMO professionals to follow. By doing so, the flywheel emphasizes the importance of customer centricity and value generation. Each step of the flywheel builds momentum, creating a self-reinforcing loop that enhances the PMO's impact and efficiency over time.

PMO professionals can learn how to create awareness about the value of the PMO, identify customer needs, develop a compelling value proposition, design tailored services, manage service deployment, measure service efficiency, enhance PMO service maturity, assess PMO value delivery, and ensure that PMO customers recognize its value. This section delves into the intricacies of each step, offering guidance on how to design, operate, and improve a PMO that not only meets—but exceeds—customer expectations.

Embracing the value-generating PMO flywheel can help ensure that a PMO remains agile, relevant, and strategically aligned with organizational goals. The flywheel steps help position the PMO as a vital asset, capable of driving organizational success through a relentless focus on delivering value. This section is crucial for any PMO professional looking to elevate their PMO's strategic importance and demonstrate its indispensable role in the organization.

Unleashing the Potential of PMOs With the Flywheel Model

The value-generating PMO flywheel represents a groundbreaking approach to PMO management, designed to drive continuous and effective value to PMO customers and organizations. This innovative model reimagines the PMO as a dynamic, customer-centric entity capable of adapting to evolving business needs while consistently demonstrating its strategic worth.

At its core, the value-generating PMO flywheel provides actionable steps for an effective implementation of the PMO Value Ring™ framework's PMO customer experience cycle. The flywheel breaks down each of the cycle's five stages into 10 actionable steps, not only providing PMO professionals with a clear roadmap for success but also emphasizing the interconnected and self-reinforcing nature of value creation in project management (see Figure 13-1).

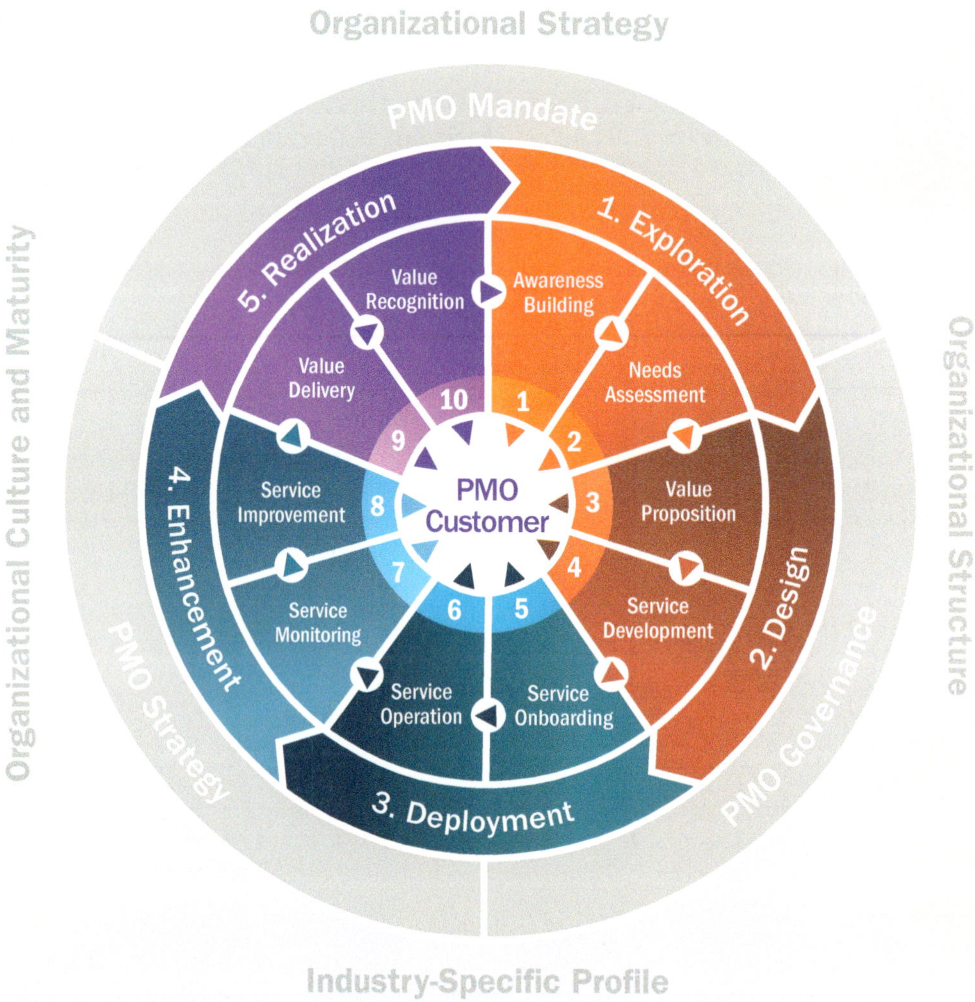

Figure 13-1. Value-Generating PMO Flywheel Model

The intricacies of the value-generating PMO flywheel model can help transform PMOs from process-oriented bureaucracies into agile, value-driven, customer-centric partners in organizational success.

The Value-Generating PMO Flywheel Dynamics

The term "flywheel" in this context is borrowed from Jim Collins' business philosophy, as outlined in his book *Good to Great*. In mechanical terms, a flywheel is a heavy wheel that requires significant effort to start spinning but, once in motion, continues to rotate with its own momentum. In business, the flywheel effect refers to the idea that sustained, incremental efforts can create a self-reinforcing loop of success.

Applied to PMOs, the flywheel concept suggests that as the PMO consistently delivers value and meets customer needs, it builds momentum. Each successful iteration of the PMO customer experience cycle makes the next one easier and more impactful, creating a virtuous circle of improvement and value generation.

The value-generating PMO flywheel is not a linear process but a dynamic, interconnected system of continuous improvement and value creation. Unlike traditional models that progress sequentially from one stage to the next, this cycle operates as a multifaceted, ever-moving mechanism. The flywheel is designed to keep the PMO in a constant state of adaptation, innovation, and value delivery, ensuring that it remains a relevant and indispensable asset to the organization.

This approach allows the PMO to simultaneously address various customer needs, develop tailored solutions, manage multiple services at different stages of maturity, measure its efficiency, continuously refine its offerings, and deliver and demonstrate effective value for its customers.

Imagine the cycle as a series of gears in constant motion. As one gear (step) turns, it engages the next while continuing its rotation. This means that the PMO is likely involved in activities across multiple cycle stages simultaneously at any given moment. For example, while the PMO is onboarding and delivering a new service (service onboard and service operation steps), it may already be gathering feedback and improving (service monitoring and service improvement steps) on other services previously implemented.

Simultaneously, the PMO can assess emerging needs (needs assessment step) in various organizational sectors while evaluating customers' perceived value of specific services (value recognition step).

This multifaceted approach allows the PMO to be highly responsive and adaptable. The flywheel model can help address the needs of different customers at various stages of their journeys, manage multiple services at different maturity levels, and continuously measure and improve its offerings.

The cycle's dynamic nature also means that learnings and insights from one step can immediately inform and influence activities in other steps. For instance, insights gathered during the value recognition step about customers' perceived benefits can immediately inform the service development step, potentially triggering the redesign of an existing PMO service.

Furthermore, this approach allows the PMO to maintain multiple touchpoints with its customers. It is not a matter of engaging with a customer once and then moving on; instead, it is about maintaining an ongoing dialogue, continually assessing needs, and refining the PMO value proposition. This continual activity across all stages can ensure that the PMO remains agile and responsive to changing organizational needs, preventing it from becoming static or outdated.

The 10 Steps of the Value-Generating PMO Flywheel

The value-generating PMO flywheel is intrinsically linked to the PMO customer experience cycle. While the cycle provides a high-level framework for customer-centric PMOs, the flywheel breaks this down into actionable steps.

The five stages of the PMO customer experience cycle—exploration, design, deployment, enhancement, and realization—each correspond to two steps in the flywheel, resulting in a 10-step process. This breakdown not only makes the cycle more practical but also emphasizes the continuous nature of the process. As the PMO completes one full rotation of the flywheel, it does not stop but continues into the next cycle, building on previous successes and learnings.

Each step of the flywheel consists of the following:

Exploration Stage

- **Step 1—Awareness building.** This initial step involves making potential customers aware of the PMO's existence and capabilities. This step is about creating visibility for the PMO and its value within the organization and educating potential and current customers about how the PMO can support their work and generate value.
- **Step 2—Needs assessment.** At this step, the PMO engages in deep discovery to understand the current landscape, customer needs, and potential opportunities. This effort involves active listening, data gathering, and insightful analysis.

Design Stage

- **Step 3—Value proposition.** Based on the insights gathered, the PMO crafts a clear value proposition for its services. This step involves articulating how the PMO will meet identified needs, deliver expected outcomes and benefits to its customers, and generate value for the organization.
- **Step 4—Service development.** This step involves creating, refining, or redesigning PMO services in comprehensive detail. It is a creative process that requires innovative thinking and collaborative problem-solving.

Deployment Stage

- **Step 5—Service onboarding.** This step focuses on introducing new or improved services to PMO customers. The effort involves change management, training, and ensuring the smooth adoption of PMO offerings.
- **Step 6—Service operation.** At this step, the PMO delivers its services, managing day-to-day operations and ensuring consistent quality and efficiency in service delivery.

Enhancement Stage

- **Step 7—Service monitoring.** This step involves monitoring and measuring the performance of PMO services. The work involves collecting data and feedback to understand how well services are being delivered and whether agreed-upon efficiency goals are being met.
- **Step 8—Service improvement.** Based on a comprehensive PMO service maturity assessment, in this step the PMO identifies opportunities for improvement and enhances its services. This step is about continuous improvement, adaptation, and service maturity evolution.

Realization Stage

- **Step 9—Value delivery.** This step focuses on measuring the promised value to customers through the expected outcomes. This step ensures that PMO services are making a tangible, positive impact on PMO customers' needs and organizational success. The step involves assessing, measuring, and communicating the value created by the PMO.
- **Step 10—Value recognition.** The final step is crucial for ensuring that PMO customers and the broader organization recognize and appreciate the PMO's contributions. By continually assessing and measuring the customers' perceptions of value, the PMO can demonstrate its ongoing relevance and impact, fostering stronger support and alignment with organizational goals and providing the momentum to initiate a new cycle in the PMO's growth and evolution journey.

The Importance of the Value-Generating PMO Flywheel

The value-generating PMO flywheel is more than just a process model; it is a paradigm shift in how PMOs operate and demonstrate their worth. The main reasons for its importance include:

- **Customer centricity.** By focusing on customer needs and experiences, the flywheel helps ensure that the PMO remains relevant and valuable to its users.
- **Value creation.** The flywheel, with explicit steps for value delivery and recognition, helps PMOs move beyond process management to genuine value generation.

- **Momentum building.** As the flywheel gains speed, the PMO's impact and efficiency increase, creating a self-reinforcing cycle of success.
- **Adaptability.** The model's emphasis on continuous assessment and improvement allows PMOs to adapt quickly to changing organizational needs.
- **Continuous improvement.** The cyclical nature of the flywheel encourages ongoing refinement and adaptation of PMO services.

The value-generating PMO flywheel represents a significant evolution in PMO operations. By breaking down the PMO customer experience cycle into actionable steps and emphasizing continuous improvement and value creation, this model offers a path for PMOs to become true strategic partners in organizational success.

By embracing the value-generating PMO flywheel, PMOs can transform from cost centers into value drivers, from process enforcers into success enablers, and from administrative overhead into indispensable partners in organizational achievement. This model offers a roadmap for PMO evolution, ensuring that these crucial organizational entities remain relevant, impactful, and valued in an ever-changing business landscape.

Looking Ahead to the Next Section

This section provided an overview of the value-generating PMO flywheel, exploring how this model can foster continuous improvement and value creation within PMOs.

The next section shifts to a detailed examination of each step in the flywheel, beginning with awareness building. This essential first step establishes the foundation for all PMO activities by making potential customers aware of the PMO's role, capabilities, and value. The following section explores strategies for effectively communicating the PMO's purpose, setting up regular stakeholder touchpoints, and educating the organization about the value the PMO brings. Implementing this step can enable PMO professionals to create a supportive environment for their initiatives, laying the groundwork for successful value delivery.

14

Step 1: Awareness Building

Why This Section Matters to PMO Professionals

Awareness building is the crucial first step in the value-generating PMO flywheel, laying the foundation for all subsequent steps. This step equips PMO professionals with the strategies and tools needed to build and sustain awareness, helping to ensure the PMO's long-term success and strategic importance within the organization.

For PMO professionals, mastering the awareness building phase is essential as it helps shape perceptions, manage expectations, and position the PMO as a key strategic partner. Effective awareness building can ensure that customers understand how the PMO supports their work and drives project success and organizational efficiency.

This understanding is critical for any PMO professional to gain buy-in, foster collaboration, and ensure that the PMO's initiatives are welcomed and supported.

Awareness Building Step at a Glance

Awareness building in the value-generating PMO flywheel is a critical and ongoing process that establishes the PMO's presence, capabilities, and value within an organization (see Figure 14-1). This foundational step goes beyond simply announcing the PMO's existence; it strategically communicates how the PMO can support various organizational functions and contribute to overall success.

This step lays the foundation for all subsequent value-generation efforts. By effectively building awareness, the PMO can more easily identify customer needs and implement its services and initiatives. This step also plays a crucial role in shaping perceptions, positioning the PMO as a strategic partner, and managing expectations.

Awareness building facilitates the creation of a supportive environment where customers not only recognize but also value the PMO's contributions. This engagement is crucial for the successful adoption of PMO services and for gaining buy-in for future initiatives. This effort encourages collaboration and fosters a culture of project management excellence.

Figure 14-1. Awareness Building Step in the PMO Flywheel

Effective awareness building can ensure that the PMO is seen as an indispensable resource for driving project success and organizational efficiency. The step enables the PMO to become a catalyst for positive change and a key player in achieving strategic goals. It is important to recognize that awareness building is not a one-time event but a continuous process that requires ongoing effort and adjustments based on continuous feedback. This process can help maintain visibility and relevance as the organization evolves throughout the PMO's life cycle.

A continuous focus on awareness is critical in laying the groundwork for the PMO's long-term success. This focus on success helps ensure that potential customers understand and appreciate the benefits of engaging with PMO services.

Implementing the Awareness-Building Step

1. Identifying Potential PMO Customers

- **Organizational structure mapping.** Start by analyzing the organizational structure and identifying key departments, teams, and individuals involved in project-related activities. Consider various roles such as executives, project managers, team leads, and functional managers. Assess each potential customer's current challenges, their level of influence on PMO adoption, and their potential impact on organizational project success.
- **Strategic segmentation.** Segment these potential customers based on multiple factors, such as their project management maturity, specific needs, pain points, and level of potential engagement with the PMO. This segmentation allows for more targeted and effective awareness-building efforts later on.
- **Organizational power dynamics.** Understanding the organization's power dynamics and decision-making processes is crucial. Identify key influencers and decision-makers who can champion PMO initiatives. This knowledge helps in prioritizing outreach efforts and tailoring messages to resonate with different stakeholder groups.
- **Developing customer personas.** Create detailed, outcome-based customer personas for each major segment, outlining their characteristics, needs, preferences, and potential objections to the PMO. These personas can guide the development of targeted awareness strategies.
- **Customer prioritization.** Prioritize the identified PMO customer groups based on their potential impact on PMO success and the organization's strategic goals. This prioritization helps focus initial awareness efforts where they can have the most significant impact.

2. Establishing Regular Touchpoints

- **Audience tailoring.** Map out customer groups' preferred communication channels through surveys or interviews. Understand how they each like to receive information and their preferred frequency. Craft clear, concise messages that convey the PMO's purpose, services, and value. Tailor these messages to different audience segments based on their needs, interests, and project management maturity.
- **Communication channels.** Choose communication channels based on the organization's culture, customer group preferences, and the nature of the information. Develop a mix of methods, such as monthly email newsletters for updates, weekly intranet posts for tips and highlights, quarterly town hall meetings for discussions and feedback, and annual reports for comprehensive reviews of PMO impact.
- **Content strategy.** Develop a content strategy with a mix of informative and engaging content about PMO services. Include success stories, infographics, short videos, and regular updates on PMO achievements. Address the "What is in it for me?" question for each customer group.

- **Content calendar.** Create a content calendar detailing topics, frequency, and channels to ensure a balanced mix and avoid repetition. Establish a reliable cadence for each type of communication. Consistency is key, and customers should know when to expect different types of updates from the PMO.

- **Interactive communication.** Incorporate mechanisms for two-way communication in touchpoints. This communication could include Q&A sessions in town halls, feedback forms in newsletters, or regular "office hours" where customers can quickly visit to discuss PMO-related matters.

- **Flexible information.** Consider creating tiered communication levels, allowing customers to opt in to different frequencies or depths of information based on their interests and needs. For instance, project managers might opt for more detailed, frequent updates, while executives might prefer higher-level quarterly summaries.

- **Tech integration.** Use technology to support your touchpoint strategy. This technology use might involve setting up automated email campaigns, leveraging collaboration platforms for real-time updates, or using project management software to share PMO dashboards.

- **Track effectiveness.** Regularly review the effectiveness of touchpoints by tracking metrics like email open rates, event attendance, and intranet post engagement. Use this data to refine the approach and be prepared to adjust the strategy based on organizational changes or feedback. Maintain consistency but remain flexible.

- **Informal engagements.** Do not underestimate the value of informal touchpoints. Encourage PMO team members to engage in casual conversations about PMO activities, attend cross-departmental meetings, or participate in company social events to build relationships and maintain visibility beyond formal communications.

3. Educating Customers About PMO Value

- **Educational library.** Develop a library of educational materials tailored to different audience segments. This library might include executive summaries for senior leadership, detailed service catalogs for project managers, and quick-reference guides for team members. Ensure that all materials are written in clear, jargon-free language that resonates with each audience.

- **Accessible training.** Develop a series of sessions or workshops to provide an overview of the PMO's purpose, explain key project management concepts, and demonstrate how the PMO can support different roles within the organization through its services. Offer these sessions regularly and make them easily accessible, perhaps through a mix of in-person and virtual formats.

- **Success stories.** Compile a collection of success stories and case studies that illustrate the PMO's impact. These should be specific, data-driven, and relatable to the organization. Include a mix of quick wins and long-term successes to show both immediate and sustained value.

- **Peer advocacy.** Establish a "PMO ambassador" program, where satisfied customers from different parts of the organization can share their experiences and the benefits they have realized from working with the PMO. Peer advocacy can be a powerful tool for building credibility and trust.
- **Benefit highlights.** Develop a series of targeted "value campaigns" that focus on specific benefits or services. For example, consider running a campaign on how the PMO improves resource allocation, followed by one on risk management benefits. This strategy allows for in-depth exploration of different value areas over time.
- **PMO portal.** Set up a PMO portal or knowledge base where customers can access information about PMO services, accepted practices, templates, and tools. Ensure this resource is user friendly, regularly updated, and promoted across the organization.

4. Measuring Effectiveness

- **Key performance metrics.** Start by establishing a comprehensive set of metrics that cover various aspects of awareness effectiveness. Implement tools and systems to collect data for these metrics. A set of key quantitative and qualitative measures that might be considered include:
  - **Reach.** Track the number of current or potential customers exposed to PMO communications through various channels.
  - **Engagement.** Measure levels of interaction with PMO content such as email open rates, click-through rates, or attendance at PMO events.
  - **Awareness levels.** Conduct regular surveys to gauge customers' familiarity with PMO services and value proposition.
  - **Inquiries.** Monitor the number and nature of requests for information about PMO services.
  - **Participation.** Track attendance and engagement in PMO workshops, training sessions, or other events.
  - **Service uptake.** Measure increases in utilization of PMO services following awareness campaigns.
  - **Feedback quality.** Analyze the nature of customer comments and questions to assess their understanding and perception of PMO value.

5. Continuous Improvement of Awareness Efforts

- **Awareness impact.** Share the measurement results with key customers, including PMO team members and organizational leadership. Use these results to demonstrate the value of awareness efforts and to secure ongoing support for PMO initiatives.
- **Continuous improvement.** Review the results of the measurements regularly to identify areas for improvement. Look for trends, patterns, or anomalies that might suggest opportunities to enhance the awareness approach.
- **Benchmarking.** Regularly benchmark awareness activities against industry practices and other successful PMOs. This external perspective can provide valuable insights and ideas for keeping the awareness approach fresh and effective.

Actionable Self-Assessment: Gauge the Effectiveness of PMO Awareness Building

The following self-assessment is designed to help PMO professionals evaluate how effectively they are building and maintaining awareness of the PMO's value within the organization. By focusing on mapping customer needs, establishing regular touchpoints, educating customers, and measuring the impact of awareness efforts, PMO professionals can drive greater engagement and support for their services. The assessment emphasizes continuous improvement to keep the PMO visible, relevant, and strategically aligned with organizational goals.

Instructions: Rate the PMO's performance in each area on a scale of 1–5, where:

1 = Not at all/ineffective

2 = Rarely/poor

3 = Sometimes/average

4 = Often/good

5 = Always/excellent

Section 1: Identifying Potential PMO Customers	
Question	**Rating**
a) We have a comprehensive map of all potential PMO customers across the organization.	
b) We have created detailed customer personas for our key PMO customer groups.	
c) We have segmented our potential PMO customers based on their project management maturity and specific needs.	
d) We understand the power dynamics within the organization and have identified key decision-makers and influencers.	
e) We understand the major needs and pain points of each major customer segment.	
Subtotal	

Section 2: Establishing Regular Touchpoints	
Question	**Rating**
a) We have a documented communication strategy tailored to different customer groups.	
b) We have identified the preferred communication channels of different customer groups through surveys or interviews.	
c) We maintain a consistent cadence of communication across various channels (e.g., newsletters, meetings, intranet).	
d) Our content strategy includes success stories, infographics, and regular updates on PMO achievements.	
e) We regularly track and analyze the effectiveness of our communication efforts.	
Subtotal	

Section 3: Educating Customers About PMO Value	
Question	**Rating**
a) We have a comprehensive library of educational materials about our PMO services and value proposition.	
b) We offer regular training sessions or workshops about PMO services and project management good practices.	
c) We actively collect and share success stories and case studies demonstrating PMO impact.	
d) We have a "PMO ambassador" program or similar peer advocacy initiative.	
e) We promote a PMO portal or knowledge base where PMO customers can access PMO-related resources, templates, and accepted practices.	
Subtotal	

Section 4: Measuring Effectiveness	
Question	**Rating**
a) We have established clear metrics for measuring the effectiveness of our awareness-building efforts.	
b) We regularly conduct surveys to gauge PMO customer awareness and perception of the PMO.	
c) We track and analyze the uptake of PMO services following awareness campaigns.	
d) We share the results of our awareness-building efforts with key PMO customers and leadership.	
e) We benchmark our awareness activities against industry practices or other successful PMOs.	
Subtotal	

Section 5: Continuous Improvement of Awareness Efforts	
Question	**Rating**
a) We analyze PMO customer feedback to understand how our awareness-building efforts are perceived.	
b) We regularly review and adjust our communication strategy based on feedback and performance metrics.	
c) We benchmark our awareness activities against industry practices and other successful PMOs.	
d) We share measurement results with key PMO customers to demonstrate the impact of awareness efforts.	
e) We implement changes to our awareness approach based on insights gained from monitoring and feedback.	
Subtotal	
Grand total	

Scoring and Interpretation: Total your scores from all 25 questions.

Excellent: 113–125 points. Your PMO excels in building awareness and maintaining visibility across the organization. Continue refining and enhancing your approach to stay ahead.

Good: 98–112 points. Your PMO demonstrates strong awareness-building efforts but may benefit from targeted improvements in certain areas.

Average: 77–97 points. Your PMO's awareness-building efforts are functional but require greater consistency and strategic focus to maximize their impact.

Poor: 51–76 points. Your PMO's awareness-building efforts are inconsistent and lack effectiveness. There are significant gaps in communication and visibility that should be addressed to improve the PMO's standing within the organization.

Critical: 25–50 points. Your PMO's awareness-building efforts are minimal or ineffective, resulting in low visibility and engagement within the organization. Immediate action is needed to build a foundation for PMO success.

Looking Ahead to the Next Section

Having explored the importance of awareness building, PMO professionals can now recognize how vital it is to establish a solid foundation of understanding and support for the PMO. With this foundation in place, the next crucial step is to gain a deep understanding of PMO customer needs and expectations.

The upcoming section focuses on the needs assessment process, which involves systematically identifying and evaluating the specific requirements, challenges, and desired outcomes of various stakeholders across the organization. By mastering this process, PMO professionals can ensure their services are truly aligned with organizational goals, laying the groundwork for impactful value propositions and service development. The section provides guidance for conducting insightful and thorough needs assessments that propel PMO success.

15

Step 2: Needs Assessment

Why This Section Matters to PMO Professionals

Needs assessment is a critical step for PMO professionals as it lays the foundation for understanding the unique requirements and challenges of the organization and PMO customers.

This step enables PMO professionals to identify the needs and expectations of PMO customers and define the outcomes that should be delivered. This approach allows the PMO to tailor its services to address the most pressing needs. By conducting a thorough needs assessment, PMO professionals can ensure that their efforts align with actual customer needs and organizational goals, resulting in a more effective and impactful PMO.

Needs assessment provides PMO professionals with a data-driven foundation for decision-making, enabling them to make informed choices about where to focus their efforts and allocate resources most effectively to enhance the customer's perception of the PMO's value.

This step is crucial for demonstrating the PMO's value to the organization, as it directly links PMO services to the specific needs of its customers. Ultimately, a well-executed needs assessment sets the stage for a successful PMO that generates tangible value and drives organizational success.

Needs Assessment Step at a Glance

Needs assessment is the second step in the value-generating PMO flywheel. As a pivotal step, it serves as a bridge between the initial awareness-building step and the subsequent value proposition step.

Its purpose is to thoroughly identify, understand, and document the explicit and implicit needs, challenges, and goals of PMO customers (see Figure 15-1). By conducting a comprehensive needs assessment, the PMO can pinpoint areas where it can add the most value, prioritize its activities, and develop targeted solutions that meet the unique requirements of the organization.

This process is crucial for maximizing the PMO's potential impact and demonstrating tangible value to the organization. A comprehensive needs assessment helps PMO professionals to design a proper value proposal for the PMO, ensuring that the most critical priorities are addressed first.

Needs assessment also fosters a collaborative environment by actively engaging customers, building trust through active listening and responsiveness, and promoting buy-in from customers, which is essential for the successful implementation of PMO initiatives.

Figure 15-1. Needs Assessment Step in the PMO Flywheel

Implementing the Needs Assessment Step

1. Outcome-Based Needs Assessment

- **Landscape mapping.** Start by mapping the organization's project landscape, identifying key customers at all levels who might be involved with or impacted by the PMO's work. This analysis provides a baseline understanding of the organization's project management maturity and identifies areas for potential improvement. Key aspects to consider in this analysis include:
  - **Existing methodologies and frameworks.** Identify which approaches (e.g., predictive, adaptive, or hybrid) are currently in use and how effectively they are being applied.
  - **Tools and technologies.** Evaluate the project management software, collaboration platforms, and other technologies being used to support delivery.

    - **Success rates.** Analyze historical data on portfolio, program, and project outcomes.
    - **Resource allocation and utilization.** Examine how human and financial resources are currently distributed across projects and assess the efficiency of this allocation.
    - **Decision-making processes.** Understand how decisions are made regarding portfolio, program, and project management.
    - **Reporting and communication practices.** Evaluate the effectiveness of current methods for sharing project status, risks, and issues.
    - **Stakeholder engagement and satisfaction levels.** Assess how well different stakeholder groups are involved in—and satisfied with—portfolio, program, and project outcomes.
    - **Alignment with organizational strategy:** Determine how well current portfolios, programs, and projects align with broader organizational goals.
- **Customer matrix.** Develop a comprehensive customer matrix, categorizing customers based on their role, influence, and potential impact on portfolio, program, or project outcomes. Employ empathy-mapping exercises to gain a deeper understanding of customers' thoughts, feelings, and motivations related to the PMO. This mapping can reveal underlying needs and expectations that customers might not explicitly state.
- **Engagement approach.** Use outcome-oriented language in all interactions. Instead of asking about desired PMO functions, focus on the results customers want to achieve. For example, rather than asking if they need a risk management process, inquire about how they can feel more confident in making decisions related to portfolios, programs, or projects.

  Note: To understand how to create a comprehensive assessment to identify the needs and expectations of PMO customers, read the section of this guide on PMO outcomes, where 30 benefits are mapped from the experiences of PMOs in the global community.

2. Data Collection and Outcome Analysis

PMO professionals can gather insights into customer needs and expectations by implementing the following methods:

- **Customer interviews.** Conduct one-on-one interviews with key customers to gather insights into their specific needs, expectations, and concerns regarding the PMO. These interviews can uncover detailed information that might not surface in group settings.
- **Surveys and questionnaires.** Distribute detailed surveys and questionnaires to a broader customer audience within the organization. This information helps to establish quantitative data on customer satisfaction, needs, and areas for improvement.
- **Focus groups.** Organize focus groups with representatives from different customer segments to discuss their experiences and expectations with the PMO. This collaborative setting can provide diverse perspectives and foster open dialogue.
- **Lessons learned reviews.** Analyze project post-mortems or lessons learned documents through the lens of the identified pain points and desired outcomes. This process can provide rich, contextual data on recurring issues and successes.

- **Feedback loops.** Establish regular feedback loops, such as periodic check-ins or feedback forms, to continuously gather and act on customer insights. This ongoing communication helps in adapting to changing needs and improving PMO services over time.

  Note: Appendix X2 of this guide provides a valuable resource for PMO professionals: the PMO Customer Expectation Assessment. This tool is based on the 30 most common potential PMO outcomes discussed earlier and offers a structured approach to understanding and addressing PMO customer needs. The assessment enables PMOs to conduct thorough needs analyses; focus services on high-impact areas; and adopt a proactive, value-driven, customer-centric strategy. The PMO Customer Expectation Assessment serves as both a diagnostic tool and a roadmap for generating value, guiding PMO professionals toward building a more responsive and impactful PMO.

3. Gap Analysis and Opportunity Identification

- **Pain and gain mapping.** Develop a "pain and gain" map for each customer group, clearly outlining their current challenges and desired positive outcomes. This map will serve as a foundation for designing the PMO value proposition and the services that will directly address customer needs.
- **Customer journey mapping.** Create customer journey maps to visualize the entire experience of different customer groups with the PMO. This process helps identify touchpoints, pain points, and opportunities to enhance the value the PMO provides to its customers.
- **Value expectation matrix.** Create a "value expectation matrix" that maps customer groups to their expected outcomes. This visual tool can help identify common themes across groups and areas where expectations might conflict.
- **Future state visioning.** Conduct "future state" visioning exercises, asking customers to describe their ideal project management environment. Focus on the outcomes they would like to realize in this ideal state, not on specific PMO services, functions, or processes.
- **Validation.** Validate the findings with PMO customers to ensure accuracy and alignment with their expectations and priorities.

4. Prioritizing and Addressing Identified Needs

- **Structured prioritization process.** Develop a systematic approach for identifying and prioritizing the most critical PMO customer needs. Evaluate the impact, urgency, and feasibility of addressing each need to focus on areas that will deliver the greatest value.
- **Alignment with organizational goals.** Ensure that prioritized needs align with the organization's strategic objectives and goals. This alignment can help guarantee that PMO initiatives contribute directly to broader organizational success.

- **Communication of findings.** Effectively communicate the results of the needs assessment to all relevant PMO customers. Transparency in sharing the findings builds trust and facilitates collaboration in addressing identified needs.
- **Action planning.** Develop clear action plans to address the top-priority PMO customer needs. Outline specific initiatives, responsible parties, timelines, and expected outcomes.
- **Progress tracking and adjustment.** Implement mechanisms to track progress in addressing identified needs. Regularly review and adjust PMO strategies as necessary to respond to changing circumstances or new insights.

5. Demonstrating the Value of Needs Assessment

- **Link findings to outcomes.** Clearly demonstrate how the needs-assessment findings contribute directly to organizational success. Connect PMO customer needs, PMO actions, and tangible results.
- **Justify PMO resource allocation.** Use data from the needs assessment to justify resource allocation and the prioritization of PMO activities. Evidence-based decision-making strengthens the case for necessary investments and support.
- **Showcase tangible benefits.** Highlight the tangible benefits and value delivered to PMO customers as a result of addressing their identified needs. Use success stories and metrics to illustrate the PMO's impact.
- **Involve PMO customers.** Involve key decision-makers and PMO customers throughout the needs-assessment process. Their engagement ensures buy-in, support for PMO initiatives, and alignment with organizational priorities.
- **Measure long-term impact.** Measure the long-term impact of the needs assessment on PMO performance. Use these insights to adjust approaches and continuously improve the PMO's effectiveness.

Actionable Self-Assessment: Gauge the Effectiveness of the PMO Needs Assessment

The following self-assessment is designed to help PMO professionals evaluate how effectively they conduct needs assessments and prioritize customer challenges. A strong needs-assessment process is the foundation for aligning PMO services with organizational goals, driving project success, and delivering tangible value to PMO customers. The assessment emphasizes the importance of data collection, outcomes-based analysis, and continuous feedback in shaping the PMO's efforts to meet customer needs and expectations. By focusing on these areas, PMO professionals can improve their impact and position themselves as strategic partners within the organization.

Instructions: Rate your PMO's performance in each area on a scale of 1–5, where:

1 = Not at all/never

2 = Rarely/poor

3 = Sometimes/average

4 = Often/good

5 = Always/excellent

Section 1: Outcome-Based Needs Assessment	
Question	**Rating**
a) We have a comprehensive map of our organization's project management landscape.	
b) We have identified and categorized all potential PMO customers across the organization.	
c) We understand the current portfolio, program, and project management practices and frameworks used in our organization.	
d) We have a clear picture of the tools and technologies used for portfolio, program, and project management across the organization.	
e) We regularly analyze historical data on portfolio, program, and project outcomes.	
Subtotal	

Section 2: Data Collection and Outcome Analysis	
Question	**Rating**
a) We conduct regular interviews with key PMO customers to gather insights into their needs and expectations.	
b) We use surveys and questionnaires to collect quantitative data on PMO customer needs and satisfaction.	
c) We organize focus groups with diverse PMO customer segments to discuss their expectations about the PMO.	
d) We analyze project post-mortems and lessons learned documents to identify recurring issues and successes.	
e) We have established ongoing feedback loops to continuously gather input from PMO customers on changing needs.	
Subtotal	

Section 3: Gap Analysis and Opportunity Identification	
Question	**Rating**
a) We use outcome-oriented language in our interactions with PMO customers.	
b) We have conducted empathy-mapping exercises to understand our PMO customers' thoughts and motivations.	
c) We have created a "pain and gain" map for each major PMO customer group.	
d) We create PMO customer journey maps to visualize the full experience of different customer groups with the PMO.	
e) We utilize a "value expectation matrix" that maps PMO customer groups to their expected outcomes to identify common themes and conflicts.	
Subtotal	

Section 4: Prioritizing and Addressing Identified Needs	
Question	**Rating**
a) We have a structured process for identifying PMO customer needs and prioritizing the most critical needs.	
b) We ensure that the identified PMO customer needs are aligned with organizational goals and strategic priorities before developing PMO services.	
c) We communicate the findings of our needs assessment effectively to all PMO customers within the organization.	
d) We have a clear plan in place for addressing the top-priority PMO customer needs identified in the assessment process.	
e) We track and regularly review progress in addressing identified PMO customer needs and continually adjust our PMO strategy, as necessary.	
Subtotal	

Section 5: Demonstrating the Value of Needs Assessment	
Question	**Rating**
a) We consistently demonstrate how the findings of a PMO customer's needs assessment link directly to improved project outcomes and organizational success.	
b) We use data from PMO customers' needs assessments to justify resource allocation and prioritization of PMO activities.	
c) We showcase the tangible benefits and value delivered to PMO customers as a result of addressing their identified needs.	
d) We involve key decision-makers in the PMO customer's needs-assessment process to ensure their buy-in and support for PMO initiatives.	
e) We measure the long-term impact of the PMO customer's needs assessment on PMO performance and adjust our approach based on these insights.	
Subtotal	
Grand total	

Scoring and Interpretation: Total your scores from all 25 questions.

Excellent: 113–125 points. Your PMO has a robust and effective needs-assessment process for PMO customers. Focus on maintaining your high standards and continually refining your approach based on evolving organizational needs.

Good: 98–112 points. Your PMO is doing well with needs assessment for PMO customers, but there is room for improvement. Identify your lowest scoring areas and create action plans to address them.

Average: 77–97 points. Your PMO has a basic needs-assessment process in place for PMO customers, but significant improvements are needed. Prioritize your lowest scoring areas for immediate attention.

Poor: 51–76 points. Your needs-assessment efforts for PMO customers require substantial work. Consider revisiting your entire approach and developing a comprehensive plan to address all areas.

Critical: 25–50 points. Your PMO urgently needs to establish basic needs-assessment practices for PMO customers. Start with the fundamentals and gradually improve your way forward.

Looking Ahead to the Next Section

Needs assessment provides key insights on understanding and prioritizing PMO customers' needs. The next essential task is articulating how the PMO will meet these needs and deliver measurable value.

The upcoming section will explore the process of building a compelling PMO value proposition. This process involves creating a clear, persuasive statement that highlights the unique benefits the PMO offers to the organization.

This process enables PMO professionals to showcase their relevance and secure stakeholder support by crafting value propositions that truly resonate with customers and fuel PMO success.

16

Step 3: Value Proposition

Why This Section Matters to PMO Professionals

The value proposition step is crucial for PMO professionals as it serves as the cornerstone of their engagement strategy with PMO customers. A strong value proposition helps PMO professionals position the PMO as a strategic partner rather than just a support function. The value proposition demonstrates the tangible and intangible benefits of the PMO by aligning the specific needs of its customers with the outcomes set as its priority goals. By clearly communicating these benefits, the PMO can build credibility and trust with its customers, who are essential for driving engagement and collaboration.

In essence, the value proposition step is about translating the insights gained from the needs assessment into a compelling narrative that resonates with PMO customers. This step sets the stage for the successful implementation of PMO initiatives by ensuring that customers understand and appreciate the value the PMO can deliver.

Value Proposition Step at a Glance

The value proposition is the third critical step in the value-generating PMO flywheel. This step focuses on creating a clear and compelling narrative that outlines how the PMO will address the identified needs and pain points of its customers (see Figure 16-1).

The value proposition demonstrates how the PMO will deliver both tangible and intangible benefits, explains why customers within the organization should engage with the PMO's services, and highlights the unique value the PMO brings. A well-crafted value proposition makes it easier to gain customer buy-in and support, especially with senior-level executives.

Implementing the Value Proposition Step

1. Synthesizing Needs Assessment Outcomes

- **Comprehensive analysis.** Review all outputs, including reports, survey results, interview transcripts, and any other relevant information.
- **Needs categorization and prioritization.** Identify recurring themes and patterns across different PMO customer groups. Create a master list of all identified needs, pains, and desired outcomes. Categorize these findings into broader areas to help identify potential services.

Figure 16-1. Value Proposition Step in the PMO Flywheel

Prioritize the identified needs based on factors such as frequency of mention, perceived impact, and alignment with organizational strategy. Use techniques like weighted scoring or the MoSCoW (must have, should have, could have, won't have) method to create a prioritized list.

- **Pain point profiles.** Develop detailed "pain point profiles" for each major identified need. These profiles should include a clear description of the pain point, its impact on customers and the organization, and any relevant quantitative data or evidence. Create a visual representation of the synthesized findings, such as a mind map or infographic, to communicate outcomes and guide the next steps.

2. Mapping Pains to Potential Solutions

- **Collaborative creation.** Conduct sessions with the PMO team to generate a wide range of potential solutions for each major pain point or need. Encourage out-of-the-box thinking without limiting ideas based on current capabilities or resources. Use the "how might we" method to frame each pain point as an opportunity.

- **Solution design.** Utilize proper techniques to map out customer duties, pains, and gains related to portfolio, program, or project management. This approach helps to clearly articulate how the PMO can alleviate pains and create gains.
- **Feasibility analysis.** Evaluate the feasibility of each potential solution by considering alignment with PMO capabilities, resource requirements, potential impacts, and ease of implementation. Use a scoring system to rate each solution on these factors. Identify patterns or commonalities among proposed solutions and group similar ideas together.

3. Defining the PMO Value Proposition

- **Solution map.** Create a visual "solution map" linking pain points to potential solutions. This mapping will help identify high-value services that can address multiple pain points.
- **Articulating PMO benefits.** For each high-priority solution, develop a service concept with a clear name, concise description, and the specific pain points or needs it addresses. Clearly articulate the value proposition for each proposed service using this format: "For [target customer], who [statement of need or opportunity], our [service name] provides [key problem-solving capability]." Identify quick wins to help build momentum and gain customer buy-in. To create an effective solution to PMO customer needs and expectations, refer to the section of this guide on PMO outcomes. This section provides invaluable insights into the most effective PMO services to generate PMO customers' expected benefits. These recommendations are grounded in real-world experience drawn from the collective wisdom of PMO leaders in the global community. Remember, the goal is not to implement every possible service but to select and adapt those that will best deliver the outcomes PMO customers value most.
- **Service outline.** Develop high-level descriptions of how each service will be delivered, considering scalability, flexibility, and potential evolution as the organization's project management maturity grows. Identify dependencies or synergies between services. To create an effective PMO service outline, refer to the section of this guide dedicated to PMO services. This comprehensive section presents a curated list of the 26 most common PMO services observed in the global community. Each service is carefully categorized and its applicable domains are specified, providing PMO professionals with a clear understanding of how these services can be most effectively deployed.
- **Service blueprint.** Create a visual, high-level representation of the core PMO services, showing how they relate to one another and to customer needs.
- **Customer validation.** Organize validation workshops or sessions with key customers to present service concepts and gather feedback.
- **Customer value agreement.** Create a "customer value agreement" for each major customer or customer group, outlining the outcomes the PMO commits to helping them achieve. Obtain formal approval to ensure alignment and buy-in.
- **Evolution roadmap.** Develop a "value proposition evolution roadmap" that outlines how the PMO's offerings will evolve over time, using a rolling wave planning approach. This roadmap is

part of the PMO strategic plan and defines how the PMO's value proposition will progressively evolve over time. It ensures that the PMO's services, capabilities, and impact remain aligned with changing organizational needs, PMO customer expectations, and business objectives. By adopting this approach, the PMO can deliver incremental benefits and value while continuously reassessing the roadmap.

- **Risk management strategy.** Develop a PMO risk management plan to specifically address the risk of failing to deliver promised value. This plan should include a detailed process for identifying, assessing, and mitigating risks that could compromise the PMO's commitments. By effectively managing this risk, the PMO can improve its reliability, strengthen customer relationships, and ensure the successful achievement of its strategic objectives.

4. Establishing and Evolving the Value Proposition

- **Review schedule.** Establish a regular cadence for reviewing the PMO's value proposition such as quarterly for minor adjustments or annually for comprehensive reviews. Align these review cycles with key organizational planning periods, if possible.
- **Review board.** Establish a diverse "value proposition review board" with representatives from various customer groups to discuss the PMO's performance and suggest refinements.
- **Feedback management.** Implement a systematic process for gathering and analyzing customer feedback through surveys, focus groups, or one-on-one interviews.
- **Lessons learned.** Document and share lessons learned from each review cycle within the PMO team to foster a culture of continuous improvement and build institutional knowledge about effective PMO value propositions.
- **Change management.** Establish clear criteria for retiring or significantly modifying existing services to ensure the PMO's service portfolio remains streamlined and focused on delivering maximum value.

5. Measuring and Refining the PMO Value Proposition

- **Systematic feedback gathering.** Collect and analyze PMO customer feedback on the effectiveness of the PMO value proposition through surveys or interviews.
- **Documentation of lessons learned.** Document lessons learned from each review cycle and share them internally to improve the PMO's approach to value delivery.
- **Prioritize improvements.** Use PMO customer feedback to prioritize enhancements to PMO services, ensuring continuous delivery of maximum value.
- **Criteria for service evolution.** Establish clear criteria for retiring, evolving, or modifying PMO services that no longer align with customer needs or goals.
- **Impact measurement and adjustment.** Regularly measure the impact of the PMO value proposition against customer expectations and adjust services accordingly.

Actionable Self-Assessment: Gauge the Effectiveness of the PMO Value Proposition

The following self-assessment helps PMO professionals to evaluate the effectiveness of their value proposition by breaking it down into essential components, from synthesizing customer needs to refining service delivery based on feedback. By identifying gaps and areas for improvement, PMOs can better position themselves as strategic partners within their organizations, ensuring their services are aligned with both customer expectations and broader business goals.

Instructions: Rate your PMO's performance in each area on a scale of 1–5, where:

1 = Not at all/never

2 = Rarely/poor

3 = Sometimes/average

4 = Often/good

5 = Always/excellent

Section 1: Synthesizing Needs Assessment Outcomes	
Question	**Rating**
a) We comprehensively analyze reports, survey results, and PMO customer feedback to develop a clear understanding of PMO customer needs.	
b) We categorize the identified PMO customer needs, pains, and desired outcomes into broader themes to structure our PMO value proposition.	
c) We prioritize PMO customer needs using objective methods aligned with organizational strategy.	
d) We develop detailed "pain point profiles" for each major identified need, including data on the impact and the PMO customer's pain.	
e) We create visual representations (e.g., mind maps) to synthesize and communicate the needs assessment outcomes.	
Subtotal	

Section 2: Mapping Pains to Potential Solutions	
Question	**Rating**
a) We conduct collaborative sessions with the PMO team to brainstorm solutions for each major pain point.	
b) We utilize tools like the "value proposition canvas" to systematically link PMO customers' pains to potential PMO solutions.	
c) We perform feasibility analysis on proposed solutions, considering PMO capabilities, resource needs, and potential impact.	
d) We systematically rate and group potential solutions based on patterns and commonalities to identify high-value services.	
e) We design PMO services that clearly articulate how they will alleviate pains and deliver gains for PMO customers.	
Subtotal	

Section 3: Defining the PMO Value Proposition	
Question	**Rating**
a) We create a clear, concise PMO service concept for each solution, linking it to specific PMO customer pain points.	
b) We develop a "solution map" that visually links pain points to PMO services, showing alignment with organizational goals.	
c) We identify and deliver quick wins to build momentum and demonstrate immediate value to PMO customers.	
d) We outline each service's delivery method, considering scalability, flexibility, and evolution as organizational maturity grows.	
e) We present PMO service concepts to key PMO customers and gather feedback in validation workshops or sessions.	
Subtotal	

Section 4: Establishing and Evolving the Value Proposition	
Question	**Rating**
a) We create a "PMO customer value agreement" for each major PMO customer group, outlining expected outcomes and securing buy-in.	
b) We maintain a "PMO value proposition evolution roadmap" to continuously adapt and enhance PMO services based on PMO customer needs.	
c) We have a documented risk management strategy to mitigate the risk of failing to deliver on our value proposition.	
d) We conduct regular reviews of our PMO value proposition, refining it quarterly and reassessing it annually to maintain relevance.	
e) We have established a diverse "PMO value proposition review board" that provides insights and suggests improvements to the PMO's value proposition.	
Subtotal	

Section 5: Measuring and Refining the PMO Value Proposition	
Question	**Rating**
a) We systematically gather and analyze PMO customer feedback on the effectiveness of the PMO value proposition through surveys or interviews.	
b) We document lessons learned from each review cycle and share them internally to improve our approach to the PMO's value delivery.	
c) We use PMO customer feedback to prioritize improvements to PMO services, ensuring the PMO continuously delivers maximum value.	
d) We establish clear criteria for retiring, evolving, or modifying PMO services that no longer align with PMO customer needs or goals.	
e) We regularly measure the impact of our PMO value proposition against PMO customers' expectations and adjust services accordingly.	
Subtotal	
Grand total	

Scoring and Interpretation: Total your scores from all 25 questions.

Excellent: 113–125 points. Your PMO has developed and successfully implemented a highly effective value proposition. Focus on maintaining high standards and continually refining your approach as the PMO customers' needs evolve.

Good: 98–112 points. Your PMO is doing well in developing its PMO value proposition but there is room for improvement. Identify your lowest scoring areas and create targeted action plans to address them.

Average: 77–97 points. Your PMO has a value proposition in place but more attention is needed to better communicate and refine the value you offer. Focus on building a more comprehensive value narrative and gathering more PMO customer feedback.

Poor: 51–76 points. Your PMO's value proposition is underdeveloped or not well communicated. Consider revisiting your entire approach to ensure it is customer centric, and leverage feedback to build stronger value alignment.

Critical: 25–50 points. Your PMO urgently needs to develop a clear value proposition. Start by thoroughly reviewing PMO customer needs and designing services that directly address pain points and align with strategic goals.

Looking Ahead to the Next Section

This section covered the importance of crafting compelling value propositions, helping a PMO professional to articulate the PMO's unique value to the organization. The next logical step is turning these propositions into actionable services.

The upcoming section explores the service development process, with a focus on designing, refining, and evolving PMO services to align with customer needs and deliver promised value. PMO professionals can learn strategies for building service catalogs, defining service levels, and ensuring alignment with organizational goals. Mastering this process equips PMO professionals with a powerful suite of value-driven services to help meet customer needs and contribute to organizational success.

17

Step 4: Service Development

Why This Section Matters to PMO Professionals

This section is pivotal for PMO professionals as it provides details on how to transform strategic insights and customer needs into actionable services that deliver tangible value.

The service development flywheel step takes the PMO value proposition and breaks it down into effective services that the PMO will provide, bridging the gap between understanding what customers need and effectively providing those solutions. In essence, the service development step is where the PMO's value proposition becomes reality. This step involves a structured process for designing services that deliver the expected outcomes and benefits.

Service Development Step at a Glance

Service development in the PMO context refers to the systematic process of developing the services that the PMO will provide to its customers. This critical step in the value-generating PMO flywheel transforms the insights gained from the needs assessment and promises made in the PMO value proposition into tangible, deliverable services (see Figure 17-1).

Through well-crafted service development, PMOs can meet the expectations set forth in their value propositions, ensuring they remain relevant and impactful within their organizations. This iterative process can ensure that the PMO is able to respond dynamically to evolving challenges and opportunities.

Implementing the Service Development Step

1. PMO Service Delivery Approach Design

- **Service delivery approach spectrum.** Review each service concept and consider a spectrum of delivery approaches, ranging from full service (where the PMO takes complete responsibility) to purely self-service (where customers operate independently using PMO-provided tools). For each service, carefully evaluate factors such as customer capability and maturity, the complexity of the service, resource availability within the PMO, and the overall organizational culture and preferences. This evaluation will help determine where on the

Figure 17-1. Service Development Step in the PMO Flywheel

spectrum each service should fall. It is crucial to recognize that the appropriate delivery approach may vary, not just between services but also between different customers or projects for the same service.

- **Service delivery matrix.** Develop a comprehensive service delivery matrix that outlines the approach for each service. This matrix should include a detailed description of the service, the chosen delivery approach, clearly defined roles and responsibilities for both the PMO and its customers, and key touchpoints and interaction models. The matrix can serve as a guide for both the PMO team and customers, ensuring clarity in how each service will be delivered and accessed.

- **Service delivery approach validation.** Validate the proposed service delivery approaches with PMO customers. Seek feedback on whether the proposed approaches align with organizational needs and expectations. Be prepared to refine the approaches based on this feedback.

- **Service delivery approach evolution.** Consider how the service delivery approaches might evolve over time. As PMO customers become more mature in portfolio, program, and project management practices, or as the PMO's capabilities expand, there may be opportunities to shift toward different types of approaches. Build this evolutionary thinking into the service delivery design, creating a roadmap for how service delivery might change over time.

2. Tailored PMO Service Process Design

- **Service process mapping.** Map out the end-to-end process for each service. This should include all steps, decision points, and handoffs. Use process-modeling techniques like flowcharts or swim lane diagrams to visualize these processes. Consider developing process variants for common scenarios to accommodate different project types, sizes, or complexity levels. For example, there may be a standard project initiation process but there may also be a need to develop variants for fast-tracked projects; complex, multiphase projects; or projects in specific domains. These variations can serve as starting points for further customization.
- **PMO service risk management.** Develop a comprehensive risk management plan for all PMO services. This plan should identify and assess potential risks to service delivery and quality, establish mitigation strategies, and create monitoring processes. The plan should integrate risk management into service operations, develop contingency plans for high-impact risks, and ensure continuous improvement. This proactive approach enhances service reliability and customer trust.
- **Process tailoring guide.** Develop a tailoring guide for each process. This guide should outline which elements of the process can be customized and under what circumstances. Include criteria for when to use different process variants and guidelines for adapting the process to specific customer needs. The aim is to provide clear direction on how to modify the process without compromising its integrity or the quality of service delivery.
- **Process documentation.** Create comprehensive process documentation for each service. This documentation should include detailed process flow diagrams, step-by-step instructions for executing each part of the process, RACI (responsible, accountable, consulted, informed) matrices to clarify roles and responsibilities, and clear specifications for the inputs and outputs of each process step. This documentation will serve as a reference for both PMO team members and PMO customers, ensuring consistent understanding and execution of each service.
- **Process change management.** Establish a governance process for managing and updating the PMO service catalog. This process should include procedures for reviewing and approving changes to processes, version control mechanisms, and a schedule for regular reviews to ensure all processes remain current and relevant. Consider appointing process owners within the PMO who are responsible for maintaining and improving specific processes.
- **Communication strategy.** Define how processes will be communicated to PMO customers. Consider developing user-friendly versions of process documentation, perhaps in the form of interactive guides or video tutorials. The goal is to make it as easy as possible for customers to understand and engage with PMO services.

3. PMO Service Catalog Development

A well-structured service catalog is essential for communicating the PMO's offerings clearly to PMO customers. Key elements in developing a service catalog include:

- **Service name and description.** The official name of the service and a brief overview of what the service entails.
- **Value proposition.** The unique value the service offers, the problems it solves, and the benefits customers can expect.
- **Target audience.** Specific customers, customer groups, or departments the service is intended to reach.
- **Service owner.** The person or team responsible for the service.
- **Service delivery model.** Details on how the service will be delivered.
- **Service features.** Specific features or components of the service.
- **Technology integration.** Appropriate technology is integrated into the service to enhance its efficiency and effectiveness.
- **Service-level agreements (SLAs).** Commitments on the level of service that customers can expect.
- **Request and access procedures.** How customers can request or access the service.
- **Delivery timeframes.** Expected timeframes for delivering the service.
- **Resource requirements.** Resources needed to deliver the service, including human resources, tools, and materials.
- **Performance metrics.** How the success of the service will be measured.
- **Feedback mechanism.** How customers can provide feedback on the service.
- **Training and documentation.** Available training materials and documentation to help customers use the service.

4. PMO-Service-Specific Performance Indicators and Goals

- **Types of metrics.** Define a set of metrics for each service. These metrics should include efficiency metrics (measuring how well the service is delivered), output metrics (quantifying the direct results of the service), and outcome metrics (assessing the impact of the service on customer and organizational goals).
- **PMO service metrics definition.** Create a detailed metrics definition for each indicator. This should include the metric name, a clear description of what it measures, the calculation method, data sources, measurement frequency, and who is responsible for data collection and reporting. Be sure to consider data availability and the effort required to collect and

analyze each metric. The goal is to create a robust set of indicators without creating an undue reporting burden.

- **Collaborative design.** Establish a process for setting customer-specific goals for each metric. This process should start with a baseline assessment of current performance. Next, conduct collaborative goal-setting sessions with each customer or customer group. These sessions should consider the customer's specific needs, priorities, and constraints. Remember that different customers may have different goals for the same service based on their unique contexts.
- **PMO performance dashboard.** Develop a flexible performance dashboard template that can be customized for each customer. This dashboard should clearly display the customer's specific metrics and goals, as well as actual performance over time. Consider using visual elements like charts or gauges to make the information easily understandable. The dashboard should differentiate between the metrics that will be used for internal service monitoring (measured in the service monitoring step) and those that measure service outcomes (assessed in the value delivery and value recognition steps). The measurement framework should capture both short-term service performance and long-term value creation.
- **Review process.** Implement a regular review process for these metrics and goals. This process might involve quarterly check-ins with customers to discuss performance, identify any issues, and adjust goals if necessary. Use these reviews as an opportunity to gather qualitative feedback as well, which can provide context to the quantitative metrics.
- **Continuous improvement.** Establish processes for analyzing trends, identifying areas for improvement, and implementing changes to enhance service delivery. This process might involve regular service review meetings within the PMO team, where performance data is discussed and improvement initiatives are planned, since the ultimate goal of these metrics is not just measurement but improvement.

5. PMO Resource Allocation and Competency Mapping

- **Competencies analysis.** Conduct a detailed analysis of each service, identifying the key competencies required for effective delivery. This analysis should go beyond just technical project management skills to include soft skills like communication and problem-solving. Create a comprehensive competency framework that outlines all of the skills needed across the PMO service portfolio.
- **Current capabilities.** Assess the PMO team's current capabilities. This assessment might involve skills assessments, performance reviews, and discussions with team members about their strengths and areas for development. Create a skills matrix that maps each team member's capabilities against the competency framework.
- **Role descriptions.** Develop detailed role descriptions for each service, outlining responsibilities, required skills, and performance expectations. These descriptions should be flexible enough to accommodate the fact that PMO team members may be involved in delivering multiple services.

- **Resource needs.** Based on the service designs and expected demand, determine the volume of resources needed for each service. Consider factors like service complexity, delivery approach, and anticipated customer demand. This assessment will help identify gaps between the current PMO team's capabilities and the resource needs.
- **Resource allocation.** Create a resource allocation plan that assigns PMO team members to services based on their skills and the service needs. Consider implementing a matrix management approach where team members may have a primary service focus but can flexibly support other services as needed. This approach can help balance workloads and provide development opportunities for team members. Implement a capacity management process to ensure that resources are efficiently utilized across services. This process might involve using resource planning tools to track PMO team member allocations and availability. Regularly review and adjust allocations based on changing service demands and priorities.
- **Managing competency gaps.** Identify any skill gaps in the current PMO team and develop a plan to address them. This plan might involve training and development programs for existing team members or recruiting new team members with specific skills. Consider both immediate needs and future requirements based on the service-evolution roadmap. Develop a cross-training program to build redundancy in key skills. This planning can help ensure service continuity in case of absences or PMO team turnover and also provides professional development opportunities for team members.

6. Service-Level Agreements (SLAs) and PMO Customer Validation

- **Creating SLAs.** Draft initial SLAs for each PMO service. These SLAs should be based on the service designs, processes, and performance indicators developed in earlier activities. For each service, clearly articulate the scope of the service including what is and is not covered; expected response times and delivery timeframes; quality standards and acceptance criteria; roles and responsibilities of both the PMO and the customer; escalation procedures for issues or disputes; performance metrics; and reporting frequency.
- **Service levels.** Define service levels for each PMO service. This definition should include specific, measurable performance metrics and quality standards. Collaborate with customers to ensure these definitions align with organizational needs and expectations. Consider factors such as response times, delivery timeframes, accuracy rates, and customer satisfaction levels.
- **Setting service goals.** Set realistic and achievable goals for each SLA metric. These goals should balance customer expectations with the PMO's capabilities and resources. Avoid the temptation to overpromise; it is better to set conservative targets that can be consistently met or exceeded than to set ambitious goals that lead to frequent shortfalls.
- **Tailoring SLAs.** When drafting these SLAs, consider different levels of service that might be appropriate for different customers or project types. For instance, there may be a standard SLA for most projects but an option of enhanced SLAs for high-priority or complex initiatives.

- **Validating SLAs.** Schedule validation sessions with PMO customers or customer groups. In these sessions, present the draft SLAs and walk through each aspect in detail. Encourage open discussion and be prepared to negotiate on specific points. The goal is to reach an agreement that is both achievable for the PMO and satisfactory for the PMO customers.

- **Building trust.** During these validation sessions, pay particular attention to the performance goals included in the SLAs. These goals should align with the service-specific metrics developed earlier, but the goals may need to be adjusted based on PMO customer expectations and priorities. Remember that different customers may have different priorities and, therefore, different performance goals for the same service. The SLAs are not just about setting goals and measuring performance. They are a tool for building trust and fostering a partnership between the PMO and its customers. Use the SLA development and validation process as an opportunity to strengthen relationships and demonstrate the PMO's commitment to delivering value.

- **Monitoring and reporting SLAs.** Consider how the SLAs will be monitored and reported. Develop templates for regular SLA performance reports and establish a process for reviewing these reports with customers. This process might involve monthly or quarterly review meetings where service performance is discussed and any issues are addressed.

- **Communicating SLAs.** Develop a communications management plan to ensure that all PMO customers are aware of the SLAs and understand their implications. This plan might involve creating summary documents or presentations highlighting key SLA points, conducting briefing sessions for project teams, or incorporating SLA information into the PMO onboarding processes.

7. PMO Service Implementation Planning

- **Implementation roadmap.** Create a comprehensive implementation roadmap for each service or group of related services. This roadmap should outline key milestones and activities from development through onboarding and into full operation. Consider dependencies among services and their impacts on the implementation sequence.

- **Implementation plan.** For each service, develop a detailed implementation plan including a timeline with specific dates for key activities and milestones, resource assignments for implementation and onboarding tasks, budget requirements for implementation and onboarding activities, risk assessments and mitigation strategies, and success criteria for implementation and onboarding.

- **Service onboarding transition plan.** Develop a transition plan from service onboarding to service operation, ensuring seamless handover and operational readiness. This plan should outline criteria for determining when a service moves from onboarding to full operation, handover procedures from the implementation team to the operations team, establishment of regular service review processes, and mechanisms for ongoing support and continuous improvement.

- **Change management strategy.** Create a comprehensive change management strategy that addresses the people side of change, helping customers understand and adapt to new services. Develop tailored communication materials, including service announcements, user guides, FAQs, and training resources.
- **Phased approach strategy.** Implement a phased approach where appropriate, starting with pilot groups or subsets of services before full implementation. This approach allows for learning and adjustment, effectively managing organizational impact.
- **Implementation governance.** Establish governance structures for overseeing implementation, onboarding, and the transition to operations. Regular check-ins with customers can ensure the process stays on track and issues are addressed promptly.

Actionable Self-Assessment: Gauge the Effectiveness of PMO Service Development

The following self-assessment provides a structured approach to evaluating the effectiveness of the PMO's service development process. By assessing key areas, PMO professionals can identify gaps, enhance service design and delivery, and ensure that PMO offerings are aligned with both customer expectations and broader organizational goals.

Instructions: Rate your PMO's performance in each area on a scale of 1–5, where:

1 = Not at all/never

2 = Rarely/poor

3 = Sometimes/average

4 = Often/good

5 = Always/excellent

Section 1: PMO Service Delivery Approach Design	
Question	**Rating**
a) We carefully evaluate different delivery approaches for each PMO service based on PMO customer needs, maturity, and organizational culture.	
b) We have developed a comprehensive PMO service delivery matrix outlining roles, responsibilities, and delivery models for each PMO service.	
c) We validate our PMO service delivery approaches with PMO customers and adjust them based on their feedback.	
d) We actively consider how PMO service delivery approaches can evolve as PMO customer capabilities and organizational maturity grow.	
e) We regularly review and update our PMO service delivery approaches to ensure they stay relevant and effective.	
Subtotal	

Section 2: Tailored PMO Service Process Design	
Question	**Rating**
a) We map out end-to-end processes for each PMO service, including decision points and handoffs.	
b) We develop PMO process variants to accommodate different project types, sizes, or complexity levels.	
c) We have implemented a comprehensive risk management plan for PMO services to mitigate risks to service delivery.	
d) We provide a clear guide for tailoring PMO processes based on specific PMO customer needs and circumstances.	
e) We maintain comprehensive documentation for each PMO service, including process flows, RACI matrices, and detailed instructions.	
Subtotal	

Section 3: PMO Service Catalog Development	
Question	**Rating**
a) We have developed a comprehensive PMO service catalog that clearly defines all available PMO services, including descriptions and key features.	
b) The PMO service catalog is segmented based on PMO customer needs, offering tailored services for different departments, project types, or levels of project management maturity.	
c) The PMO service catalog includes a clear and accessible guide for PMO customers on how to request and access each service.	
d) We regularly update the PMO service catalog to reflect new offerings, service improvements, and organizational changes, ensuring it remains relevant and valuable to PMO customers.	
e) We actively promote the PMO service catalog across the organization, ensuring that all PMO customers are aware of the available PMO services and how they can leverage them to meet their needs.	
Subtotal	

Section 4: PMO-Service-Specific Performance Indicators and Goals	
Question	**Rating**
a) We have defined clear efficiency, output, and outcome metrics for each PMO service.	
b) We have created detailed metric definitions including how each metric is calculated, who is responsible, and how frequently data is collected.	
c) We conduct collaborative goal-setting sessions with PMO customers to establish performance metrics for each PMO service.	
d) We use customized performance dashboards to visually represent PMO service metrics and goals for each PMO customer.	
e) We regularly review PMO service metrics with customers and adjust goals or services based on feedback and performance trends.	
Subtotal	

Section 5: PMO Resource Allocation and Competency Mapping	
Question	**Rating**
a) We have conducted a comprehensive analysis of the skills required for each PMO service, including technical and soft skills.	
b) We have assessed the current capabilities of the PMO team and mapped them against a PMO competency framework.	
c) We have developed clear role descriptions that outline responsibilities, required skills, and performance expectations for PMO each service.	
d) We regularly review resource needs and adjust PMO team allocations based on PMO service demand and PMO team capacity.	
e) We have implemented a training and development plan to address skill gaps and ensure continuous professional growth within the PMO team.	
Subtotal	

Section 6: Service-Level Agreements (SLAs) and PMO Customer Validation	
Question	**Rating**
a) We draft detailed SLAs for each PMO service, outlining service scope, delivery timeframes, quality standards, and performance metrics.	
b) We set realistic and achievable PMO service targets, balancing PMO customer expectations with the PMO's capacity and resources.	
c) We tailor SLAs based on the specific needs of different PMO customer groups.	
d) We validate our SLAs through PMO customer feedback and adjust them accordingly to ensure alignment with PMO customers' needs.	
e) We regularly monitor and report SLA performance to PMO customers and discuss adjustments during review meetings.	
Subtotal	

Section 7: PMO Service Implementation Planning	
Question	**Rating**
a) We develop detailed implementation roadmaps for each PMO service, outlining key milestones, dependencies, and timelines.	
b) We create comprehensive implementation plans that include PMO team resource assignments, PMO budget requirements, and PMO risk assessments.	
c) We have established a transition plan from PMO service onboarding to service operation, ensuring seamless handovers and operational readiness.	
d) We implement a phased rollout strategy for complex or high-impact PMO services, starting with pilot groups before full-scale implementation.	
e) We have established clear PMO governance structures to oversee PMO service implementation, PMO service onboarding, and PMO ongoing operations.	
Subtotal	
Grand total	

Scoring and Interpretation: Total your scores from all 35 questions.

Excellent: 154–160 points. Your PMO has developed a highly effective service-development process, with a clear focus on designing and delivering valuable, customer-centric services. Continue refining and evolving your services as customer needs and organizational priorities shift.

Good: 131–153 points. Your PMO is doing well in service development but there is room for further refinement. Focus on areas with lower scores to improve service design and implementation.

Average: 102–130 points. Your PMO has a basic service-development process in place but significant improvements are needed. Prioritize enhancing your process documentation, customer validation, and SLA monitoring.

Poor: 68–101 points. Your PMO's service-development process requires substantial improvement. Revisit key areas such as resource allocation, performance metrics, and customer engagement to strengthen your approach.

Critical: 35–67 points. Your PMO urgently needs to establish a structured service-development process. Begin by designing clear processes, validating the processes with customers, and building strong SLAs to drive service quality and alignment with organizational needs.

Looking Ahead to the Next Section

Creating a comprehensive suite of PMO services is just the beginning. Even the most well-crafted offerings will not deliver value unless they are properly implemented.

The next section details service onboarding, a vital phase where new or enhanced PMO services are introduced to users within the organization. The section explores strategies for managing change, offering training, and ensuring a smooth transition.

Mastering this step is essential for PMO professionals to embed their services into an organization's operations, setting the stage for effective service delivery and value creation.

18

Step 5: Service Onboarding

Why This Section Matters to PMO Professionals

Mastering service onboarding is essential for PMO professionals for several reasons. Firstly, it ensures a smooth adoption of new services. Effective onboarding helps users understand the benefits and functionalities of the new services, reducing resistance and increasing acceptance. This process maximizes the value and impact of PMO services, ensuring that they are utilized effectively and efficiently within the organization.

Secondly, service onboarding plays a crucial role in building credibility and trust in the PMO. By providing comprehensive training, clear communication, and robust support during the onboarding process, the PMO can demonstrate its commitment to helping stakeholders succeed. This commitment helps foster positive relationships and enhances the PMO's reputation as a reliable and valuable partner within the organization.

A well-executed onboarding process sets the stage for long-term service success. By addressing potential issues early, gathering feedback, and making necessary adjustments, the PMO can ensure that services continue to meet user needs and deliver expected outcomes. This proactive approach minimizes disruptions and ensures that the new services integrate smoothly into existing workflows and processes.

Service Onboarding Step at a Glance

Service onboarding in the PMO context is a structured process that introduces newly developed or improved PMO services to their intended users within the organization. This critical phase bridges the gap between service development and full-scale implementation, ensuring PMO customers are prepared, educated, and supported in adopting new PMO services (see Figure 18-1).

Effective service onboarding is vital for ensuring the smooth adoption of new services, maximizing the value and impact of PMO services, building credibility and trust in the PMO, minimizing resistance to change, and setting the stage for long-term service success.

A well-executed onboarding process significantly influences the perception and utilization of PMO services, directly impacting their effectiveness and the PMO's overall value to the organization. By carefully guiding its customers through the initial stages of service engagement, the PMO can foster a positive user experience, encourage consistent usage, and ultimately drive the realization of intended benefits from its services.

Figure 18-1. Service Onboarding Step in the PMO Flywheel

Implementing the Service Onboarding Step

1. PMO Customer Preparation and Engagement

- **Engagement strategy.** Identify all relevant customers who will be impacted by—or involved in—the new services. Develop a comprehensive customer map that outlines each group's current level of awareness, potential concerns, and expected benefits from the new services. Create a tailored engagement strategy for each customer group. This strategy should outline how the PMO will communicate with customers, what key messages need to be conveyed, and the plans to address specific needs and concerns.

- **Building awareness.** Develop a series of awareness-building activities to generate interest and excitement about the new services. These activities might include teaser campaigns, showcases of service benefits, or early adopter testimonials. The goal is to create a positive buzz around the services before they are fully launched. Organize kickoff events or town hall meetings to formally introduce the new services. These events should provide an overview of the services, explain how they align with organizational goals, and outline the onboarding process. Use these events as an opportunity to address any initial questions or concerns from customers.

- **Customer feedback.** Establish feedback mechanisms to capture customer input throughout the onboarding process. This effort could include surveys, feedback sessions, or a dedicated email address for questions and comments. Regularly review and act on this feedback to refine the onboarding approach and address emerging concerns.
- **Identify champions.** Identify and engage "service champions" within different PMO customer groups. These individuals can help promote the new services, provide peer support during the onboarding process, and serve as a bridge between the PMO and its respective teams or departments.

2. PMO Service Training Program Development

- **Needs analysis.** Start by conducting a training-needs analysis for each customer group. This analysis should consider their current knowledge levels, the specific skills required to use the new services, and any gaps that need to be addressed.
- **Training curriculum.** Develop a multitiered training curriculum that caters to different user roles and proficiency levels. This curriculum might include basic orientation sessions for all customers, in-depth technical training for power customers, and specialized modules for managers or executives who need to understand the strategic implications of the services.
- **Training materials.** Create a variety of training materials to support different learning styles and preferences. The materials could include user manuals, quick reference guides, video tutorials, interactive eLearning modules, and hands-on workshops. Ensure that all materials are clear, concise, and focused on the practical application of the services.
- **Learning approach.** Design a blended learning approach that combines self-paced learning with instructor-led sessions. This approach allows for flexibility while also providing opportunities for direct interaction and Q&A. Consider incorporating real-world scenarios and case studies into the training to make it more relevant and engaging.
- **Recognize competencies.** Develop a certification or competency assessment process to ensure that customers have acquired the necessary skills. This assessment might involve practical tests, quizzes, or a demonstration of service use in real project scenarios. Certificates or badges can be used to recognize and motivate user proficiency.
- **Train the trainers.** Establish a train-the-trainer program to build internal capacity for ongoing training and support. Identify potential trainers within different departments or teams and provide them with additional training and resources to coach their colleagues effectively.
- **Ongoing education.** Create a plan for ongoing education and skill development. This plan should include refresher courses, advanced training modules, and regular updates on new features or industry practices. By fostering a culture of continuous learning, customers can continue to maximize the value of the PMO services over time.

3. **Pilot Implementation and Feedback Loops**
   - **Pilot groups.** Identify suitable pilot groups or projects that represent a cross-section of the PMO's target customers. These groups should be diverse enough to provide comprehensive feedback but manageable enough to allow for close monitoring and support.
   - **Pilot implementation plan.** Develop a detailed pilot implementation plan that outlines the scope, duration, and objectives of the pilot. This plan should include specific metrics for measuring the success of the pilot, such as user adoption rates, service performance indicators, and customer satisfaction scores. Ensure that mechanisms are in place to collect both quantitative data and qualitative feedback throughout the pilot period.
   - **Pilot support.** Provide enhanced support for the pilot participants. This support might include dedicated help desk resources, regular check-in meetings, and on-site support during critical service-usage phases. The goal is to closely monitor the user experience and quickly address any issues or challenges that arise.
   - **Pilot feedback loop.** Establish a structured feedback loop to capture insights from the pilot implementation. This effort should include regular surveys, focus group sessions, and one-on-one interviews with customers. Encourage customers to provide honest, detailed feedback on all aspects of the service, from usability to perceived value.
   - **Pilot feedback analysis.** Analyze the feedback and data collected during the pilot to identify areas for improvement or refinement. Look for patterns in customer behavior, common pain points, or unexpected ways that customers are leveraging the services. Use these insights to make necessary adjustments to the services, training materials, or support processes before full-scale implementation.
   - **Pilot feedback review.** Conduct a comprehensive review at the end of the pilot period. This review should involve all key customers, including pilot participants, PMO team members, and relevant decision-makers. Present the findings from the pilot, discuss lessons learned, and collaboratively decide on any final adjustments needed before proceeding with full implementation.
   - **Leverage success.** Leverage the experiences and successes from the pilot to build momentum for the wider rollout. Encourage pilot participants to become advocates for the new services, sharing their experiences and good practices with their colleagues. This peer-to-peer promotion can be a powerful tool in driving adoption and enthusiasm for the services across the organization.

4. **Service Support Infrastructure Establishment**
   - **Support levels.** Define the different levels of support that will be required, from basic customer assistance to more complex problem-solving and service optimization. Develop a clear support model that outlines how users can access help, how issues will be escalated, and what response times they can expect.

- **Knowledge base.** Create a comprehensive knowledge base that includes FAQs, troubleshooting guides, good practices, and detailed documentation for each service. This resource should be easily accessible to all customers and regularly updated based on common issues and user feedback. Consider implementing a search function to help customers quickly find the information they need.
- **Help desk.** Establish a help desk or support team for the new services. This team should be well trained in both the technical aspects of the services and customer service skills. Develop clear processes for logging, tracking, and resolving support requests. Consider implementing a ticketing system to manage and prioritize support cases effectively.
- **Support channels.** Set up multiple channels for customers to access support, such as email, phone, online chat, and self-service portals. Artificial intelligence (AI) chatbots can also be implemented for this purpose. Different customers may prefer different methods of seeking help, so offering a variety of options can improve the overall support experience. Ensure that these channels are well integrated to provide a consistent support experience regardless of how users reach out.
- **Customer communities.** Consider establishing a user community or forum where service customers can share experiences, tips, and solutions. This peer-to-peer support can be a valuable complement to formal support channels and can help foster a sense of community around the PMO services.

5. Performance Monitoring and Evaluation Framework

- **Success criteria review.** Revisit the KPIs and success criteria defined during the service development phase. Refine these metrics to ensure they accurately reflect the onboarding process's goals and align with organizational objectives.
- **Performance dashboard.** Develop a comprehensive performance dashboard that provides real-time visibility into service adoption, usage patterns, and impact. This dashboard should include metrics such as user-engagement rates, service-utilization levels, time savings, error reduction, and customer satisfaction scores. Ensure that the dashboard is accessible to customers and provides both high-level overviews and the ability to drill down into specific details.
- **Data collection and analysis.** Implement tools and processes for data collection and analysis. This data collection and analysis might involve integrating analytics capabilities into the services themselves, setting up user surveys, or implementing usage-tracking systems. Ensure that data-collection methods are compliant with privacy regulations and organizational policies.
- **Performance reviews.** Establish regular performance review meetings with customers. These meetings should focus on analyzing the performance data, identifying trends, and making data-driven decisions about necessary adjustments to the onboarding process or the services themselves. Develop a standard agenda and reporting format for these meetings to ensure consistency and efficiency.

6. **Transitioning to Full-Service Operation**

- **Successful onboarding criteria.** Define what constitutes a successful transition. These criteria might include achieving certain adoption rates, reaching specific performance benchmarks, or completing a set of critical milestones.
- **Transition plan.** Develop a detailed transition plan that outlines the steps required to move from onboarding to full operation. This plan should include timelines, resource allocation, risk mitigation strategies, and a clear delineation of responsibilities between the onboarding team and the ongoing operations team. Consider a phased transition approach, gradually shifting responsibilities and focus areas.
- **Handover strategy.** Create a comprehensive handover document that captures all key information about the services, including design specifications, user feedback, known issues, and lessons learned during the onboarding process. This document will be crucial for ensuring continuity as the services move into regular operation.
- **Knowledge transfer.** Organize knowledge-transfer sessions between the onboarding team and the operations team. These sessions should cover not just the technical aspects of the services but also insights into user behavior, common challenges, and effective support strategies. Consider implementing a shadowing period where operations team members work alongside the onboarding team before taking full responsibility.
- **Continuous monitoring and support.** Establish ongoing monitoring and support processes that will continue beyond the onboarding phase. This process includes defining long-term performance metrics, setting up regular service reviews, and creating mechanisms for continuous improvement and user feedback.
- **Communication strategy.** Develop a communications management plan to inform all customers about the transition to full-service operation. This plan should include what customers can expect in terms of support, any changes to service access or processes, and how they can provide ongoing feedback or request enhancements.
- **Onboarding success celebration.** Plan a formal launch or celebration to mark the successful completion of the onboarding phase and the transition to full operation. This event can serve to recognize the efforts of all involved, reinforce the value of the services, and generate enthusiasm for their continued use and evolution within the organization.

Actionable Self-Assessment: Gauge the Effectiveness of PMO Service Onboarding

The following self-assessment allows PMO professionals to gauge the effectiveness of their service-onboarding processes and identify areas for improvement. By focusing on key elements such as customer engagement, training, support, and performance monitoring, PMOs can ensure a smooth transition from service development to full-scale adoption, maximizing the impact of new services on organizational success.

Instructions: Rate your PMO's performance in each area on a scale of 1–5, where:

1 = Not at all/never

2 = Rarely/poor

3 = Sometimes/average

4 = Often/good

5 = Always/excellent

Section 1: PMO Customer Preparation and Engagement	
Question	**Rating**
a) We have identified all relevant PMO customers impacted by or involved in the new PMO services.	
b) We have developed tailored engagement strategies for each PMO customer group based on their needs and concerns.	
c) We regularly communicate with PMO customers to build awareness and generate excitement about new PMO services.	
d) We collect and act on PMO customer feedback during the PMO-service-onboarding process.	
e) We have identified PMO service champions within PMO customer groups to promote the new PMO services and support peers.	
Subtotal	

Section 2: PMO Service Training Program Development	
Question	**Rating**
a) We conduct a thorough training needs analysis for each PMO customer group before service onboarding.	
b) We have developed a multitiered training curriculum tailored to different user roles and proficiency levels.	
c) We provide a variety of training materials, including guides, video tutorials, and interactive modules.	
d) We use a blended learning approach, combining self-paced materials with instructor-led sessions.	
e) We offer certification or competency assessments to ensure PMO customers have mastered the necessary skills.	
Subtotal	

Section 3: Pilot Implementation and Feedback Loops	
Question	**Rating**
a) We have selected diverse pilot groups to represent different PMO customer segments.	
b) We have a detailed pilot-implementation plan with defined objectives and success metrics.	
c) We provide enhanced support for pilot participants to monitor the PMO customer experience closely.	
d) We collect both quantitative data and qualitative feedback from pilot participants.	
e) We analyze pilot feedback and data to identify patterns, pain points, and areas for improvement.	
Subtotal	

Section 4: Service Support Infrastructure Establishment	
Question	**Rating**
a) We have established clear levels of support, from basic PMO customer assistance to advanced problem-solving.	
b) We have developed a comprehensive knowledge base, including FAQs and troubleshooting guides.	
c) We offer multiple support channels (email, phone, online chat) for customers to seek help.	
d) We have established a help desk or support team trained in both technical and PMO customer service skills.	
e) We have created a PMO customer community or forum for peer-to-peer support and knowledge sharing.	
Subtotal	

Section 5: Performance Monitoring and Evaluation Framework	
Question	**Rating**
a) We have clearly defined KPIs and success criteria for measuring the PMO-service-onboarding process.	
b) We use a performance dashboard to provide real-time visibility into PMO service adoption.	
c) We have tools in place to collect and analyze data on PMO customer engagement and PMO service utilization.	
d) We hold regular performance review meetings with PMO customers to assess the onboarding progress.	
e) We adjust the PMO-service-onboarding process or PMO services based on data-driven insights and feedback.	
Subtotal	

Section 6: Transitioning to Full-Service Operation	
Question	**Rating**
a) We have clear criteria for defining the successful transition from service onboarding to full operation.	
b) We have a detailed transition plan that outlines steps, timelines, and PMO team resource allocation.	
c) We conduct knowledge-transfer sessions between the service-onboarding team and the PMO operations team.	
d) We have established ongoing monitoring and support processes for post-onboarding operations.	
e) We communicate clearly with PMO customers about the transition to full-service operation and any changes they can expect.	
Subtotal	
Grand total	

Scoring and Interpretation: Total your scores from all 30 questions.

Excellent: 134–150 points. Your PMO has mastered service onboarding, ensuring smooth adoption, engagement, and continued success of new services. Maintain this high standard while refining and evolving your approach based on ongoing feedback.

Good: 114–133 points. Your PMO is performing well in onboarding but there are opportunities for improvement. Focus on areas with lower scores to further enhance training, support, and customer engagement.

Average: 89–113 points. Your PMO's onboarding process is functional but requires significant improvement. Prioritize training development, pilot feedback, and service-support enhancements to increase effectiveness.

Poor: 59–88 points. Your PMO's onboarding process needs considerable work. Revisit key areas such as customer engagement, support infrastructure, and transition planning to ensure a more successful onboarding experience.

Critical: 30–58 points. Your PMO urgently needs to establish a structured service onboarding process. Begin by focusing on comprehensive training, customer feedback mechanisms, and support systems to drive successful service adoption.

Looking Ahead to the Next Section

This section explored service onboarding and how to successfully introduce new or improved PMO services to the organization. The next section details the day-to-day management of these PMO services.

Service operation is where the real work of delivering PMO services begins. This step of the value-generating PMO flywheel is where plans take shape and the PMO creates value for the organization. The next section discusses strategies for managing service delivery, handling PMO customer requests, allocating resources, and ensuring service quality. By mastering this phase, PMO professionals can ensure that their services consistently meet PMO customer needs and deliver measurable value.

19

Step 6: Service Operation

Why This Section Matters to PMO Professionals

Mastering service operation is critical for PMO professionals because it is where the PMO's promises and value propositions are realized. The ability to consistently deliver high-quality services is essential for establishing and maintaining trustworthiness within the organization. Effectively managing service operations allows the PMO to demonstrate its value and become an integral part of the business strategy, directly impacting project success and organizational performance.

PMO professionals can significantly enhance project management capabilities across the organization by ensuring that PMO services are available, reliable, and meet quality standards. Consistent service delivery fosters customer satisfaction and confidence in the PMO's ability to support and drive organizational goals.

The service operation step in the PMO context represents the culmination of strategy formulation, service design, and implementation efforts. This step involves the day-to-day execution and management of PMO services, delivering tangible value to the organization and its customers (see Figure 19-1).

This critical step marks the point where the PMO transitions from preparation to action, putting its carefully crafted services into practice. It is in this step that the PMO builds its reputation, demonstrating its worth through consistent, reliable, and high-quality service delivery. By successfully managing service operations, the PMO can ensure that its offerings are readily available, dependable, and aligned with quality standards that directly impact project success and organizational performance.

Service operation serves as a real-world testing ground for PMO services. Through direct interaction with customers, the PMO gains invaluable insights that drive continuous improvement. As the PMO consistently delivers value through its services, it cements its position as an integral part of the organization's strategic framework.

Implementing the Service Operation Step

1. Daily PMO Service Delivery Management

- **PMO services delivery.** Ensure that each PMO service is delivered according to its defined processes, meeting the quality standards and service-level agreements established during the service development and onboarding steps.

Figure 19-1. Service Operation Step in the PMO Flywheel

- **PMO service daily management.** Start each day by reviewing the service schedule and prioritizing tasks. Daily service-delivery management requires a proactive approach but is crucial to maintain a balance between scheduled services and ad hoc requests that may arise throughout the day.
- **Communication channels.** Establish clear channels for service requests and maintain open lines of communication with all customers. This communication might involve managing a service desk, responding to email inquiries, or conducting regular check-ins with key customers.
- **Delivery monitoring.** Actively monitor service delivery, identifying any issues or bottlenecks that may impact quality or timeliness. Quick problem-solving and decision-making skills are essential. When issues arise, address them promptly and transparently, keeping customers informed of any potential impacts on service delivery.

- **Delivery performance review.** Review service-delivery performance, update service logs, prepare daily reports, or brief team members on completed tasks and upcoming priorities. Reflect on any lessons learned or potential improvements that could enhance service delivery in the future.

2. Executing PMO Service-Level Agreements (SLAs)

- **SLA regular reviews.** Review the active SLAs and their associated performance targets. A regular check helps to prioritize tasks and allocate resources effectively to meet SLA commitments. Use a dashboard or report that provides an at-a-glance view of current SLA performance across all services.
- **Service request prioritization.** Develop and maintain a system for prioritizing service requests based on SLA commitments. This system can ensure that services with more stringent SLA requirements, or those approaching breach thresholds, receive appropriate attention. Train PMO staff on this prioritization system and ensure it is consistently applied in day-to-day operations.
- **Escalation process.** Create a clear escalation process for addressing potential SLA breaches. This process should outline the steps to be taken when a service is at risk of not meeting its SLA targets, including who needs to be notified and what actions should be taken at each escalation level. Ensure all PMO staff are familiar with this process and can initiate it when necessary.
- **SLA records.** Maintain detailed records of all SLA-related activities and decisions. This recordkeeping includes logging any instances where SLAs are at risk, the actions taken to address these situations, and the outcomes of these actions.
- **SLA-oriented culture.** Foster a culture of SLA awareness within the PMO team. Regularly reinforce the importance of meeting SLA commitments and recognize PMO team members who consistently achieve or exceed SLA targets. Consider implementing visual management techniques, such as SLA performance boards, to keep SLA commitments at the forefront of daily operations.
- **Exceptions management.** Be prepared to handle exceptions or special circumstances that may impact SLA performance. This planning might involve situations where meeting an SLA for one service could jeopardize performance on another or where organizational priorities shift unexpectedly. Develop guidelines for making informed decisions in these scenarios, always keeping the overall value delivery to the organization in mind.

3. Handling Service Requests and Inquiries

- **Request-tracking system.** Implement a robust system for tracking and managing requests from submission to resolution. This system should allow for the categorization of requests, assignment to appropriate PMO team members, and real-time status updates. Consider using a dedicated service management tool to integrate with other PMO systems for seamless data flow and reporting.

- **Request prioritization.** Develop a prioritization framework to ensure that high-impact or urgent requests receive timely attention. This framework should consider factors such as the request's alignment with organizational priorities, potential impacts on project success, and the requesting customer's role. However, be sure to maintain a balance to ensure that all requests receive appropriate attention.
- **Response time.** Establish clear SLAs for initial response times and resolution timeframes for different types of requests. Communicate these standards to customers and ensure the PMO team is equipped to meet them consistently. Regularly monitor and report on adherence to these SLAs.
- **Extraordinary requests.** Implement escalation procedures for complex or time-sensitive requests that cannot be resolved through standard processes. Clearly define the criteria for escalation and the path it should follow, ensuring that senior PMO staff or subject matter experts are involved when necessary.

4. PMO Resource Allocation and Workload Management

- **PMO resource pool.** Maintain a clear overview of the PMO resource pool. This effort includes understanding each team member's skills, availability, and current workload. Regularly update this information to account for changes in capacity due to leave, training, or other commitments.
- **Resource allocation.** Develop a robust resource allocation process. This process should take into account the priority and complexity of different services, as well as the specific skills required for each task. Aim to match tasks with the most appropriate PMO team members, considering both their expertise and their development needs. Look for opportunities to assign tasks that stretch PMO team members' abilities and contribute to their professional growth. This process not only enhances the PMO team's overall capabilities but also contributes to job satisfaction and retention.
- **Workload management.** Implement a workload management system that allows the PMO to track and balance tasks across the PMO team. This system might involve using project management software or a custom-built dashboard. The goal is to ensure that work is distributed equitably and that no team member is over- or underutilized. Be prepared to adjust resource allocations dynamically in response to changing demands or unexpected events. This adjustment might involve reallocating resources from lower-priority tasks to address urgent needs or bringing in additional resources during peak periods.
- **PMO team communication.** Regular communication with the team is crucial for effective resource and workload management. Hold daily or weekly team meetings to discuss workloads, identify any capacity issues, and collaboratively solve resource allocation challenges. Encourage PMO team members to speak up if they feel overwhelmed or if they have the capacity to take on additional tasks.
- **Resource utilization monitoring.** Monitor resource utilization and productivity regularly. Look for patterns or trends that might indicate the need for additional resources, training, or process improvements. Use this data to inform future resource planning and to justify resource requests to senior management if necessary.

5. **PMO Customer Engagement and Communication**

- **Communication strategy.** Develop and maintain a customer communications management plan. This plan should outline regular touchpoints with different customer groups, such as weekly updates to project managers, monthly reports to executives, or quarterly review sessions with department heads. Tailor the communication style and content to each group's needs and interests.
- **Communication channels.** Implement a variety of communication channels to effectively reach customers. These channels might include email newsletters, intranet updates, face-to-face meetings, or digital collaboration platforms. The key is to make information about PMO services easily accessible and to encourage two-way communication.
- **Customer feedback.** Regularly seek feedback from customers on their experiences with PMO services. This feedback could involve formal surveys, informal check-ins, or dedicated feedback sessions. Act on this feedback promptly, demonstrating the PMO's responsiveness and commitment to continuous improvement.
- **Trusted advisor role.** Establish the PMO team members as trusted advisors to key customers. This effort involves not just delivering services but also providing insights, recommendations, and strategic guidance. Look for opportunities to add value beyond the scope of defined services, such as sharing industry trends or good practices.
- **Expectation management.** Manage customer expectations effectively. Be clear about what the PMO can and cannot do and be transparent about any limitations or challenges in service delivery. If issues arise, communicate them promptly, along with a plan for resolution.
- **Collaboration culture.** Foster a culture of collaboration among the PMO and its customers. Encourage customers to view the PMO as a partner in achieving project and organizational goals. This collaborative approach can lead to more effective service delivery and greater overall impact.

6. **PMO Risk and Issue Management**

- **Risk management framework.** Develop a comprehensive risk management framework for PMO services. This framework should include risk identification, assessment, mitigation, and monitoring processes. Regularly conduct risk assessments for each service, considering factors such as resource availability, technological changes, and organizational priorities.
- **Issue management.** Establish a clear process for escalating and managing issues that arise during service delivery. This process should include defining what constitutes an issue, how issues should be reported, who is responsible for addressing them, and how their resolution will be communicated to customers.
- **Risk and issue log.** Implement a risk and issue log to track potential threats to service delivery and ongoing challenges. Regularly review and update this log, ensuring that mitigating actions are taken and that lessons are learned from resolved issues.
- **Contingency plan.** Develop contingency plans for high-impact risks. These plans should outline specific steps to be taken if a risk materializes, ensuring quick and effective responses to minimize service disruption. Regularly test and update these contingency plans to ensure they remain relevant and effective.

- **Transparent communication.** Communicate transparently about risks and issues with customers. While it is important to avoid creating unnecessary alarms, keeping customers informed about potential challenges and how they are being addressed can build trust and demonstrate the PMO's proactive approach to service management.
- **Analyze patterns.** Regularly analyze patterns in risks and issues to identify underlying causes or systemic problems. Use these insights to drive longer-term improvements in service design or delivery processes.
- **PMO team development.** Foster a proactive risk management culture within the PMO team. Encourage team members to identify and report potential risks or issues early. Provide training on risk management techniques and make risk discussions a regular part of team meetings.

7. Knowledge Management and Capacity Building

- **Knowledge management system.** Develop a comprehensive knowledge management system for the PMO. This system should include a centralized repository for documenting processes, good practices, lessons learned, and service-specific knowledge. Ensure that this system is easily accessible to all team members and is kept current.
- **Knowledge capture.** Implement processes for capturing knowledge from day-to-day service operations. These processes might involve regular debriefing sessions, project retrospectives, or a system for PMO team members to easily document insights or solutions as they arise. Encourage a culture where knowledge sharing is valued and rewarded.
- **Service documentation.** Create and maintain detailed documentation for each PMO service. This documentation should include process maps, job aids, troubleshooting guides, and FAQs. Regularly review and update this documentation to reflect any changes in service delivery or new insights gained.
- **PMO team member onboarding.** Develop a structured approach to onboarding new PMO team members and cross-training existing staff. This approach ensures that knowledge is effectively transferred and that the PMO has the flexibility to cover all services, even if key team members are unavailable.
- **PMO team member development.** Regularly assess the skills and knowledge within the PMO team. Identify any gaps in capabilities and develop targeted training or development plans to address these gaps. These plans might involve internal training sessions, external courses, or on-the-job learning opportunities. Implement mentoring within the PMO team, pairing less-experienced team members with seasoned professionals to facilitate knowledge transfer and accelerate skill development.
- **Learning culture.** Foster a learning culture within the PMO. Encourage team members to stay current with industry trends, pursue professional certifications, or attend relevant conferences. Allocate time and resources for continuous learning and development.
- **Technology support.** Leverage technology to support knowledge management and capacity building. This technology may include implementing collaboration tools, eLearning platforms, or AI-powered knowledge bases that make it easier to capture, share, and access critical information.

Actionable Self-Assessment: Gauge the Effectiveness of PMO Service Operation

The following self-assessment provides a comprehensive tool for PMO professionals to evaluate their effectiveness in service operation and identify areas for improvement. By focusing on key operational aspects such as SLA execution, resource management, and customer engagement, PMOs can ensure they not only meet—but exceed—organizational expectations for service delivery.

Instructions: Rate your PMO's performance in each area on a scale of 1–5, where:

1 = Not at all/never

2 = Rarely/poor

3 = Sometimes/average

4 = Often/good

5 = Always/excellent

Section 1: Daily PMO Service Delivery Management	
Question	**Rating**
a) We ensure each PMO service is delivered according to its defined processes and quality standards.	
b) We prioritize tasks effectively and maintain a balance between scheduled services and ad hoc requests.	
c) We have established clear communication channels for handling PMO service requests.	
d) We actively monitor PMO service delivery to identify and address issues promptly.	
e) We regularly review PMO service delivery performance to identify improvement opportunities.	
Subtotal	

Section 2: Executing PMO Service-Level Agreements (SLAs)	
Question	**Rating**
a) We regularly review SLAs and their performance targets to ensure compliance.	
b) We have a systematic approach for prioritizing PMO service requests based on SLA commitments.	
c) We have a clear escalation process for addressing potential SLA breaches.	
d) We maintain detailed records of SLA-related activities and decisions.	
e) We foster an SLA-oriented culture within the PMO team.	
Subtotal	

Section 3: Handling Service Requests and Inquiries	
Question	**Rating**
a) We have a robust system for tracking and managing PMO service requests from submission to resolution.	
b) We prioritize PMO customer requests to ensure timely attention based on organizational priorities and impact.	
c) We have clear SLAs for response times and resolution timeframes that we consistently meet.	
d) We have established procedures for escalating complex or urgent PMO customer requests.	
e) We regularly review and update our management processes for service requests to improve efficiency and PMO customer satisfaction.	
Subtotal	

Section 4: PMO Resource Allocation and Workload Management	
Question	**Rating**
a) We maintain an updated overview of the PMO resource pool and individual PMO team member capacities.	
b) We effectively match tasks with PMO team members based on their skills and workloads.	
c) We use tools or systems to balance and track workloads across the PMO team.	
d) We communicate regularly with the PMO team to manage resources and address capacity issues.	
e) We monitor resource utilization and productivity to ensure efficient use of PMO capabilities.	
Subtotal	

Section 5: PMO Customer Engagement and Communication	
Question	**Rating**
a) We have a well-defined PMO customer communications management plan that aligns with different groups' needs.	
b) We use diverse communication channels to effectively reach all PMO customers.	
c) We actively seek and promptly act on PMO customer feedback regarding PMO services.	
d) We manage PMO customer expectations transparently and effectively.	
e) We foster a collaborative culture between the PMO team and PMO customers.	
Subtotal	

Section 6: PMO Risk and Issue Management	
Question	**Rating**
a) We have a comprehensive risk management framework for PMO services.	
b) We have an established process for escalating and managing issues during service delivery.	
c) We maintain a detailed risk and issue log, regularly updating and mitigating actions.	
d) We have developed and regularly test contingency plans for high-impact risks.	
e) We communicate transparently with customers about risks and issues.	
Subtotal	

Section 7: Knowledge Management and Capacity Building	
Question	**Rating**
a) We have developed a centralized knowledge management system accessible to all PMO team members.	
b) We have implemented processes to capture and share knowledge from daily PMO operations.	
c) We maintain updated PMO service documentation and facilitate ongoing training and development.	
d) We leverage technology to enhance PMO knowledge management and capacity building.	
e) We regularly review and improve PMO knowledge management practices to ensure they remain aligned with evolving PMO team and organizational needs.	
Subtotal	
Grand total	

Scoring and Interpretation: Total your scores from all 35 questions.

Excellent: 154–175 points. Your PMO excels in service operation, consistently delivering high-quality services and maintaining strong customer relations. Continue to innovate and refine your processes.

Good: 131–153 points. Your PMO is effective in service operation but can improve in certain areas to enhance service delivery and customer satisfaction.

Average: 102–130 points. Your PMO has foundational service-operation processes in place but significant improvements are necessary to meet higher standards.

Poor: 68–101 points. There are critical gaps in your PMO's service-operation practices that need immediate attention to prevent service disruption.

Critical: 35–67 points. Urgent action is required to establish basic service-operation capabilities and stabilize your PMO's service delivery.

Looking Ahead to the Next Section

This section explored the details of the service operation step of the value-generating PMO flywheel, demonstrating how to manage the daily delivery of PMO services while ensuring these services continue to meet PMO customer needs and provide value. This step requires a structured method for tracking and evaluating the PMO's delivery performance.

The next section details the service monitoring step—the process of measuring and assessing the effectiveness of PMO services. The section explores strategies for defining KPIs, collecting and analyzing data, and using the results to drive ongoing improvements. By mastering this step, PMO professionals can help ensure their services stay aligned with customer expectations and organizational objectives.

20

Step 7: Service Monitoring

Why This Section Matters to PMO Professionals

The service monitoring step in the value-generating PMO flywheel is essential for PMO professionals as it emphasizes the efficacy and efficiency of service delivery. Mastering service monitoring is crucial because it provides concrete evidence of the PMO's ability to meet its commitments and deliver the services defined in the PMO value proposition.

For PMO professionals, effective service monitoring differentiates between service outputs and outcomes, offering a clear understanding of immediate results and broader impacts. This step is crucial for PMO professionals as it helps maintain high service standards, build customer trust, and drive PMO processes and maturity improvement, reinforcing the PMO's value within the organization.

Service Monitoring Step at a Glance

Service monitoring in the PMO context is a critical process that provides real-time insights into service delivery effectiveness and efficiency. This systematic approach to tracking, measuring, and evaluating PMO services against predetermined standards ensures that the PMO consistently meets or exceeds its commitments to PMO customers (see Figure 20-1).

At its core, service monitoring focuses on the tangible outputs of PMO services, providing concrete evidence of performance. By regularly tracking KPIs and compliance with SLAs, this process helps ensure consistency and quality in service delivery. Service monitoring serves as an early warning system, allowing for the identification of potential issues before they escalate into significant problems.

The data gathered through service monitoring enables informed, real-time decision-making about resource allocation and service refinement. This data-driven approach not only enhances operational efficiency but also demonstrates the PMO's commitment to accountability and continuous improvement. By consistently meeting or exceeding performance targets, the PMO builds credibility and trust with customers across the organization.

In essence, service monitoring acts as the pulse of PMO performance, providing vital signs that indicate the health and efficiency of PMO services. This step transforms abstract concepts of quality and efficiency into measurable metrics, offering a clear picture of the PMO's immediate impact and value. By maintaining this constant vigilance on service performance, the PMO positions itself as

Figure 20-1. Service Monitoring Step in the PMO Flywheel

a reliable, high-performing entity capable of adapting to changing organizational demands and consistently delivering value.

Tracking the effectiveness of services provided by a PMO is essential to help ensure these services are delivered efficiently and are meeting the intended standards, processes, SLAs, and PMO customer expectations.

The SLAs establish specific performance benchmarks that the PMO commits to achieving, making them a critical framework for both setting and measuring service expectations. However, it is important to distinguish between two types of performance indicators in this context: those focused on service delivery and those centered on outcomes. While outcome-based indicators evaluate the ultimate value or impact generated by a service—such as enhanced project success rates or ROI—indicators focused on service delivery measure the PMO's efficiency and proficiency in providing the service itself, often against SLA commitments.

Service delivery indicators primarily assess how well the PMO executes its services according to SLAs and internal standards. These indicators address questions such as:

- Is the service being provided consistently and on schedule?
- Are methodologies being followed?
- Are SLAs being met?

For example, in resource management, a service delivery indicator might measure the timeliness and accuracy of resource allocation, ensuring that skilled personnel are available where and when needed. While this metric does not directly measure project success or customer satisfaction, it does provide essential insights into the quality of the resource management process and SLA compliance.

Focusing on service delivery indicators tied to SLAs offers several benefits for a PMO. First, these indicators help identify inefficiencies or areas for improvement within the service itself. For instance, if the PMO's methodology management service frequently fails to meet SLAs related to timeliness or consistency, it may indicate a need for refining processes, offering additional training, or establishing clearer guidelines. This insight allows the PMO to take corrective action and streamline its processes, ensuring that all services are delivered at a consistently high standard. Additionally, these indicators support accountability, providing concrete metrics that measure whether each service meets agreed-upon SLAs, reinforcing the PMO's commitment to delivering reliable and efficient support.

Another significant benefit of service delivery indicators is that they establish a foundation for outcome-focused performance. Efficient, SLA-compliant service delivery often lays the groundwork for achieving desired outcomes. For instance, a PMO that meets SLA benchmarks in change control management (such as processing a set percentage of change requests within a specified timeframe) is better positioned to avoid project delays and budget overruns. This proficiency in service execution creates a stable environment where project outcomes are more likely to align with strategic goals.

In addition to service delivery indicators, PMOs also require indicators focused on outcomes, which provide insights into the value generated by the services over time. These outcome indicators are key to assessing the broader impact and alignment of services with strategic goals. These indicators address questions such as:

- Does the service improve project success rates?
- Are customers more satisfied with project outcomes?
- Has there been a measurable increase in ROI or resource utilization efficiency?

Outcomes are specifically assessed in Steps 9 and 10 of the PMO Value Ring™ framework, respectively known as value delivery and value recognition.

Together, SLA-focused service delivery indicators and outcome indicators offer a comprehensive view of PMO performance. Service delivery indicators ensure that the PMO operates efficiently within established SLAs, while outcome indicators validate the PMO's value to the organization. This balanced approach enables the PMO to refine its processes, consistently deliver on promises, and demonstrate quantifiable value, aligning more closely with the organization's strategic goals.

Table 20-1 provides examples of indicators tailored to specific PMO services. Each indicator highlights the importance of objective, results-oriented metrics in demonstrating the PMO's commitment to operational excellence and effective service delivery.

Organizing service delivery indicators into specific categories allows the PMO to manage day-to-day performance systematically, aligning each activity with defined SLA commitments. This structured approach creates a clear framework for monitoring and enhancing operational effectiveness, enabling the PMO to consistently deliver high-quality services, meet customer expectations, and promptly address any arising issues. The main types of service delivery indicators, organized by their focus and impact, include:

- **Efficiency indicators.** Efficiency indicators ensure that resources, such as time, budget, and personnel, are used effectively in delivering PMO services. By tracking metrics like time taken to complete tasks, budget adherence, and resource utilization, the PMO can identify bottlenecks and optimize processes to meet SLA requirements for resource use, ensuring services are delivered on schedule and within budget.

Table 20-1. Examples of PMO Service Delivery Performance Indicators

Service	Performance Indicator	Objective
Methodologies and frameworks management	Adherence rate to standardized methodologies	Measures the percentage of projects following the standardized methodologies and frameworks set by the PMO
Systems and tools management	Average response time for system support requests	Tracks the average time taken to respond to and resolve issues or support requests related to PMO systems and tools
Training and development	Participation rate in training programs	Tracks the percentage of targeted employees who attend scheduled training and development sessions
Project management	On-time delivery rate of project milestones	Measures the percentage of project milestones delivered on schedule
Stakeholder engagement	Frequency of stakeholder communication	Measures the number of formal communications or updates provided to stakeholders within a specified period

- **Quality indicators.** Quality indicators assess whether PMO services meet predefined standards for accuracy, consistency, and reliability. Compliance with quality standards, rates of errors or rework, and customer satisfaction with service quality are tracked to maintain high standards and build trust. These indicators help ensure that services consistently align with SLA quality commitments, reducing errors and supporting reliability.
- **Compliance indicators.** Compliance indicators measure the PMO's adherence to internal policies, regulatory requirements, and governance standards as specified in the SLA. Metrics like adherence to methodologies, audit compliance rates, and regulatory adherence protect the organization from risks and help ensure that all service delivery practices align with necessary standards, which is crucial for operational integrity.
- **Productivity indicators.** Productivity indicators evaluate how effectively PMO team members complete tasks associated with service delivery. By tracking task completion rates, output per hour, and the number of deliverables produced, the PMO can optimize workflows and ensure team members meet productivity targets specified in SLAs. This helps the PMO meet service delivery expectations within set timelines.
- **Satisfaction indicators.** Satisfaction indicators capture customer perceptions of PMO service delivery, providing insights into whether the services meet delivery expectations outlined in SLAs. Using tools like satisfaction surveys, service feedback, and ratings on service quality, the PMO can make adjustments to better align with satisfaction standards, ensuring customers are consistently pleased with the service.
- **Timeliness indicators.** Timeliness indicators measure the PMO's responsiveness and speed in delivering services, meeting the SLA commitments related to response times and deadlines. Metrics like response time, issue resolution time, and the percentage of projects completed on schedule can help the PMO to maintain consistent, prompt delivery as expected in the SLA.
- **Adaptability indicators.** Adaptability indicators evaluate the PMO's ability to respond to changing requirements while staying within the SLA. Tracking metrics like successful change implementation rates, time to reallocate resources, and flexibility in priority adjustments, the PMO can help ensure it meets changing needs without compromising service quality or timeliness.
- **Communication indicators.** Communication indicators monitor the clarity, transparency, and frequency of communication between the PMO and customers, as specified in the SLA. These indicators track metrics such as the frequency of updates, clarity of reports, and customer feedback on communication effectiveness, ensuring customers remain informed and aligned.
- **Risk management indicators.** Risk management indicators assess the PMO's ability to identify, evaluate, and mitigate risks in service delivery, maintaining service stability in line with SLAs. Tracking metrics like frequency of risk assessments, percentage of mitigated risks, and customer confidence in risk management practices can help prevent disruptions and ensure a stable and reliable service.

Implementing the Service Monitoring Step

1. Establishing a Comprehensive PMO Service Monitoring Framework

- **Service performance measurement process.** Develop a standardized data-collection and analysis methodology. This process might involve implementing automated tracking systems, creating custom reporting tools, or integrating existing project management software with monitoring capabilities. The goal is to establish a consistent and reliable method for gathering performance data across all PMO services.
- **Service performance dashboard.** Create a centralized dashboard or reporting system that provides real-time visibility into service performance. This dashboard should offer both high-level overviews and the ability to drill down into specific services or metrics. Consider using data-visualization techniques to make the information easily digestible and actionable.
- **Monitoring schedule.** Develop a schedule for regular monitoring activities. This schedule may include daily checks of critical metrics, weekly performance reviews, and monthly comprehensive analyses. The frequency of monitoring should be tailored to the nature of each service and the requirements should be specified in the SLAs.
- **PMO team roles and responsibilities.** Establish clear roles and responsibilities within the PMO team for monitoring activities. This process includes designating individuals responsible for data collection, analysis, and reporting for each service. Provide training to ensure that all team members understand the monitoring framework and their roles within it.

2. Managing SLA Compliance

- **SLA compliance system.** Implement a system for tracking SLA compliance. This system should provide visibility into how current performance compares to SLA goals. Consider using a traffic light system (red, amber, green) to quickly highlight services that are meeting, at risk of breaching, or already breaching their SLAs.
- **SLA performance review process.** Establish a process for regular SLA performance reviews. This process may involve weekly checks of all SLAs and more in-depth monthly reviews. During these reviews, assess not only whether SLAs are being met but also how close performance is to the agreed goals. Look for trends that could indicate future compliance issues.
- **SLA breaches.** Develop a clear escalation process for addressing SLA breaches or near misses. This process should outline the steps to be taken when a service is at risk of not meeting its SLA, including who needs to be notified and what actions should be taken. Ensure this process is well documented and understood by all PMO team members.
- **SLA noncompliance documentation.** Create a system for documenting all instances of SLA noncompliance, including the circumstances that led to the breaches, actions taken to address them, and measures implemented to prevent recurrences. This documentation is crucial for demonstrating accountability and informing future improvement efforts.
- **SLA reviews.** Periodically review the relevance and appropriateness of existing SLAs. As organizational needs and PMO capabilities evolve, some SLAs may need to be adjusted.

Use the insights gained from ongoing monitoring to inform these reviews and negotiate any necessary changes to SLA terms.

- **Service development.** Ensure that learnings from SLA reviews feed back into the service development step. Insights gained about realistic performance targets, changing customer needs, or emerging service priorities should inform the ongoing evolution of PMO services.

3. SLA Performance Reporting and Communication

- **Performance reporting.** Regularly communicate SLA performance to PMO customers. This communication may include monthly or quarterly SLA compliance reports that provide clear overviews of performance against all SLAs. Be transparent about any breaches or challenges faced and use these communications as opportunities to demonstrate the PMO's commitment to meeting its service commitments.
- **Reporting schedule.** Establish a regular reporting schedule that aligns with organizational rhythms and decision-making cycles. This reporting schedule might involve daily performance snapshots, weekly summary reports, monthly detailed analyses, and quarterly strategic reviews. Ensure that the frequency and depth of reporting is appropriate for each PMO customer group.
- **Reporting content.** Implement data visualization techniques to make monitoring results more accessible and impactful. Use charts, graphs, and infographics to highlight key trends, comparisons, and performance against targets. Consider using interactive dashboards that allow PMO customers to explore the data themselves. Develop a clear and consistent narrative around the monitoring results. This narrative should explain what the data means, why it matters, and what actions are being taken as a result. Use this narrative to reinforce the link between service performance and organizational value.
- **Reporting channels.** Establish multiple channels for communicating monitoring results. These channels may include email reports, presentations in management meetings, updates on internal collaboration platforms, or dedicated performance review sessions. Tailor the communication method to the preferences and needs of different PMO customer groups.

4. Gathering and Analyzing PMO Customer Feedback

- **Customer satisfaction measurement.** Develop a standardized set of questions or metrics for measuring PMO customer satisfaction across different services. This standardized measurement will help ensure consistency in feedback collection and allow for meaningful comparisons over time and between services.
- **Customer feedback collection.** Implement a system for collecting and analyzing PMO customer feedback. This system may involve using survey tools that provide instant notifications of low satisfaction scores or negative comments, allowing for quick follow-up and resolution of issues.
- **Customer feedback analysis.** Regularly analyze the feedback collected to identify trends, common issues, or areas of excellence. Look for correlations among PMO

customer satisfaction data and other performance metrics to gain a more comprehensive understanding of service quality. Use text analysis techniques to extract insights from qualitative feedback. This analysis can help identify recurring themes or issues that may not be captured by quantitative metrics alone. Consider using sentiment analysis tools to gauge the overall tone of customer feedback.

- **Customer feedback response.** Develop a process for acting on PMO customer feedback. This process should include steps for addressing individual complaints or issues, as well as mechanisms for incorporating broader feedback trends into service improvement initiatives. Close the feedback loop by communicating back to customers about how their input has been used to improve services. This feedback loop demonstrates that the PMO values customer feedback and is committed to continuously enhancing its services based on user needs and experiences.

Actionable Self-Assessment: Gauge the Effectiveness of PMO Service Monitoring

The following self-assessment enables PMO professionals to evaluate their effectiveness in monitoring service delivery, managing SLA compliance, and addressing PMO customer feedback. By focusing on key operational metrics, PMOs can ensure they consistently meet performance targets, foster trust with PMO customers, and continuously improve service quality.

Instructions: Rate your PMO's performance in each area on a scale of 1–5, where:

1 = Not at all/never

2 = Rarely/poor

3 = Sometimes/average

4 = Often/good

5 = Always/excellent

Section 1: Establishing a Comprehensive PMO Service Monitoring Framework	
Question	**Rating**
a) We have a standardized and reliable data-collection process for all PMO services.	
b) We use a centralized dashboard or reporting system to monitor real-time service performance.	
c) We maintain a regular schedule for activities related to monitoring PMO service performance (e.g., daily, weekly, monthly).	
d) We have clear roles and responsibilities for data collection, analysis, and reporting within the PMO team.	
e) We provide training to ensure all PMO team members understand the PMO service monitoring framework.	
Subtotal	

Section 2: Managing SLA Compliance	
Question	**Rating**
a) We have a system in place for tracking SLA compliance across all services.	
b) We regularly review SLA performance and address areas at risk of noncompliance.	
c) We have an escalation process for potential SLA breaches that is well documented and understood by all PMO team members.	
d) We document all instances of SLA noncompliance and use these records for future improvements.	
e) We periodically review and adjust SLAs to ensure they remain relevant to organizational needs.	
Subtotal	

Section 3: SLA Performance Reporting and Communication	
Question	**Rating**
a) We regularly communicate SLA performance to PMO customers with transparency.	
b) Our reporting schedule aligns with organizational rhythms and decision-making cycles.	
c) We use data-visualization techniques (e.g., charts, graphs) to make PMO service monitoring results more accessible.	
d) We develop clear narratives around PMO service monitoring results, explaining their relevance and actions taken.	
e) We use multiple channels (e.g., email, meetings, dashboards) to communicate PMO service performance results effectively.	
Subtotal	

Section 4: Gathering and Analyzing PMO Customer Feedback	
Question	**Rating**
a) We use standardized questions or metrics for measuring PMO customer satisfaction across services.	
b) We have a feedback-collection system in place to capture real-time PMO customer feedback.	
c) We regularly analyze PMO customer feedback to identify trends, issues, and areas of excellence.	
d) We use both quantitative and qualitative feedback to enhance our understanding of PMO service quality.	
e) We close the feedback loop by communicating back to PMO customers about how their input has influenced service improvements.	
Subtotal	
Grand total	

Scoring and Interpretation: Total your scores from all 20 questions.

Excellent: 89–100 points. Your PMO excels in service monitoring, ensuring a high standard of service delivery and building customer trust through transparency and accountability.

Good: 76–88 points. Your PMO has a solid monitoring framework but can refine specific areas for improved service management and communication.

Average: 59–75 points. Your PMO has basic monitoring processes in place but needs significant improvements to enhance transparency, SLA management, and customer satisfaction.

Poor: 39–58 points. There are gaps in your PMO's service monitoring capabilities. Focus on building a structured framework and improving reporting mechanisms to enhance service reliability.

Critical: 20–38 points. Immediate attention is required to establish a monitoring framework. Begin by developing essential data collection, SLA compliance, and reporting processes.

Looking Ahead to the Next Section

This section examined service monitoring and specific ways to track and evaluate PMO service performance. The following section focuses on PMO service improvement and maturity growth.

The service improvement step in the value-generating PMO flywheel is a methodical approach to enhancing PMO service maturity through the use of performance data, customer feedback, and organizational change adaptation. The section covers strategies for identifying areas for enhancement, prioritizing key improvements, and implementing changes that increase the value and effectiveness of services. By refining this process, PMO professionals can ensure their services continually adapt to meet evolving PMO customer demands and organizational goals.

21

Step 8: Service Improvement

Why This Section Matters to PMO Professionals

The service improvement step of the value-generating PMO flywheel is critical for PMO professionals as it directly enhances the PMO's ability to deliver value to PMO customers and the organization. This step focuses on increasing the maturity of PMO services, enabling PMO professionals to elevate PMO offerings from basic functions to sophisticated services. As services mature, they significantly increase the likelihood of achieving desired outcomes and delivering effective value.

This maturity enhancement is crucial for PMO professionals aiming to transition from operational efficiency to value impact. Service improvement allows PMO professionals to develop services that not only meet current needs but also anticipate future challenges, positioning the PMO as a proactive, value-driving entity.

The focus on service maturity provides PMO professionals with a structured approach to continuous improvement, enabling them to quantifiably demonstrate the evolution of PMO services over time. This tangible progress in PMO service sophistication and effectiveness serves as compelling evidence of the PMO's growing value, strengthening its position within the organization and securing ongoing support and resources for further development and impact.

Service Improvement at a Glance

The service improvement step is a structured approach aimed at enhancing the maturity, effectiveness, and overall value generated by PMO services. This step in the value-generating PMO flywheel emphasizes a continuous cycle of assessing current service maturity levels, identifying key areas for evolution, and implementing targeted improvements to elevate service maturity (see Figure 21-1).

Service improvement involves a continuous cycle of assessment, planning, implementation, and review. Key aspects include analyzing data, gathering customer feedback, benchmarking against industry standards, and leveraging emerging practices in PMOs.

The improvement process may involve refining existing services, developing new services, or retiring obsolete ones. The refinement of services often requires cross-functional collaboration within the organization and may necessitate changes in processes, tools, or skills. Successful service improvement results in more sophisticated PMO services that are better aligned with organizational strategy, more efficient in their execution, and more effective in delivering expected outcomes.

Figure 21-1. Service Improvement Step in the PMO Flywheel

Implementing the Service Improvement Step

1. Conducting a Comprehensive PMO Service Maturity Assessment

- **PMO service maturity assessment.** Evaluate each PMO service's current maturity level using a clear PMO maturity model. Define specific criteria for each level of maturity in the model. Assess each service against these criteria to determine its current state. Note that organizational maturity models and PMO maturity models are different instruments: The former measures the organization's maturity in portfolio, program, and project management, while the latter measures the maturity level of each PMO service in terms of the sophistication with which it is provided. Appendix X3 in this guide offers a PMO Service Maturity Assessment, a comprehensive model for evaluating the maturity of the 26 most common PMO services.

- **PMO service maturity reporting.** Document the assessment findings in a comprehensive report, including detailed analyses of each service and overall PMO maturity. This report will serve as a baseline for measuring future progress and as a foundation for developing the service improvement roadmap.

2. Analyzing Maturity Gaps and PMO Service Improvement Opportunities

- **PMO service maturity gap analysis.** Conduct a gap analysis comparing the current maturity state with the desired future state. This gap analysis will help identify the most critical areas for improvement and inform the prioritization of enhancement initiatives. This activity involves a deep dive into the assessment results to understand the root causes of maturity gaps and identify the most impactful areas for enhancement. When defining the desired maturity levels, consider both the immediate needs of the organization and long-term strategic objectives.
- **Identify and detail improvement opportunities.** Analyze the identified gaps and pinpoint specific improvement opportunities. Prioritize the improvement opportunities based on multiple factors. Consider the potential impact on service effectiveness, alignment with PMO customer needs, alignment with organizational strategy, complexity of implementation, and resource requirements. Analyze the interdependencies among different services and improvement opportunities. Some enhancements may have cascading effects, positively impacting multiple services or maturity dimensions. Identifying these synergies can help in developing a more efficient improvement strategy.
- **Quick wins.** Look for quick wins—improvements that can be implemented rapidly and with minimal resources while still providing noticeable benefits. These opportunities can help build momentum and demonstrate early value from the improvement process.
- **Feasibility analysis.** Conduct a cost-benefit analysis for each major improvement opportunity. Estimate the resources required for implementation and the potential benefits in terms of increased efficiency, effectiveness, and value delivery. This analysis will be crucial in building a business case for improvement initiatives.
- **Reporting the maturity improvement proposal.** Document the findings of this analysis in a detailed report, including prioritized improvement opportunities, their potential impacts, and recommendations for addressing them. This report will serve as a key input for developing the service improvement roadmap.

3. Developing a PMO Service Improvement Roadmap

- **Setting objectives and goals.** Set clear, measurable objectives for each service improvement initiative and directly link the objectives to the goals of increasing value delivery. Align these objectives with the overall PMO goals.
- **Phased implementation approach.** Develop a phased approach to implementing improvements. Begin with quick wins that can demonstrate immediate value, followed by

medium-term enhancements and long-term transformational changes. This phased approach helps manage resources effectively and maintains momentum throughout the improvement journey.

- **Implementation timeline.** Create a detailed timeline for each phase of the improvement process. Include key milestones, deliverables, and decision points. Consider using Gantt charts or other project management tools to visualize this timeline and the dependencies among different initiatives.
- **Ownership and responsibilities.** Assign clear ownership and responsibilities for each improvement initiative. Identify who will be responsible for leading each initiative, who needs to be involved, and who should be kept informed. This clarity in roles and responsibilities is crucial for successful implementation.
- **Resource planning.** Develop resource plans for each improvement initiative. This includes estimating required budgets, personnel, technology, and other resources needed for successful implementation. Ensure that these resource requirements are realistic and aligned with organizational constraints.
- **Overall PMO maturity.** Integrate plans for enhancing the PMO's implementation of the PMO Value Ring™ framework into the overall improvement roadmap. This planning can help ensure a holistic approach to PMO maturity enhancement.

4. Implementing PMO Service Enhancement Initiatives

- **Implementation team.** Establish an implementation team or task force responsible for driving the enhancement initiatives. This team should have a mix of skills including project management, change management, and specific expertise related to the services being improved. Ensure this team has the necessary authority and resources to effectively lead the implementation efforts.
- **Implementation plans.** Develop detailed implementation plans for each enhancement initiative. These plans should break down the improvement process into specific tasks, assign responsibilities, set timelines, and identify key dependencies. Use project management methodologies to structure these plans, ensuring all aspects of implementation are considered. Implement a rolling planning process for service improvement while maintaining a long-term vision, focusing on detailed planning for the near term (e.g., the next 3–6 months) and developing broader, more flexible plans for the longer term.
- **Pilot approach.** Start with pilot implementations where appropriate. This approach allows for testing and refining enhancements in a controlled environment before full-scale rollout. Select pilot groups that are representative of the broader user base and can provide valuable feedback.
- **Change management.** Implement a robust change management strategy to support the adoption of enhanced services. This strategy includes developing a comprehensive communications management plan to keep all customers informed about the changes, their

benefits, and their potential impacts. Conduct training sessions to ensure users are prepared for new or modified processes and tools.

- **Be flexible.** Build flexibility and adaptability into the implementation. While it is important to have a clear plan, also recognize that priorities may shift and new opportunities may emerge. Include regular review points where the roadmap can be reassessed and adjusted if necessary.
- **Implementation progress metrics.** Establish clear metrics for tracking implementation progress. These metrics should include both process metrics (e.g., milestones achieved, tasks completed) and outcome metrics (e.g., improvements in service performance and user satisfaction). Regularly monitor these metrics and report progress to customers.
- **Risk management.** Manage risks proactively throughout the implementation process. Regularly reassess potential risks and develop mitigation strategies. Be prepared to quickly address any issues that arise during implementation to minimize disruption to ongoing PMO operations.

5. Managing Feedback and Lessons Learned

- **Customer feedback.** Create feedback mechanisms to gather insights from PMO customers throughout the implementation process. This process may include regular check-ins, surveys, or feedback sessions. Use this input to make real-time adjustments to the implementation approach as needed.
- **Lessons learned.** Document lessons learned throughout the implementation process. Regularly review what is working well and what can be improved in the implementation approach. Use these insights to refine future enhancement initiatives and contribute to the PMO's overall knowledge base.

6. Transitioning to PMO Service Operations or Onboarding

- **Define clear transition criteria.** Establish explicit criteria for when and how to transition from the service improvement phase to ongoing service operations. This clarity helps ensure that everyone understands the benchmarks that signify readiness for operation or the need for further onboarding.
- **Develop a transition plan.** Create a comprehensive transition plan that outlines the processes and responsibilities for handovers from the implementation team to the operations team. This plan should detail timelines, key activities, and communication strategies to facilitate a seamless handover.
- **Maintain continuous support and monitoring.** Implement continuous support mechanisms and monitoring practices to ensure the enhanced services integrate successfully into daily operations. Ongoing support helps address any issues promptly and maintains service quality.
- **Establish ongoing service reviews.** Set up regular service reviews to assess the long-term success and performance of the service improvements. These reviews enable the team to

identify opportunities for further enhancement and ensure the services continue to meet organizational needs.

- **Ensure customer communication and support.** Keep PMO customers well informed and provide support throughout the transition to full-service operations. Effective communication helps manage expectations, fosters trust, and encourages PMO customer engagement with the new services.
- **Plan for continuous improvement.** Develop strategies for maintaining and continually improving the enhanced services, even after the initial implementation phase is complete. This proactive approach helps ensure that the services remain relevant and valuable over time.

Actionable Self-Assessment: Gauge the Effectiveness of PMO Service Monitoring

The following self-assessment provides a structured way for PMO professionals to evaluate the effectiveness of their service-improvement initiatives. The assessment helps ensure that the PMO can enhance service maturity, identify critical improvement opportunities, and continuously deliver value to the organization by refining its services and aligning them with strategic objectives.

Instructions: Rate your PMO's performance in each area on a scale of 1–5, where:

1 = Not at all/never

2 = Rarely/poor

3 = Sometimes/average

4 = Often/good

5 = Always/excellent

Section 1: Conducting a Comprehensive PMO Service Maturity Assessment	
Question	**Rating**
a) We have a clear PMO maturity model to assess the current state of each PMO service.	
b) Our PMO maturity assessments identify specific strengths and gaps in each PMO service.	
c) We maintain detailed reports of our PMO service maturity assessments for future reference.	
d) We use PMO maturity assessments to inform PMO service improvement initiatives and roadmaps.	
e) We regularly review and update our PMO service maturity criteria to reflect evolving business needs.	
Subtotal	

Section 2: Analyzing PMO Maturity Gaps and PMO Service Improvement Opportunities	
Question	**Rating**
a) We conduct a thorough gap analysis to identify the most critical areas for PMO service improvement.	
b) Our PMO service improvement opportunities are prioritized based on impact, PMO customer needs, and strategic alignment.	
c) We regularly identify quick wins to demonstrate PMO service value early in the improvement process.	
d) We conduct feasibility analyses to ensure that PMO service improvement opportunities are realistic and achievable.	
e) We document and communicate our findings and proposed PMO service improvements to key PMO customers.	
Subtotal	

Section 3: Developing a PMO Service Improvement Roadmap	
Question	**Rating**
a) We set clear, measurable objectives and goals for each PMO service improvement initiative.	
b) Our PMO service improvement roadmap includes a phased approach, balancing quick wins with long-term enhancements.	
c) We have established timelines and milestones for each phase of the PMO service improvement process.	
d) We assign clear ownership and responsibilities for each PMO service improvement initiative.	
e) We allocate PMO resources realistically, ensuring sufficient personnel, budget, and technology to support PMO service improvements.	
Subtotal	

Section 4: Implementing PMO Service Enhancement Initiatives	
Question	**Rating**
a) We have a dedicated PMO implementation team with the necessary skills to drive PMO service improvements.	
b) We have detailed implementation plans that break down the PMO service improvement process into manageable tasks.	
c) We pilot improvements with small, representative groups before full-scale rollout.	
d) Our change management strategy supports PMO customers and PMO team members in adopting enhanced PMO services.	
e) We establish clear progress metrics and regularly monitor PMO service implementation progress.	
Subtotal	

Section 5: Managing Feedback and Lessons Learned	
Question	**Rating**
a) We collect customer feedback throughout the service-improvement process.	
b) Feedback from customers is used to make real-time adjustments to service improvements.	
c) We proactively manage risks during the implementation of service enhancements.	
d) Lessons learned from each improvement initiative are documented and shared across the PMO.	
e) We use lessons learned to refine future improvement initiatives and contribute to continuous PMO development.	
Subtotal	

Section 6: Transitioning to PMO Service Operations or Onboarding	
Question	**Rating**
a) We define clear criteria for transitioning from service improvement to ongoing operations.	
b) We have a transition plan that ensures smooth handovers between the implementation and operations teams.	
c) We maintain continuous support and monitoring to ensure successful integration into operations.	
d) We establish ongoing service reviews to track the long-term success of service improvements.	
e) Our customers are well informed and supported throughout the transition to full-service operations.	
Subtotal	
Grand total	

Scoring and Interpretation: Total your scores from all 30 questions.

Excellent: 134–150 points. Your PMO excels in PMO service improvement, continuously enhancing PMO service maturity and delivering measurable value to the organization.

Good: 114–133 points. Your PMO has a solid framework for PMO service improvement but can refine specific areas to improve its overall impact and PMO maturity.

Average: 89–113 points. Your PMO service improvement efforts are underway but need significant enhancements to increase PMO service maturity and align with strategic goals.

Poor: 59–88 points. There are notable gaps in PMO service improvement processes. Focus on building a structured improvement roadmap and addressing the most critical gaps in PMO service maturity.

Critical: 30–58 points. Immediate attention is required to establish a robust PMO service improvement framework. Begin by developing a PMO maturity assessment and prioritizing key improvement opportunities.

Looking Ahead to the Next Section

This section detailed the service monitoring and improvement activities, helping PMO professionals to continuously refine their PMO services. However, improving services alone is not enough—the real test of a PMO's effectiveness is the tangible value it brings to the organization.

The next section explores the value delivery step of the value-generating PMO flywheel, focusing on how to measure and demonstrate the outcomes and value that PMO services can generate. The section provides strategies for measuring and communicating value and ensuring that PMO efforts result in meaningful impact. By mastering this critical process, PMO professionals can clearly prove the PMO's value and secure lasting support for the PMO.

22

Step 9: Value Delivery

Why This Section Matters to PMO Professionals

The value delivery step of the value-generating PMO flywheel is crucial for PMO professionals as it directly demonstrates the tangible impact of their efforts on organizational success. This stage transforms service outputs into concrete benefits for PMO customers and the organization, providing justification for the PMO's existence and investments.

By effectively delivering and showcasing value, PMO professionals can validate their role as strategic assets, build credibility with PMO customers, and secure ongoing support and resources. This focus on measurable outcomes drives alignment with organizational goals.

Mastering value delivery is essential for PMO professionals to maintain relevance in a results-driven business environment. Value generation enables professionals to quantify their contributions in tangible terms, linking PMO activities to improved performance and broader organizational success.

Furthermore, the insights gained from value-delivery-step assessments provide a foundation for data-driven decision-making and service refinement. Ultimately, excelling in value delivery positions PMO professionals as indispensable contributors to organizational success, elevating their status and influence within the organization.

Value Delivery Step at a Glance

The value delivery step in the PMO context is the process of realizing and demonstrating the tangible benefits that PMO services provide to organizations. This step involves identifying specific, measurable metrics that showcase the PMO's impact on expected outcomes and organizational success (see Figure 22-1).

PMO professionals should balance short-term wins with long-term strategic improvements, consistently tracking and reporting on value delivery over time. This process also involves establishing clear baselines for comparison and leveraging insights for continuous improvement of PMO services.

Ultimately, the value delivery step serves as a bridge between PMO services and organizational success, transforming PMO contributions into recognizable business benefits and positioning the PMO as a key driver of organizational growth and success.

Figure 22-1. Value Delivery Step in the PMO Flywheel

The value delivery step is dedicated to measuring the tangible outcomes that demonstrate the PMO's value. This step focuses on evaluating whether the PMO is successfully delivering on the specific outcomes promised to the organization. The outcomes should be aligned with PMO customer needs and the organization's strategic goals, and each outcome should represent a direct, measurable impact that the PMO contributes toward achieving these goals.

Indicators used in the value delivery step are inherently tangible and results-oriented, as they track the degree to which the PMO has achieved predefined benefits and goals. These metrics are essential because they provide concrete evidence of the PMO's efficiency and enable the PMO to communicate its impact in terms that resonate with executive leadership and other customers. For instance, indicators might include metrics such as increased project success rates, reduced operational costs, optimized resource allocation, or accelerated project timelines. These results can be quantified and linked directly to the PMO's influence, making them essential tools for demonstrating the PMO's contributions.

While this step focuses on tangible outcomes, it does not ignore qualitative elements, as these can enhance the story of value delivered. For instance, a higher project success rate is often a tangible metric, but underlying factors like improved project team collaboration or project stakeholder satisfaction can provide valuable context, supporting the interpretation of the PMO's impact on these outcomes. Although these qualitative aspects may appear in value recognition (Step 10), they still add depth to the assessment of value delivery, helping the PMO to highlight not only what was achieved but also the supporting factors that contributed to those achievements.

In this sense, the value delivery step sets a foundation for the next step—value recognition—by providing a measurable baseline of results. Once the PMO has established these tangible outcomes, it is better positioned to move into Step 10, where the focus shifts toward understanding how these outcomes meet PMO customers' expectations and fulfill their perceived needs. Although value delivery centers on quantifiable impact, this step acknowledges that both tangible and intangible indicators play a role in capturing the full picture of value creation.

Value delivery indicators demonstrate the PMO's effectiveness in achieving expected outcomes, with each type of indicator in this step providing concrete, measurable insights into the PMO's contributions and capturing its impact through direct results. While customer satisfaction indicators are often associated with perception (measured in Step 10), in Step 9 they serve to measure direct satisfaction with the specific outcomes delivered. This distinction is essential, as satisfaction here is closely tied to the tangible, measurable delivery of promised results, rather than to a broader, more subjective recognition of the value emphasized in Step 10.

Table 22-1 provides examples of value delivery indicators tailored to specific PMO outcomes. Each indicator underscores the PMO's effectiveness in delivering quantifiable results, allowing it to demonstrate its value through clear, objective data.

By categorizing indicators related to value delivery, the PMO can systematically assess how well it achieves concrete, measurable outcomes. This structured approach provides clear metrics for evaluating the PMO's effectiveness in delivering tangible results. The most common types of indicators for the value delivery step that emphasize the tangible achievement of outcomes include:

- **Performance impact indicators.** These indicators capture the PMO's direct influence on improving program and project success, measuring adherence to scope, schedule, and budget. For instance, project success rates, on-time completion percentages, and budget-adherence rates reveal the PMO's effectiveness in helping projects meet critical performance targets, providing stakeholders with measurable evidence of reliability and consistency.
- **Operational efficiency indicators.** Operational efficiency indicators assess the PMO's ability to streamline processes, reduce waste, and enhance project cycle efficiency. Metrics such as reduced project cycle times, improved resource utilization rates, and minimization of rework show how the PMO helps optimize operations, directly contributing to smoother, faster project completion and improving workflow efficiency.

Table 22-1. Examples of Value Delivery Performance Indicators

Outcome	Performance Indicator	Objective
Better availability of skilled resources	Percentage of projects staffed with skilled project managers	Measures the availability of qualified personnel for critical projects
Better quality of project results	Rate of rework or revisions needed after delivery	Tracks the effectiveness of quality control measures by counting revisions required after project completion
Effective knowledge transfer	Stakeholder feedback on knowledge accessibility and utility	Gathers input on the availability and usefulness of project management knowledge resources
Enhanced resource management	Rate of resource conflicts or overallocation issues resolved	Tracks how efficiently the PMO handles resource conflicts, minimizing disruptions
Greater alignment with strategic objectives	Percentage of projects aligned with strategic organizational goals	Tracks the extent to which projects support the organization's broader mission

- **Cost management indicators.** These indicators measure the PMO's impact on cost control and savings, focusing on budget adherence and resource allocation efficiency. Metrics like cost savings from optimized resources, reduction in budget overruns, and cost avoidance through risk management highlight the PMO's role in maintaining financial discipline and maximizing resource use, ensuring that projects stay within financial expectations and deliver value without excess spending.

- **Risk mitigation indicators.** Risk mitigation indicators reflect the PMO's success in identifying, assessing, and reducing project risks. By tracking the reduction in high-impact risks, percentage of risks mitigated before affecting project outcomes, and frequency of unplanned project disruptions, these indicators illustrate the PMO's proactive role in maintaining project stability and predictability, ensuring that potential challenges are addressed before they can impact success.

- **Resource optimization indicators.** These indicators measure how effectively the PMO allocates and utilizes resources, ensuring the right talent and tools are in place across projects. Metrics such as resource allocation efficiency, percentage of projects staffed optimally, and improvements in skill-utilization rates demonstrate how the PMO strategically deploys resources to maximize their impact, minimizing resource conflicts and ensuring project teams are adequately supported.

- **PMO customer satisfaction indicators.** In Step 9, customer satisfaction indicators measure direct satisfaction with specific outcomes achieved by the PMO. Examples include satisfaction ratings related to delivery quality, feedback on the timeliness of project support, contributions to the executive decision-making process, and ratings on cost management success. Satisfaction indicators in this step specifically reflect PMO customer satisfaction with the outcome delivery itself, not general perceptions of value. This distinction is crucial because it separates concrete satisfaction with results from the broader recognition of impact on PMO customer needs, which is the focus of Step 10, value recognition.

- **Strategic alignment indicators.** Strategic alignment indicators assess how closely the PMO's outcomes support organizational goals and priorities. Metrics like the percentage of projects contributing to strategic objectives, alignment scores for key initiatives, and frequency of strategic goal attainment underscore the PMO's role in ensuring that projects deliver results aligned with the organization's vision, reinforcing its strategic relevance.

Implementing the Value Delivery Step

1. Establishing a Comprehensive Value Measurement Framework

- **Outcomes review.** Review the expected outcomes for each PMO service, as defined in the SLAs and customer expectations gathered during earlier steps. Develop a set of specific, measurable indicators for each outcome. These indicators should be directly tied to organizational goals and portfolio, program, or project success metrics.
- **Data collection method.** Create a detailed methodology for data collection, ensuring consistency and reliability across different PMO services. Focus on quantitative metrics, such as cost savings, time reduction, or increased productivity.
- **Value-delivered reporting.** Design a standardized reporting format that clearly presents the value delivered, making it easy for customers to understand the PMO's impact. This reporting might include dashboards, scorecards, or detailed reports tailored to different audience needs. Establish a regular cadence for data collection and reporting, aligning with organizational reporting cycles where possible.

2. Conducting Quantitative Impact Analysis

- **Data collection.** Collect quantitative data to determine the tangible impact of PMO services. Conduct financial impact assessments, translating PMO contributions into monetary terms wherever possible.
- **Trend analysis.** Perform trend analyses to identify patterns in value delivery across different services, project types, or organizational units. Look for areas of consistent high performance as well as potential improvement opportunities.
- **Report findings.** Create detailed reports summarizing findings, including visualizations that make the data easily understandable to various customers. Be sure to clearly articulate the methodology used and any assumptions made in the analysis.

3. Evaluating PMO Customers' Expected Benefits Realization

- **Revisit expectations.** Revisit the PMO customers' expectations and desired outcomes identified during earlier steps of the framework. Create a comprehensive list of expected outcomes for each PMO customer group and key PMO customers.

- **Tracking process.** Develop a process for tracking a PMO customer's expected benefits realization, monitoring progress toward expected outcomes over time. This process might involve creating individual benefit profiles for each expected outcome, detailing the metrics used to measure the outcome, the timeline for realization, and any dependencies or assumptions.
- **Establish baselines.** Conduct before-and-after analyses for major PMO interventions or service implementations. This analysis involves establishing clear baselines before the PMO's involvement and then measuring the changes in relevant metrics after a sufficient period of time has passed.
- **Case studies.** Use case studies to deeply examine specific instances of high-value delivery. This methodology involves selecting representative cases, conducting in-depth analyses of the value delivered, and documenting the processes and factors that contributed to success.
- **Benefits reporting.** Regularly synthesize and report on the overall benefits delivered to PMO customers. This reporting may involve creating customer value scorecards, developing detailed benefits realization reports, or presenting case studies that showcase significant value-delivery instances.

4. Synthesizing and Communicating PMO Value Delivery Results

- **Collect data.** Gather all relevant data from the various value-delivery activities, including quantitative analyses, strategic assessments, customer benefit evaluations, and audit results.
- **Value narrative.** Develop a comprehensive narrative that tells the story of the PMO's value delivery. This narrative should go beyond just presenting data to explaining how PMO services have contributed to project success, strategic goal achievement, and overall organizational performance.
- **Communication materials.** Create a suite of communication materials tailored to different stakeholder groups. These materials may include executive summaries for senior leadership, detailed technical reports for project managers, and visually engaging presentations for broader organizational communication.
- **Data visualization.** Use data-visualization techniques to make complex value-delivery information easily understandable. This effort may involve creating infographics, interactive dashboards, or video presentations that highlight key value metrics and trends.
- **Reporting schedule.** Develop a regular reporting schedule that aligns with organizational rhythms and decision-making cycles. This reporting schedule may include monthly value delivery updates, quarterly in-depth reviews, and annual comprehensive value reports.
- **Communication strategy.** Implement a multichannel communication strategy to ensure wide dissemination of value-delivery results. This strategy may include email newsletters, intranet posts, town hall presentations, and one-on-one briefings with customers.

- **Future priorities.** Communicate the value-delivery results to gather input on future PMO priorities and services. Encourage stakeholders to share their perspectives on where the PMO can deliver even greater value in the future, creating a feedback loop that informs ongoing PMO strategy and service development.

5. Iterative Refinement and Process Realignment

- **Value gap analysis.** This critical activity involves analyzing the value-delivery results against initial expectations and, if necessary, revisiting earlier steps in the PMO Value Ring™ framework to ensure alignment and maximize value delivery. Begin by conducting a comprehensive gap analysis between the expected outcomes defined in the value proposition step and the actual results measured during the value delivery step.
- **Root cause identification.** For each significant discrepancy identified, perform a root cause analysis to understand why the expected outcomes were not achieved. This analysis may involve reviewing the initial assumptions made during the value proposition step, reassessing the service design from the service development step, or examining the implementation process from the service operation step.
- **Action plan development.** Based on the insights gained, develop action plans for refining various elements developed in the previous steps. This may include:
    - **Value proposition step.** Adjust the PMO value proposition to better align with realistic outcomes and evolving organizational needs.
    - **Service development step.** Redesign specific PMO services to deliver the expected value more effectively.
    - **Service delivery step.** Modify service delivery processes to address identified bottlenecks or inefficiencies.
- **Improving metrics.** Refine the metrics and measurement approaches used in the value delivery step to more accurately capture the PMO's impact. Prioritize these refinement actions based on their potential impact on value delivery and the resources required for implementation.
- **Change management.** Establish a formal change management process for implementing these refinements. This process should include a clear communications management plan to inform all customers about the changes, training programs to support new processes or service designs, and feedback mechanisms to monitor the impact of the changes.
- **Continuous improvement.** Use the insights gained from this process to inform continuous learning and improvement within the PMO team. Conduct lessons learned sessions to capture key takeaways from each iteration and use these insights to refine the overall PMO strategy and approach to value delivery.

Actionable Self-Assessment: Gauge the Effectiveness of PMO Value Delivery

The following self-assessment enables PMO professionals to evaluate their effectiveness in delivering measurable value to their organization. By focusing on clear metrics, quantitative analysis, and robust communication strategies, PMO professionals can ensure their PMO services have a tangible impact on organizational performance.

Instructions: Rate your PMO's performance in each area on a scale of 1–5, where:

1 = Not at all/never

2 = Rarely/poor

3 = Sometimes/average

4 = Often/good

5 = Always/excellent

Section 1: Establishing a Comprehensive Value Measurement Framework	
Question	**Rating**
a) We have clearly defined and measurable outcomes for each PMO service.	
b) We collect consistent and reliable data to measure the impact of PMO services.	
c) Our value reporting is clear, standardized, and tailored to various PMO customer needs.	
d) We regularly review value metrics to ensure they align with organizational goals.	
e) We have a formalized schedule for data collection and reporting on value delivery.	
Subtotal	

Section 2: Conducting Quantitative Impact Analysis	
Question	**Rating**
a) We routinely collect and analyze quantitative data to measure the PMO's impact.	
b) We perform financial impact assessments to quantify PMO contributions in monetary terms.	
c) We conduct trend analyses to identify consistent patterns in value delivery.	
d) Our reports include visualizations that make complex data easily understandable.	
e) Our analyses clearly articulate assumptions and the methodology used to derive value metrics.	
Subtotal	

Section 3: Evaluating PMO Customers' Expected Benefits Realization	
Question	**Rating**
a) We revisit the expected benefits and outcomes for each PMO customer group regularly.	
b) We track the realization of PMO customer benefits over time with clear metrics.	
c) We conduct before-and-after analyses to measure the impact of PMO interventions.	
d) We use case studies to document and highlight high-value PMO delivery examples.	
e) We regularly report on overall PMO benefits delivered, using detailed and comprehensive reports.	
Subtotal	

Section 4: Synthesizing and Communicating PMO Value Delivery Results	
Question	**Rating**
a) We collect comprehensive data from all PMO value-delivery activities, including quantitative and qualitative insights.	
b) We develop a clear value narrative that links PMO services to organizational success.	
c) We tailor communication materials for different PMO customer groups, including senior leadership and project managers.	
d) We use data-visualization techniques to simplify complex PMO value-delivery information.	
e) We have a well-established reporting schedule that aligns with organizational decision-making cycles.	
Subtotal	

Section 5: Iterative Refinement and Process Realignment	
Question	**Rating**
a) We conduct regular value gap analyses to identify discrepancies between expected and actual PMO outcomes.	
b) We perform root cause analysis for any significant discrepancies in PMO value delivery.	
c) We develop action plans to refine the PMO value proposition, PMO service design, or PMO delivery processes.	
d) We continuously improve our metrics and measurement approaches to better capture the PMO's impact.	
e) We follow a structured change management process to implement refinements and communicate changes to PMO customers.	
Subtotal	
Grand total	

Scoring and Interpretation: Total your scores from all 25 questions.

Excellent: 113–125 points. Your PMO excels in value delivery, effectively demonstrating and communicating its contributions to organizational success.

Good: 98–112 points. Your PMO delivers strong value but could benefit from refining its metrics and communication strategies to further enhance its impact.

Average: 77–97 points. Your PMO is delivering value but lacks consistency or sophistication in tracking and communicating it. Focus on improving data collection and analysis techniques.

Poor: 51–76 points. Your PMO needs significant improvement in tracking, analyzing, and demonstrating value. Reassess your framework for value measurement and reporting.

Critical: 25–50 points. Your PMO is struggling to demonstrate its value. Start by developing clear value-measurement frameworks and engaging stakeholders to define key metrics.

Looking Ahead to the Next Section

This section explored the value delivery step of the value-generating PMO flywheel, helping PMO professionals to achieve and showcase the tangible benefits of PMO services. However, delivering value is just one part of the equation; ensuring that this value is recognized and appreciated by PMO customers and the wider organization is equally important.

The final step of the flywheel focuses on value recognition—the process of ensuring PMO contributions are acknowledged and valued. The next section explores strategies for communicating PMO achievements; fostering a culture that appreciates project management excellence; and building strong, value-oriented relationships with stakeholders. By mastering this step, PMO professionals can solidify their roles as essential partners in organizational success.

23

Step 10: Value Recognition

Why This Section Matters to PMO Professionals

The value recognition step is critical for PMO professionals as it directly impacts the PMO's perceived worth and sustainability within the organization. This step focuses on ensuring that PMO customers not only receive value but also recognize and appreciate it.

For PMO professionals, mastering value recognition is essential for maintaining customer support, justifying resources, and driving continuous improvement. The value recognition step provides insights into how well the PMO's efforts align with customer expectations and organizational goals. By understanding and influencing value perception, PMO professionals can better tailor their services, communicate their impact more effectively, and strengthen their strategic position within the organization.

This step also helps in identifying any gaps between delivered value and perceived value, allowing for targeted improvements in service delivery or communication strategies.

Ultimately, effective value recognition enhances the PMO's credibility, secures ongoing support, and ensures that the PMO remains a valued and integral part of the organization's success strategy.

Value Recognition at a Glance

Value recognition in the PMO context is a critical process that goes beyond the mere delivery of services. Value recognition focuses on ensuring that PMO customers receive benefits from the PMO and fully acknowledge, appreciate, and internalize these benefits. This step is about bridging the gap between the actual value delivered and the perceived value, making it a crucial link in the value-generating PMO flywheel (see Figure 23-1).

This step is important because it can transform tangible outcomes into recognized organizational assets. While the value delivery step (Step 9) focuses on producing measurable results, value recognition ensures that these results are recognized and valued by PMO customers. This recognition is vital for the PMO's long-term sustainability and growth within the organization.

Value recognition connects closely with other steps in the PMO Value Ring™ framework. This step builds upon the foundations laid in the awareness building (Step 1) and needs assessment (Step 2)

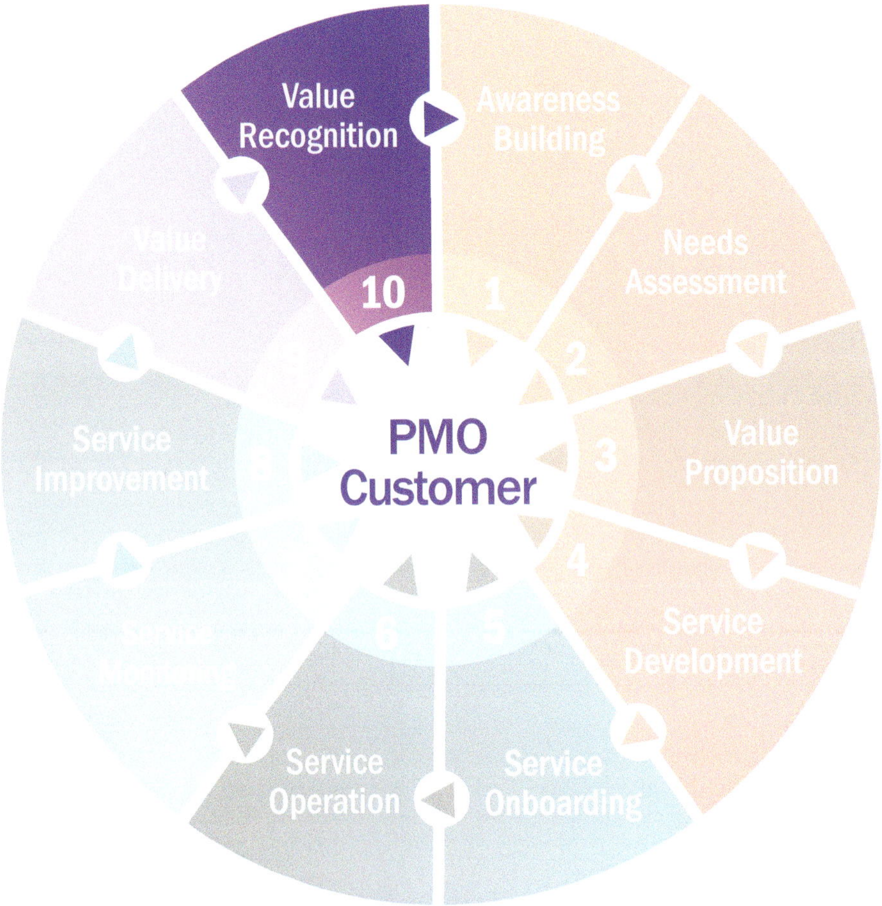

Figure 23-1. Value Recognition Step in the PMO Flywheel

phases, ensuring that the initial promises and identified needs are not just met but recognized. This step also complements the value proposition (Step 3), service development (Step 4), and value delivery (Step 9) steps, acting as a validation mechanism for the PMO's efforts.

Moreover, effective value recognition sets the stage for a more impactful awareness-building phase in the next cycle. When customers recognize and appreciate the PMO's value, they become more receptive to future awareness campaigns and more likely to engage with the PMO services proactively.

Value recognition fosters a culture that values project management excellence by creating a shared understanding and appreciation of the PMO's role in organizational success. This cultural shift can lead to increased support for PMO initiatives, better resource allocation, and a stronger strategic position for the PMO within the organization.

Ultimately, effective value recognition acts as a catalyst, propelling the value-generating PMO flywheel forward. This step reinforces the PMO's relevance, justifies its existence and resource allocation, and provides the momentum needed to begin the next cycle of value creation with renewed energy and customer buy-in. This continuous cycle of delivery, recognition, and renewed engagement is key to the PMO's ongoing evolution and its ability to consistently align with and contribute to organizational objectives.

In the previous step, value delivery, the PMO's primary objective is to measure and communicate tangible outcomes that reflect its ability to meet predefined goals. Indicators in that step are predominantly quantitative and results-focused, aimed at providing concrete, measurable evidence of the PMO's effectiveness in delivering on specific outcomes.

In contrast, value recognition shifts focus from quantitative outcomes to the "perceived value" the PMO brings to its customers. While the previous step demonstrates what the PMO has achieved in concrete terms, this step explores how these achievements are understood, valued, and appreciated by those whom the PMO serves. The indicators in this step are largely qualitative, centering on PMO customer satisfaction, alignment with strategic goals, and the PMO's reputation for reliability. Metrics here might include customer satisfaction ratings, feedback on the PMO's strategic relevance, and testimonials from executive leadership. These are inherently subjective measures that capture how PMO customers feel about the PMO's contributions, adding a layer of trust, credibility, and relational depth that goes beyond objective outcomes.

While Step 9, value delivery, is evidence-oriented, providing PMO customers with objective performance measures and focusing on the PMO's ability to meet specified targets (thus directly answering questions like "Has the PMO achieved its goals?"), Step 10, value recognition, is perception-oriented, offering insights into how these results are received and appreciated, and addressing a different set of questions such as: "Do PMO customers feel that the PMO is a valuable partner?"

Value recognition shows how well the PMO's impact resonates on both relational and reputational levels, and solidifies the PMO's reputation by emphasizing customer trust, satisfaction, and alignment with the organization's vision. In this way, this step becomes essential for building long-term loyalty and securing executive support, as it reflects the PMO's value beyond raw numbers.

Together, the value delivery and value recognition steps provide a holistic view of the PMO's contributions. Value delivery gives the PMO a solid foundation of quantitative results, proving that it meets targets. Value recognition adds depth to this foundation, showing that beyond achieving goals, the PMO also cultivates a strong, positive presence within the organization. By addressing both the measurable outcomes and the perceived value of its services, the PMO can not only validate its success but also reinforce its importance, trustworthiness, and customer focus.

Table 23-1 provides examples of value recognition indicators tailored to specific PMO outcomes. Each indicator highlights the importance of PMO customer feedback and perception in capturing the full scope of the value of a PMO.

In addition to indicators tied to specific outcomes, value recognition can also include "general indicators" that capture a broader view of the PMO's reputation and perceived value within the

Table 23-1. Examples of Value Recognition Performance Indicators

Outcome	Performance Indicator	Objective
Better availability of skilled resources	PMO customer perception of resource expertise	Gauges PMO customer satisfaction regarding the expertise and skill levels of program and project managers, reflecting confidence in resource quality
Better project prioritization	PMO customer perception of project prioritization effectiveness	Measures executives' satisfaction with the alignment of project prioritization to strategic goals, reflecting the PMO's strategic focus
Improved availability of information	PMO customer satisfaction with information accessibility	Assesses how accessible and useful users find project data, indicating the PMO's support for informed decision-making
Improved success rates	PMO customer perception of project success consistency	Assesses PMO customers' confidence in the PMO's ability to consistently enable successful projects
Reduction of risk exposure	PMO customer confidence in risk management	Measures how confident PMO customers feel in the PMO's proactive risk mitigation efforts

organization. These indicators go beyond measuring success in individual areas, focusing instead on the PMO's overall impact as a strategic and trusted partner. By assessing these high-level perceptions, the PMO can gain insights into its general standing with customers, its alignment with organizational strategies, and its contributions to long-term goals.

The following are examples of general-value-recognition indicators that reflect the PMO's broader influence and reputation:

- **Net Promoter Score℠ (NPS®) for the PMO.**[1] The NPS® measures the likelihood that PMO customers would recommend the PMO's services to others. This indicator captures overall satisfaction and loyalty, reflecting the PMO's standing within the organization.
- **General trust level in the PMO.** This indicator assesses the degree of trust that executive leaders and other key customers place in the PMO's ability to deliver valuable, reliable services. This indicator is essential for understanding the PMO's credibility and reputation across the organization.
- **Perception of the PMO as a strategic partner.** This indicator evaluates whether customers see the PMO as aligned with the organization's long-term goals and as a critical player in achieving

[1] Net Promoter®, NPS®, NPS Prism®, and the NPS-related emoticons are registered trademarks of Bain & Company, Inc., NICE Systems, Inc., and Fred Reichheld. Net Promoter Score℠ and Net Promoter System℠ are service marks of Bain & Company, Inc., NICE Systems, Inc., and Fred Reichheld.

strategic objectives. This indicator reflects the PMO's influence and strategic importance beyond operational metrics.

- **Overall satisfaction score with PMO services.** This indicator captures a high-level view of customer satisfaction across all PMO services, offering insight into general perceptions about the quality, relevance, and effectiveness of the PMO's support.
- **Reputation for innovation and adaptability.** This indicator assesses the perception of the PMO's ability to evolve with changing organizational needs and introduce new, beneficial practices or tools. This indicator demonstrates the PMO's role in driving progress and adapting to new challenges.
- **Alignment with organizational culture and values.** This indicator measures how well customers feel the PMO embodies and supports the organization's core values and cultural norms. This indicator reflects the PMO's ability to integrate and reinforce the broader organizational ethos.
- **PMO contributions to organizational learning and maturity development.** This indicator evaluates the perception of the PMO's role in fostering a learning culture through knowledge sharing, good practices, and continuous improvement initiatives to evolve the organizational project management maturity. This indicator showcases the PMO as a facilitator of growth and knowledge development.
- **Customer perceptions of the PMO's impact on organizational success.** This indicator measures how customers perceive the PMO's contributions to overall organizational success, beyond individual projects or initiatives. This indicator provides a comprehensive view of the PMO's perceived value as a critical organizational asset.

While all indicators in this step focus on perception and customer satisfaction, grouping them into distinct categories highlights the different facets of the PMO's relationships with its customers and its perceived impact within organizations. By categorizing these indicators, the PMO can collect more focused feedback, gaining deeper insights into specific areas of its reputation and customer experience. Some possible categories for value recognition indicators include:

- **Delivery satisfaction indicators.** These indicators capture customer perceptions of the quality of results delivered by the PMO. For instance, the satisfaction level regarding the quality of completed projects can be assessed.
- **Strategic alignment indicators.** These indicators assess how well the PMO's efforts are perceived to align with organizational strategic goals. For instance, the executives' perceptions of the PMO's contribution to achieving organizational objectives can be assessed.
- **Trust and credibility indicators.** These indicators measure the trust that customers place in the PMO, reflecting its reliability and reputation. For instance, the customers' confidence in the accuracy and reliability of the PMO's reports and data can be assessed.
- **Relationship and collaboration indicators.** These indicators evaluate the interaction quality between the PMO and its customers, especially in areas like communication and support.

For instance, the customers' satisfaction with the support and communication provided by the PMO throughout the project stages can be assessed.

- **Innovation and continuous improvement indicators.** These indicators focus on customer perceptions of the PMO's ability to innovate and continuously improve. For instance, the feedback on the PMO's responsiveness to changing needs and its implementation of innovative solutions can be assessed.

Implementing the Value Recognition Step

1. Conducting PMO Customer Value Perception Surveys

- **Survey design and analysis.** Develop a comprehensive survey covering various PMO value aspects. Include both quantitative rating scales and open-ended questions to capture nuanced feedback. Ensure the survey design allows for segmentation of responses by customer group to identify any variations in value perception. Analyze the survey results thoroughly, looking for patterns, trends, and any discrepancies between expected and perceived value.

- **Survey reporting.** Prepare detailed reports of the findings, including visualizations that make the data easily digestible for different audiences. Use these insights to inform future PMO strategies, service improvements, and communication plans. Consider implementing a longitudinal approach, repeating the survey at regular intervals to track changes in value perception over time. Pay special attention to areas where there is a significant gap between delivered value (as measured in the previous step) and perceived value. Any gaps can highlight communication issues or misalignments in expectations.

- **Customer engagement.** Use the survey process itself as a tool for engagement and value recognition. The act of seeking feedback demonstrates the PMO's commitment to customer satisfaction and continuous improvement. Follow up with participants to share key findings and action plans, reinforcing the message that their input is valued and acted upon. This comprehensive approach to customer-value-perception surveys provides a solid foundation for understanding how well the PMO's efforts are recognized and appreciated across the organization, setting the stage for targeted improvements and enhanced value recognition.

2. Facilitating PMO Value Recognition Workshops

- **Interactive workshops.** Organize and facilitate interactive workshops designed to explore and enhance customers' recognition of PMO value. These workshops should bring together diverse groups of customers to discuss and reflect on the PMO's contributions. Start by carefully planning the workshop structure, including activities that encourage open dialogue, critical thinking, and collaborative problem-solving. Begin each workshop with a brief presentation of key PMO achievements and metrics to set the context. Then engage participants in exercises such as value mapping, where they visually represent how PMO services connect to organizational outcomes.

- **Insights documentation.** Document all insights, suggestions, and feedback meticulously. After the workshop, synthesize the information gathered and share a summary with participants and other relevant customers. Use the workshop outcomes to inform PMO strategy, service development, and communication plans. Consider making these workshops a regular event, perhaps quarterly or biannually, to maintain an ongoing dialogue about PMO value.
- **Post-workshop engagement.** Follow up with participants after the workshop to see how their perceptions or actions have changed. This post-workshop engagement can reinforce the workshop's impact and provide additional data on its effectiveness in enhancing value recognition. These interactive sessions not only gather valuable insights but also serve to reinforce and expand customers' recognition of PMO value, creating a shared understanding and appreciation of the PMO's role in organizational success.

3. Developing and Maintaining a PMO Value Recognition Dashboard

- **Value recognition dashboard.** Create a dynamic, visual dashboard that consolidates and displays key indicators of PMO value recognition. Begin by identifying the most crucial metrics that reflect how well PMO value is recognized across the organization. These metrics might include customer satisfaction scores, utilization rates of PMO services, number of requests for PMO involvement in new initiatives, or mentions of PMO contributions in executive communications. Design the dashboard to be visually appealing and easily understandable, using charts, graphs, and infographics to represent data.
- **Dashboard accessibility.** Make the dashboard easily accessible to PMO team members and customers, perhaps through a dedicated intranet page or regular email updates. Use the dashboard in PMO team meetings to guide discussions on value recognition strategies and in stakeholder meetings to demonstrate the PMO's impact. Regularly review and refine the dashboard based on feedback and changing organizational priorities.
- **Customized dashboards.** Consider creating customized views of the dashboard for different customer groups, highlighting the metrics most relevant to their interests. This customization can increase engagement and relevance for various users. Implement a feature that allows customers to input their own observations or feedback directly into the dashboard, creating a more interactive and inclusive tool.
- **Provide visibility of the PMO.** Create a "value story of the month" feature on the dashboard, highlighting a specific example of PMO impact. This engagement opportunity can help bring the metrics to life and reinforce the tangible benefits of PMO services. Implement alerts or notifications for significant changes in key metrics, ensuring that the PMO can respond quickly to shifts in value perception.
- **Gamification approach.** Consider gamification elements, such as departmental competitions or individual recognition for high engagement with PMO services, to encourage active participation in value-creating activities. Finally, use the dashboard as a learning tool, incorporating explanations of metrics and their significance to educate customers about different aspects of PMO value. This value recognition dashboard serves as a powerful tool for monitoring, communicating, and enhancing the recognition of PMO value across the organization, providing a central point of reference for all value-related discussions and decisions.

4. **Conducting PMO Value Storytelling Campaigns**
   - **Storytelling campaigns.** Develop and execute comprehensive storytelling campaigns that bring the PMO's value to life through compelling narratives. Start by collecting a diverse range of stories that illustrate the PMO's impact across different customers, projects, departments, and organizational goals. Train PMO team members in effective storytelling techniques, focusing on how to structure narratives that resonate with different audiences. Create a variety of storytelling formats, such as written case studies, video testimonials, podcasts, or infographic journey maps.
   - **Storytelling content calendar.** Develop a content calendar that ensures a steady stream of fresh stories across various communication channels. Collaborate with the marketing or communications department to enhance these stories' production quality and reach. Encourage customers to share their own stories of PMO value, providing them with templates or guidelines to ensure consistency.
   - **Storytelling events.** Leverage, for example, the globally recognized International PMO Day, which is celebrated on the second Tuesday of May each year, to organize storytelling events such as a "PMO Impact Day," where successes are shared through presentations and interactive displays. Integrate these stories into regular organizational communications, such as newsletters, town hall meetings, or the company intranet. Create a searchable repository of PMO success stories that customers can easily access and reference.
   - **Storytelling campaign measurement.** Measure the impact of the storytelling campaign through metrics like story engagement rates, changes in PMO service requests, or improvements in value perception surveys. Use these insights to continuously refine the storytelling approach, focusing on the types of stories and formats that resonate most strongly with audiences. This storytelling-campaign approach makes PMO value tangible and relatable, enhancing recognition across the organization through the power of narrative and personal connection.

5. **Implementing a 360-Degree PMO Value Feedback System**
   - **Feedback process.** Develop and implement a comprehensive feedback process that captures insights on PMO value from all angles within the organization. Start by mapping out all touchpoints between the PMO and various customers, from project initiation to closure and beyond. Create a range of feedback mechanisms tailored to different interaction types and customer preferences. These feedback mechanisms may include quick pulse surveys after specific PMO interactions, in-depth interviews at project milestones, online feedback forms accessible through the PMO portal, and AI-powered chatbots for gathering real-time feedback.
   - **Identifying trends.** Use the feedback to identify trends in value perception, uncover hidden pain points, and highlight areas of exceptional value delivery. Implement a closed-loop system where customers are informed about how their feedback has been used to enhance PMO services or processes. Regularly review and refine the feedback system itself, ensuring it remains user-friendly and relevant.

- **Feedback forums.** Organize regular "feedback forums" where customers can discuss their experiences with the PMO in a facilitated group setting. These sessions can uncover collective insights and foster a shared understanding of PMO value. Develop a system of "value alerts" that notifies PMO leadership of significant positive or negative feedback, allowing for rapid responses to critical issues or opportunities.

6. Organizing PMO Value Recognition Events

- **PMO value recognition events.** Plan and execute a series of events specifically designed to showcase and celebrate the value delivered by the PMO. Organize smaller, more frequent events like monthly "PMO Value Spotlight" sessions where specific PMO successes are presented to relevant stakeholders. These sessions can be informal, perhaps over lunch or as part of regular team meetings, to maintain ongoing awareness of PMO value. Create interactive showcase events where customers can explore PMO tools, methodologies, and success stories through hands-on demonstrations and displays. This type of "PMO Value Expo" could feature booths highlighting different aspects of PMO value, interactive technology demonstrations, and mini workshops on PMO services.
- **Spreading PMO value recognition within the organization.** Develop a "PMO Value Roadshow" that travels to different departments or locations, tailoring the presentation of PMO value to each specific audience. This mobile approach ensures that all parts of the organization, regardless of location, have the opportunity to engage with and recognize PMO value. Incorporate elements of gamification or competition into these events to boost engagement, such as a "PMO Value Challenge," where teams compete to demonstrate their understanding and application of PMO principles.
- **External collaboration.** Invite external speakers or industry experts to these events to provide perspective on the PMO's value relative to industry standards. This external validation can significantly enhance the credibility of the PMO's value proposition. Use these events as opportunities to gather additional feedback on PMO value perception, perhaps through interactive polling or feedback walls. This real-time input can provide valuable insights and demonstrate the PMO's commitment to customer opinions.
- **Executive engagement.** Ensure high-level executive participation in these events to underscore the organizational importance of the PMO. Consider having executives share their perspectives on how the PMO has contributed to strategic objectives. Document these events through videos, photos, and written summaries, and share these materials widely to extend the reach of the value recognition message beyond the immediate attendees.
- **Impact measurement.** Measure the impact of these events through attendance rates, engagement levels, and follow-up surveys on PMO value perception. Use these metrics to continuously refine and improve the events, ensuring they remain effective tools for value recognition. These recognition events serve not only to celebrate PMO achievements but also to reinforce and expand the recognition of PMO value across the organization, creating a culture of appreciation for project management excellence.

Actionable Self-Assessment: Gauge the Effectiveness of PMO Value Recognition

The following self-assessment helps PMO professionals evaluate their effectiveness in ensuring that the value provided by their services is recognized and appreciated across the organization. By focusing on structured feedback, engaging workshops, storytelling campaigns, and real-time dashboards, PMOs can enhance visibility and appreciation of their contributions, driving sustained customer support and organizational success.

Instructions: Rate your PMO's performance in each area on a scale of 1–5, where:

1 = Not at all/never

2 = Rarely/poor

3 = Sometimes/average

4 = Often/good

5 = Always/excellent

Section 1: Conducting PMO Customer Value Perception Surveys	
Question	**Rating**
a) We regularly survey PMO customers to assess their perception of the value we provide.	
b) Our surveys include both quantitative and open-ended questions to capture nuanced feedback from PMO customers.	
c) We segment survey responses by PMO customer group to identify variations in value perception.	
d) We thoroughly analyze survey results to identify discrepancies between delivered value and PMO customers' perceived value.	
e) We use survey findings to inform future PMO strategies, service improvements, and communication plans.	
Subtotal	

Section 2: Facilitating PMO Value Recognition Workshops	
Question	**Rating**
a) We organize interactive workshops to help PMO customers recognize and reflect on PMO contributions.	
b) Our workshops encourage open dialogue, collaborative problem-solving, and value-mapping exercises.	
c) We document insights and feedback from workshops and share them with participants.	
d) We follow up with workshop participants to gauge changes in perception or behavior.	
e) Our workshops are held regularly (e.g., quarterly or biannually) to maintain ongoing dialogue about PMO value.	
Subtotal	

Section 3: Developing and Maintaining a PMO Value Recognition Dashboard	
Question	**Rating**
a) We have a dynamic dashboard that consolidates key metrics of PMO value recognition.	
b) Our dashboard includes critical indicators such as PMO customer satisfaction, service utilization, and requests for PMO involvement.	
c) We make the dashboard easily accessible to both PMO team members and PMO customers.	
d) We regularly review and refine the dashboard based on PMO customer feedback and changing priorities.	
e) Our dashboard highlights specific success stories or "value stories of the month" to illustrate the PMO's impact.	
Subtotal	

Section 4: Conducting PMO Value Storytelling Campaigns	
Question	**Rating**
a) We develop storytelling campaigns that highlight real examples of PMO value across different projects and departments.	
b) We train PMO team members in storytelling techniques to communicate our value effectively.	
c) Our storytelling campaigns leverage various formats, such as case studies, videos, and infographics.	
d) We organize PMO storytelling events (e.g., "PMO Impact Day") to celebrate and share PMO successes.	
e) We measure the engagement and impact of storytelling campaigns, using the results to refine future efforts.	
Subtotal	

Section 5: Implementing a 360-Degree PMO Value Feedback System	
Question	**Rating**
a) We have a comprehensive feedback system that captures insights from all PMO customer touchpoints across the project life cycle.	
b) Our feedback system includes quick pulse surveys, in-depth interviews, and online forms to collect PMO customer feedback.	
c) We analyze PMO customer feedback to identify trends in value perception and areas of improvement.	
d) We close the PMO customer feedback loop by informing customers about how their input has been used to enhance PMO services.	
e) We regularly refine the PMO customer feedback system to ensure it remains user friendly and relevant.	
Subtotal	

Section 6: Organizing PMO Value Recognition Events	
Question	**Rating**
a) We organize PMO value recognition events to showcase and celebrate the PMO's contributions to organizational success.	
b) Our events range from small sessions (e.g., "PMO Value Spotlights") to larger showcases (e.g., "PMO Value Expo").	
c) We use these events to foster a culture of recognition and appreciation for PMO achievements.	
d) We involve senior leadership in these events to emphasize the strategic importance of the PMO.	
e) We measure the impact of these events through metrics such as attendance rates, engagement, and follow-up surveys.	
Subtotal	
Grand total	

Scoring and Interpretation: Total your scores from all 30 questions.

Excellent: 134–150 points. Your PMO excels at ensuring that value is recognized and appreciated throughout the organization, fostering strong customer relationships and support.

Good: 114–133 points. Your PMO effectively recognizes and communicates value but there may be opportunities to refine certain communication strategies or improve engagement further.

Average: 89–113 points. Your PMO demonstrates value but more consistent and sophisticated approaches are needed to ensure that customers fully recognize and appreciate the impact of PMO services.

Poor: 59–88 points. Significant improvement is needed in communicating and showcasing the value the PMO provides. Focus on customer engagement and feedback mechanisms to drive better recognition.

Critical: 30–58 points. Your PMO is struggling to ensure that its value is acknowledged within the organization. Begin by establishing clear communication channels, regularly measuring perception, and addressing gaps in recognition.

Completing the PMO Flywheel Journey and Preparing for Future Cycles

Value recognition is the final phase of the journey through the value-generating PMO flywheel. This final step closes the loop, ensuring that the value delivered by the PMO is fully acknowledged and appreciated.

By mastering value recognition, PMO professionals can create a positive feedback loop that reinforces the PMO's importance and drives continued support for its initiatives. This recognition sets the stage for the next cycle of the flywheel, informing future awareness-building efforts and needs assessments.

The PMO journey is ongoing. Each rotation of the flywheel brings new opportunities for improvement and value creation. By consistently applying these principles, PMO professionals can ensure their PMOs remain dynamic, value-driven entities that are crucial to organizational success.

24

Conclusion

As we reach the end of this comprehensive practice guide, it is clear that the landscape of PMOs has evolved significantly, demanding a new approach to their design, implementation, and operation. This guide, developed by PMO Global Alliance, the Project Management Institute global community of PMO professionals, represents a significant leap forward in understanding how PMOs can deliver real value to organizations in an increasingly complex business environment.

At the heart of this guide lies the innovative PMO Value Ring™ framework, a groundbreaking approach that reimagines the role of PMOs within organizations. This framework shifts the focus from traditional, process-centric PMO models to dynamic, customer-focused entities that drive continuous improvement and tangible value creation. By breaking down the PMO customer experience cycle into 10 actionable steps, the value-generating PMO flywheel provides PMO professionals with a clear roadmap for success, emphasizing the importance of customer centricity, continuous improvement, and value generation.

One of this guide's key strengths is its practical approach. Throughout its pages, PMO professionals will find not just theoretical concepts but actionable strategies, assessments, and tools that can be immediately applied to enhance their PMO's effectiveness. The guide provides practical insights on all areas of PMO service, including conducting comprehensive needs assessments, developing compelling value propositions, managing service operations, and continuously improving PMO service maturity—all grounded in real-world experience.

The guide's customer-centric approach, embodied in the detailed exploration of PMO outcomes, marks a paradigm shift in how PMOs interact with their customers. By focusing on the specific benefits that PMO customers expect and value, this guide enables PMO professionals to tailor their services more effectively, ensuring that they deliver outcomes that truly matter to their organizations.

The comprehensive overview of PMO services and the innovative service-approaches model help give PMO professionals a versatile toolkit for designing and delivering PMO services. This flexible approach allows PMOs to adapt their service-delivery methods based on customer maturity and organizational needs, ensuring maximum impact and value creation.

The emphasis on PMO service maturity represents another significant contribution to the field. By providing a comprehensive framework for assessing and improving the sophistication of PMO services, this guide enables PMO professionals to continuously enhance their offerings and deliver greater value to their organizations. This focus on maturity and continuous improvement ensures that PMOs can evolve alongside their organizations, remaining relevant and impactful in the face of changing business needs.

Finally, the guide's detailed exploration of core PMO competencies provides PMO professionals with valuable guidance on developing the essential skills needed to excel in this evolving landscape, helping to ensure that they can effectively design, operate, and continually improve their PMOs.

Looking to the future, *Project Management Offices: A Practice Guide* will play a crucial role in shaping the development of PMOs over the next decade. By providing effective support to PMO professionals and setting clear directions for future PMO evolution, this guide serves as a beacon for those navigating the complex world of portfolio, program, and project management.

The guide's innovative approach to PMO design and operation, embodied in the PMO Value Ring™ framework, represents a significant step forward in understanding how PMOs can deliver value in today's dynamic business environment. By emphasizing customer centricity, value creation, and continuous improvement, this framework provides a solid foundation for building PMOs that are truly aligned with organizational needs and capable of driving strategic success.

Looking ahead, future editions of this guide will likely build upon the solid foundation laid here, further exploring emerging trends in PMOs and project management, delving deeper into the application of technologies like artificial intelligence and machine learning in PMO operations, and providing even more detailed insights into PMO value measurement and communication. As the business landscape continues to evolve, so too will the role of PMOs, and this guide will evolve alongside them, always striving to provide the most current, practical, and valuable insights for PMO professionals worldwide.

The future of PMOs is bright and filled with opportunities to drive organizational success through effective portfolio, program, and project management. With this guide as a foundation, PMO professionals are well equipped to lead their organizations into this future, creating PMOs that are not just administrative centers but true strategic partners in achieving organizational goals.

PMO professionals are encouraged to reflect on how these insights can be applied in their own PMO journeys. Whether establishing a new PMO, revitalizing an existing one, or seeking to take the PMO to the next level of maturity and effectiveness, the principles and practices outlined here provide a robust framework for success.

Part 4

Appendices, Bibliography, Glossary, and Index

Appendix X1
Contributors and Reviewers

The volunteers who contributed to the development of *Project Management Offices: A Practice Guide* deserve special recognition and gratitude for their invaluable efforts.

These experienced PMO professionals come from diverse backgrounds, industries, and regions, but they are all united by their passion for PMO excellence. Their collective contributions helped to develop a guide that addresses the real challenges and opportunities that PMO professionals face worldwide. Their dedication to advancing PMO practices and their generosity in sharing knowledge for the benefit of the global PMO community are deeply valued.

Throughout the guide's development, these volunteers played crucial roles at every stage—from the initial generation of ideas to the practical implementation of recommendations. They reviewed articles and manuscripts, provided essential feedback, presented at global events, and ensured that each proposal was aligned with the practical needs of PMO professionals.

The following list of contributors and reviewers stands as a reflection of the collaborative spirit that has guided this project from the very beginning. Each person listed has played a vital role in ensuring that *Project Management Offices: A Practice Guide* is both practical and forward-looking. Their contributions have been essential in creating a guide that is grounded in reality and designed to help PMOs thrive. Together, they have created a resource that focuses on delivering real value to organizations and will undoubtedly influence PMOs around the world for years to come.

PMI deeply values both their individual contributions and the remarkable impact of their collective collaboration. Each volunteer's unique expertise and dedication enriched the development process, while their teamwork amplified these efforts, resulting in a guide that truly reflects the diverse needs and insights of the PMO community. PMI recognizes that it is through this powerful blend of individual effort and collaborative spirit that meaningful, high-impact resources are created.

Farhad Abdollahyan, PMI-RMP, PMP, PMO-CP

Saadi Adra, PhD, PgMP, PfMP

Mounir A. Ajam

Fola F. Alabi, MBA, PMI-ACP, PMP

Mohammed Dawood AlAssafi, PMP, PMO-CP, PfMP

Thaer Fathi AlAthamneh, PMP, PMO-CP, PMO-CC

Haitham Alrasheed, PhD, VMA, PMO-CC

Heba ALShehhi, PMP, PMO-CP, PMO-CC

Abdulrahman Alulaiyan, MBA, PMO-CC

Edgar Alvarez, MBA, PMP, PMO-CC

Amireh Amirmazaheri, PMI-PBA, PMO-CP, PMO-CC

Ala' Yacoub Amr, PMP, PMO-CC

Tony El-Khoury Antonios, MBA, PMO-CP, PMO-CC
Charalampos Apostolopoulos, PhD, PgMP, PfMP
Bruno Otaviano Ferreira Araújo, MSc, PMP, PMO-CP
Alfredo Armijos, PMP, PMO-CP, PMI-CP
Kara Ayn Austin, PMI-ACP, PMP, PMO-CP
Mete Aydin
Hilary Aza, PhD, PgMP, PfMP
Robert Azanero, PM4R, PMP, PMO-CP
Akbar Azwir, Prosci CCP, PMP, PMO-CC
Ahmed Saleh Said Bahakim, P3O, PMP, PMO-CC
Abdulrahman Balubaid, PMP, PMO-CC, PfMP
Maria Cristina Barbero, PMI-ACP, PMP, PMO-CP
Emilio Augusto Barbosa
Paulo de Tarso Barros, PMP, PMO-CP
Ahmed Ibrahim Battisha
Mikhail Belov, PMO-CC, PgMP, PfMP
Maria Belyaeva, PMO-CP, PMO-CC
Abdelilah Benhmidi
Xavier Billingsley, PMO-CC
Claudio C. Boros
Claudia Martins Bueno
Hazell Hassan Melendez Cabrera, PMI-ACP, PMP, PMO-CP
Carolina Vázquez Camarano, PMP, PMO-CP
Joe Campa, PMI-RMP, PMP, PMO-CP
Rodolfo Campos
Gart Capote
Julio Cesar Gusmão Carvalho
Frederic L. Casagrande
Alessandro Cavalcanti, PTE, PMP, PMO-CP
Porfirio Chen Chang, PMP, PMO-CP, PgMP
Brendan Cody, PMO-CC
Davi Cohen
Ana Maria da Graça Costa, PMP, PMO-CP
Marcelo Cota, DSc
Fabio Cruz
Gilnei de Assis
Elmarie-Louise de Beer
Jose Abitia Nilo de Rivera, PMO-CP, PMO-CC
Estelle Detrembleur, MBA, ChPP, PMO-CP
Gaurav Dhooper, PAL-I, CSAPM, PMI-ACP
Dimitar Georgiev Dimitrov
Abdelrahman Elsheikh
Clive N. Enoch, PhD, PMO-CP, PfMP
Carlos Alexandre Espanha
Alexandres Hoyos Espinoza
Fernando Andrés de Cortillas Farías, MBA, PMI-ACP, PMP
Galen Garrison, CSM, PMP, PMO-CP
Ahmed Kamel Ghanem, PMP, PMO-CC, PgMP
Paula Cunha Lima Giudicelli
Jackie Glynn, MPM, PMP, PfMP
Giorgi Gogishvili, PMP, PMO-CP, PMO-CC
Bernardo Jose Marquez Gonzalez, PMP, PMO-CP, PMO-CC
Nanysma I. Guerra-Flores, MEd, PMP, PMO-CP
Katinka Halasz, PMP, PMO-CP
Ganie Hanifan, CBAP, PMO-CC, PgMP
Heberth Campos Hernández, PMI-RMP, PMP, PMO-CP
Christoph Hirnle, PhD, PMO-CP
Tarik Yassin Al Hraki
Mohammed Ahmed Hummadi, MPM, PMP, PMO-CC
Evgenii Ishchenkov, PMP, PMO-CP
Ebtihal Al Jassim, PMP, PMO-CP, PMO-CC
Alamir Paulo Júnior

Rami Kaibni, CBAP, PMP, PgMP
Gergely Keki, Prosci, PMP, PMO-CP
Vahagn Keshishyan, PMP, PMO-CP
Sridihar Kethandapatti, PMI-RMP, PMO-CP, PgMP
Deborah Kupty, PMO-CP
Ginger Levin, DPA, PMP, PgMP
Hugo Magalhães Lourenço
Neeta Manghnani, MBA, PMP, PMO-CP
Antonio Canas Martinez, PMO-CC, PgMP, PfMP
Vitor Massari
Yosra Torjmen Mekni
Claudio Mello, PMP, PMO-CP, PMO-CC
Hatem Abdel-Wahab Metwalli
Peter Botond Mihok
David Miller, PMI-ACP, PMP, PMO-CP
Walla S. E. Mohamed, PMO-CC, PgMP, PfMP
Lincoln Sant'Ana Morales
Jose Luiz Augusto Gomes Moreira, PMP, PMO-CP
Brayden Mueller, PMI-ACP, PMP, PMO-CP
Rakhmat Mulyanto, PMP, PMO-CP, PMO-CC
Luis Negreiros, MSc, PMP, PMO-CP
Trevor K. Nelson, PhD, PMP, PMO-CP
Laura Lazzerini Neuwirth, Agile PgM, PMP, PMO-CP
Novelly Intan Nursavitri, PMP, PMO-CP
Michael O'Connor, PMP, PgMP, PfMP
Volodymyr Oros, PMI-RMP, PMP, PMO-CP
Fernand Washington Padilha
Marc Pauwels, PMP, PMO-CP, PfMP
Alfredo de Barros Pereira
Sergio Fernando Ferraz Perez
Miguel Pascual Perez-Alfaro
Carlos Victor Salvarez Pestana, CSM, PMP, PMO-CC
Americo Pinto, PMP, PMO-CP, PMO-CC
Adilson Pize, DASSM, PMP, PMO-CP
Monika Podkowińska, PMP, PMO-CP
Roberto Henrique Pons, MSc, PMO-CP
Juliana Prado, PMP, PMO-CP
Adi Prasetyo, PhD, PMP, PMO-CP
Tony Prensa, PhD, PMP, PMO-CC
Wael Ramadan, PhD, PMP, PMO-CC
Mahmoud Fathy Rashed, MBA, PMP, PMO-CP
Vladimir Rasovic, PMP, PMO-CP
Claudia T. Rassalski, CA, PMP, PMO-CP
Betsy Redden, PMO-CP
Luis Antonio Guardado Rivera
Adeline Rodier
Alessandra Almeida Rodrigues
Eleftherios (Lefteris) Rousoudis, PMP, PMO-CP, PMO-CC
Ahmet Rumiye, PhD, PgMP, PfMP
Julio Cesar Samorini
Kelly Sandstrom, PMI-ACP, PMP, PMO-CP
Natalia Slynko, PMP, PMO-CP
Cristian Soto, MPM, PMP, PMO-CP
Kris Sprague, MBA, PMO-CP, PfMP
Sheldon St. Clair, PhD, FRSA, PMO-CP
Abdurrahman Syahrawi, PhD, PMO-CP, PMO-CC
Fuad Tahhan
Rogerio Tamassia
Regis Mattos Teixeira, MSc
Rodrigo Thahira, PMP, PMO-CP, PfMP
Sofia Tissera, PMP, PMO-CP, PMI-CP
Meiko Tourista, EPC, Prosci CCP, PMO-CP
Żydra Tubelytė, PMP, PMO-CP, PMO-CC
Bharatkumar Unercat, PMO-CP, PgMP, PfMP
Kidian Germán Chavarría Velásquez, PMI-ACP, PMP, PMO-CC

Michelle Venezia, PMI-ACP, PMP, PfMP
Eddy Vertil, PhD, PMP, PMO-CP
Ana Victoria Villalta, Mgt.
Ievgen Vyshnevetskyi, PMP, PMO-CP
Kelvin Wan, PhD, PMP, PMO-CP
Leonardo Boles Wanderkoke
Jack Wu, RSM, PMI-ACP, PMP
Abdalla Yassin, MBA, PMP, PMO-CC
Krzysztof Zaborowski, PMP, PgMP, PfMP
Daniel Zitter, BSc, PMP
Joseane de Fatima Zoghbi
Humberto Zuleta

Appendix X2
PMO Customer Expectation Assessment

Building on the customer-centric approach, this section presents a powerful resource for PMO professionals: a curated list of 30 potential PMO outcomes. This comprehensive list has emerged from extensive research within the global PMO community, encompassing PMOs from diverse regions and industries. The insights gathered represent a broad spectrum of experiences, challenges, and good practices observed across various organizational contexts.

The outcomes listed have been distilled from interactions with PMO leaders, project managers, and stakeholders from multinational corporations, government agencies, nonprofit organizations, and small- to medium-sized enterprises. This diverse sample ensures that the list captures a wide range of potential needs and pain points that PMOs might encounter, regardless of their specific industry or geographical location.

Each outcome in the list is meticulously structured to provide maximum utility:

- The "evidence of need" highlights signs or symptoms suggesting a customer may grapple with challenges in a specific area. This information empowers PMO professionals to identify potential pain points proactively.
- The "how to question the customer" section provides thoughtfully designed questions that serve as conversation starters. These questions enable PMO professionals to delve deeper into the customers' needs, challenges, and expectations.
- The "recommended services" section is derived from a comprehensive analysis of the most common PMO services implemented globally. This analysis draws upon the collective experiences and insights of the diverse, international PMO community.

This comprehensive list of potential outcomes serves as a versatile tool for PMO professionals. The list offers a structured approach to needs assessment, ensuring no critical areas are overlooked. This approach aids in prioritizing PMO services based on the most urgent customer needs and helps align PMO services with specific outcomes.

By understanding which services have the greatest potential to generate the desired outcome, PMOs can make informed decisions about where to focus their resources and efforts. This targeted approach allows for more efficient and effective PMO operations, ensuring that the services implemented are those most likely to address the customers' most pressing needs and deliver tangible value.

Moreover, this alignment between outcomes and services facilitates a more strategic approach to PMO design and operation. This approach enables PMOs to build a service portfolio that is directly tied to organizational needs and expected outcomes rather than implementing services based on generic PMO models or assumptions.

The inclusion of recommended services transforms this list from a diagnostic tool into a comprehensive guide for PMO development and optimization. The recommended services bridge the gap between identifying needs and implementing solutions, providing PMO professionals with a roadmap for creating high-impact, customer-centric PMO operations tailored to their unique organizational contexts.

The assessment includes 30 outcomes, all carefully structured to offer maximum utility when interviewing or surveying PMO customers to identify their top priorities and needs.

1. **Better Availability of Skilled Resources**

   - **Evidence of need**: Difficulty finding and retaining skilled program or project management resources.
   - **How to question the customer**:

     a) How challenging is it for your organization to find and retain skilled program and project managers?

     b) Do you often experience issues in projects due to a lack of experienced project management personnel?

     c) How satisfied are you with the current skill level of your program and project management teams?

   - **Most recommended services:**
     - **Service 10—Resource management.** Effective resource management ensures optimal allocation of skilled personnel across projects, maximizing their availability and utilization while identifying skill gaps for targeted development.
     - **Service 12—Training and development.** By offering comprehensive training programs, the PMO directly enhances the skills of existing program and project managers and team members, creating a larger pool of skilled resources within the organization.
     - **Service 18—Mentoring and coaching.** One-on-one mentoring and coaching programs help develop and refine the skills of program and project managers and team members, creating a more skilled workforce over time.

2. **Better Organizational Change Management**
   - **Evidence of need:** Resistance to change, disrupted processes, and reduced efficiency during transitions.
   - **How to question the customer:**

     a) How smoothly does your organization typically handle major organizational changes in processes or systems?

     b) To what extent do you experience resistance to change among your employees during new initiatives?

     c) How would you rate your organization's current change management practices in terms of effectiveness?
   - **Most recommended services:**
     - **Service 3—Foster project culture.** Promoting a project-centric culture enhances overall adaptability to change, making the organization more receptive to new practices and transitions.
     - **Service 5—Organizational change management.** This service directly addresses the need by implementing structured change management practices, ensuring smooth transitions and minimizing disruptions across programs and projects.
     - **Service 26—Stakeholder engagement.** Effective stakeholder engagement is crucial for successful organizational change, ensuring buy-in and support from all affected parties throughout the transition process.
3. **Better Control Over Project Teams**
   - **Evidence of need:** Lack of accountability, unclear reporting lines, and difficulty managing project teams.
   - **How to question the customer:**

     a) How clear are the reporting structures within your project teams?

     b) Do you face challenges in holding team members accountable for their responsibilities?

     c) How would you describe the overall effectiveness of your project team management?
   - **Most recommended services:**
     - **Service 9—Methodologies and frameworks management.** Implementing standardized methodologies provides a consistent structure for team management, enhancing control and accountability across all projects.
     - **Service 10—Resource management.** Efficient resource management ensures teams are correctly staffed and resources are allocated based on skills and availability. This improves workflows and communication, leading to better control over project teams, smoother project execution, and effective goal attainment.

- **Service 19—Performance management.** Regular monitoring and managing of project performance helps maintain control over teams by setting clear expectations and tracking progress against objectives.
- **Service 21—Project management.** By providing project managers, the PMO establishes clear reporting structures and accountability measures, directly contributing to better control over project teams.

4. **Better Definition of Roles and Responsibilities**

- **Evidence of need:** Confusion, overlapping responsibilities, and inefficiencies within project teams.
- **How to question the customer:**

a) How often do you encounter confusion or overlapping responsibilities within your project teams?

b) To what extent do project team members clearly understand their roles and contributions to projects?

c) How would you rate the efficiency of your project teams in terms of task allocation and execution?

- **Most recommended services:**
  - **Service 4—Governance oversight.** Establishing governance frameworks includes defining roles and responsibilities at various levels, ensuring clarity in decision-making and accountability throughout the organization.
  - **Service 9—Methodologies and frameworks management.** Standardized methodologies typically include clear definitions of roles and responsibilities, providing a consistent structure across projects and ensuring team members understand their duties.

5. **Better Project Prioritization**

- **Evidence of need:** Misallocated resources, conflicting priorities, and inability to focus on high-impact projects.
- **How to question the customer:**

a) How confident are you in your organization's ability to focus on the most strategically important projects?

b) Do you often find resources being misallocated or spread too thin across multiple projects?

c) How effectively does your organization balance and manage competing project priorities?

- **Most recommended services:**
  - **Service 1—Advice to executive level.** Strategic guidance to executives helps align project prioritization with organizational goals, ensuring high-level support for prioritization decisions.
  - **Service 2—Benefits realization management.** This service helps to prioritize projects by assessing their potential to deliver benefits. By monitoring outcomes, benefits realization management allows organizations to prioritize the projects that align with strategic goals and deliver proven value, ensuring efficient resource allocation and portfolio success.
  - **Service 6—Portfolio management.** Portfolio management directly addresses project prioritization, ensuring projects are selected and prioritized based on their strategic value and impact on the organization.
  - **Service 7—Strategic planning support.** This service ensures that project prioritization is aligned with long-term organizational goals, supporting more effective resource allocation and strategic focus.

6. **Better Quality of Project Results**
   - **Evidence of need:** Substandard deliverables, dissatisfied stakeholders, and negative impacts on the organization's reputation.
   - **How to question the customer:**
     a) How satisfied are your stakeholders typically with the quality of project deliverables?
     b) Have you experienced any negative impacts on your organization's reputation due to substandard project results?
     c) How consistently do your projects meet or exceed quality expectations?
   - **Most recommended services:**
     - **Service 9—Methodologies and frameworks management.** Standardized methodologies often include good practices for quality management, ensuring consistency in approach across projects and improving overall quality.
     - **Service 13—Audit assessments.** This service contributes to a better quality of project results by conducting thorough audits and assessments. These evaluations ensure compliance with standards, identify potential issues early, and recommend targeted improvements.
     - **Service 19—Performance management.** Regular monitoring and management of project performance helps identify and address quality issues early, leading to better final results.

- **Service 23—Quality assurance.** This service directly focuses on ensuring project deliverables meet defined quality standards through systematic processes, directly contributing to higher-quality project results.
- **Service 25—Specialized services.** The PMO can provide expert knowledge in specific areas, leading to higher-quality outcomes in complex or specific projects.

7. **Better Talent Management**

- **Evidence of need:** High turnover rates and difficulty in attracting and retaining skilled project managers.
- **How to question the customer:**
  a) What challenges do you face in attracting and retaining skilled project managers?
  b) How would you rate your organization's ability to internally develop and grow project management talent?
  c) What is your current turnover rate for project management practitioners and how does it impact your operations?
- **Most recommended services:**
  - **Service 10—Resource management.** Effective resource management includes strategies for attracting and retaining talent, ensuring optimal allocation of skilled personnel across projects.
  - **Service 12—Training and development.** This service directly contributes to developing top talent by offering programs to enhance skills and competencies in portfolio, program, and project management.
  - **Service 18—Mentoring and coaching.** Providing mentoring and coaching helps develop and retain talent by offering personalized guidance and support to project managers and team members.

8. **Effective Knowledge Transfer**

- **Evidence of need:** Inconsistent practices, loss of knowledge when employees leave, and lack of shared expertise.
- **How to question the customer:**
  a) How effectively does your organization capture and share project management good practices?
  b) To what extent do you experience loss of critical knowledge when key employees leave?
  c) How consistent are project management practices across different teams or departments in your organization?

- **Most recommended services:**
  - **Service 8—Knowledge management.** Enables effective knowledge transfer by establishing systematic processes for capturing, organizing, and sharing project insights and good practices. This service ensures that valuable experience and expertise are readily accessible across the organization, promoting continuous learning, preventing repeated mistakes, and enhancing overall project performance through improved decision-making and execution.
  - **Service 9—Methodologies and frameworks management.** Standardized methodologies act as repositories of organizational knowledge, ensuring good practices are documented and consistently applied across projects.
  - **Service 12—Training and development.** Training programs serve as a structured method for transferring knowledge and good practices across the organization, ensuring consistency in project management approaches.
  - **Service 18—Mentoring and coaching.** One-on-one mentoring facilitates direct knowledge transfer from experienced professionals to less experienced team members, preserving and spreading expertise within the organization.

9. **Enhanced Decision-Making**

- **Evidence of need:** Difficulty making informed decisions due to a lack of accurate and up-to-date project data.
- **How to question the customer:**
  a) How timely and accurate is the project data available to decision-makers in your organization?
  b) Do you often face challenges in making informed decisions due to lack of up-to-date project information?
  c) How confident are you in the quality of data used to support project-related decision-making?
- **Most recommended services:**
  - **Service 1—Advice to executive level.** Strategic guidance to executives ensures high-level decisions are aligned with organizational goals and based on comprehensive portfolio and project information.
  - **Service 4—Governance oversight.** Established governance frameworks provide clear decision-making processes and accountability, enhancing the quality and consistency of decisions across programs and projects.

- **Service 7—Strategic planning support.** Providing support for strategic planning ensures that decisions are data driven and aligned with the organization's long-term goals. This service enables leaders to make informed, well-considered decisions.
- **Service 16—Data analytics and reporting.** This service provides accurate, timely data and insights to support informed decision-making, enabling project managers and executives to make better choices based on real-time information.

10. Enhanced Project Customer Experience

- **Evidence of need:** Low customer satisfaction due to poor project delivery and unmet expectations.
- **How to question the customer:**
  a) How consistently do your projects meet or exceed customer expectations?
  b) What level of customer satisfaction do you typically achieve with your project deliveries?
  c) Have you experienced any loss of business or loyalty due to poor project delivery or unmet customer expectations?
- **Most recommended services:**
  - **Service 15—Customer relationship management.** This service directly focuses on maintaining and enhancing relationships with project customers, ensuring their needs and expectations are met throughout the project life cycle.
  - **Service 17—Issue management.** This service contributes to an enhanced project customer experience by promptly identifying, addressing, and resolving issues that could impact customer satisfaction. This proactive approach minimizes disruptions, maintains project quality, and demonstrates responsiveness to customer needs.
  - **Service 23—Quality assurance.** Ensuring project deliverables meet defined quality standards directly contributes to meeting or exceeding customer expectations, enhancing their overall experience.
  - **Service 26—Stakeholder engagement.** Effective stakeholder engagement ensures customer expectations are well understood and managed, leading to higher satisfaction with project outcomes.

11. Enhanced Resource Management

- **Evidence of need:** Inefficient resource allocation, underutilized or overburdened resources, and project bottlenecks.
- **How to question the customer:**
  a) How efficiently does your organization allocate resources across projects?
  b) Do you often experience bottlenecks or delays due to resource constraints?
  c) How well balanced is the workload among your project team members?

- **Most recommended services:**
  - **Service 6—Portfolio management.** This service helps to strategically allocate resources across multiple projects, ensuring alignment with organizational priorities and optimal use of available resources.
  - **Service 10—Resource management.** This service directly addresses optimizing resource allocation across projects, ensuring adequate staffing and support while minimizing conflicts and maximizing utilization.
  - **Service 14—Change control management.** By efficiently managing changes to project scope and objectives, change control management ensures that resources are allocated optimally, avoiding overuse or underuse.
  - **Service 19—Performance management.** Monitoring project performance helps to identify resource-related issues early, allowing for timely adjustments to resource allocation and utilization.

12. **Greater Alignment With Strategic Objectives**

- **Evidence of need:** Projects not contributing to organizational goals, misaligned priorities, and wasted investments.
- **How to question the customer:**

  a) How confident are you that all of your projects directly contribute to your organization's strategic goals?

  b) Have you experienced instances where completed projects did not deliver the expected strategic value?

  c) How effectively does your organization prioritize projects based on their alignment with strategic objectives?
- **Most recommended services:**
  - **Service 1—Advice to executive level.** Providing strategic guidance to senior executives helps to ensure that portfolio and project decisions are consistently aligned with overarching organizational goals.
  - **Service 2—Benefits realization management.** By measuring and managing project benefits, the PMO ensures that outcomes align with strategic goals. This service tracks alignment throughout the project, allowing for adjustments as needed to maintain focus on broader organizational priorities.
  - **Service 4—Governance oversight.** This service enhances alignment with strategic objectives by establishing and maintaining governance frameworks that link project activities to organizational goals.

- **Service 6—Portfolio management.** Portfolio management oversees the selection and prioritization of projects to ensure they align with strategic objectives and deliver optimal value to the organization.
- **Service 7—Strategic planning support.** This service directly ensures that programs and projects align with long-term organizational goals, maximizing their strategic impact and value.

13. Greater Integration Among Organizational Areas

- **Evidence of need:** Lack of cross-functional collaboration, disjointed project execution, and failure to leverage organizational capabilities.
- **How to question the customer:**
  a) How would you rate the level of collaboration among different departments on project work?
  b) Do you face challenges in leveraging diverse organizational capabilities in your projects?
  c) How often do you experience issues due to a lack of integration among different organizational areas?
- **Most recommended services:**
  - **Service 3—Foster project culture.** Promoting a project-centric culture across the organization enhances collaboration and integration among different departments, fostering a unified approach to project execution.
  - **Service 11—Systems and tools management.** This service provides common platforms and tools that facilitate collaboration and information sharing across different parts of the organization.
  - **Service 26—Stakeholder engagement.** Effective stakeholder engagement ensures collaboration and support across various departments and levels of the organization, promoting integration in project execution.

14. Higher Return on Investment (ROI)

- **Evidence of need:** Low program or project ROI, inability to demonstrate the value of programs or projects, and a lack of business growth.
- **How to question the customer:**
  a) How satisfied are you with the overall ROI of your organization's project portfolio?
  b) Do you face challenges in demonstrating the value of completed projects to stakeholders?
  c) How effectively does your organization track and measure the business benefits of projects?

- **Most recommended services:**
  - **Service 2—Benefits realization management.** This service directly focuses on managing and measuring the realization of benefits from programs and projects, ensuring they deliver expected value and maximize ROI.
  - **Service 6—Portfolio management.** Effective portfolio management ensures the selection and prioritization of projects with the highest potential ROI, optimizing overall investment returns for the organization.
  - **Service 19—Performance management.** Monitoring and managing project performance helps to identify and address issues that could impact ROI, ensuring projects stay on track to deliver maximum value.
  - **Service 20—Program management.** By providing program managers, the PMO can coordinate interrelated projects, optimize resources and benefits across initiatives, and potentially increase overall ROI.

15. **Improved Availability of Information**
    - **Evidence of need:** Limited access to project information, leading to uninformed or delayed decisions.
    - **How to question the customer:**
      a) How timely is project information for decision-makers in your organization?
      b) How often do you face situations where critical project data is not readily available when required?
      c) How quickly can decision-makers in your organization access the project information they need?
    - **Most recommended services:**
      - **Service 11—Systems and tools management.** Managing and maintaining effective project management systems ensures that information is consistently captured, stored, and made readily accessible to stakeholders.
      - **Service 16—Data analytics and reporting.** This service directly addresses needs by providing timely, accurate data and insights on project performance, supporting informed decision-making across the organization.
      - **Service 22—Project support services.** Providing administrative support for documentation and coordination helps ensure that project information is consistently recorded and available when needed.

16. **Improved Collaboration and Communication**
    - **Evidence of need:** Miscommunication, lack of transparency, and poor collaboration among team members and stakeholders.

- **How to question the customer:**
  a) How would you rate the overall effectiveness of communication within your project teams?
  b) Do you often encounter misalignments or misunderstandings among team members or stakeholders?
  c) How satisfied are you with the current tools and processes for project-related communication?
- **Most recommended services:**
  - **Service 3—Foster project culture.** Promoting a project-centric culture enhances overall communication and collaboration within the organization, creating an environment where information sharing is valued and practiced.
  - **Service 11—Systems and tools management.** Implementing and managing collaborative tools and systems facilitates better communication and information sharing among team members and stakeholders across projects.
  - **Service 26—Stakeholder engagement.** Effective stakeholder engagement ensures clear communication channels and fosters collaboration among all project participants, keeping everyone aligned and informed.

17. Improved Organizational Commitment to Results

- **Evidence of need:** Lack of focus on project outcomes, insufficient accountability, and weak performance culture.
- **How to question the customer:**
  a) How would you describe the level of accountability for project outcomes in your organization?
  b) Do you face challenges in maintaining focus on achieving project results?
  c) How strong is the performance culture within your project teams?
- **Most recommended services:**
  - **Service 1—Advice to executive level.** Strategic guidance to executives helps ensure a top-down commitment to results, setting the tone for the entire organization and aligning project outcomes with strategic objectives.
  - **Service 2—Benefits realization management.** This service helps to maintain organizational commitment to tangible results by focusing on the actual benefits delivered by programs and projects.
  - **Service 3—Foster project culture.** This service directly contributes to cultivating a culture of accountability and results across the organization, aligning project outcomes with organizational goals.

- **Service 6—Portfolio management.** This service ensures that projects are selected and prioritized based on their potential to deliver results aligned with organizational strategy, reinforcing the commitment to outcomes.
- **Service 19—Performance management.** Regular monitoring and management of project performance reinforces the focus on achieving results and helps to maintain accountability throughout the project life cycle.

18. **Improved Project Budget Management**

- **Evidence of need:** Frequent budget overruns and financial inefficiencies in project execution.
- **How to question the customer:**
  a) How often do your projects experience budget overruns?
  b) How satisfied are you with the current financial oversight of your projects?
  c) Do you have clear visibility into project spending and budget utilization?
- **Most recommended services:**
  - **Service 14—Change control management.** Managing changes effectively helps to control scope creep and unexpected costs, which are often major factors in budget overruns.
  - **Service 16—Data analytics and reporting.** Providing accurate financial data and analysis helps project managers and stakeholders to make informed decisions about budget allocation and control throughout the project life cycle.
  - **Service 17—Issue management.** Unresolved issues cause many budget overruns; effective issue management can help control costs.
  - **Service 19—Performance management.** By consistently tracking project objectives against performance metrics, any cost or resource inefficiencies can be identified early. This tracking helps to keep expenditures in check and prevents budget overruns, leading to improved project budget management through proactive adjustments.
  - **Service 21—Project management.** By providing project managers, the PMO can implement robust budget control and financial oversight, ensuring projects stay within financial constraints.
  - **Service 22—Project support services.** Support services often assist in tracking expenses and preparing budget reports, contributing to better budget management.
  - **Service 25—Specialized services.** This service enhances project budget management by providing highly specialized expertise in budget development and control. The PMO offers dedicated professionals with advanced skills in financial planning, cost estimation, and budget tracking specific to project environments.

19. **Improved Project Customer Relationships**

- **Evidence of need:** Strained customer relationships due to unmet expectations and poor communication.
- **How to question the customer:**
  a) How would you rate your organization's relationships with project customers?
  b) Do you often receive feedback about unmet expectations from project customers?
  c) How effectively does your team communicate with project customers throughout the project life cycle?
- **Most recommended services:**
  - **Service 15—Customer relationship management.** This service directly focuses on maintaining and enhancing relationships with project customers, ensuring their needs are met and expectations are managed throughout the project life cycle.
  - **Service 17—Issue management.** Quickly resolving issues fosters trust and transparency with project customers. By addressing concerns promptly and keeping customers informed, the PMO strengthens and improves the project customer relationship, ensuring a responsive and collaborative project experience.
  - **Service 19—Performance management.** Monitoring project performance against project customer expectations helps to ensure that projects stay on track to meet or exceed customer requirements, leading to improved relationships.
  - **Service 26—Stakeholder engagement.** Effective stakeholder engagement includes strategies for engaging and communicating with project customers, helping to build and maintain strong relationships.

20. **Improved Performance Management**

- **Evidence of need:** Lack of performance tracking leading to unnoticed issues and suboptimal program and project outcomes.
- **How to question the customer:**
  a) How effectively does your organization track and monitor program and project performance?
  b) Do you often encounter unexpected issues that could have been identified earlier with better performance tracking?
  c) How satisfied are you with your current ability to ensure successful program and project delivery?

- **Most recommended services:**
  - **Service 13—Audit assessments.** Thorough audits help to identify performance issues and areas for improvement, contributing to better performance management overall.
  - **Service 16—Data analytics and reporting.** Providing data analytics and reporting services supports performance management by offering insights into project trends and enabling the early identification of issues.
  - **Service 17—Issue management.** Tracking and resolving issues is a key aspect of managing overall project performance.
  - **Service 19—Performance management.** This service directly addresses the need for improved performance management by monitoring and managing the performance of programs and projects, ensuring that they meet objectives and deliver expected outputs and outcomes.
  - **Service 20—Program management.** This service enhances performance management by providing experienced program managers through the PMO. These professionals oversee multiple related projects, implementing comprehensive performance-monitoring systems across the program. The program managers coordinate cross-project dependencies, optimize resource allocation, and ensure alignment with strategic goals, leading to improved overall performance tracking and management at both the program and project levels.
  - **Service 21—Project management.** This service enhances performance management by providing skilled project managers through the PMO. These professionals apply good practices, implement effective performance-tracking systems, conduct regular reviews, and take proactive measures to address issues, ensuring that projects consistently meet or exceed performance targets and organizational objectives.
  - **Service 22—Project support services.** By handling project management tasks to assist project managers, support services contribute to more effective performance management.

21. **Improved Success Rates**

- **Evidence of need:** Frequent program and project failures, delays, missed deadlines, and budget overruns.
- **How to question the customer:**

  a) How often do your programs and projects meet their time, budget, and objective targets?

  b) What percentage of your projects would you consider successful?

  c) How significantly do project delays or failures impact your organization's overall success?

- **Most recommended services:**
  - **Service 5—Organizational change management.** Managing changes ensures that projects integrate smoothly into the business, reducing resistance and disruptions. Aligning project outcomes with organizational objectives encourages quicker adoption and smoother transitions.
  - **Service 8—Knowledge management.** By capturing and sharing good practices and lessons learned, teams can apply proven strategies and avoid repeating mistakes. This knowledge sharing leads to more efficient project execution and improved success rates as teams make better-informed decisions, reducing errors and increasing project success.
  - **Service 9—Methodologies and frameworks management.** Implementing standardized methodologies helps to ensure consistency in project execution, leading to higher success rates across multiple programs and projects.
  - **Service 14—Change control management.** Change control management ensures that all changes are carefully reviewed and approved, avoiding unnecessary scope creep or disruptions that could derail the project. This disciplined approach to managing alterations helps in maintaining project stability and alignment with objectives, thus contributing to improved success rates.
  - **Service 17—Issue management.** Proactive issue management helps to prevent small problems from becoming major obstacles to project success.
  - **Service 20—Program management.** This service contributes to improved success rates by providing experienced program managers through the PMO. These professionals coordinate and oversee multiple related projects, ensuring strategic alignment and efficient resource allocation across the program. By managing interdependencies, mitigating risks at a higher level, and leveraging synergies among projects, program managers significantly enhance the likelihood of successful outcomes for both individual projects and the overall program objectives.
  - **Service 21—Project management.** This service enhances project success rates by providing skilled project managers through the PMO. By applying good practices, PMO-provided project managers significantly increase the likelihood of projects meeting their objectives.
  - **Service 24—Risk management.** Identifying, assessing, and managing risks throughout the project life cycle helps to mitigate potential issues that could derail project success, improving overall success rates.
  - **Service 25—Specialized services.** For projects requiring specific expertise, the PMO's specialized services can significantly improve the likelihood of success.

22. Improved Reliability of Information Provided

- **Evidence of need:** Inaccurate, outdated, or inconsistent project data, leading to poor decision-making.

- **How to question the customer:**
  a) How confident are you in the accuracy and timeliness of your project information?
  b) How often do you encounter decision-making challenges due to unreliable or outdated project data?
  c) What impact does the quality of project information have on your organization's decision-making processes?
- **Most recommended services:**
  - **Service 11—Systems and tools management.** Implementing and maintaining robust project management systems helps to ensure consistent capture and storage of reliable information across all projects.
  - **Service 16—Data analytics and reporting.** This service focuses on providing accurate, timely data and analysis, ensuring that project information is reliable and current to support informed decision-making.
  - **Service 23—Quality assurance.** Applying quality assurance processes to information management helps to maintain high standards of accuracy and reliability in project data and reporting.

23. Improved Stakeholder Engagement

- **Evidence of need:** Disconnected stakeholders, lack of buy-in, and misaligned program or project expectations.
- **How to question the customer:**
  a) How effectively does your organization engage stakeholders throughout the program or project life cycle?
  b) Do you often face challenges with stakeholder buy-in or misaligned expectations?
  c) How would you rate your current stakeholder engagement practices?
- **Most recommended services:**
  - **Service 5—Organizational change management.** Managing the impact of organizational changes helps to engage stakeholders affected by projects, ensure their concerns are addressed, and manage expectations during transitions.
  - **Service 15—Customer relationship management.** While primarily focused on project customers, this service also contributes to overall stakeholder engagement by maintaining and enhancing relationships with key project participants.
  - **Service 26—Stakeholder engagement.** This service directly focuses on identifying and managing stakeholder expectations and engagement, ensuring their support and involvement throughout the project life cycle.

24. **Increased Organizational Learning**

- **Evidence of need:** Repeated mistakes and inability to leverage past successes due to poor knowledge management.
- **How to question the customer:**

  a) How effectively does your organization capture and apply lessons learned from past projects?

  b) Do you often see the same mistakes being repeated across different projects?

  c) How would you describe your organization's culture of continuous improvement in project management?

- **Most recommended services:**
  - **Service 8—Knowledge management.** This service significantly contributes to increased organizational learning by systematically capturing, organizing, and sharing experiences and good practices. Knowledge sharing enables the organization to build on past successes, ultimately enhancing overall project performance and organizational capability.
  - **Service 12—Training and development.** This service directly contributes to organizational learning by offering programs to enhance skills and knowledge, as well as helping to incorporate lessons learned from past projects into training materials.
  - **Service 13—Audit assessments.** Conducting thorough audits of projects helps to identify lessons learned and areas for improvement, contributing to organizational learning and continuous improvement.
  - **Service 18—Mentoring and coaching.** One-on-one mentoring and coaching can facilitate the transfer of knowledge and lessons learned from experienced professionals to others in the organization.

25. **Increased Productivity on Projects**

- **Evidence of need:** Low team performance, inefficient processes, and suboptimal project outcomes.
- **How to question the customer:**

  a) How would you rate the overall productivity and efficiency of your project teams?

  b) What are the main factors affecting your project team's performance?

  c) How effectively are you implementing good practices and tools to boost project productivity?

- **Most recommended services:**
  - **Service 9—Methodologies and frameworks management.** Implementing standardized methodologies and frameworks provides project teams with proven, efficient processes, directly contributing to increased productivity across projects.
  - **Service 10—Resource management.** Optimal allocation and management of resources can ensure that project teams are well staffed and supported, leading to increased productivity and efficiency.
  - **Service 11—Systems and tools management.** Providing and maintaining effective project management tools can significantly boost team productivity by streamlining tasks, communication, and information sharing.
  - **Service 22—Project support services.** By handling administrative and logistical tasks, support services can allow project team members to focus on their core responsibilities, increasing overall productivity.
  - **Service 25—Specialized services.** The PMO offers expert professionals who excel in specific aspects of project management, thereby enhancing productivity by performing specialized activities for the project manager.

26. Increased Visibility of Project Progress

- **Evidence of need:** Limited insight into project status, leading to uninformed decision-making and potential project delays.
- **How to question the customer:**
  a) How clear and regular are your projects' progress updates to stakeholders?
  b) Do you often encounter situations where stakeholders are not aligned due to a lack of project visibility?
  c) How satisfied are you with your current projects' progress-reporting mechanisms?
- **Most recommended services:**
  - **Service 11—Systems and tools management.** Implementing and maintaining project management systems with robust reporting capabilities enhances visibility into project progress across the organization.
  - **Service 16—Data analytics and reporting.** This service directly addresses the need for visibility by providing regular, clear updates on project progress through data-driven reports and analytics, ensuring all stakeholders are well informed.
  - **Service 26—Stakeholder engagement.** This service ensures that project progress is effectively communicated to all relevant stakeholders, increasing overall visibility.

27. **More Accurate Project Forecasting**

- **Evidence of need:** Inaccurate project forecasts, leading to budget overruns and missed deadlines.
- **How to question the customer:**
  a) How often do your project forecasts align with actual outcomes?
  b) What impact do inaccurate forecasts have on your project budgets and timelines?
  c) How confident are you in your current project forecasting methodologies?
- **Most recommended services:**
  - **Service 9—Methodologies and frameworks management.** Implementing standardized methodologies often includes good practices for project estimation and forecasting, leading to more consistent and accurate predictions across projects.
  - **Service 16—Data analytics and reporting.** This service provides accurate, data-driven insights that form the basis for reliable project forecasting, enabling better planning and decision-making based on historical and current project data.
  - **Service 22—Project support services.** By maintaining accurate project records and assisting in data collection, support services can contribute to more accurate project forecasting.
  - **Service 24—Risk management.** Effective risk management contributes to more accurate forecasting by identifying and quantifying potential issues that could impact project timelines and outcomes.
  - **Service 25—Specialized services.** This service enhances project-forecasting accuracy by providing expert resources with advanced skills in predictive analytics and forecasting techniques specific to project management. The PMO offers specialized professionals who bring an in-depth knowledge of statistical modeling, trend analysis, and industry-specific forecasting methodologies.

28. **Reduction of Risk Exposure**

- **Evidence of need:** High uncertainty levels and unexpected setbacks negatively impact project outcomes.
- **How to question the customer:**
  a) How comprehensive is your current risk management strategy?
  b) How often do unexpected setbacks significantly impact your project outcomes?
  c) How confident are you in your organization's ability to identify, assess, and mitigate project risks?

- **Most recommended services:**
  - **Service 4—Governance oversight.** Establishing and maintaining governance frameworks ensures that risk management processes are consistently applied across projects, reducing overall organizational risk exposure.
  - **Service 13—Audit assessments.** Conducting thorough audits helps to identify potential risks and areas of vulnerability, contributing to more effective risk mitigation strategies.
  - **Service 17—Issue management.** Many issues, if left unmanaged, can evolve into significant risks. Effective issue management is a key part of risk reduction.
  - **Service 24—Risk management.** This service directly addresses the need to reduce risk exposure by identifying, assessing, and managing risks throughout the project life cycle, implementing comprehensive strategies to mitigate potential issues.

29. Stronger Governance and Compliance

- **Evidence of need:** Noncompliance with industry regulations or organizational policies, leading to penalties or reputational damage.
- **How to question the customer:**

  a) How well does your organization adhere to relevant regulations and policies in portfolio, program, and project management?

  b) Have you experienced any compliance-related issues or penalties in recent projects?

  c) How confident are you in your current governance frameworks?

- **Most recommended services:**
  - **Service 4—Governance oversight.** This service directly addresses the need for stronger governance by establishing and maintaining governance frameworks and ensuring programs and projects are managed in accordance with organizational policies and relevant regulations.
  - **Service 9—Methodologies and frameworks management.** Implementing standardized methodologies often includes governance and compliance elements, ensuring consistent application of good practices across all projects.
  - **Service 13—Audit assessments.** Conducting regular audits helps to identify compliance issues and areas for improvement in governance practices, contributing to stronger overall governance.
  - **Service 14—Change control management.** This service adds a layer of structured oversight to any project. Every proposed change should go through formal approval processes, which helps to ensure that governance policies and compliance standards are maintained. Change control minimizes the risk of unauthorized changes and can ensure adherence to organizational rules.

30. **Reduction of Project Life Cycle**

- **Evidence of need:** Prolonged project durations, delays in delivering results, and slow time-to-market releases.
- **How to question the customer:**
  a) How satisfied are you with the current durations of your project life cycles?
  b) What impact do the lengths of your project life cycles have on your organization's competitiveness?
  c) How effectively are you streamlining project processes to reduce time to market?
- **Most recommended services:**
  - **Service 9—Methodologies and frameworks management.** Implementing efficient, standardized methodologies can significantly streamline project processes, reduce unnecessary steps, and accelerate the overall project life cycle.
  - **Service 10—Resource management.** Optimal resource allocation and management can ensure that projects are adequately staffed at critical points, preventing delays and reducing the project life cycle.
  - **Service 14—Change control management.** By ensuring that changes are managed efficiently and unnecessary modifications are avoided, change control management prevents delays caused by mismanagement of project scope and focus. Change control helps to keep projects on track, resulting in a reduction of project life cycles by eliminating avoidable extensions and rework.
  - **Service 17—Issue management.** Quickly identifying and resolving issues can prevent delays and keep projects on schedule, potentially reducing overall project durations.
  - **Service 21—Project management.** This service contributes to reducing project life cycles by providing experienced project managers through the PMO. By leveraging their expertise in efficient project execution and continuous improvement, PMO-provided project managers may significantly decrease project durations.
  - **Service 22—Project support services.** Efficient project support can streamline administrative processes, potentially reducing overall project durations.
  - **Service 25—Specialized services.** This service contributes to reducing project life cycles by providing highly skilled experts in specific areas of project management and execution. This targeted expertise allows for faster problem-solving, more efficient resource utilization, and the ability to fast track critical project components without compromising quality or scope.

Appendix X3
PMO Service Maturity Assessment

The PMO service maturity assessment is designed to be a practical tool for assessing current capabilities, identifying areas for improvement, and guiding PMO development. Organizations can effectively use this model for:

1. **Assessment.** Begin by assessing the PMO's current service maturity level across each dimension. This assessment involves gathering data through surveys, interviews, and performance metrics to determine where the PMO stands in relation to the defined service maturity levels.
2. **Gap analysis.** Identify gaps between the current service maturity level and the desired level for each dimension. The desired level should be determined based on organizational needs and strategic objectives, recognizing that the highest maturity level may not always be necessary or appropriate for every dimension.
3. **Prioritization.** Based on the gap analysis, prioritize areas for improvement. Consider both the size of the gap and the potential impact on organizational performance when setting priorities.
4. **Action planning.** Develop detailed action plans for increasing service maturity levels in priority areas. These plans should include specific initiatives, resource requirements, timelines, and success metrics.
5. **Implementation.** Execute the action plans, ensuring proper change management practices are in place to support the transition.
6. **Monitoring and adjustment.** Regularly monitor progress and be prepared to adjust plans as needed. PMO service maturity development is an ongoing process, and flexibility is key to long-term success.
7. **Reassessment.** Periodically reassess the PMO's service maturity levels to track progress and identify new areas for improvement.

This comprehensive assessment outlines the 26 most common PMO services and their five levels of maturity. Each maturity level reflects increasing complexity, capability, and impacts on value generation for overall organizational success. Understanding these services and their progression helps PMO professionals to strategically enhance their PMOs, ensuring they deliver maximum value and align with evolving business objectives.

This assessment should be used as an instrument for applying Step 8 of the value-generating PMO flywheel, which is part of the PMO Value Ring™ framework. More details on this step can be found in Section 21 on service improvement.

To calculate the PMO service maturity, follow these steps:

1. **Identify the services.** List all of the strategic, tactical, and operational services provided by the PMO.
2. **Assign points.** Assign a maturity score based on predefined criteria for each service. The scoring system might range from 1 to 5, with 1 indicating low maturity and 5 indicating high maturity.
3. **Sum the scores.**
    - **Strategic services.** Add the points obtained for all of the strategic services.
    - **Tactical services.** Add the points obtained for all of the tactical services.
    - **Operational services.** Add the points obtained for all of the operational services.
4. **Calculate the total possible points.**
    - **Strategic services.** Multiply the number of strategic services by the highest possible score (i.e., 5).
    - **Tactical services.** Multiply the number of tactical services by the highest possible score.
    - **Operational services.** Multiply the number of operational services by the highest possible score.
5. **Compute the maturity percentages.**
    - **Strategic maturity percentage.** (Sum of strategic services points / total possible strategic points) × 100
    - **Tactical maturity percentage.** (Sum of tactical services points / total possible tactical points) × 100
    - **Operational maturity percentage.** (Sum of operational services points / total possible operational points) × 100

These percentages provide a clear view of the maturity levels across the strategic, tactical, and operational dimensions of the PMO, helping to identify areas for improvement.

PMO Service Maturity Assessment

Strategic Services

1. **Advice to Executive Level**

    - **Level 1—Reactive advisory.** Advice is provided only when explicitly requested by executives. It is often based on limited information and may not align consistently with organizational strategy. The PMO lacks a proactive approach and does not offer unsolicited insights, potentially missing opportunities to add value.
    - **Level 2—Structured consultation.** The PMO implements scheduled consultations with executives, providing more consistent advice. These sessions follow a basic structure but the advice may still lack depth or comprehensive data backing. While more regular, the advice might not fully integrate all aspects of portfolio, program, and project management.
    - **Level 3—Data-driven guidance.** The PMO leverages robust data analytics to provide insights. Advice becomes proactive based on trends identified in portfolio, program, and project performance data. There is a clear link between the advice given and organizational objectives, with recommendations supported by concrete evidence.
    - **Level 4—Strategic integration.** The PMO's advice becomes a key input in strategic decision-making. There is a bidirectional flow of information, with the PMO both informing and being informed by organizational strategy. Scenario planning and predictive analytics are used to provide forward-looking advice, enabling executives to make more informed decisions.
    - **Level 5—Transformational leadership.** The PMO is seen as a strategic partner, actively shaping organizational strategy through its advice. The guidance provided leads to transformational changes in how the organization approaches portfolios, programs, and projects. Advanced techniques like artificial intelligence and machine learning are used to provide predictive and prescriptive advice, positioning the PMO as an industry thought leader.

2. **Benefits Realization Management**

    - **Level 1—Ad hoc tracking.** The PMO identifies potential benefits for portfolios and programs, but there is no structured process for tracking or measuring them. Benefits realization is largely left to chance, with little to no follow-up work performed after project completion. The organization has limited visibility into whether expected benefits are actually realized.
    - **Level 2—Structured monitoring.** The PMO establishes a formal process for identifying and tracking benefits. There is a consistent approach to documenting expected benefits at the outset of programs and projects. Basic metrics are defined and monitored but the focus is primarily on tracking rather than active management. Some benefits may be measured after implementation but the process is not comprehensive.
    - **Level 3—Active management.** The PMO actively manages benefits throughout the life cycle of portfolios and programs. Regular benefits reviews are conducted, with clear processes for making adjustments to ensure benefits are realized. The PMO works closely with program and project managers to identify risks to benefits realization and develop mitigation strategies. There is a strong focus on accountability, with clear ownership assigned for each expected benefit.

- **Level 4—Integrated approach.** Benefits realization becomes a key factor in program and project selection, prioritization, and continuation decisions. The PMO provides regular benefits realization reports to senior management, which directly inform strategic planning. There is a sophisticated understanding of the interdependencies among different benefits across the portfolio. The organization has a clear view of how program and project benefits contribute to overall strategic objectives.
- **Level 5—Continuous optimization.** The PMO employs advanced analytics and artificial intelligence to forecast and optimize benefits realization. Sophisticated modeling techniques predict the likelihood of benefits realization and identify influencing factors. Complex scenarios are run to optimize the portfolio for maximum benefits realization. A culture of continuous learning exists, with insights from benefits realization feeding back into project selection and execution processes. The organization is recognized as a leader in benefits realization management.

3. **Foster Project Culture**

- **Level 1—Basic awareness.** The PMO introduces basic project management concepts to the organization. Outside of dedicated project teams, there is limited understanding of project management principles. Training and communication efforts are sporadic and lack a coherent strategy. The value of project management is not widely recognized across the organization.
- **Level 2—Structured education.** The PMO implements regular training sessions to improve project management skills across the organization. There is a structured curriculum covering key project management concepts. However, the focus is primarily on technical skills rather than fostering a broader project culture. Participation may be limited to those directly involved in projects.
- **Level 3—Embedded practices.** Project management principles are widely understood and applied across the organization beyond just project teams. The PMO promotes the use of project management tools and techniques in various business contexts. There is growing recognition of how project management contributes to organizational success. Cross-functional collaboration in project contexts becomes more common.
- **Level 4—Cultural alignment.** Project management is seen as a core competency and is factored into performance evaluations across the organization. The PMO works with human resources to integrate project management skills into job descriptions and career development paths. There is a strong emphasis on continuous improvement in project management practices. Leadership actively champions the project management culture.
- **Level 5—Innovative project culture.** Project management culture drives innovation and is a key differentiator for the organization. The PMO facilitates a culture of experimentation and learning from both successes and failures. Advanced project management practices are developed internally and are often shared with the wider industry. The organization attracts top talent due to its strong project management culture and is seen as a benchmark by others.

4. **Governance Oversight**

   - **Level 1—Basic rules.** The PMO introduces basic rules for project management but they are not consistently followed across the organization. Governance is largely reactive, addressing issues as they arise. There is limited understanding of governance's role in project success. Documentation of governance processes is minimal and not widely accessible.
   - **Level 2—Structured framework.** The PMO establishes clear governance structures that are generally adhered to across portfolios, programs, and projects. Roles and responsibilities within the governance framework are defined. Regular governance meetings are held but they may focus more on reporting than decision-making. There is improved documentation of governance processes but it may not cover all scenarios.
   - **Level 3—Active enforcement.** The PMO conducts regular audits to ensure compliance with governance standards. There are clear consequences for noncompliance, balanced with support for improvement. Governance processes are well documented and easily accessible. The PMO provides training on governance to ensure widespread understanding. Governance data is used to identify trends and areas for improvement.
   - **Level 4—Adaptive governance.** The PMO regularly reviews and updates the governance framework to reflect changing organizational needs and lessons learned. Governance processes are flexible enough to accommodate different types of programs and projects while maintaining consistency. There is a strong focus on governance as an enabler of project success, not just a control mechanism. Advanced tools are used to support governance processes and decision-making.
   - **Level 5—Value-driven governance.** Governance is seen as a value-adding activity, not just a control mechanism, and drives organizational performance. The PMO uses advanced analytics to demonstrate the link between strong governance and project success. Governance processes are highly efficient, minimizing bureaucracy while maximizing value. The organization's governance approach is recognized as good practice in the industry and is often benchmarked by others.

5. **Organizational Change Management**

   - **Level 1—Reactive approach.** The PMO responds to change impacts reactively, with no formal process in place. Change management is seen as a project-specific activity rather than a portfolio- or program-level concern. There is limited understanding of how changes in one area can impact others. Resistance to change is often high due to a lack of preparation.
   - **Level 2—Planned approach.** The PMO establishes a formal change management process for portfolios and programs. Changes are anticipated and planned for, but not consistently across all initiatives. Basic change-impact assessments are conducted. There is some stakeholder analysis and communication planning but it may not be comprehensive. Change readiness is assessed at a high level.

- **Level 3—Integrated management.** A comprehensive change management approach is consistently applied across all portfolios and programs. The PMO works closely with program and project managers to integrate change management into all plans. Detailed stakeholder analyses and tailored communication strategies are developed. Change readiness is thoroughly assessed and addressed. There is a focus on building change capability within the organization.
- **Level 4—Proactive enablement.** The PMO uses change management to proactively enable and accelerate organizational transformations. Advanced change-impact modeling is used to predict and mitigate potential issues. There is a strong focus on building organizational change resilience. Change management metrics are linked to portfolio and program success metrics. The PMO acts as a center of excellence for change management, providing guidance across the organization.
- **Level 5—Cultural embedding.** The organization is highly adaptable, with change management embedded in its culture. The PMO facilitates continuous change-readiness assessments and improvement initiatives. Advanced analytics and artificial intelligence are used to predict change impacts and optimize change strategies. The organization's approach to change is seen as a competitive advantage, allowing for rapid adaptation to market shifts. The PMO is recognized as an industry leader in organizational change management.

6. **Portfolio Management**
    - **Level 1—Basic project listing.** The PMO maintains a basic inventory of programs and projects. Selection and prioritization are ad hoc, with limited consideration of strategic alignment. Resource allocation is not optimized and portfolio performance is minimally monitored. The focus is on individual projects rather than the overall portfolio.
    - **Level 2—Structured selection and prioritization.** The PMO establishes project selection and prioritization criteria. There is a structured process for evaluating new project proposals. Basic portfolio monitoring is in place but it may not be comprehensive. Resource allocation is considered but not optimized across the portfolio. Strategic alignment is acknowledged but not consistently enforced.
    - **Level 3—Active portfolio management.** The PMO actively manages the portfolio, optimizing resource allocations on an ongoing basis. Regular portfolio reviews are conducted to assess performance and alignment. There is a clear process for adding, changing, or terminating projects based on portfolio performance. Strategic alignment is a key factor in decision-making. Basic portfolio analytics are used to inform decisions.
    - **Level 4—Strategic alignment and optimization.** The portfolio is a key tool for executing organizational strategy. Advanced portfolio analytics are used to optimize resource allocations and maximize strategic value. There is a sophisticated understanding of interdependencies among programs and projects. The PMO provides regular, insightful portfolio performance reports to senior management. Scenario planning is used to inform portfolio decisions.

- **Level 5—Dynamic portfolio optimization.** The portfolio is dynamically optimized using predictive models and scenario analysis. Artificial intelligence and machine learning are employed to forecast portfolio performance and recommend adjustments. The portfolio is highly responsive to changes in the business environment. The PMO's portfolio management approach is recognized as industry leading, often driving innovation in the field.

7. **Strategic Planning Support**

- **Level 1—Basic input provision.** The PMO's involvement in strategic planning is limited to providing basic project status information. There is little to no analysis of how projects contribute to strategic goals. The PMO is not actively involved in strategic discussions. The link between projects and strategy is not clearly articulated or understood.
- **Level 2—Structured contribution.** The PMO provides regular, structured inputs to the strategic planning process. There is a basic analysis of how programs and projects align with strategic objectives. The PMO participates in strategic planning meetings but primarily in a supporting role. Project proposals include basic information on strategic alignment.
- **Level 3—Active participation.** The PMO actively contributes to shaping strategic plans based on portfolio insights. There is a clear understanding of how programs and projects drive strategic outcomes. The PMO provides valuable data and analysis to inform strategic decisions. Strategic alignment is a key factor in project selection and prioritization.
- **Level 4—Strategic integration.** The PMO plays a key role in translating strategy into executable portfolio plans. There is a bidirectional flow of information between portfolio management and strategic planning. The PMO uses advanced analytics to model how different portfolio scenarios impact strategic outcomes. Senior management sees the PMO as a valuable strategic partner.
- **Level 5—Strategy cocreation.** The PMO is seen as a strategic partner, with portfolio insights driving strategic direction. The PMO uses advanced predictive analytics and scenario modeling to inform long-term strategy. There is a deep integration between strategic planning and portfolio management processes. The PMO's strategic planning support is recognized as a key competitive advantage for the organization.

Tactical Services

8. **Knowledge Management**

- **Level 1—Ad hoc documentation.** Knowledge capture is sporadic and unstructured. Lessons learned are sometimes documented at project closure but are rarely shared or used. There is no centralized repository for project knowledge. Knowledge transfer relies primarily on informal, person-to-person interactions.
- **Level 2—Basic knowledge repository.** The PMO establishes a central repository for project documents and lessons learned. There is a standard template for capturing project knowledge but usage is inconsistent. Some knowledge sharing occurs but it is not systematic. The focus is mainly on explicit knowledge, with little attention to tacit knowledge.

- **Level 3—Active knowledge sharing.** Regular knowledge-sharing sessions are implemented. The PMO facilitates cross-project learning through structured debriefs and case studies. A user-friendly knowledge base is maintained and actively used. There is growing recognition of the value of knowledge management in improving project outcomes.
- **Level 4—Integrated knowledge management.** Knowledge management is integrated into all phases of the program and project life cycles. The PMO implements advanced tools for knowledge capture, including AI-assisted systems. There is a strong culture of knowledge sharing, with incentives tied to contributions. Tacit knowledge transfer is facilitated through mentoring programs and communities of practice.
- **Level 5—Knowledge-driven organization.** Knowledge management becomes a key strategic asset and competitive advantage. The PMO leverages advanced analytics to derive insights from the knowledge base, informing strategic decision-making. Knowledge management is seamlessly integrated with innovation processes. The organization is recognized as a thought leader, often sharing insights with the wider industry. Continuous learning and adaptation based on accumulated knowledge are ingrained in the organizational culture.

9. **Methodologies and Frameworks**

- **Level 1—Basic guidelines.** The PMO provides basic project management guidelines but they are not comprehensive or consistently followed. Methodologies and frameworks are loosely defined and may vary across the organization. There is limited training or support for methodology implementation and documentation is minimal.

  Trigger: Basic project management guidelines are in place.
- **Level 2—Standardized methodology.** The PMO establishes a standardized methodology for project management. Basic templates and tools are provided. Some training on the methodology is provided but adoption may be inconsistent. The methodology is primarily focused on project-level processes, with limited consideration for portfolio or program management.
- **Level 3—Comprehensive framework.** The PMO implements a comprehensive framework that addresses portfolio, program, and project management. The methodology is well documented and supported by a full set of tools and templates. Regular training and support are provided. There is a process for methodology-compliance audits.
- **Level 4—Adaptive methodology.** The PMO's methodology is regularly updated based on lessons learned and emerging practices. The framework is flexible, allowing for tailoring to different project types and organizational needs. Advanced training programs, including certification paths, are in place.
- **Level 5—Innovative good practice.** The PMO's methodologies and frameworks are at the forefront of industry practices, often driving innovation in the field. The approach seamlessly integrates portfolio, program, and project management. Advanced technologies, including artificial intelligence, are incorporated into the methodology.

10. **Resource Management**

- **Level 1—Basic allocation.** The PMO provides basic support for resource allocation. There is limited visibility into resource availability and utilization across projects. Resource conflicts are addressed reactively. Resource planning is short term and often inaccurate. There is minimal consideration of skills matching in resource allocation.
- **Level 2—Centralized tracking.** The PMO establishes a centralized resource management system. There is improved visibility into resource availability and utilization. Basic resource forecasting is in place. Resource conflicts are identified earlier but are still managed reactively. Skills are considered in resource allocation.

  Trigger: A centralized system for resource tracking is implemented.
- **Level 3—Proactive management.** The PMO implements proactive resource management practices. Advanced resource forecasting and capacity planning are in place. There is effective management of resource conflicts across programs and projects. Skills matching is a key factor in resource allocation. Resource utilization is optimized at the portfolio level.
- **Level 4—Strategic alignment.** The PMO aligns resource management with organizational strategy. Sophisticated modeling optimizes resource allocation across the portfolio. There is a strong focus on developing and retaining key resources. Resource management decisions consider long-term strategic impacts. Advanced analytics predict and prevent resource bottlenecks.
- **Level 5—Dynamic optimization.** The PMO employs artificial intelligence and machine learning for dynamic resource optimization. Real-time adjustments are made to resource allocations based on changing project and organizational needs, and predictive modeling of future resource needs is used. The organization's approach to resource management is recognized as industry leading.

11. **System and Tools Management**

- **Level 1—Basic tool provision.** The PMO offers basic project management tools, often with minimal integration. Tool selection is ad hoc and may vary across projects. There is limited training or support for tool usage. System maintenance is reactive. The impact of tools on project performance is not systematically measured.
- **Level 2—Standardized tool set.** The PMO establishes a consistent tool set for portfolio, program, and project management. There is improved integration between tools. Basic training and support for tool usage are provided. Regular system maintenance is conducted. Some tracking of tool utilization and impact begins.
- **Level 3—Integrated management systems.** The PMO provides comprehensive, integrated management systems. There is seamless data flow across portfolio, program, and project levels. Advanced training and support ensure high tool adoption and proficiency. Proactive system optimization and enhancement occur regularly. Tool impact on management effectiveness is systematically measured and analyzed.

- **Level 4—Strategic technology enablement.** The PMO aligns systems and tools with organizational strategy. There are sophisticated modeling and predictive analytics capabilities. Systems significantly enhance decision-making and execution at all levels. The PMO drives continuous innovation in management technologies. System capabilities become a source of competitive advantage.
- **Level 5—Intelligent management ecosystems.** The PMO employs artificial intelligence and machine learning for intelligent, adaptive management systems. Processes and decision-making support are optimized in real time. Systems autonomously identify improvement opportunities and suggest enhancements. The organization's approach to project management systems sets new standards in the industry.

12. **Training and Development**
    - **Level 1—Basic skill training.** The PMO offers basic, sporadic training sessions. Training content is general and may not be tailored to organizational needs. Training effectiveness is limitedly assessed. Training is not linked to career development or organizational strategy. There is minimal ongoing skill-development support.
    - **Level 2—Structured training program.** The PMO implements a structured training program covering key project management areas. There is some tailoring of content to organizational needs. Basic assessments of training effectiveness are conducted. Training begins to link with career development paths. Regular training sessions are scheduled and well attended. Certifications are considered in the career development paths.
    - **Level 3—Comprehensive competency development.** The PMO provides a robust, multitiered competency development program. There is a sophisticated assessment of individual and organizational skill gaps. Training is closely aligned with career development and organizational needs. Advanced learning methodologies, including experiential and peer learning, are employed. Continuous learning is encouraged and supported.
    - **Level 4—Strategic capability building.** The PMO aligns training and development with strategic organizational capabilities. The PMO also performs predictive analysis of future skill needs. Development programs significantly enhance portfolio, program, and project management capabilities across the organization. Thus, the PMO plays a key role in organizational knowledge management and innovation.
    - **Level 5—Transformational learning ecosystem.** The PMO employs advanced technologies for adaptive, personalized learning experiences. There is real-time skill-gap analysis and automated learning path adjustment. The organization's approach to project management development drives industry innovation. Learning and development become key sources of competitive advantage and organizational transformation.

Operational Services

13. Audit Assessments

- **Level 1—Basic compliance checks.** The PMO performs basic audits focusing primarily on policy compliance. Audits are infrequent and often reactive. Assessment criteria are limited and may not be consistently applied. Audit findings are documented but follow-up may be limited. There is minimal integration of audit insights into project practices.
- **Level 2—Standardized audits.** The PMO establishes a consistent audit methodology. Audits are conducted more regularly and cover a broader range of project aspects. Findings and recommendations are better documented. Basic follow-up processes are in place. Audit insights begin to inform project management practices.
- **Level 3—Comprehensive assessments.** The PMO conducts thorough assessments covering all aspects of program and project management. There is a strong focus on performance improvement alongside compliance. Sophisticated assessment tools and techniques are used. Findings are systematically tracked and inform continuous improvement initiatives.
- **Level 4—Proactive performance optimization.** The PMO uses audits proactively to optimize program and project performance. Predictive analytics are used to identify potential issues before they occur. There is seamless integration of audit insights into portfolio, program, and project management practices. Audits significantly contribute to organizational learning and capability development.
- **Level 5—Continuous intelligent oversight.** The PMO employs artificial intelligence and machine learning for continuous, real-time program and project oversight. Intelligent systems automatically identify issues and suggest improvements. There is sophisticated modeling of how audit findings impact organizational performance. The organization's approach to project audits and assessments sets new standards in the industry.

14. Change Control Management

- **Level 1—Reactive change handling.** The PMO responds to changes as they occur, with no standardized process. Change documentation is minimal and inconsistent. Impact assessments are superficial. There is limited control over scope, schedule, and resource changes. Stakeholders are not consistently informed about changes.
- **Level 2—Basic change process.** The PMO establishes a basic change control process with defined steps. Changes are documented more consistently. There is a simple impact-assessment process. A change control board is formed but its effectiveness may be limited. Stakeholder communication about changes improves but may not be comprehensive.
- **Level 3—Integrated change management.** The PMO implements a comprehensive change control system integrated with other processes. Detailed impact assessments cover scope, schedule, resources, and risks. The change control board functions effectively. There is a clear escalation process for significant changes. Stakeholders are systematically informed and involved in the change process.

- **Level 4—Proactive change management.** The PMO uses advanced analytics to predict potential changes and their impacts. Change trends are analyzed to inform program and project planning. There is a strong focus on change prevention and minimization. The change process is highly efficient, with automated workflows. Change data is used to continuously improve program and project management practices.
- **Level 5—Strategic change enablement.** The PMO's change management approach is seen as a strategic asset, enabling organizational agility. Advanced artificial intelligence and machine learning are used to model complex change scenarios and their strategic impacts. The change process is fully integrated with strategic planning and portfolio management. The organization's ability to manage change becomes a competitive advantage.

15. **Customer Relationship Management**
    - **Level 1—Basic customer interaction.** The PMO provides basic support for project customer interactions. Customer requirements are gathered but may not be systematically managed. Communication with project customers is reactive and often inconsistent. There is limited tracking of project customer satisfaction. Project customer relationship management is not integrated with project processes.
    - **Level 2—Standardized customer management.** The PMO establishes consistent processes for managing project customer relationships. There is improved documentation of project customer requirements and expectations. Basic customer satisfaction tracking is in place. Some integration with project management processes occurs. Regular project customer updates have become more common.
    - **Level 3—Integrated customer engagement.** The PMO implements comprehensive customer engagement strategies. There is a sophisticated analysis of project customer needs and satisfaction. Advanced techniques are used to manage customer expectations. Project customer relationship management is seamlessly integrated with program and project processes. There is a strong focus on proactive project customer communication.
    - **Level 4—Strategic customer partnership.** The PMO aligns project customer relationship management with organizational strategy. There is a predictive analysis of project customer needs and behaviors. Project customer partnerships significantly enhance program and project outcomes. The PMO plays a key role in managing strategic project customer relationships. There is a focus on cocreation and long-term value delivery to project customers.
    - **Level 5—Transformational customer collaboration.** The PMO employs advanced technologies for dynamic project customer insight and engagement. There is real-time adjustment of project customer strategies based on AI-driven analytics. The organization's approach to project customer relationship management in projects drives industry innovation. Project customer collaboration becomes a key source of competitive advantage and organizational transformation.

16. **Data Analytics and Reporting**

- **Level 1—Basic reporting.** The PMO provides basic, often manual, reporting on project status. Data analysis is limited and primarily descriptive. Reports are typically static and may not be timely. There is limited consistency in reporting across projects. Data quality issues are common. Analytics provide minimal strategic insights.
- **Level 2—Standardized reporting.** The PMO establishes consistent reporting templates and processes. There is improved data collection and validation. Basic data visualization tools are used. Reports are more timely and accurate. Some basic trend analysis is conducted. Reporting begins to cover portfolio and program levels but may not be comprehensive.
- **Level 3—Integrated analytics.** The PMO implements comprehensive analytics and reporting systems. Sophisticated data visualization and business intelligence tools are used. There is effective integration of data across portfolios, programs, and projects. Predictive analytics begin to inform decision-making. Real-time dashboards provide up-to-date performance insights.
- **Level 4—Strategic insight generation.** The PMO uses advanced analytics to generate strategic insights. There is sophisticated modeling of how program and project performance impacts organizational outcomes. Prescriptive analytics guide decision-making at all levels. Analytics capabilities significantly enhance the organization's competitive advantage.
- **Level 5—Intelligent performance optimization.** The PMO employs artificial intelligence and machine learning for intelligent performance optimization. There is automated generation of insights and recommendations. Advanced predictive and prescriptive models drive continuous performance improvement. The organization's approach to project analytics and reporting is recognized as industry leading, often driving innovation in the field.

17. **Issue Management**

- **Level 1—Reactive issue handling.** The PMO responds to issues reactively. There is no standardized system for tracking or managing issues. Resolution is often ad hoc and may not consider broader impacts. Communication about issues is inconsistent. There is limited analysis of issue trends or root causes.
- **Level 2—Basic issue tracking.** The PMO establishes a basic issue log and tracking process. Issues and their resolutions are better documented. Basic prioritization of issues is in place. Some trend analysis begins but it may not be comprehensive. Communication about issues becomes more consistent.
- **Level 3—Proactive issue management.** The PMO implements comprehensive issue management processes. Potential issues are identified and mitigated proactively. Advanced prioritization and escalation procedures are in place. A thorough root cause analysis is conducted. Issue management is integrated with risk management processes.

- **Level 4—Strategic issue prevention.** The PMO employs predictive analytics to identify potential issues before they occur. Issue impacts are sophisticatedly modeled across the portfolio. Issue management significantly enhances program and project success rates. Lessons learned from issues systematically inform organizational practices.
- **Level 5—Continuous improvement ecosystem.** The PMO maintains a centralized knowledge base of all issues and their resolutions, accessible organization-wide. Regular cross-departmental review sessions identify systemic patterns and implement permanent fixes. Issue management metrics directly influence strategic planning and resource allocation. The PMO implements automated early warning systems that detect issues at their earliest stages, enhanced by AI analysis for pattern recognition and solution recommendation. Third-party vendors and stakeholders are integrated into the issue tracking system, creating end-to-end visibility and accountability.

18. **Mentoring and Coaching**

- **Level 1—Ad hoc support.** The PMO provides basic, informal mentoring to program and project managers. Support is reactive and inconsistent. There is no structured coaching program. Knowledge transfer relies heavily on individual initiatives. The impact of mentoring is not measured or tracked.
- **Level 2—Structured mentoring program.** The PMO implements a structured mentoring program. Mentoring relationships are formally established and tracked. Basic guidelines for mentoring are provided. Mentors receive some training. The program focuses primarily on new or struggling project managers. Basic feedback is collected on mentoring effectiveness.
- **Level 3—Comprehensive coaching framework.** The PMO establishes a robust coaching and mentoring framework. Mentoring and coaching services are clearly differentiated. Mentors and coaches receive advanced training. The program covers all levels of program and project management. Performance improvements from coaching are systematically tracked.
- **Level 4—Strategic talent development.** The PMO aligns mentoring and coaching with strategic talent development goals. There is sophisticated matching of mentors/coaches with mentees based on skills and career paths. The program significantly enhances project management capabilities across the organization. Mentoring and coaching outcomes directly inform succession planning.
- **Level 5—Transformational leadership development.** The PMO employs artificial intelligence to create highly personalized mentoring and coaching experiences. There is continuous, real-time feedback and development guidance. The program drives transformational leadership development. The organization's approach to project management mentoring and coaching sets new standards in the industry.

19. **Performance Management**

- **Level 1—Basic monitoring.** The PMO provides basic monitoring of project timelines and budgets. Performance metrics are limited and primarily focused on time and cost. There is minimal analysis of performance trends. Reporting is inconsistent and often reactive. Performance management is not linked to strategic objectives.

- **Level 2—Standardized tracking.** The PMO establishes consistent performance metrics and tracking processes. Key performance indicators are regularly reported, basic trend analysis is conducted, performance reviews become more frequent and structured, and some linkage to strategic objectives is established.
- **Level 3—Integrated performance management.** The PMO implements comprehensive performance management processes. Performance data is sophisticatedly analyzed, including earned value management. Performance management is closely linked to strategic objectives. Proactive interventions based on performance trends become common. Program-level performance management is well established.
- **Level 4—Predictive performance optimization.** The PMO employs predictive analytics to forecast program and project performance. There is real-time performance tracking as well as automated alerts and sophisticated modeling of how project performance impacts organizational outcomes. Performance management significantly enhances program and project success rates.
- **Level 5—Intelligent performance enhancement.** The PMO uses artificial intelligence and machine learning for continuous performance optimization. There is an automated generation of performance insights and improvement recommendations. Advanced predictive and prescriptive models drive real-time performance enhancements. The organization's approach to project performance management is recognized as industry leading.

20. **Program Management**

    - **Level 1—Basic coordination.** The PMO provides program managers on an ad hoc basis for basic coordination among related projects. These program managers have limited authority and mainly focus on basic information sharing among projects. Program objectives are broadly defined but not consistently aligned with strategic goals. There is minimal integration of project management plans and resources. Program benefits are identified but not actively managed.
    - **Level 2—Structured program management.** The PMO assigns program managers more consistently, implementing a structured approach to program management. These program managers establish clearer program objectives linked to strategic goals. The program managers improve the integration of project management plans and resources within the program. Basic program-level reporting is implemented. Program risks and issues are identified and managed, though the process may not be comprehensive.
    - **Level 3—Integrated program governance.** The PMO provides experienced program managers who implement comprehensive program governance aligned with organizational structures. These program managers ensure strong integration among projects within the program, with clear management of interdependencies. The program managers actively manage program benefits throughout the life cycle and provide robust, program-level reporting with meaningful insights to stakeholders.

- **Level 4—Strategic program alignment.** The PMO deploys highly skilled program managers who position programs as critical drivers of strategic objectives. These program managers use sophisticated modeling to demonstrate how programs contribute to strategic outcomes. The program managers leverage advanced analytics to optimize program performance and resource allocation and ensure tight integration with portfolio management and strategic planning processes.
- **Level 5—Transformational program leadership.** The PMO provides elite program managers capable of driving significant organizational transformations. These leaders use programs to drive innovation and create new organizational capabilities. The program managers have a strong focus on realizing complex, long-term benefits. The program management practices implemented by these leaders are recognized as industry leading, often setting new standards in the field.

21. Project Management

- **Level 1—Basic execution.** The PMO provides part-time project managers with limited skills on an as-needed basis. These project managers execute projects with minimal standardization. The project managers implement basic scope, time, and budget tracking but their approach is often reactive. Project documentation is inconsistent and there is limited proactive management of project constraints.
- **Level 2—Standardized processes.** The PMO assigns part-time project managers with improved skills more consistently. These project managers implement standardized project management processes using consistent templates and tools. The project managers provide better tracking of scope, time, and budget. Project documentation becomes more uniform. The project managers implement basic risk and stakeholder engagement processes.
- **Level 3—Integrated management.** The PMO deploys skilled, part-time project managers who implement comprehensive project management practices integrated with organizational strategies. These project managers use advanced planning techniques to proactively manage all project constraints. The project managers also implement robust risk and stakeholder engagement processes and consistently measure and report project performance.
- **Level 4—Optimized performance.** The PMO provides a mix of part-time and full-time skilled project managers who employ sophisticated project management techniques to optimize performance. These project managers use predictive analytics for planning and control. The project managers focus strongly on continuous improvement of project management practices. Projects led by these managers consistently deliver high value and align closely with strategic objectives.
- **Level 5—Innovative leadership.** The PMO assigns highly experienced part-time and full-time project managers whose practices are at the forefront of the industry. These leaders use innovative techniques to manage projects, often leveraging artificial intelligence and machine learning. The project managers set new standards in project management that others in the industry study and emulate. Projects led by these managers consistently deliver transformational value to the organization.

22. **Project Support Services**

- **Level 1—Basic administrative support.** The PMO offers basic administrative support on request. Services are inconsistent and not standardized. Support is primarily reactive. There is limited proactive planning or coordination of support services. Documentation and recordkeeping are minimal.
- **Level 2—Standardized support services.** The PMO implements a defined set of support services. There is improved consistency in service delivery. Basic templates and tools are provided for common administrative tasks. Some proactive support is offered but it may not be comprehensive. Service levels are defined but may not be consistently met.
- **Level 3—Comprehensive project enablement.** The PMO provides a full range of proactive support services. There is seamless integration of administrative support with project management processes. Advanced tools and technologies are used to enhance support efficiency. Service levels are consistently met and regularly reviewed. Support services significantly contribute to project efficiency.
- **Level 4—Strategic support optimization.** The PMO aligns support services with strategic project objectives. There is sophisticated resource allocation to maximize support impact. Advanced analytics are used to predict support needs and optimize service delivery. Support services significantly enhance project success rates and organizational agility.
- **Level 5—Intelligent project assistance.** The PMO employs artificial intelligence and machine learning for intelligent project assistance. There is automated handling of routine administrative tasks. Predictive models anticipate project support needs. The organization's approach to project support services sets new standards in efficiency and effectiveness.

23. **Quality Assurance**

- **Level 1—Basic quality checks.** The PMO conducts basic quality checks, primarily at project completion. Quality standards are not well defined or consistently applied. Quality assurance is reactive and often focuses on defect detection rather than prevention. There is limited documentation of quality processes.
- **Level 2—Standardized quality processes.** The PMO establishes consistent quality standards and processes. Quality checks are conducted at defined project milestones. Basic quality metrics are tracked. There is improved documentation of quality processes. Some focus on defect prevention begins but it may not be comprehensive.
- **Level 3—Integrated quality management.** The PMO implements comprehensive quality management processes. There is a strong focus on defect prevention alongside detection. Advanced quality metrics and analysis techniques are used. Quality assurance is fully integrated with other project management processes. Continuous quality improvement becomes a key focus.

- **Level 4—Predictive quality optimization.** The PMO employs predictive analytics to identify potential quality issues before they occur. The PMO also uses sophisticated modeling to understand how quality impacts project and organizational outcomes. Quality assurance significantly enhances project success rates and deliverable value, and the organization's quality standards become benchmarks in the industry.
- **Level 5—Intelligent quality enhancement.** The PMO uses artificial intelligence and machine learning for continuous quality optimization. The PMO automates the identification of quality trends and real-time adjustments to quality processes. Advanced predictive and prescriptive models drive ongoing quality enhancements. The organization's approach to project quality assurance is recognized as industry leading, often driving innovation in the field.

24. Risk Management

- **Level 1—Basic identification.** The PMO supports basic risk identification for projects. Risk documentation is minimal and inconsistent. There is limited analysis of risk impacts. Risk responses are typically reactive. Risk management is not integrated with other project processes. There is minimal ongoing risk monitoring.
- **Level 2—Standardized process.** The PMO establishes a consistent project risk management process. There is improved risk documentation and categorization. A basic qualitative risk analysis is conducted. Risk responses are more proactive but may not be comprehensive. There is some integration with other project processes. Regular risk reviews are conducted.
- **Level 3—Integrated approach.** The PMO implements an integrated risk management approach. Sophisticated risk analysis techniques, including quantitative methods, are used. Risk management is fully integrated with other program and project processes. There is effective risk aggregation at the program level. Risk responses are comprehensive and proactive.
- **Level 4—Strategic risk management.** The PMO aligns risk management with organizational strategy. Advanced analytics are used for risk modeling and scenario analysis. There is a strong focus on opportunity management alongside risk mitigation. Risk appetite is clearly defined and informs decision-making. Risk management significantly enhances program and project success rates.
- **Level 5—Predictive risk intelligence.** The PMO employs artificial intelligence and machine learning for predictive risk intelligence. Real-time risk identification and assessment are in place. There is sophisticated modeling of risk interactions and cascading impacts. The organization's approach to risk management provides a significant competitive advantage. Risk management practices are at the forefront of industry innovation.

25. Specialized Services

- **Level 1—Ad hoc expertise.** The PMO provides specialized services reactively on a case-by-case basis. Experts are sourced ad hoc, often externally, to meet specific project needs. There is no structured process for identifying or delivering specialized services. The impact of these services is not systematically measured and there is limited integration with overall project management processes.
- **Level 2—Defined specialty areas.** The PMO establishes a defined set of specialized services and begins to build a pool of internal experts. There is a basic process for requesting and delivering these services. The PMO tracks service utilization and starts to integrate specialized support with project management processes. Internal expertise in key specialty areas is developed and cultivated.
- **Level 3—Integrated specialized support.** The PMO maintains a comprehensive range of specialized services with a robust network of internal and external experts. There is proactive identification of projects requiring specialized support. The PMO implements advanced tracking and analysis of service impact. Specialized experts are seamlessly integrated into project teams, significantly enhancing program and project outcomes.
- **Level 4—Strategic capability enhancement.** The PMO aligns specialized services with strategic organizational capabilities, providing high-level experts contributing to competitive advantage. There is sophisticated matching of specialized services to strategic project needs. The PMO becomes a center of excellence for key specialized areas, with experts often leading industry discussions. Service offerings continuously evolve based on emerging needs and technologies.
- **Level 5—Innovative specialization leadership.** The PMO provides world-class experts who are at the forefront of developing and implementing cutting-edge specialized services. These experts seamlessly integrate emerging technologies like artificial intelligence and machine learning into their offerings. The specialized services provided set new standards in the industry, with the PMO's experts recognized as thought leaders in multiple specialty areas. The organization's approach to specialized project services is studied and emulated by others in the field.

26. Stakeholder Engagement

- **Level 1—Basic stakeholder identification.** The PMO supports basic stakeholder identification. There is limited analysis of stakeholder needs or influence. Communication with stakeholders is reactive and inconsistent. Stakeholder engagement is not integrated with other project management processes. There is minimal ongoing stakeholder engagement planning.
- **Level 2—Structured stakeholder analysis.** The PMO establishes consistent stakeholder analysis and management processes. There is improved documentation of stakeholder needs and expectations. Basic stakeholder engagement plans are developed. Some integration with project communication processes occurs. Regular stakeholder updates are becoming more common.

- **Level 3—Comprehensive stakeholder engagement.** The PMO implements comprehensive stakeholder engagement strategies. The PMO uses a sophisticated means of analyzing stakeholder influence and interests and uses advanced engagement techniques for different stakeholder groups. Stakeholder engagement is fully integrated with portfolio, program, and project management processes. The PMO also continuously monitors and adjusts stakeholder relationships.
- **Level 4—Strategic stakeholder alignment.** The PMO aligns stakeholder engagement with organizational strategy. There is a predictive analysis of stakeholder behaviors and needs. Stakeholder relationships significantly enhance program and project outcomes. The PMO plays a key role in managing strategic stakeholder relationships at the portfolio level. There is a strong focus on creating long-term stakeholder value.
- **Level 5—Transformational stakeholder collaboration.** The PMO employs advanced technologies for dynamic stakeholder analysis and engagement. Based on AI-driven insights, stakeholder strategies are adjusted in real time. The organization's approach to stakeholder engagement drives industry innovation. Stakeholder collaboration becomes a key source of competitive advantage and organizational transformation.

Appendix X4
Critical Competency Profiles for PMO Service Delivery

Presented in this appendix is an in-depth analysis of the most critical competencies—selected from the 30 core competencies identified—that are essential for the effective delivery of each of the 26 most common PMO services. This list is based on the collective experience and insights of the global PMO community, reflecting the competencies that are deemed critical for the effective delivery of each service.

It is important to note that other competencies not listed under each service are not necessarily unimportant or unnecessary; rather, they were not specifically emphasized in the mapped experiences with the same significance as those listed.

The purpose of this list is to serve as a practical guide for PMO professionals looking to enhance their skills in alignment with the services they provide. By focusing on these key competencies, PMO professionals can tailor their competency development efforts to areas that will have the most significant impact.

(S) Services/(C) Competencies

S1: Advice to Executive Level

- Analytical skills (C3): Critical for providing data-driven advice
- Business acumen (C4): Essential for understanding strategic objectives
- Communication (C6): Necessary for effectively conveying insights to executives
- Decision-making (C11): Important for making informed recommendations
- Interpersonal intelligence (C12): Vital for navigating executive relationships
- Integrity and ethics (C13): Builds trust with senior leadership
- Leadership (C15): Establishes credibility as a strategic advisor
- Objectivity (C17): Helps ensure unbiased advice

- Relationship building (C22): Key for fostering trust with executives
- Stakeholder engagement (C25): Crucial for understanding executive needs
- Strategic influence (C26): Important for impacting strategic decisions
- Strategic thinking (C27): Essential for aligning advice with long-term goals

S2: Benefits Realization Management

- Accuracy (C1): Critical for the precise measurement of benefits
- Analytical skills (C3): Necessary for evaluating benefit data
- Business acumen (C4): Important for aligning benefits with strategy
- Communication (C6): Essential for reporting to stakeholders
- Continuous improvement (C8): Key for enhancing benefits realization processes
- Customer focus (C10): Helps ensure benefits meet customer expectations
- Decision-making (C11): Vital for optimizing benefit delivery
- Integrity and ethics (C13): Builds credibility in reporting
- Objectivity (C17): Important for unbiased benefits assessment
- Problem-solving (C19): Necessary for addressing benefits realization challenges
- Process management (C20): Critical for systematic benefits tracking
- Risk management (C24): Essential for mitigating risks to benefits
- Stakeholder engagement (C25): Key for aligning stakeholder expectations
- Strategic thinking (C27): Important for linking benefits to strategic goals

S3: Foster Project Culture

- Adaptability (C2): Necessary for adjusting to diverse environments
- Collaboration (C5): Essential for promoting teamwork
- Communication (C6): Critical for advocating project culture
- Cultural awareness (C9): Vital for respecting organizational diversity
- Leadership (C15): Key for inspiring cultural change
- Project management (C21): Helps ensure consistent project practices
- Stakeholder engagement (C25): Important for gaining support
- Teamwork (C28): Crucial for building a collaborative culture

S4: Governance Oversight

- Accuracy (C1): Essential for monitoring compliance precisely
- Analytical skills (C3): Necessary for evaluating governance data
- Business acumen (C4): Important for understanding policy impacts
- Communication (C6): Critical for articulating governance standards
- Decision-making (C11): Vital for enforcing policies effectively
- Integrity and ethics (C13): Builds trust in oversight activities
- Objectivity (C17): Helps ensure impartial governance
- Process management (C20): Key for maintaining governance frameworks
- Risk management (C24): Important for identifying governance risks
- Strategic thinking (C27): Necessary for aligning governance with strategy

S5: Organizational Change Management

- Adaptability (C2): Essential for managing transitions
- Collaboration (C5): Important for working with diverse teams
- Communication (C6): Critical for informing stakeholders
- Conflict resolution (C7): Necessary for addressing resistance
- Cultural awareness (C9): Vital for understanding organizational dynamics
- Customer focus (C10): Helps ensure changes meet stakeholder needs
- Leadership (C15): Key for guiding through change
- Proactivity (C18): Important for anticipating challenges
- Project management (C21): Drives structured change implementation
- Stakeholder engagement (C25): Crucial for securing buy-in

S6: Portfolio Management

- Accuracy (C1): Critical for precise portfolio analysis
- Analytical skills (C3): Necessary for evaluating project proposals
- Business acumen (C4): Essential for aligning with business strategy
- Communication (C6): Important for reporting portfolio status
- Continuous improvement (C8): Key for optimizing portfolio performance

- Decision-making (C11): Vital for portfolio prioritization
- Integrity and ethics (C13): Builds trust in portfolio decisions
- Process management (C20): Necessary for systematic portfolio management
- Risk management (C24): Crucial for balancing portfolio risks
- Strategic thinking (C27): Important for aligning the portfolio with strategic goals

S7: Strategic Planning Support

- Analytical skills (C3): Essential for data-driven planning
- Business acumen (C4): Necessary for understanding strategic context
- Collaboration (C5): Important for cross-functional planning
- Communication (C6): Critical for articulating strategic plans
- Continuous improvement (C8): Key for refining strategies
- Decision-making (C11): Vital for making strategic choices
- Innovation (C14): Important for creative strategic solutions
- Leadership (C15): Essential for guiding planning efforts
- Process management (C20): Necessary for structuring planning activities
- Stakeholder engagement (C25): Crucial for aligning interests
- Strategic influence (C26): Key for impacting strategic directions
- Strategic thinking (C27): Vital for long-term planning
- Teamwork (C28): Important for collaborative strategy development

S8: Knowledge Management

- Accuracy (C1): Critical for reliable knowledge resources
- Collaboration (C5): Essential for knowledge sharing
- Communication (C6): Important for disseminating information
- Continuous improvement (C8): Key for updating knowledge bases
- Process management (C20): Necessary for organizing knowledge systems
- Teamwork (C28): Vital for collective learning
- Training skills (C30): Crucial for educating others

S9: Methodologies and Frameworks Management

- Accuracy (C1): Essential for precise methodologies
- Collaboration (C5): Important for developing frameworks
- Communication (C6): Critical for explaining methodologies
- Continuous improvement (C8): Key for evolving frameworks
- Innovation (C14): Necessary for introducing new approaches
- Process management (C20): Vital for implementing methodologies
- Project management (C21): Establishes reliable process standards
- Teamwork (C28): Crucial for collaborative development
- Training skills (C30): Important for teaching methodologies

S10: Resource Management

- Adaptability (C2): Necessary for adjusting resource management plans
- Continuous improvement (C8): Important for optimizing resource use
- Decision-making (C11): Critical for allocating resources effectively
- Process management (C20): Essential for managing resource processes
- Project management (C21): Optimizes resource allocation efficiency
- Time management (C29): Vital for scheduling resources efficiently

S11: Systems and Tools Management

- Accuracy (C1): Crucial for maintaining data integrity
- Adaptability (C2): Necessary for adopting new tools
- Continuous improvement (C8): Important for enhancing systems
- Process management (C20): Essential for system governance
- Project management (C21): Integrates essential project management technologies
- Time management (C29): Key for timely system updates

S12: Training and Development

- Collaboration (C5): Important for working with trainees
- Communication (C6): Critical for effective instruction
- Continuous improvement (C8): Necessary for updating training content
- Project management (C21): Enhances skills through structured learning
- Training skills (C30): Essential for designing impactful programs

S13: Audit Assessments

- Accuracy (C1): Critical for precise assessments
- Analytical skills (C3): Necessary for evaluating audit data
- Communication (C6): Important for reporting findings
- Integrity and ethics (C13): Essential for unbiased audits
- Objectivity (C17): Crucial for impartial evaluations
- Problem-solving (C19): Key for identifying issues
- Process management (C20): Vital for systematic audits

S14: Change Control Management

- Accuracy (C1): Essential for precise documentation
- Communication (C6): Critical for informing stakeholders
- Integrity and ethics (C13): Necessary for fair change management
- Objectivity (C17): Important for unbiased evaluations
- Problem-solving (C19): Key for resolving change issues
- Process management (C20): Vital for standardized procedures
- Project management (C21): Maintains structured change oversight

S15: Customer Relationship Management

- Adaptability (C2): Necessary for meeting diverse customer needs
- Collaboration (C5): Important for working with customers
- Communication (C6): Critical for effective interactions
- Customer focus (C10): Essential for prioritizing customer satisfaction

- Interpersonal intelligence (C12): Vital for understanding customers
- Leadership (C15): Key for guiding customer engagements
- Relationship building (C22): Crucial for long-term partnerships
- Stakeholder engagement (C25): Important for managing expectations

S16: Data Analytics and Reporting

- Communication (C6): Essential for presenting data insights
- Continuous improvement (C8): Necessary for refining analytics
- Problem-solving (C19): Important for interpreting data challenges
- Time management (C29): Critical for timely reporting

S17: Issue Management

- Analytical skills (C3): Necessary for identifying root causes
- Communication (C6): Critical for informing stakeholders
- Decision-making (C11): Essential for resolving issues promptly
- Problem-solving (C19): Key for finding effective solutions
- Risk management (C24): Important for mitigating impacts
- Teamwork (C28): Vital for collaborative resolution

S18: Mentoring and Coaching

- Adaptability (C2): Necessary for tailoring approaches
- Collaboration (C5): Important for working with mentees
- Communication (C6): Critical for clear guidance
- Continuous improvement (C8): Essential for ongoing development
- Interpersonal intelligence (C12): Vital for understanding mentees
- Leadership (C15): Key for inspiring growth
- Problem-solving (C19): Important for addressing challenges
- Project management (C21): Guides professional growth effectively
- Teamwork (C28): Crucial for supportive relationships
- Training skills (C30): Necessary for effective coaching

S19: Performance Management

- Accuracy (C1): Essential for precise performance data
- Analytical skills (C3): Necessary for evaluating metrics
- Communication (C6): Important for feedback delivery
- Continuous improvement (C8): Key for enhancing performance
- Decision-making (C11): Vital for performance-related actions
- Problem-solving (C19): Critical for addressing performance issues
- Process management (C20): Necessary for systematic evaluations
- Risk management (C24): Important for identifying performance risks
- Teamwork (C28): Crucial for collaborative improvement

S20: Program Management

- Accuracy (C1): Important for precise program data
- Analytical skills (C3): Necessary for program evaluation
- Business acumen (C4): Essential for aligning with strategy
- Collaboration (C5): Critical for coordinating projects
- Communication (C6): Vital for stakeholder updates
- Decision-making (C11): Key for program decisions
- Leadership (C15): Necessary for guiding program teams
- Problem-solving (C19): Important for resolving program issues
- Process management (C20): Essential for program processes
- Project management (C21): Aligns projects within strategic programs
- Risk management (C24): Crucial for managing program risks
- Stakeholder engagement (C25): Important for securing support
- Strategic thinking (C27): Vital for program alignment
- Teamwork (C28): Key for effective collaboration
- Time management (C29): Necessary for program scheduling

S21: Project Management

- Accuracy (C1): Essential for precise project execution
- Analytical skills (C3): Necessary for project analysis
- Business acumen (C4): Important for project alignment
- Collaboration (C5): Critical for team coordination
- Communication (C6): Vital for stakeholder communication
- Decision-making (C11): Key for project decisions
- Leadership (C15): Necessary for leading project teams
- Problem-solving (C19): Important for overcoming challenges
- Process management (C20): Essential for project processes
- Project management (C21): Fundamental competency
- Risk management (C24): Crucial for handling project risks
- Stakeholder engagement (C25): Important for managing expectations
- Strategic thinking (C27): Vital for project alignment
- Teamwork (C28): Key for collaborative success
- Time management (C29): Necessary for meeting deadlines

S22: Project Support Services

- Collaboration (C5): Essential for assisting project teams
- Communication (C6): Important for clear coordination
- Continuous improvement (C8): Necessary for enhancing support
- Process management (C20): Critical for efficient support processes
- Portfolio/program/project management (C21): Fundamental competency
- Teamwork (C28): Vital for effective support

S23: Quality Assurance

- Accuracy (C1): Essential for precise quality checks
- Analytical skills (C3): Necessary for evaluating quality data
- Communication (C6): Important for reporting quality issues
- Integrity and ethics (C13): Builds trust in quality assessments

- Objectivity (C17): Helps ensure unbiased evaluations
- Problem-solving (C19): Key for resolving quality problems
- Process management (C20): Critical for quality procedures

S24: Risk Management

- Accuracy (C1): Essential for precise risk identification
- Analytical skills (C3): Necessary for risk analysis
- Communication (C6): Important for informing stakeholders
- Decision-making (C11): Critical for risk responses
- Problem-solving (C19): Key for mitigating risks
- Process management (C20): Vital for risk processes
- Risk management (C24): Fundamental competency
- Strategic thinking (C27): Necessary for aligning risk strategy
- Teamwork (C28): Important for collaborative risk management
- Time management (C29): Crucial for timely risk actions

S25: Specialized Services

- Accuracy (C1): Important for precise, specialized work
- Adaptability (C2): Necessary for customizing services
- Analytical skills (C3): Critical for specialized analysis
- Business acumen (C4): Essential for aligning with business needs
- Collaboration (C5): Key for working with specialists
- Communication (C6): Vital for conveying specialized information
- Customer focus (C10): Crucial for meeting specific needs
- Leadership (C15): Important for guiding specialized teams
- Problem-solving (C19): Necessary for addressing unique challenges
- Process management (C20): Essential for specialized procedures
- Project management (C21): Fundamental competency
- Stakeholder engagement (C25): Important for aligning expectations
- Strategic thinking (C27): Key for aligning specialized work

S26: Stakeholder Engagement

- Communication (C6): Critical for engaging stakeholders
- Conflict resolution (C7): Necessary for addressing disputes
- Interpersonal intelligence (C12): Essential for understanding stakeholders
- Integrity and ethics (C13): Builds trust with stakeholders
- Leadership (C15): Important for influencing stakeholders
- Negotiation (C16): Key for balancing interests
- Objectivity (C17): Helps ensure fair treatment
- Project management (C21): Builds and maintains stakeholder relationships
- Relationship building (C22): Vital for long-term engagement
- Stakeholder engagement (C25): Fundamental competency
- Strategic influence (C26): Necessary for impacting stakeholder decisions
- Strategic thinking (C27): Important for aligning stakeholder goals
- Teamwork (C28): Crucial for collaborative relationships

Bibliography

Benefits Management

- Bradley, G. (2010). *Benefit realisation management*. Gower.
- Melton, T., Ilês-Smith, P., & Yates, J. (2008). *Project benefits management: Linking projects to the business*. Butterworth-Heinemann.
- Project Management Institute (PMI). (2019). *Benefits realization management: A practice guide*. PMI.
- Serra, C. E. M. (2020). *Benefits realization management for PMO practitioners*. The BRM Academy.

Business Agility and Agile Approaches to Project Management

- Agile Alliance. (2001). *Principles behind the agile manifesto.* http://agilemanifesto.org/principles.html
- Beck, K., Beedle, M., van Bennekum, A., Cockburn, A., Cunningham, W., Fowler, M., Grenning, J., Highsmith, J., Hunt, A., Jeffries, R., Kern, J., Marick, B., Martin, R. C., Mellor, S., Schwaber, K., Sutherland, J., & Thomas, D. (2001). *Manifesto for agile software development*. Agile Alliance. http://agilemanifesto.org
- Nir, M. (2013). *The agile PMO: Leading the effective, value driven, project management office*. CreateSpace Independent Publishing Platform.
- Project Management Institute (PMI). (2017). *Agile practice guide*. PMI.

Customer Centricity

- Collins, J. (2011). *Good to great: Why some companies make the leap...and others don't*. Random House Business Books.
- Dodkins, J. (2014). *Foundations for customer centricity*. Lulu.com.

- Eggert, A., & Ulaga, W. (2002). Customer perceived value: A substitute for satisfaction in business markets? *Journal of Business & Industrial Marketing, 17*(2/3), 107–118.
- Fader, P., & Toms, S. E. (2018). *The customer centricity playbook: Implement a winning strategy driven by customer lifetime value*. Wharton School Press.
- Harrin, E. (2017). *Customer-centric project management*. Routledge.
- McDougall, G. H. G., & Levesque, T. (2000). Customer satisfaction with services: Putting perceived value into the equation. *Journal of Services Marketing, 14*(5), 392–410.
- Tarling, K. (2023). *The service organization: How to deliver and lead successful services, sustainably*. London Publishing Partnership.

Governance

- Knapp, M. (2018). *Enterprise portfolio governance: How organisations optimise value from their project portfolios*. Springer.
- Müller, R. (2011). Project governance. In P. W. G. Morris, J. K. Pinto, & J. Söderlund (Eds.), *The Oxford handbook of project management* (pp. 297–320). Oxford University Press.
- Müller, R. (Ed.). (2016). *Project governance*. Gower.
- Müller, R., Shao, J., & Pemsel, S. (2016). *Organizational enablers for project governance*. Project Management Institute.
- Project Management Institute (PMI). (2016). *Governance of portfolios, programs, and projects: A practice guide*. PMI.

Organizational Change and Culture

- Cameron, K. S., & Quinn, R. E. (2006). *Diagnosing and changing organizational culture: Based on the competing values framework*. Jossey-Bass.
- Cameron, K. S., Quinn, R. E., DeGraff, J., & Thakor, A. V. (2006). *Competing values leadership: Creating value in organizations*. Edward Elgar Publishing.
- Project Management Institute (PMI). (2013). *Managing change in organizations: A practice guide*. PMI.

Performance Management

- Keyes, J. (2011). *Implementing the project management balanced scorecard*. CRC Press.
- Spitzer, D. R. (2007). *Transforming performance measurement: Rethinking the way we measure and drive organizational success*. AMACOM.

Portfolio, Program, and Project Management

- AXELOS Limited. (2011). *Management of portfolios (MoP®)*. The Stationery Office (TSO).
- AXELOS Limited. (2011). *Managing successful programmes (MSP®)*. The Stationery Office (TSO).
- Lock, D., & Wagner, R. (Eds.). (2020). *Gower handbook of programme management*. Routledge.
- Project Management Institute (PMI). (2017). *The standard for portfolio management*—Fourth edition. PMI.
- Project Management Institute (PMI). (2021). *A guide to the project management body of knowledge (PMBOK® guide)*—Seventh edition. PMI.
- Project Management Institute (PMI). (2024). *Risk management in portfolios, programs, and projects: A practice guide*. PMI.
- Project Management Institute (PMI). (2024). *The standard for program management*—Fifth edition. PMI.

Project Management Maturity and Capabilities

- AXELOS Limited. (2015). *Portfolio, programme, and project management maturity model (P3M3®) v3.0*. The Stationery Office (TSO).
- Forrester, E., Buteau, B., & Shrum, S. (2011). *CMMI for services: Guidelines for superior service*. Addison-Wesley Professional.
- Kerzner, H. (2005). *Using the project management maturity model*. John Wiley & Sons.
- Mullaly, M. E. (2006). Longitudinal analysis of project management maturity. *Project Management Journal, 37*(3), 62–73.
- Mullaly, M., & Thomas, J. L. (2010, June). *Re-thinking project management maturity: Perspectives gained from explorations of fit and value*. Paper presented at PMI Research® Conference: Defining the Future of Project Management, Washington, D.C., USA. Project Management Institute.
- Niazi, M., & Ali Babar, M. (2009). Identifying high perceived value practices of CMMI level 2: An empirical study. *Information and Software Technology, 51*(8), 1231–1243.
- Project Management Institute (PMI). (2018). *The standard for organizational project management (OPM)*. PMI.
- Software Engineering Institute. (2000). *The capability maturity model: Guidelines for improving the software process*. Carnegie Mellon Software Engineering Institute.
- Yazici, H. J. (2009). The role of project management maturity and organizational culture in perceived performance. *Project Management Journal, 40*(3), 14–33.

Project Management Offices

- Artto, K., Kulvik, I., Poskela, J., & Turkulainen, V. (2011). The integrative role of the project management office in the front end of innovation. *International Journal of Project Management, 29*(1), 408–421.
- Aubry, M., Hobbs, B., & Thuillier, D. (2007). A new framework for understanding organisational project management through the PMO. *International Journal of Project Management, 25*(4), 328–336.
- Aubry, M., Hobbs, B., & Thuillier, D. (2008). Organisational project management: An historical approach to the study of PMOs. *International Journal of Project Management, 26*(1), 38–43.
- Aubry, M., Hobbs, B., & Thuillier, D. (2009). The contribution of the project management office to organisational performance. *International Journal of Managing Projects in Business, 2*(1), 141–148.
- Aubry, M., & Hobbs, B. (2010). A fresh look at the contribution of project management to organizational performance. *Project Management Journal, 42*(1), 3–16.
- Aubry, M., Hobbs, B., Müller, R., & Blomquist, T. (2010). Identifying forces driving PMO changes. *Project Management Journal, 41*(4), 30–45.
- Aubry, M., Müller, R., Hobbs, B., & Blomquist, T. (2010). Project management offices in transition. *International Journal of Project Management, 28*(8), 766–778.
- Aubry, M., Hobbs, B., Müller, R., & Blomquist, T. (2011). *Identifying the forces driving frequent change in PMOs*. Project Management Institute.
- Aubry, M., Müller, R., & Glückler, J. (2011). Exploring PMOs through community of practice theory. *Project Management Journal, 42*(5), 42–56.
- Aubry, M., Müller, R., & Glückler, J. (2012). *Governance and communities of PMOs*. Project Management Institute.
- Aubry, M., Richer, M., Lavoie-Tremblay, M., & Cyr, G. (2011). Pluralism in PMO performance: The case of a PMO dedicated to a major organizational transformation. *Project Management Journal, 42*(6), 60–77.
- Augustine, S., Cuellar, R., & Scheere, A. (2021). *From PMO to VMO: Managing for value delivery*. Berrett-Koehler Publishers.
- AXELOS Limited. (2020). *Portfolio, programme and project offices (P3O®)*. The Stationery Office (TSO).
- Bolles, D. (2002). *Building project management centers of excellence*. AMACOM.
- Crawford, J. K. (2010). *The strategic project office*. CRC Press.
- Dai, C. X., & Wells, W. G. (2004). An exploration of project management office features and their relationship to project performance. *International Journal of Project Management, 22*(7), 523–532.
- Dietrich, P., Artto, K., & Kujala, J. (2010, October). *Strategic priorities and PMO functions in project-based firms*. Paper presented at PMI® Research Conference: Defining the Future of Project Management, Washington, D.C., USA. Project Management Institute.

- Dixon, S. (2021). *PMO service catalogue: An insight into what PMOs do*. EHC Consulting.
- Dow, W. (2017). *The PMO lifecycle: Building, running, and shutting down*. Dow Publishing LLC.
- Dow, W. (2021). *PMO service offerings: How do I select the right services for my PMO?* Dow Publishing LLC.
- Duggal, J. (2018). *The DNA of strategy execution: Next generation project management and PMO*. John Wiley & Sons.
- Englund, R. L., Graham, R. J., & Dinsmore, P. C. (2003). *Creating the project office: A manager's guide to leading organizational change*. Jossey-Bass.
- Hill, G. M. (2013). *The complete project management office handbook*. Auerbach Publications.
- Hobbs, B., & Aubry, M. (2007). A multi-phase research program investigating project management offices (PMOs): The results of phase 1. *Project Management Journal, 38*(1), 74–86.
- Hobbs, B., & Aubry, M. (2008). An empirically grounded search for a typology of project management offices. *Project Management Journal, 39*(1), 69–82.
- Hobbs, B., & Aubry, M. (2010). *The project management office (PMO): A quest for understanding*. Project Management Institute.
- Hobbs, B., & Aubry, M. (2011). *A typology of PMOs derived using cluster analysis and the relationship with performance*. In Proceedings of the IRNOP Conference, June 20–22, 2011, Montreal, Canada.
- Hobbs, B., Aubry, M., & Thuillier, D. (2008). The project management office as an organisational innovation. *International Journal of Project Management, 26*(5), 547–555.
- Hurt, M., & Thomas, J. L. (2009). Building value through sustainable project management offices. *Project Management Journal, 40*(1), 55–72.
- Julian, J. (2008). How project management office leaders facilitate cross-project learning and continuous improvement. *Project Management Journal, 39*(3), 43–58.
- Kendall, G. I., & Rollins, S. C. (2003). *Advanced project portfolio management and the PMO: Multiplying ROI at warp speed*. J. Ross Publishing.
- Kerzner, H. (2003). Strategic planning for a project office. *Project Management Journal, 34*(2), 13–25.
- Kerzner, H., Zeitoun, A., & Vargas, R. V. (2022). *Project management next generation: The pillars for organizational excellence*. Wiley.
- Letavec, C. J. (2006). *The program management office: Establishing, managing and growing the value of a PMO*. J. Ross Publishing.
- Letavec, C. J., & Bolles, D. (2011). *The PMOSIG program management office handbook: Strategic and tactical insights for improving results*. J. Ross Publishing.
- Müller, R., Aubry, M., & Glückler, J. (2010). *A relational typology of project management offices*. In Proceedings of the IRNOP Conference, June 20–22, 2009, Montreal, Canada.

- Pellegrinelli, S., & Garagna, L. (2009). Towards a conceptualisation of PMOs as agents and subjects of change and renewal. *International Journal of Project Management, 27*(7), 649–656.
- Perry, M. P. (2009). *Business driven PMO setup: Practical insights, techniques and case examples for ensuring success*. J. Ross Publishing.
- Perry, M. P. (2013). *Business driven PMO success stories: Across industries and around the world.* J. Ross Publishing.
- Pinto, A., Cota, M. F. M., & Levin, G. (2010). The PMO maturity cube, a project management office maturity model. In Proceedings of PMI Research & Education Conference, July 10–14, 2010, Washington, D.C., USA.
- Pinto, A., Cota, M. F. M., & Levin, G. (2010). The PMO maturity cube, a project management office maturity model. In C. Letavec & D. Bolles (Eds.), *The PMOSIG program management office handbook* (pp. 383–402). J. Ross Publishing.
- Project Management Institute (PMI). (2023, March). *The evolution of PMOs: Delivering value through xMOs*. PMI.
- Spivak, E. (2023). *PMO governance: Practical strategies to govern portfolio, program, and project delivery*. FriesenPress.
- Taylor, P. (2011). *Leading successful PMOs: How to build the best project management office for your business*. Gower Publishing.
- Taylor, P. (2023). *Projects: Methods: Outcomes: The new PMO model for true project and change success*. Routledge.
- Tjahjana, L., Dwyer, P., & Habib, M. (2009). *The program management office advantage: A powerful and centralized way for organizations to manage projects*. AMACOM.

Stakeholder Engagement

- Bourne, L. (2016). *Stakeholder relationship management: A maturity model for organisational implementation*. Routledge.
- Holloway, J., & Bryde, D. (2016). *A practical guide to dealing with difficult stakeholders*. Routledge.

Value Management

- AXELOS Limited. (2010). *Management of value (MoV®)*. The Stationery Office (TSO).
- Besner, C., & Hobbs, B. (2006). The perceived value and potential contribution of project management practices to project success. *Project Management Journal, 37*(3), 37–48.
- Hubbard, D. W. (2007). *How to measure anything: Finding the value of intangibles in business*. John Wiley & Sons.

- Mengel, T., Cowan-Sahadath, K., & Follert, F. (2008). The value of project management to organizations in Canada and Germany, or do values add value? Five case studies. *Project Management Journal, 40*(1), 28–41.
- Mullaly, M., & Thomas, J. L. (2009). Exploring the dynamics of value and fit: Insights from project management. *Project Management Journal, 40*(1), 124–135.
- Phillips, J. J., Brantley, W., & Phillips, P. P. (2012). *Project management ROI: A step-by-step guide for measuring the impact and ROI for projects*. Wiley.
- Phillips, J. J., & Phillips, P. P. (2007). *Show me the money: How to determine ROI in people, projects, and programs*. Berrett-Koehler Publishers.
- Schnapper, M., & Rollins, S. (2006). *Value-based metrics for improving results: An enterprise project management toolkit*. J. Ross Publishing.
- Seiden, J. (2019). *Outcomes over output: Why customer behavior is the key metric for business success*. Sense & Respond Press.
- Thomas, J., & Mullaly, M. (2007). Understanding the value of project management: First steps on an international investigation in search of value. *Project Management Journal, 38*(3), 74–89.
- Thomas, J., & Mullaly, M. (2008). *Researching the value of project management*. Project Management Institute.
- Thomas, J., & Mullaly, M. (2009). Explorations of value: Perspectives of the value of project management. *Project Management Journal, 40*(1), 2–3.
- Zhai, L., Xin, Y., & Cheng, C. (2009). Understanding the value of project management from a stakeholder's perspective: Case study of mega-project management. *Project Management Journal, 40*(1), 99–109.

Glossary

agility-driven PMO. A PMO that adopts business agility principles to remain flexible and responsive to changing organizational needs.

awareness building. The initial step in the value-generating PMO flywheel focused on educating stakeholders about the PMO's role, capabilities, and potential value.

customer perception of value. A subjective evaluation by PMO customers of the benefits they receive from PMO services relative to their expectations and needs.

customer value agreement. A formal document outlining the specific outcomes and value the PMO commits to delivering to each major customer or customer group.

deployment stage. The third phase in the PMO customer experience cycle where designed services are implemented and rolled out to customers.

design stage. The second phase in the PMO customer experience cycle where insights from exploration are transformed into service concepts and plans.

enhancement stage. The fourth phase in the PMO customer experience cycle focused on continuously improving and refining PMO services.

evidence of need. Signs or symptoms indicating that a customer may be facing challenges in a specific area; used to identify potential PMO service opportunities.

exploration stage. The initial phase in the PMO customer experience cycle focused on understanding the current landscape, customer needs, and potential opportunities.

industry-specific profile. The unique characteristics, challenges, and good practices of the organization's industry that influence PMO operations.

needs assessment. The process of identifying and evaluating the specific requirements and pain points of PMO customers.

organizational baseline elements. Foundational components that influence PMO design and operation, including organizational strategy, structure, culture, and industry-specific profile.

organizational contextual scenarios. Distinct states or situations that an organization may experience, influencing how a PMO operates and delivers value.

PMO as a service provider. A perspective that views the PMO as an internal service provider, focusing on meeting customer needs and delivering value rather than just enforcing processes.

PMO capability building. The ongoing process of enhancing the skills, knowledge, and abilities of the PMO team to improve service delivery and value creation.

PMO competency domains. Areas of expertise required for effective PMO operation, including design, operation, and improvement.

PMO customer. Stakeholders within an organization that directly receive, use, or benefit from the services provided by the PMO.

PMO customer experience cycle. A model representing the stages a PMO goes through in interacting with and delivering value to its customers.

PMO customer segmentation. The practice of dividing PMO customers into groups based on their needs, maturity levels, or other relevant characteristics.

PMO governance. The framework that defines decision-making processes, roles, responsibilities, and accountability measures within the PMO.

PMO mandate. A formal declaration that defines the PMO's purpose, scope, authority, and responsibility within the organizational context.

PMO outcomes. The specific benefits or results that PMO customers expect to achieve through the use of PMO services.

PMO risk management plan. A strategy for identifying, assessing, and mitigating risks specific to PMO operations and value delivery.

PMO service approaches. Different methods of delivering PMO services, ranging from consultative to directive, and tailored to customer needs and organizational context.

PMO service catalog. A comprehensive list of services offered by the PMO, including their descriptions, benefits, and delivery approaches.

PMO service maturity. The level of sophistication and effectiveness of individual PMO services, assessed on a scale to guide improvement efforts.

PMO service performance metrics. Specific, measurable indicators used to assess the effectiveness and efficiency of PMO services.

PMO strategy. A comprehensive plan outlining how the PMO will deliver value to its stakeholders over the short, medium, and long term.

PMO structural components. Essential elements that form the foundation of a PMO, including PMO mandate, PMO strategy, and PMO governance.

PMO value journey. A mapped progression of how the PMO's value proposition to its customers will evolve over time.

PMO Value Ring™ framework. A comprehensive model for creating and operating value-driven, customer-centric PMOs.

realization stage. The final phase in the PMO customer experience cycle where the PMO's impact on the organization comes into sharp focus and value is demonstrated.

service development. The process of creating, refining, and evolving PMO services to meet customer needs and organizational objectives.

service improvement. The process of enhancing the maturity and effectiveness of PMO services to increase their value and impact.

service-level agreement (SLA). A formal agreement between the PMO and its customers defining the expected level of service.

service monitoring. The process of tracking, measuring, and evaluating PMO services against predetermined standards.

service onboarding. The process of introducing newly developed or improved PMO services to their intended users within the organization.

service operation. The day-to-day management and execution of PMO services to deliver value to customers.

strategic alignment. The process of ensuring PMO activities and services directly support and contribute to the organization's strategic objectives.

value delivery. The process of realizing and demonstrating the tangible benefits that PMO services provide to the organization.

value proposition. A clear statement articulating how the PMO will address identified needs and add value to the organization.

value recognition. The process of ensuring that customers not only receive value from PMO services but also acknowledge and appreciate it.

value-generating PMO flywheel. A model that breaks down the PMO customer experience cycle into 10 actionable steps.

Index

D

N

O

P

Q

R

S

T

Tales for All Seasons

Also by Elizabeth Clark

STORIES TO TELL
COUNTRY TALES TO TELL

Elizabeth Clark

Tales for All Seasons

Illustrated by
CARA LOCKHART SMITH

HODDER AND STOUGHTON
LONDON SYDNEY AUCKLAND TORONTO

British Library Cataloguing in Publication Data

Clark, Elizabeth
Tales for all seasons.
I. Title II. Lockhart Smith, Cara
823'.912[J] PZ7

ISBN 0-340-38039-X

This compilation first published 1986

Published by Hodder and Stoughton Children's Books,
a division of Hodder and Stoughton Ltd,
Mill Road, Dunton Green, Sevenoaks, Kent TN13 2YJ

Photoset by Rowland Phototypesetting Ltd,
Bury St Edmunds, Suffolk

Printed in Great Britain by T.J. Press (Padstow) Ltd,
Padstow, Cornwall

Contents

The Tale of a Tail

It was eleven o'clock at night on Midsummer Eve (which is the twenty-third of June). A fine large moon was sailing high in the sky and Mrs Spriggins' garden looked all silvery in the moonlight. The stones of the garden path shone as white as snow and the grass in the meadow beyond seemed frosted with moonshine.

There was a warm spicy smell from the deep red clove pinks that grew under the kitchen window. Mrs Spriggins could sniff it as she leaned out. But she was not thinking of clove pinks. She was vexed and worried and every few minutes she said to herself, 'Dear, dear, dearie me – wherever can he be?' And she shook her head and looked across the meadow where a big fairy-ring showed quite plain in the moonlight.

'If the Good Folk catch him up to his tricks on Midsummer Eve, he'll get into trouble, so he will,' said Mrs Spriggins. And she leaned out of the window and called very loud, 'Kitty, kitty, kitty! Mr Wickens, Mr Wickens, kitty, kitty-cat!'

'Mr Wickens', as perhaps you have guessed, was the name of Mrs Spriggins' cat. It is an odd name for a cat, but it seemed to suit him very well indeed. He was large and dignified, with a wise, kind face and a satin-smooth dark tabby coat. His tail was long and thick (but not fluffy). Mrs Spriggins liked to draw her hand down his shining back and along his beautiful smooth tail. When she reached the tip of his tail Mr Wickens would stand firmly on his toes and pull softly against her hand, purring with pleasure and delight. They loved each other dearly and they liked each other's ways.

Mr Wickens wore a little leather collar round his neck, like a dog. Fastened to the collar was a tiny tinkling bell; that was to keep him from catching birds. However quietly he crept, the bell tinkled as he moved and the birds heard it and flew away before he reached them. It kept him from catching mice of course, but Mrs Spriggins kept her cat for company, not for mice, so that did not matter.

But on moonlight nights in summer-time Mr Wickens liked to take a walk in the fields, and several times, in spite of his tinkling bell, he had brought back a baby rabbit in his mouth. He carried it quite gently, as a mother-cat carries a kitten, and it was not hurt though it was very frightened. He always trotted in, looking very proud and pleased, and laid the rabbit down in Mrs Spriggins' kitchen and mewed and purred till Mrs Spriggins came to see what he had brought. She could never make him understand that baby rabbits were no use at all to her. Each time, she had to make a nest in a basket and feed the rabbit till it was old enough to scamper away.

But she could not explain to Mr Wickens that he really gave her a good deal of trouble. He was always quite sure that he had brought her a very nice present.

So Mrs Spriggins sat by her kitchen window waiting, and hoping there would not be a baby rabbit that night, because she wanted to go to bed. It was getting very late. She got up from her chair to look at the time and the hands of the tall grandfather clock were almost together. It was very nearly twelve o'clock. 'Dear, dear,' said Mrs Spriggins. But as she leaned out of the window again she heard a little far-off tinkling sound in the stillness, and she said to herself, '*There* he is!'

She could see a little black shadow on the far side of the meadow, slipping along in the moonlight. She called again, 'Mr Wickens, Mr Wickens, kitty, kitty-cat,' and the little black shadow turned and came running across the field, jumping over the big tufts of coarse grass that the cows had left standing here and there. It was Mr Wickens.

'Oh dear,' said Mrs Spriggins, 'he's brought me another.' She could see a little bundle in his mouth. 'Be quick,' she called, 'you naughty cat. It's nearly twelve o'clock.' Just as she spoke the big church clock began to strike, and just as the clock began to strike, Mr Wickens reached the edge of the fairy-ring.

He gave a jump because the grass grew tall and thick round the ring; and as he jumped – he was gone. There was the meadow all white in the moonshine. There was the fairy-ring, like a ring of shadow rather ragged at the edges. But where were Mr Wickens and his baby rabbit? They were nowhere at all!

Mrs Spriggins got up from her chair and ran – all in a hurry – down the garden path, out of the gate and along the little trodden path that led through the meadow beyond. Her long black shadow ran beside her in the moonlight.

She left the path and hurried across to the fairy-ring and stood looking at it. There it was, all quiet and empty; there was not a sound of a tinkling bell, not a shadow, not a purr, not a mew. 'Oh dear, oh dearie me, wherever can he be!' said Mrs Spriggins; and she sat down all in a heap at the edge of the fairy-ring, because quite suddenly she felt all shaky at the knees.

'The Good Folk have taken away my Kitty Wickens,' she said to herself, 'and I don't know what to do about it.'

She was so upset that she was almost crying, and then something touched her face and tickled her nose and made her sneeze instead. It was something velvety and soft as silk. Mrs Spriggins rubbed her nose and looked to see what it could be. Then she rubbed her eyes and looked and looked again. There was no doubt about it. Waving in the moonlight, quite close to her and just outside the fairy-ring, was the tip of Mr Wickens' long smooth tail – only the tip, there was no more of the tail. It ended where the fairy-ring began. Mrs Spriggins put out her hand to seize it, but it whisked away and was gone.

Then she knew what had happened. She had heard her grandmother say that once you stepped inside a fairy-ring on a Midsummer moonlight night, the Good Folk had power over you. If they chose, no one could see you or hear you. There you stayed as long as they willed. They charmed your feet, and they charmed your eyes and your ears. You could only walk and see and hear as the Good Folk chose.

'But they forgot to charm my Kitty Wickens' tail,' said Mrs Spriggins, 'or perhaps it was too long for them. And I'll get him out again, that I will.'

But she could do nothing that night. She waited and watched and waited, but there was never another glimpse of even the tip of Mr Wickens' tail. So at last Mrs Spriggins went back to her cottage and up to bed. At any rate, she knew where her dear cat was, and that was half-way to getting him back again.

She went to bed, but she did not sleep much, as you may guess. She woke very early, while the birds were still whispering to one another, and she lay thinking. Presently she said to herself, 'I'll ask Mrs Featherstone to help me.' And when she had eaten her breakfast, she put on her bonnet and went away down the lane to Mrs Featherstone's cottage.

Mrs Featherstone was large and fat. Mrs Spriggins was small and thin. But they were very good friends, and Mrs Featherstone thought Mr Wickens was a dear good cat – as indeed he was – so she was quite ready to help. She came along to Mrs Spriggins' cottage at sunset; and as the Midsummer moon came up in the east, large and round and golden-red, Mrs Spriggins and Mrs Featherstone came down the garden path. They each carried a little three-legged wooden stool and they had brought their knitting with them to pass the time away. Mrs Featherstone had a long blue stocking, Mrs Spriggins had a thick grey sock. They could knit by moonlight, or starlight, or any other kind of light. They could even knit in the dark. And moonlight or starlight or dark they meant to stay by the fairy-ring till they saw Mr Wickens' waving tail. 'And *then*,' said

Mrs Spriggins, 'we'll see what we'll see!'

So there they sat, on their wooden stools at the edge of the fairy-ring, and their shadows lay beside them, growing shorter and shorter as the moon came creeping up the sky like a golden ball of light. Bats came out of the hollows in the elm-trees and flitted across the field. A great owl came after them, shouting, 'Hoo-hoo. Hoo-hoo-hoo-hoo-oo-oo.' But there was no sound from the fairy-ring. Nothing moved there, not even a blade of grass.

Ten o'clock struck and still they knitted and waited. Eleven o'clock passed and there was no sign of Mr Wickens or his tail. Twelve o'clock began to strike from the church tower, and as it struck Mrs Spriggins shouted, 'There it is!'

She dropped her knitting and leaned forward and snatched at something that floated in the air just in front of her. It was the tip of Mr Wickens' tail! She held it fast and she could feel him dig in his toes and pull gently against her as he always did when she held his tail. And then – as she leaned forward – the three-legged stool tilted (three-legged stools are very easily upset, you know) and Mrs Spriggins fell, right into the fairy-ring. And what would have been the end of this story if Mrs Featherstone had not been there, I really cannot tell.

There was Mrs Spriggins inside the fairy-ring. She had tight hold of Mr Wickens, it is true; she could feel him as she fell, and she grabbed him with one hand and held him fast. But he seemed as heavy as lead, and her hands and her knees and her toes felt full of pins and needles and would not move; and thousands of tiny shining, sparkling wings were dancing before her eyes.

Mrs Spriggins blinked and shut her eyes because they dazzled so, but she held firm and she could feel that Mr Wickens was purring, so she was sure there was nothing to be really afraid of. 'It's just the Good Folk playing tricks on us,' she said to herself. Then she felt a tug and she knew what was happening. Mrs Featherstone had caught her by the arm as she fell and she was pulling her out of the fairy-ring. It was a very good thing that Mrs Featherstone was large and stout and that Mrs Spriggins was small and thin. Mrs Featherstone could see nothing of Mrs Spriggins except her hand, but she held that and pulled and tugged with all her might. And all in a moment – just like a fish out of a pool – out came Mrs Spriggins into the moonlight and out came Mr Wickens too.

And Mrs Featherstone said, *'Well!'* She had no breath to say anything more. And Mrs Spriggins said, *'Well!'* She had no breath either. Then they picked up their three-legged stools and carried them to the path, quite away from the edge of the fairy-ring. They sat down side by side in the moonlight and looked at each other and nodded their heads, while Mr Wickens walked round them in the moonlight, purring and rubbing against them, saying thank you with all his might.

Mrs Spriggins said, 'Thank you, Mrs Featherstone, my dear.'

Mrs Featherstone said, 'Mrs Spriggins, my dear, I'm sure you're very welcome.'

Then they picked up their three-legged stools and walked across the field and up the garden path to Mrs Spriggins' door. And they each had a large bowl of bread-and-milk, and Mr Wickens – who was very hungry, poor cat – had one too.

It was one o'clock in the morning by the time they had finished their bread-and-milk and their talk about the very queer things that had happened. They said good night at last, and Mrs Spriggins lit the lantern for Mrs Featherstone because the moon was setting and it was really very dark under the trees.

She stood at her cottage door and watched Mrs Featherstone and the lantern go bobbing away down the garden path. Then she shut the door and stroked Mr Wickens, feeling very glad she had him there safe and sound to stroke. Mr Wickens nudged her with his nose, which was *his* way of stroking, and he jumped into the cushioned arm-chair and curled himself up to sleep and Mrs Spriggins climbed the stairs to bed.

What became of the baby rabbit that Mr Wickens carried with him into the fairy-ring, I do not know. But no doubt the Good Folk cared for it and sent it back to its mother. As Mr Wickens never brought another to Mrs Spriggins, they must certainly have explained to him that no really kind cat would steal a baby rabbit. And being a really kind cat, Mr Wickens stole no more. And I expect that pleases you almost as much as it pleased Mrs Spriggins.

The Tale of Mrs Puffin's Prize Pumpkin

Mrs Puffin stood on her door-step one fine morning early in June, and looked at her garden and said, 'Oh dear! Oh dear! Dearie, dearie me.'

You could not really say there was much garden to look at. There had been no rain for weeks and everything was dried up. The rose that climbed over the house was covering the ground with white petals like snow; the honeysuckle was drooping, and the tall foxgloves by the door hung their heads. Even the pinks in the border looked shrivelled, and Mrs Puffin's neat rows of young cabbages and potatoes and peas were thirsty and dry.

'I'll go down the hill,' said Mrs Puffin, 'and get a bucket or two of water and give the peas a soaking before the sun gets hot.'

Mrs Puffin lived in a little white cottage half-way up a hill. If you went down a lane between tall green hedges you came to another little white house at the bottom of the hill where her nearest neighbour lived. His name was Peter Pinch. Peter had a garden too, but in spite of the hot dry weather it was still fresh and green. A tiny spring of clear, bright water came out of the hillside just by Peter's gate. It made a little pool there and then ran on, right through his garden, past his old apple-trees and away through fields till I suppose it came to a river and went down with it to the sea.

So Peter had all the water that he needed for his garden. His roses were pink and white and covered with buds; his flowers stood up straight and strong, his cabbages and potatoes and peas looked fresh and green. You would not think Peter had anything to grumble about. But he had. He grumbled every day and every time when Mrs Puffin came to fetch water from his little pool.

'Don't take too much, Mrs Puffin,' he would say, 'you'll empty the pool and leave none for me. Two buckets full in the morning and two in the evening is a-plenty,' said Peter.

He knew quite well that the little spring went on running, and that however much water Mrs

Puffin took, the pool would soon fill again. But Peter Pinch always wanted to keep everything for himself. Even the birds made him angry. He threw stones at them to drive them away from his garden in summer, and he never gave them even a crumb in winter.

On the morning that I am telling you about, Mrs Puffin hoped that Peter Pinch would still be asleep. She went quietly down the hill with her buckets. It was not really very far, though it seemed a long way when you came uphill with a heavy bucket in each hand. She looked up at Peter's window and saw that it was shut and the curtains were drawn. So she did not hurry. She dipped the water out of the little pool, slowly and comfortably with her big tin mug, till the pails were nearly full. Then she carried them up and watered her thirsty peas and went down again to get water for the house.

She had filled one bucket and she was stooping over the second when somebody laughed and something fell with a loud splash into her pail. Mrs Puffin jumped, and said, 'Bless me!' and looked round. Peter Pinch was leaning over his gate, laughing to himself. He had just dropped a large toad into the full bucket. Toads do not like being dropped into water any more than you or I would, so Mrs Puffin said, 'Poor thing!' and picked him out in a hurry and wrapped him in two dock-leaves and put him in her apron pocket. She was sure Peter did not mean to be kind to the toad, so she would not leave him there.

Peter only laughed again and said, 'There's a bit of company for you, Mrs Puffin. I've got no room for him in *my* garden.'

And Mrs Puffin said politely in a dignified voice, 'Good *morning*, Mr Pinch,' and picked up her pails and went up the hill. She put the toad down in a cool corner under some ferns by the door; and she used the water from the pail he had been in for scrubbing. There was enough in the other pail to make several cups of tea, so she did not have to go down the hill again till the cool of the day was come.

When she came back with her pails in the evening, she found the toad sitting on her door-step. He looked at her with his bright eyes, and Mrs Puffin nodded at him, 'Good evening, Master Toad,' she said, 'I hope I see you well.'

When she had finished watering her garden he was still there, and she said good night to him when she shut the door. He was among her rows of peas next morning when she watered them, and Mrs Puffin said, 'Nice morning' to him. The toad never made a sound – as you know, toads are quiet creatures – but he looked fat and comfortable, and as the days went by Mrs Puffin talked to him more and more. When she came panting up the hill with her buckets, she used to tell him how hot it was and how heavy the pails were. She told him how green Peter Pinch's garden was looking, how fat his peas were and how rosy and ripe his strawberries were getting. And at last, one evening, poor Mrs Puffin sat down and burst into tears. Peter Pinch had been so cross, she was so tired, and her garden looked so dried up and withered. 'If only I had a little spring of water of my own,' said poor Mrs Puffin, 'just a little tiny spring, to keep the garden green!'

She cried and cried and the toad looked at her

solemnly. He was sitting in the corner of the door-step where he always sat in the evening. Presently he crawled off the door-step and went slowly down the garden path. He wriggled under Mrs Puffin's gate; she thought he must be going down the lane, but she was too tired and miserable to go and look. She cried a little more, because she was really fond of her toad and she was afraid he was tired of her dried-up garden, and then she went to bed.

But when she came out with her pails very early next morning, she saw the toad again. He had not gone down the hill, after all. He was crawling under the gate of a field, a little way down the lane.

'Good morning, Master Toad,' said Mrs Puffin. The toad sat in the lane and looked wisely at her, and Mrs Puffin looked over the gate. The grass in the field was short because Farmer Brown's cows fed there, and she could see very plainly that there was a big fairy-ring in the middle of the field. And from the fairy-ring to the gate there was a little ruffled pathway through the dew, as if something had crawled across the grass.

'It seems to *me*,' said Mrs Puffin to herself as she went down the hill, 'that my Master Toad has been talking to the Fairies!'

When she came back the toad was in the garden again, and in the evening he was on the door-step as usual, so Mrs Puffin knew he had come back to stay.

It was not long after this that a fat, juicy green shoot came up in the corner of Mrs Puffin's garden, in a little hollow by the hedge. Mrs Puffin looked at it and wondered what it could be, and gave it all the water she could spare to encourage it to grow.

It grew very fast and presently Mrs Puffin said, 'It's a pumpkin plant. Wherever did it come from!' She looked at the toad as if he could tell her. She thought perhaps he could, if only he could talk. She had not forgotten the morning when she saw him coming away from the fairy-ring. 'And maybe,' she said to herself, 'the Good Folks sent me a pumpkin to make up for the rest of my things being spoiled this year!'

Pumpkins are rather like vegetable marrows. They like plenty of water. Mrs Puffin gave her pumpkin every drop she could spare. She emptied her scrubbing-pail and her washing-bowl into the hollow. She put all her tea-leaves round the root to keep it damp. And the pumpkin grew big green leaves and long green stalks and it blossomed with large yellow flowers.

Mrs Puffin watched it grow with joy and

pride. She was so proud of it that she even told Peter Pinch about it, and he used to walk up the lane to look at it and count the flowers and wonder how many pumpkins there would be. He had none of his own, and to tell the truth he was rather jealous of Mrs Puffin. So I am afraid he was really pleased to find that when all the yellow flowers had fallen, there was only one little green pumpkin left.

Mrs Puffin was very disappointed. She had hoped she was going to have half a dozen pumpkins at least. But she only said, 'One is a deal better than none,' and she went on watering her pumpkin plant. And the little pumpkin grew and grew and *grew* larger and larger, rounder and rounder till it was a most enormous pumpkin! Mrs Puffin watched it grow. She went to look at it so often that her footsteps made quite a deep little pathway across her garden. Very often she found the toad sitting in the little hollow, and she thought to herself, 'He's as proud of it as I am.'

When September came the pumpkin was ripe. It had turned from green to pale yellow and from yellow to bright orange. The leaves and stalks dried up and withered, but the pumpkin almost filled the little hollow. It lay there like a large round golden moon. And it was heavy. Mrs Puffin moved it gently and felt sure she could not lift it. She said to Peter Pinch, 'My pumpkin's ripe, Master Pinch. I shall cut it this evening for fear it should spoil. If you like to come up the hill, I'll give you half of it. There's more than I can use.'

Peter Pinch was pleased. He liked having presents given to him, though he never gave any himself. So about six o'clock that evening he went up the hill and found Mrs Puffin with a knife, all ready to cut the pumpkin.

'I'll cut it in half in the garden,' said Mrs Puffin, 'it's too heavy to carry into the house.'

She stooped down to cut it. But as the point of her knife went into the big yellow pumpkin, Mrs Puffin said *'Oh!'* in a startled voice. 'Oh!' she said. 'Oh dear! It's quite hollow. There's nothing in it, Master Pinch!'

She pulled out the knife and there was a little bubbling sound. A tiny stream of water ran out of the hole that the knife had made.

Peter Pinch looked at it angrily. 'That pumpkin's *bad*,' he said. And he turned round and stumped away down the hill, very cross indeed. He was really a very grumpy old man.

Poor Mrs Puffin! She was dreadfully disappointed. She went in and sat down and made herself a large cup of tea for comfort; and she did not go out into the garden again that evening.

She could not bear to look at her beautiful pumpkin.

But she looked out of her window that night before she got into bed. She remembered she had not said good night to the toad. It was a clear night with a great bright moon, and she could see Master Toad quite plainly sitting by the little hollow. The pumpkin lay there, but she could only see part of it. The hollow was almost filled with clear water that shone in the moonlight and the pumpkin was nearly covered.

'It must have held a lot of water. It's a very queer pumpkin,' said Mrs Puffin. Then she called 'Good night' to the toad and she got into bed and went to sleep.

When she came out early next morning with her pails, the first thing she noticed was a little stream – a tiny sparkling stream of water, running from the pumpkin hollow, along the little path that her footsteps had made right across her garden.

'Bless me!' said Mrs Puffin, 'where did that come from? That pumpkin gets queerer and queerer.'

She hurried across her garden to see what could have happened. When she came to the hollow, Master Toad sat by it looking at it solemnly and importantly. Mrs Puffin looked

too; she was looking for her big pumpkin. But there was no pumpkin to be seen. The little hollow was filled with clear water that stirred and rippled gently as if it bubbled up softly from beneath.

'Oh-h-h-h!' said Mrs Puffin – and she said no more for quite a long while – she stood there looking and thinking.

Presently she stooped down and looked close; under the ripples she thought she could see just a gleam of yellow shining. 'Yes,' said Mrs Puffin, and she nodded her head. 'Yes, that's it, there's my pumpkin. It was a fairy pumpkin, sure enough. The Good Folks sent it to me with a spring of water in it for my garden!'

She turned and curtseyed very deeply and gratefully to the toad and said, 'Thank you, Master Toad, my dear.' She was sure he was pleased because his eyes sparkled like little diamonds in the sunlight.

Then Mrs Puffin put her pails on her door-step and hurried down the hill. She stopped to make a curtsey and to say 'Thank you with all my heart,' in the middle of the fairy-ring; and then she ran to Peter Pinch's cottage. She knocked on the door and threw little stones at the window till Peter Pinch opened it and put out his head (with a night-cap on it), very cross indeed at being waked so early.

Mrs Puffin said, 'Peter Pinch! I've got a spring of water in my garden. It's come from my big pumpkin,' which surprised him so much that he came running downstairs in two minutes, all dressed, with his night-cap still on his head.

They went up the hill together; and there was no doubt about it, there really was a spring. The water bubbled up softly in the pool in the hollow and flowed through Mrs Puffin's garden and into the field and down the hill.

'I shall never have to carry pails of water up the hill again,' said Mrs Puffin. And she never did. Spring, summer, autumn, and winter, the water flowed and Mrs Puffin's garden was green and blossoming every year.

She and Master Toad lived there in great happiness and contentment for many years after. And I am glad to say that even Peter Pinch grew better-tempered when Mrs Puffin no longer needed to draw water from his spring. On summer evenings he would often hobble up the hill for a chat; and they would talk together of Mrs Puffin's prize pumpkin, while Master Toad sat by them on the door-step.

The Hill-man's Little Bag

It was a very cold day, just about the time of the New Year. The sun shone brightly, but the north wind blew cold over the moor, and hurried ragged white clouds across a pale blue sky; and as the day went on the clouds came thicker and heavier, till there was scarcely any blue sky left.

'Snow before morning – snow before morning!' said old Mother Jennifer to herself as she sat spinning brown sheep's wool into yarn for stockings, at the door of her little house. It was a very tiny house, tucked away under a hill, built of grey stones piled together, with moss and heather stuffed between them to keep out wind and rain. The roof was of boughs covered with turf and flat stones, and it almost looked like part of the hill except for the smoke that curled out of its chimney. But it was warm and weather-tight, and if you had peeped inside you would have seen that there was a good fire on the hearth, and all along one wall were piled turf and tough old twisted roots for burning. There was room in the little house for Mother Jennifer and her family, and that was all that mattered. The family were close beside her as she sat and spun. There was a nanny-goat nibbling grass, two hens – one brown and one speckled – and a little black cat was washing himself by the warm hearth. They were very good company, Mother Jennifer thought, and she talked to herself and to them most of the day.

Every now and again she looked up and down the road that ran across the moor to see if anyone was in sight. It was a long straight road – as straight as if it had been ruled with a ruler. The Romans had made it long before Mother Jennifer's time, and it ran over hill and dale without a bend or a turning and dropped down into the hollow where the stream flowed and the village lay, and then it climbed the farther hill and stretched away and away to the Great Wall that the Romans built. There the road is still, and you can see it and travel on it if ever you cross the moorland. But there was no sign of anyone upon it that day, and old Mother Jennifer was troubled. 'The miller's man should have been here by now,' she said, 'with the bag of meal. There's not much left in the meal chest, and if it snows deep tonight we shall all be hungry here before the roads are clear again.'

She stayed by the door watching till the sun went down in the west, and shone out under a bank of heavy grey clouds with one last blaze of red light that made the heather and bracken look as though they were lit by the glow of a great fire. Then she went inside and shut the door and stirred the turf on the hearth and put on a piece of wood to make a blaze. Nanny the goat came too, and Speckle and Brownie the hens. Nanny lay down by the turf pile; Speckle and Brownie fluttered to the top of it; and the little black cat stretched himself and looked round and yawned till his little tongue looked like a curly pink feather, and blinked his eyes at Mother Jennifer as much as to say, 'Here we are, all snug and warm together, this cold winter's night.'

Mother Jennifer sat down by the fire and went on spinning. Presently she looked up. 'Is it the wind,' she said, 'that whistles so loudly through the crack of the door?'

The little black cat opened his eyes and stared too; then he got up from his place by the fireside and walked across to the door. He seemed to listen a moment and then he looked at Mother Jennifer and said as plainly as a cat could say with his eyes, 'Open the door, Mother Jennifer!' and Mother Jennifer did as she was bid. She could see nothing at first except darkness, and she could hear nothing but the wind whistling and moaning over the moor. Then suddenly, from somewhere down by her feet, came a long shrill squeal, 'Oe-ee-oo-ee-oo-ee-ee-ee!' Mother Jennifer jumped and somebody gave a little cackling laugh. And the little black cat pounced into the dark as if he was catching a rat, and whisked back again with a little kicking brown bundle and laid it at Mother Jennifer's feet. And as Mother Jennifer stooped to look the brown bundle uncurled

and shook itself and scrambled to its feet. It was a tiny man in brown – the colour of withered bracken – with a red cap and a brown wrinkled face that looked as if he might be as 'old as the hills', as the saying goes.

'Cats never can take a joke,' said the little man in a shrill, squeaky voice. The little black cat walked away in a dignified manner and sat down with his back turned and his tail folded over his toes.

'All I wanted,' said the little man, 'was just to ask for a little meal for my little bag, and he treats me like a rat!'

'People that squeal and squeak like rats should be treated like rats,' said Mother Jennifer severely. 'Last time I saw one of you hill-folk' (a hill-man is a fairy-man, as we should say) '*he* was in mischief too, tangling up my wool as fast as I spun it, and the time before he was tweaking the hens' tails, and they've never laid an egg since, poor creatures. How do I know what mischief you may be up to tonight?'

'Nothing at all – nothing at all, Mother Jennifer,' said the little man. 'I only want to borrow a little meal to make a little cake for my mother's birthday. A thousand years old she is tonight, as you count time, and she fancies an oaten cake. You shall have the meal back in no time at all, I promise you.'

Mother Jennifer stood considering. There was very little meal in the meal-chest, as you know, and every little counts when you have yourself and your cat and a goat and two hens to feed, as she certainly would if the snow came down that night. But it did seem as if a person who had had nine hundred and ninety-nine birthdays, and who was going to have another, ought to have what she wanted. So Mother Jennifer opened the lid of the meal-chest and said to the little brown man, 'Help yourself and welcome.' He scrambled in and began to fill his bag in a great hurry. It was surprising how long he took and how much his bag seemed to hold. Now and again he looked at Mother Jennifer with his sharp brown eyes; but she said nothing to stop him, and at last he had stuffed in every grain there was room for. And then he gave a sudden jump, just like a brown cricket, and was gone, bag and all, out of the door, which was still a crack open, and into the dark. And the little black cat got up and rubbed himself against Mother Jennifer, as much as to say, 'Never mind, *we* know what manners are, even if he doesn't!' Then he curled himself up by the fire, and presently Mother Jennifer went to bed too, and she and all her family slept snug and warm that night.

But outside it snowed and snowed. The heather and the furze and the grass were covered deep; so was the long, straight road, and there were drifts in all the hollows. When Mother Jennifer woke in the morning the little house was almost dark, and she could scarcely open the door for the weight of snow against it. And still the air seemed full of snow, falling, falling, like cold grey feathers from the cold grey sky.

Mother Jennifer milked the nanny-goat and gave her a piece of oatcake, and she gave some to the hens too. Then she set some porridge on to boil, and by and by she and the little black cat had breakfast. There was a little porridge for dinner too, and some for supper as well. But the meal chest was nearly empty, and what could she do when all the meal was gone! She sat by the fire a long time that evening, wondering unhappily whether poor Speckle and Brownie, who had never laid an egg since the hill-man tweaked their tails, would have to be made into chicken broth before the snow melted and the roads were clear again. At last she fell asleep and woke once in the night to hear a little scratching sound as if a rat was burrowing under the hearthstone. She could just see the little black cat sitting beside the red embers, with his ears pricked, watching; so she said, 'Good Pussy' and went to sleep again.

When she woke in the morning and went to the meal-chest to see if she could scrape a little meal together, the first thing she saw was the hill-man's little bag lying on the lid of the chest, stuffed as fat and tight as when he took it away. 'The good little creature!' said Mother Jennifer, 'it will give the hens a meal, poor things.' She opened the bag and began to pour out a little stream of oatmeal for the hens to peck at. It trickled steadily out of the little brown bag – more and more came out till there was quite a little heap; and the bag seemed as full as ever.

'They give good measure,' said Mother Jennifer to the little black cat and the nanny-goat and the hens, who were all watching her. And still the meal poured out and the bag felt fat and firm.

'There's enough to make porridge for today,' she said presently. So she put the little brown bag away in the meal-chest – it still seemed as full as ever – and she cooked a large potful of porridge and they all had some for breakfast and dinner and supper. (You might have been tired of porridge, but Mother Jennifer and the little black cat and the goat and the hens didn't mind; besides, it was very good porridge – very good indeed.) And would you believe it, next day Speckle laid

an egg! The little brown bag still poured out oatmeal to feed them all; and the next day but one Brownie laid an egg! The fairy porridge must have quite cured them of their fright, you see, and there was no more need to think of making them into chicken broth.

So it went on all through the long dark days and nights when the snow lay deep on the moor till one day the wind changed and the sun shone and the drifts melted, and by and by the miller's man was able to come ploughing through the snow with Mother Jennifer's bag of meal.

And what became of the hill-man's bag, do you ask? It vanished away somehow, when the meal-chest was full again. Some folk thought that the nanny-goat had eaten it – goats will eat *anything*, you know. But most people said the hill-man had taken it away again, and I think they were right. Most likely the little black cat knew, but cats don't talk, and he never told anyone what really happened.

The Tale of Mr T. Toad and Mr Littlefrog

THERE was once a pleasant little pool that lay in the corner of a large green field. Tall reeds and rushes grew round it in a ring, and beyond them were thorn bushes and brambles. So the little pool was hidden away from everyone but the birds who flew over it and the dragonflies that sometimes floated above it.

Down among the reeds and rushes on the edge of the pool lived Mr T. Toad and his friend Mr Littlefrog. There were little fishes in the pool and snails and beetles and water spiders and other creepy crawly things, but Mr T. Toad was far larger than any of them – even Mr Littlefrog looked a very small fellow beside him – and there was no doubt he thought himself far more important, and so did everyone else. Nobody ever thought of calling him just 'Mr Toad'; they always called him 'Mr T. Toad'. But no one knew what the T. stood for. It might have been Thomas or it might have been Timothy, or even Theophilus; nobody, not even Mr Littlefrog, quite liked to ask him. But the fishes and the beetles and the water snails and spiders all believed it really stood for 'Tremendous'. He was so very proud and grand.

He would sit for hours by the edge of the pool looking at himself in the clear shining water and puffing himself out to look as large as possible. Mr Littlefrog would sit by his side admiring him too, while the fishes popped their heads out of the water to watch, and said to each other, 'How wonderful to have such a great gentleman living amongst us. He must be quite the largest creature in the whole world.' They really believed it. So did Mr T. Toad and Mr Littlefrog, and nobody ever came near them to tell them they were wrong. The ground was so marshy and the reeds and rushes so tall and thick that no animals came to drink at the little pool.

So there they all lived together – Mr T. Toad, Mr Littlefrog, the beetles, the snails, the water spiders and the fishes – and they would have been as happy as the day was long if it had not been for Mr T. Toad's temper. No one could call him a good-tempered toad. You see, he was quite sure that the pool belonged to him, and was meant for him to use as a looking-glass. And if a fish ruffled it, or a water spider ran across it while he was sitting there, or if Mr Littlefrog jumped in 'plop' and made rings all over it, Mr T. Toad was very angry indeed. Then he would sit scolding while everyone shivered and shook to listen to him; and they were all very thankful when he stopped talking and hopped slowly and grumpily away among the bulrush roots and went to sleep.

The times that everyone looked forward to and enjoyed were the days on which Mr T. Toad changed his coat. He did not change it very often, because you see his coat was not like yours or mine would be. It grew upon his back and fitted him very comfortably, and his new coat grew underneath the old one. When he was ready to change, 'pop' went the old coat and it split, and Mr T. Toad wriggled out of it and rolled it up into a neat little ball and *swallowed* it.

But he did not wish the fishes or the beetles or the water spider or snails – or even his friend Mr Littlefrog – to see him half in and half out of his coat. So when the time came he always hopped away among the reeds and rushes and spent the day where no one could watch him.

Those were beautiful days. The fishes swam

round and round the pool; the water spiders raced across and across; Mr Littlefrog dived in and out; the snails and beetles crawled up and down the stems of the water plants. Everyone played and was happy till Mr T. Toad came hopping heavily out of the bulrushes in his fine new coat and sat down to admire himself in the clear water.

Now Mr Littlefrog, as his name tells you, was quite a small fellow. He was a little brown and yellow frog, very slim and quick in the water and very good-natured and kind to everyone. The fishes and the beetles, the water snails and the spiders all liked him. He had plenty of friends to talk to and play with. Sometimes he felt sorry for Mr T. Toad. 'Poor fellow!' he said to himself. 'It must be very lonely to be so much greater than everyone else that you have nobody grand enough to talk to.'

Well, one day – it was early in the summer and everyone was feeling happy and bright – Mr T. Toad's temper seemed worse than usual. I think it may have been because his coat was growing tight and uncomfortable; it was almost time for him to change it. And as Mr Littlefrog looked at poor sulky Mr T. Toad he said to himself, 'A little friendly conversation would do him a world of good. After all, there may be someone to keep him company. I will see what I can do.' And he turned his back on the pleasant little pool and his happy companions and hopped bravely away through the bulrushes to the edge of the marsh. It was just like travelling through a tall forest would be to you or me, and he had never been so far before. Presently he came to thorn bushes and brambles, and it was not easy to find his way through them; but he managed it at last and found himself in a field of grass and tall yellow buttercups. Through the field there ran a little stream which came from the pool where Mr Littlefrog lived. And munching the long grass by the side of the stream was a creature so much larger than Mr T. Toad that Mr Littlefrog could hardly believe his eyes. It had a brown and white coat and large brown eyes; it had two horns on its head and a long tail. And as Mr Littlefrog stared at it, the creature lifted its head and said, 'Moo-oo-oo-oo-oo,' and from the other end of the field another creature answered, 'Moo-oo-oo-oo-oo!'

It was only a cow, of course, talking to another cow, but it seemed terribly large and noisy to Mr Littlefrog, and he turned round and hopped back to the marsh as quickly as his legs could carry him, with his heart beating very fast and his long legs shaking with fright. He scrambled through the bushes and scuffled through the reeds till he reached the edge of the pool; and there sat Mr T. Toad admiring himself in the clear water while the fishes nudged each other and whispered, 'Keep quiet, he is very cross today.'

'Oh, Mr T. Toad! Mr T. Toad,' said Mr Littlefrog, all out of breath and in a great hurry, 'I have some wonderful news for you.'

And Mr T. Toad, without even turning his head, said, 'Pray do not be so noisy. You disturb me.'

'But Mr T. Toad,' said Mr Littlefrog, 'you need not be lonely any longer, for you are not the largest creature in the world. There are others far larger to keep you company.' And all the fishes poked out their heads to listen, and whispered to each other, 'Fancy that!'

But Mr T. Toad, still without turning his head, said, 'Pooh!' which was very rude of him. One should not say 'Pooh' to kind people who are trying to tell one things.

'But it is quite true, Mr T. Toad,' said Mr Littlefrog. 'I have seen the creature.'

'Pooh!' said Mr T. Toad again. 'Is it as large as this?' And he puffed out his sides till he looked like a fat little puppy-dog.

'*Much* larger,' said Mr Littlefrog.

'Rubbish!' said Mr T. Toad, and he puffed out his sides till he looked like a football.

'Much, *much* larger, dear Mr T. Toad,' said Mr Littlefrog earnestly.

'*Stuff!*' said Mr T. Toad very loudly. And he gave a great puff, and 'pop!' his coat split all down the middle of his back. And a small fish, whose manners were not very good, laughed till it swallowed some water and choked, and then all the other fishes laughed too. They really could not help it.

But Mr T. Toad was very angry and very much upset, and he turned round and hopped away among the bulrush roots as fast as he could go, with his torn coat flapping round him like a mackintosh.

And he never came back! Perhaps he hopped

away and found the cow and settled down in the field by the side of the stream; perhaps he found another pond where nobody could laugh at him, and lived there all alone. Perhaps he tried so hard to blow himself up as big as a cow that he blew himself up altogether and flew into little bits. Nobody knows.

Mr Littlefrog and the fishes and the beetles and the water spiders and the snails often used to wonder what had become of him, but they could never really be sorry he had gone. He had been so cross and they were so comfortable without him. So they talked and played their games and chased each other round and round, and ruffled the water just as much as they pleased. And they all lived as happy as the day was long in that pleasant little pool down among the reeds and bulrushes, where nobody ever came to trouble them or scold them.

Papa Hedgehog and the Hare

It had been a very wet day. The rain had poured steadily from the grey sky; the birds had stayed quiet in the trees and hedges; and all the little creatures of the woods and fields had kept snug in their holes and burrows. But towards evening the rain had stopped, the sky cleared, and the sun shone out as if he was pleased to see all the world looking so bright and clean after the washing the clouds had given it.

Papa Hedgehog came creeping out of his hole (it was underneath a thick blackthorn bush, just on the edge of the wood). He looked round him. 'I think,' he said to his wife, 'I shall take a little walk in the cabbage field. It is a fine evening and so fresh after the rain. Really it is a pleasure to watch those cabbages grow, so large and handsome as they are and so cool and shady when the sun is hot. Besides,' said Papa Hedgehog, 'one finds delightful company there. The beetles are quite the pleasantest I have ever met.'

(I am afraid the beetles were more pleasant to Papa Hedgehog than he was to the beetles. For to tell the truth, he liked them so much that he *ate* them! But that has nothing to do with this story.)

'Do go, my love,' said Mamma Hedgehog. 'I will follow you as soon as possible. As you say, it is a fine evening, and a walk will do you good.'

So Papa Hedgehog trotted off on his four little legs, with his bright eyes and sharp nose, finding all kinds of good things to see and smell. The cabbages certainly were very handsome; their leaves were so broad and firm and green, and large, round, shining raindrops lay on them, sparkling like the clearest crystal. Papa Hedgehog sipped a little water from the hollow of a leaf and trotted on, keeping a sharp look-out for the beetles whose company he enjoyed so much.

Suddenly there was a scurry and a scuffle among the cabbages, and – almost on top of Papa Hedgehog – out bounced a large brown Hare, sending a shower of raindrops flying and upsetting quite a little pool of water from a big leaf over Papa Hedgehog's head and into his eyes and nose. Papa Hedgehog was startled, and he did as he always does when anything frightens him – he rolled himself into a tight little ball and stayed quite still for some minutes. Then he cautiously began to unroll, and the first thing his little bright eyes lit upon was the Hare sitting there laughing.

Papa Hedgehog sneezed and shook his head. He was a good-natured little fellow, and though the Hare had startled him he was not vexed. But if you or I had upset water all over a respectable old gentleman who was out for an evening walk we should at least say, 'I am sorry.' The Hare did nothing of the kind. He laughed and laughed till he nearly fell over with laughing. 'You can't think how funny you looked,' he said. 'You hedgehogs are funny anyhow, all just alike, with your round bodies and crooked legs. But I never saw you look so ridiculous as you did just now. Oh, dear! Oh, dear! Oh, dear!' said the Hare. And this time he really did fall over sideways with laughing.

'My legs are very good and useful legs,' said Papa Hedgehog in a dignified voice, 'and they are much better than your *manners*, which are very bad indeed. Good evening,' said Papa Hedgehog, and he turned round to go home again, for the Hare had quite upset him and spoiled his evening walk. But the Hare shouted

'Crooked-legs' so loudly after him that he stopped. A thought came into his little head, and he smiled to himself. 'The Hare says we are all alike and all ridiculous, does he? Well, he shall see. It is time he had a lesson,' said Papa Hedgehog.

So he came trotting back. 'My legs may be crooked,' said he to the Hare, 'but that is no reason why you should laugh at them. Let us run a race and see who is the winner. You may be very much surprised!'

'A race indeed,' said the Hare; 'I can run a mile while you creep a yard.'

'Try and see,' said Papa Hedgehog. 'It is moonlight tonight, and the next field has been ploughed. I will run up one furrow. You shall run up the next. When you get to the end you shall see!'

'Very well, old Crooked-legs,' said the rude Hare; 'I'll be there, waiting to laugh at you.' And away he went with a hop, skip and jump of his long legs, over the bank, through the hedge, and across the fields, while Papa Hedgehog trotted home to his wife.

'My love,' said he, 'we are to play a little game with the Hare tonight,' and he told Mamma Hedgehog his plan; and they both chuckled so much that they rolled themselves into tight balls with laughing.

Presently – just a little while before the moon rose – Mamma Hedgehog trotted out and away into the dark. Papa Hedgehog had told her where to go and what to do, and by-and-by, when the moon was up, he followed. Past the cabbage field, where the cabbages looked as if they were made of ivory and silver in the moonlight, he scuttled – through the hedge – and there lay the ploughed field with its long, deep, dark furrows. A minute or two later the Hare came running swiftly along the edge of the field. 'Hullo, old Crooked-legs,' he said, 'are you ready to start?'

'Yes,' said Papa Hedgehog. 'I am quite ready. I will take the furrow nearest the hedge. You take the next. Are you ready? *Off!*'

Away went the Hare, bounding easily up the furrow. He did not hurry very much; he thought there was no need. 'Poor fellow,' he said scornfully to himself, 'his crooked legs must be working very hard to carry that fat little round body. Probably he will die for want of breath before he is half-way up the furrow. Well, it is not my fault,' said the Hare. And with one long jump he reached the end of the course. But just as he got there, a little head with two bright eyes and a sharp nose peeped out of the next furrow, and a little voice said, 'Here I am, you see!' It was Mamma Hedgehog who was waiting for him;

but the Hare did not know that. One hedgehog looked just like another to him, especially by moonlight, and he thought Papa Hedgehog had got there first! His big eyes nearly popped out of his head with surprise. He did not wait one minute to think. 'I'll beat you next time,' he said in a great hurry; and he turned round and flew down the furrow, leaving Mamma Hedgehog chuckling behind him.

'Fancy old Crooked-legs running so fast,' said the Hare to himself as he ran, 'but he can never keep it up. He is probably dead by now!'

But when he was nearly at the end of the course a little head with a sharp nose and two bright eyes peeped out of the next furrow, and a little voice said, 'Here I am, you see!' It was Papa Hedgehog, who had been sitting there very comfortably, waiting for him.

'You!' said the Hare, very much out of breath. 'Yes, *me*,' said Papa Hedgehog. 'I'll beat you next time,' said the Hare, and he raced up the furrow again. But Mamma Hedgehog was ready for him, and back went the Hare once more. Up and down he raced, up and down. The time went by, and the full moon came sailing higher and higher up the sky. It seemed as if there was a broad smile on its face at the sight of the Hare running so fast along the furrow, while Papa and

Mamma Hedgehog waited for him, one at each end. Up and down he went, up and down; he was all out of breath, he was giddy and panting and puzzled. It was really a terrible race! And at last he was so tired he really could run no more; right in the middle of the furrow he tumbled down and went to sleep, and never woke up till sunrise next morning. And Papa and Mamma Hedgehog trotted off chuckling, to find their supper, and then they went home to sleep.

As for the Hare, next time he saw Papa Hedgehog coming, he went a long way round to avoid meeting him. He was afraid Papa Hedgehog would laugh! How the tale of the race came to be told I do not know; Papa and Mamma Hedgehog are quiet folk and do not talk much, and certainly the Hare never spoke of it. Perhaps it was the Man in the Moon! But whoever told it first, it has certainly been told a great many times since, and now I am telling it again for you.

The Tale of the Tiny Tree

THIS is a story about a beech-tree that I know.

You would be surprised if you could see it, I think. As you know, most beech-trees are tall, with silvery-grey trunks and strong branches that stretch far and wide, and their beautiful sprays of green leaves toss and wave in the wind. But this is a very tiny beech-tree – only thirty centimetres tall and its little trunk is about as thick as my wrist and its branches do not stretch any farther than a very small umbrella. But it is not a baby tree. It is quite grown up. In fact, before long it will be twenty years old. I will tell you its story, and then you will understand how it comes to be so small.

Twenty years ago, high up on the side of one of the great green hills that are called the Downs, there stood a beech-wood of large and lovely trees. Their branches swept down almost to the ground. If you crept under them when the leaves were out, it was like being in a great green tent.

Every year in summer-time, beech-nuts, in their pointed furry, green sheaths, grew thick on the leafy sprays. There were so many of them that they weighed the branches down. When autumn came, the ground beneath the trees was covered with beech-nut sheaths. They had curled back their pointed tips and opened, and inside each, on a pale brown satiny lining, were four glossy brown beech-nuts. The beech-nuts fell out and lay scattered on the ground all ready to grow into beech-trees.

But very few of them ever got the chance. Beech-nuts are very good to eat, and flocks of big grey pigeons came flying over the Downs to settle down and gobble them. Squirrels frolicked down from the upper branches of the beech-trees and gathered the nuts with quick busy little paws, and hurried up the tree-trunks to store them away in hollows for their winter food. Wood-mice nibbled them and carried them away to their holes. And big bright-coloured pheasants with their brown wives came strutting and stalking, to swallow the nuts as fast as they could peck them up.

So, not very many beech-nuts were left to sink down into the soft thick carpet of fallen leaves and lie there till spring came. But some were lucky; and one little beech-nut fell in a very good place, right into the middle of a patch of thick, soft green moss. It slipped down among the moss stems and was hidden. No mouse or squirrel spied it with his bright black eye and no sharp beak of pigeon or pheasant pecked it out. There it lay, snug and safe from frost and cold when winter came; and the rain soaked it till its brown coat grew soft and split.

Presently spring came round again and the sunshine warmed the earth and the beech-nut woke up and put out a little white root through the hole in its brown coat. The root drank up food from the warm wet earth and the beech-nut swelled till its coat burst quite in two and a pale green shoot pushed out of it, up through the moss towards the light. Two strong thick little leaves unfolded and spread themselves out, in the sunshine and air. The beech-nut was getting ready to grow into a tree.

All through that summer the two little leaves stretched themselves out like two little wings. They gathered strength from air and rain and light and they drank food from the earth beneath. They were not a bit like beech-leaves; they were more like the first two leaves of a bean. But late in the summer a tiny green leaf-bud pushed up between them and uncurled itself, and then came another. They were real baby beech-leaves. When winter came the little leaves curled up and fell off, but a strong little brown stem was left standing in the clump of green moss. It had a brown bud at the top and its little root went down into the soft brown earth. And when spring came again the brown bud unfolded and the little stem put out its green leaves. It was only six centimetres tall, but it had begun to be a tree!

It grew another three centimetres that year and its stem was thicker. When next spring came its little leaves fluttered in the wind, and it looked like a fairy beech-tree from a tiny fairy forest.

Then, one sunshiny day in June, two people on bicycles came riding slowly along the green grass road that led to the beech-wood. Their names were Mr and Mrs Berry-Brown and they were out for a holiday. They leaned their bicycles against the silvery-grey trunk of a big beech-tree on the edge of the wood, and they sat down in the shade and ate sandwiches and cake from the neat little white packets that Mr Berry-Brown had carried in his bicycle basket. When they had finished they dug a little hole deep down under the roots of the trees, and there they buried all the sandwich papers and covered them tidily with earth and moss.

Then they sat still very comfortably under the tree. It was like the nicest kind of summer-house, with a floor of red-brown leaves with spots and splashes of sunlight, and a roof of green leaves with sparkles and gleams of sunshine. If you stooped down quite low and looked out you could see the green country going up hill and down dale, with the soft wind blowing, and the grass and flowers nodding and dancing, and hot bright light everywhere under the bright blue sky.

It was so cool and pleasant that they stayed there quite a long while – much longer than they meant to stay – for to tell the truth, they both fell fast asleep. And presently Mrs Berry-Brown woke up and blinked because a sunbeam was tickling her nose. She was lying with her head on a mossy root, and just in front of her eyes was a patch of bright green moss. And in the middle of the moss grew a tiny beech-tree just ten centimetres high.

Mrs Berry-Brown said, 'That is the dearest little tree I have ever seen. I must take it home with me!' She woke Mr Berry-Brown and they dug very carefully with their pocket-knives and a stick till they came safely to the end of the little

beech-tree's root, which was surprisingly long and strong. At last, they lifted it up with plenty of earth and soft green moss, and they wrapped it in long grass to keep it cool and put it in the bicycle basket. Then they mounted their bicycles and rode away.

So the little beech-tree left its mother-tree and its home in the wood and went to live with Mr and Mrs Berry-Brown. They lived in a town and they had no garden, so the little tree was planted in a large Japanese bowl and kept in the house. They were very kind to it. They watered it well and washed its leaves and put it out on the window-ledge to give it a bath of air and sunshine. I think at first it was lonely and it missed all the other little green things that lived near it in the beech-wood; but it was a cheerful little tree and it went on growing and doing its best.

Every year in spring-time its slender pointed buds opened and fresh young green beech-leaves spread themselves out. Every year it grew a little taller and its little trunk was thicker, and its little branches crooked themselves and stretched wider like a real little forest tree.

So the years went by and presently Mr and Mrs Berry-Brown moved to another town and settled down in a house with a fine large garden. Next door to them lived Mrs Berry-Brown's sister, whose garden was larger still.

The beech-tree went with them to the new house of course, but it did not live indoors any longer. 'It will be lovely for it to be out of doors again,' said Mrs Berry-Brown. So they carried it into the garden, and placed it, still in its Japanese bowl, in a sunny spot.

It was very happy at first, out in the air and sunshine. The sparrows came and chattered to it. The bees buzzed past and said, 'Plee-ee-ee-z-z-z-ed to zee-ee you,' to it. Sometimes a white butterfly floated by and settled on a leaf for a little talk. A robin-redbreast made great friends with the little tree and a pair of thrushes made a nest in a bush near-by. The tree spread out its leaves and fluttered them in the spring wind and enjoyed it all.

But as the days grew hotter, the sun blazed down on the garden and the tree felt very thirsty and dry. Mr and Mrs Berry-Brown were very busy that summer. Mr Berry-Brown was writing a book and Mrs Berry-Brown was making curtains and cushions and chair-covers for the new house. Nobody seemed to have time to remember to water the little beech-tree. The earth in its bowl grew hard and dusty, its roots were shut up tight, all pressed together inside the bowl, and they grew cramped and dry. Its gay green leaves curled up and fell off. Long before winter came the little tree was quite bare. That was sad enough and very uncomfortable too. But what troubled the tree most was that it had scarcely been able to get any buds ready for the next spring.

'I can't *think* what they will think of me next year,' it said anxiously to the robin one day. 'I have only two buds that are fit to be seen. The others are so tiny and so dry. I have done my best, but I am afraid I shall look very shabby.'

The robin was very sorry for the poor little tree. He came every day to sing to it, which was very comforting. But that seemed all that he could do.

Then came winter, with rain and cold and snow. Nobody remembered the tree. Mr Berry-Brown was still busy with his book and Mrs Berry-Brown was busy too with all kinds of things, in the house and out of the house.

The tree held up its little bare branches bravely, but it had been hungry and thirsty all through the summer, and the cold pinched it hard. When spring came most of the little dried-up buds had no strength to unfold, and even if they did the little leaves soon curled up and died; it could only manage two good green leaves that spring. They were at the very end of the tip-top bough. But they were fresh and strong, and they danced and fluttered in the wind as if they were saying, 'Here we are – still a-blowing and a-growing – here we are!'

One morning in early summer, Mrs Berry-Brown and her sister were walking down the garden path. They came where the little tree stood – looking very brown and dry, but bravely holding out its leaves like two little green flags.

Mrs Berry-Brown looked at it and said, 'Oh *dear*!'

Mrs Berry-Brown's sister looked at it and she said in a firm voice, 'That little tree wants taking care of. Would you like me to see what I can do?'

And Mrs Berry-Brown, who was really very sorry she had forgotten the poor little tree, said, 'Yes, *please* do.'

'We will plant it in the Rock Garden,' said Mrs Berry-Brown's sister.

So they picked up the tree in its bowl and they carried it through the gate in the wall into the next garden. The little beech-tree wondered where it was going.

They went past the lily-pond where tall irises, purple and white, and yellow, and blue were unfolding their lovely flowers. They went past the long border, where big scarlet poppies grew and blue and white campanulas, and columbines, pink and yellow and white, purple and plum-colour and blue, nodded at the white pinks that smelled so sweet. They came to a little twisty path that wound in and out among big, rough, grey stones, and all among the stones were flowers that spread out like little bright mats and carpets of colour. They were blue, they were yellow, they were pink, they were orange, they were red. The beech-tree had never seen anything half so gay. It felt even its roots curling with happiness when Mrs Berry-Brown's sister said, 'We will put it *here*,' and she pointed to a bare place by the side of a big stone.

So Mrs Berry-Brown and her sister pushed the stone to one side to make a larger space. They fetched a fork and dug, and loosened the soil.

They scooped a hole and dug deeper to make a nice soft place. They filled a large watering-can with water and soaked the earth.

Then they carefully lifted the little tree out of the bowl where it had lived so long, and they spread out its dry roots in the soft wet earth. They poured more water for the thirsty roots to drink, and they put back the earth and pressed it firmly round the tree. There stood the little beech-tree in the middle of the Rock Garden with the bright carpet of many coloured flowers spread round it. It held up its two little leaves to the sunshine, and it said thank you with all its little heart.

And that is where it is standing now. I saw it myself this year. It is still a tiny tree, and it always will be. It has grown so accustomed to living in a bowl and to being very small, that it does not want to be any bigger. But each year it has as many green leaves as any little tree could possibly wish for. The birds (especially the robin) and the bees and the butterflies and the flowers are its friends. Mr Berry-Brown and Mrs Berry-Brown and Mrs Berry-Brown's sister come to look at it very often, and they bring their friends to see it too.

It is a happy, friendly, contented little tree.

The Home in the Hood

Once upon a time there was a little house that stood by the seashore. If you think of the very tiniest house you ever saw, that would still be too big for this little house. It was so small that all it held was a heap of dry branches and fern for a bed and a log for a seat. It was built of grey stone piled together without mortar, the roof was of boughs thatched with golden-brown reeds from the marshes near, and it had neither a chimney nor a door.

But outside the little grey house there was a gay little garden, and at the time the story happened it was very gay indeed. There were wallflowers, yellow and brown – smelling so sweet in the sunshine – there were big yellow double daffodils and little blue hyacinths, sweet yellow alyssum and cushiony white arabis. The little honey bees hummed and the big bumble bees buzzed in and out, and the man who lived in the little grey house sang to himself as he worked in the garden.

Who was the man, do you say? Well, his name was St Malo, and this story happened so long ago that nobody knows very much about him, but we do know that he came from Britain to teach the poor people of Brittany. And it was in Brittany, just where the town of St Malo stands now, that he built his tiny house and made his gay little garden.

St Malo was very busy in his garden that spring morning. There was so much to be done. A little rose bush had nearly been blown away by the winds from the sea. That must be tied up. The weeds were coming up thick among the flowers, and the grass was trying to choke them: all that must be cleared away. Then there were the vines in his little vineyard to be tied up to strong sticks driven deep into the earth. St Malo worked hard, the spring sun was hot. Presently he took off his long brown robe, with its pointed hood that he pulled over his head in cold, wet weather, and hung it up on the bough of a tree. Then he went on with his work.

A little while after two small brown wrens

came flying into the garden. Wrens are tiny birds, but they have quite big voices, and these wrens were talking very loud indeed.

'My dear,' said Father Wren, 'I cannot think why you won't settle this year. The blackbirds and the thrushes and the starlings are all building, the swallows will be here soon, and we have not even chosen a place. You know it is quite time we began to build.'

'Well,' said Mrs Wren, in a high, shrill chirp, 'you must remember, Father Wren, that *I* have to sit on the nest. It is all very well for you. You can fly about, but I must find a really *comfortable* place to sit, and I have not seen anything that pleases me yet . . . But what is that over there?' chirped Mrs Wren suddenly, and with a quick little flit and flutter she flew – where do you think? Straight into the pointed brown hood of St Malo's robe as it hung on the bough of the tree. She dived right down to the very bottom, and Father Wren heard her giving little surprised chirps of delight. 'So soft,' said Mrs Wren, 'so warm, so sheltered, so well hidden. I shall certainly stay here in this beautiful nest I have found. It is not the least use your talking like that, Father Wren.' (Father Wren was trying to say something which sounded like, 'But – but – but, my *dear* . . .') 'Go and find me something to eat;

all this excitement has made me quite hungry.'

Father Wren knew it was no use to talk. Mrs Wren was a sweet little brown bird, but she could be very obstinate. So he flew away talking to himself. 'Those brown feathers hanging on that tree' (he meant St Malo's robe. Of course he thought all clothes were feathers) – 'those brown feathers belong to that two-legged creature that is scratching and pecking about this place. Mother Wren will be very much surprised and upset when he comes to take them away. But it is no use my talking. I will go and find something for her to eat. She will need it!'

So Father Wren flew away and came back and busily fed Mother Wren. The wallflowers and the daffodils nodded in the wind, the bees buzzed among the flowers, and St Malo worked away in his garden. And all the time Mother Wren sat quiet, tucked away deep down in the bottom of St Malo's hood. The sun sank lower and lower in the blue sky, and presently the bees went home, and he too went to sleep with his head under his little brown wing.

So there the hood hung all through the weeks that followed. Sometimes there was rain, sometimes the wind blew stormy and cold, and St Malo must have missed his warm woollen robe, but he left it hanging on the bough, and never

thought of taking it away. He knew about the little family that lived there; he watched Father and Mother Wren fly in and out feeding them, there were a great many baby wrens, quite ten, or perhaps twelve, I think. At last they peeped out and learned to flutter about the garden, and after that they all flew away; and not till then did kind St Malo take down his robe from the bough where it had hung so long to make a home for Father Wren and Mother Wren and all their fluffy family.

Nowadays there is a busy town on the place where St Malo's little house stood and his garden and vineyard grew. The vineyard is gone long, long ago, and there are families of boys and girls in the town instead of families of wrens! But St Malo is not forgotten, for the town is called by his name, and in the country round you will find plenty of people who can tell you the story of the saint who was so kind to little Father and Mother Wren.

The Tale of Mrs Button's Christmas Tree

ONCE upon a time – and not very long ago – a little old woman lived in a little house in a little green lane. Her name was Mrs Button and she was rather like her name. She was small and very neat, with round, rosy cheeks and two bright blue eyes. She was smiling and cheerful; and the day this story begins she was very busy indeed, because she was getting ready to go to town by the twelve o'clock bus to do her Christmas shopping.

Her two grandchildren, Billie and Bella, were staying with her for Christmas. Billie was six and Bella was four. Mrs Button had made up her mind that it should be an extra-special kind of Christmas. She had been saving up her money and she was going to have a Christmas tree. It was to be a big surprise for Billie and Bella.

She finished everything in the house and then she swept the garden path. 'Just to leave everything straight,' said Mrs Button. There had been a wind in the night and the last dry leaves from the hedges had blown across the garden. I think perhaps you might have smiled if you had seen Mrs Button sweeping, because she was so small and her broom was so big. It was not a broom with bristles; it was a long-handled broom made of a big bunch of birch twigs, long and shaggy, and bushy – the kind of broom that gardeners use. That is the best kind for sweeping a garden and by the time Mrs Button had finished, the path looked as if it had been brushed and combed and *scrubbed*, it was so clean.

Mrs Button set the broom in the corner of the porch. It was a new one, and she was careful to put it with its twigs upwards, which is the way a birch-broom should always stand, so that the twigs do not get bent or broken.

'There,' she said, 'that's all tidy, and now I must get my things on and catch the bus.'

Ten minutes later, Mrs Button and her shopping-bag, with Billie and Bella beside her, went hurrying down the lane that led to the high-road. Billie and Bella were going to have dinner with old Mr Peck, who lived at the corner of the lane. They were going to stay with him until their granny came home. Mr Peck had a tabby cat and a tame jackdaw and a brown spaniel and a large fat rabbit called Susan, so they would have plenty of company all the afternoon.

Mrs Button put them in at Mr Peck's gate and saw them go trotting up the garden path. Then she stood by the signpost and waited for the bus.

It was a very cold day, with a very grey sky – not a very cheerful kind of day. But Mrs Button was so excited to think of all the things she was going to buy, that she scarcely thought about the weather, except to say to herself, 'I'm sure I hope it won't snow before I get home.'

Presently the long, red bus came rumbling along the road and Mrs Button, with her shopping-bag and her purse, climbed into it – there was just one seat to spare – and away she went to town. She had a little list in her pocket and she put on her spectacles and began to read it over. Then she counted her money and then she put away her spectacles. Then she got them out again and read the list again and counted her money once more. And after that, she discovered she had been sitting next to a friend of hers all the time; so they chatted very pleasantly all the way to town.

When Mrs Button got out of the bus, the very first thing she did was to buy her Christmas tree.

It was a nice sturdy, little green fir-tree in a smart red pot. The man in the shop rolled it round carefully in a big sheet of brown paper and put a label on it addressed to 'Mrs Button, Rose Cottage, Green Lane,' and he promised to send it to the Red Bus Station in plenty of time to catch the four o'clock bus.

Then Mrs Button went to the toyshop and bought a doll for Bella and a horse and cart for Billie. Then she went to the sweet-shop and bought half a pound of mixed sweets – pear-drops and acid-drops, raspberry drops and barley-sugar-drops, some toffee and some coconut ice. And then she went to the department store to buy the decorations for the Christmas tree.

It was lovely in the department store. The big shop was warm and full of people all talking and laughing and buying Christmas things. There were long wreaths of coloured paper, red and white and green and blue, across and across the shop. There were all kinds of bright-coloured sparkling decorations. Mrs Button looked and looked and then she began to buy.

She bought a box of little lights – red and green and white and pink and yellow and blue. She bought bright little ornaments to fasten to the branches. She bought long, shining strings of silvery tinsel. She bought some crackers and

NTA'S GROTTO
IXPEN
ORE
PY
MA

some little gold and silver balls to dangle from the tree. She bought little painted angels and some red and green paper and a packet of sparkling powder that looked like hoar-frost on the grass. And then she saw a tiny fairy doll, all in white with silvery wings and a wand with a star, and she said, 'I *must* have that.' So she bought the fairy, too, and then she said to herself, 'Selina Button, that's *enough*!'

She looked at the big clock in the High Street as she came out of the department store, and it was just five minutes to four.

'Dear, dear, *dear*,' said Mrs Button, 'I shall miss the bus.' She hugged all her parcels very tight and ran down the High Street like a hen in a hurry. She scrambled into the bus just as it was moving off. There was no seat to spare and Mrs Button had to stand. She was so busy holding on to all her parcels and trying to find the money for her fare that she could think of nothing else for a time. But all of a sudden, as the bus came to the turning where the shops ended and the little houses and gardens began, poor Mrs Button gave a loud shriek. 'Oh dear! Oh dear! Oh dear,' she said, 'I've left the Christmas tree behind. I quite forgot to ask for it at the parcel office.' And so she had!

Everybody in the bus was very sorry for her.

But nobody could do anything about it. The bus could not go back, and neither could Mrs Button. There was no other bus that night. So she was obliged to stay where she was while the big red bus carried her farther and farther away from her Christmas tree.

The conductor was very kind about it. He said, 'I'll bring the tree and leave it at the corner house next time I come this way.' But that would not be till after Christmas, and what was the use of a Christmas tree when Christmas was over and gone?

Poor Mrs Button felt as if she could cry. But she said to herself, 'Now, Selina Button, just you make the best of it and never mind the rest of it.' She thanked the conductor and when she got to Mr Peck's corner she said good night to him and to all the other kind people on the bus; and she trotted up the garden path and called for Billie and Bella.

It had just begun to snow, and when Billie and Bella came running out, all warm and wrapped-up and rosy, they thought that was great fun. Mr Peck and Mrs Button were not so sure about it. 'It looks like a big snow,' said Mr Peck; and Mrs Button said, 'So it does. We must hurry home. Thank you kindly, Mr Peck, for looking after my chicks and a very good night to you.' Then they all three went hurrying home with Mrs Button's little electric torch switched on to light the way. Billie carried it and it certainly was a help.

When they got home Mrs Button put all her parcels in the parlour and shut the door. 'That's a Christmas secret,' she said. Then they all had hot bread-and-milk for supper and Billie and Bella climbed into their warm beds and went fast asleep.

When they were safely in bed, Mrs Button sat down to think. 'Whatever can I do?' she said. 'A Christmas tree I *will* have, by hook or by crook. Perhaps I could get a bough from the hedge. It would be better than nothing.'

She went to the door and opened it – and she could see nothing but snow! It was coming down like a curtain. There was no wind, not a breath, but the tiny flakes fell fast and thick. Mrs Button stood in the porch and looked out.

'If I went out in that,' she said, 'even as far as the hedge, I might lose myself and never get back. *That* would never do.' She shook her head sadly – and something tickled her cheek. It was the birch-broom. It was standing where she had left it in the corner of the porch. It looked very big and bushy in the lamplight.

Mrs Button looked at it. '*Well*,' she said,

'Selina Button, make the best of it and never mind the rest of it. I declare,' said Mrs Button, 'I've got an idea!'

She picked up the broom and carried it into the house. She got her little saw and sawed off a good bit of the broom-stick. She took the kitchen pail and stood the birch-broom in it and wedged it tight with two bricks from the scullery and an old cushion and some dusters.

'I believe it will *do*,' said Mrs Button, and she put the pail and the broom in the parlour and locked the door and went to bed.

Next day, as you know, was Christmas, and in the evening Mr Peck was coming to tea. Billie and Bella were put to sleep in the afternoon because they were going to sit up later than usual in the evening. While they were asleep Mrs Button was very busy in the parlour. She came out, looking pleased and smiling at tea-time and after tea she popped in again. They could hear her striking matches. Then she called, 'Come in, Mr Peck. Come in, my duckies.'

So in they came, and what do you think they saw? The candles on the mantelpiece had been lighted. There was a lovely fire in the grate. The round table had been pushed back and in the middle of the room there stood a Christmas tree!

It was in a large, magnificent pot, wrapped in

red and white and blue. You would never have guessed that the pot was Mrs Button's kitchen pail with her Coronation decorations round it. The tree was taller than Billie – it came about up to Mrs Button's shoulder. It was a bare, bushy little tree with a short, thick stem – but it sparkled most beautifully all over, as if it was covered with silver frost. On the very tip-top twigs of the tree stood a shining fairy with silver wings and a wand; and fastened to the twigs, in a ring round the fairy, were six little angels. There were lots of tiny lanterns, all different colours – red, green

and white, pink, yellow and blue, and they were all alight.

Below them sparkling strings of silver hung down like silver rain and were looped up round the sides of the tree. Little balls of gold and silver bobbed and dangled from its slender branches and shiny little bags of red and green paper hung from loops of bright green string. They looked as if they were full of something good, and if you remember Mrs Button's shopping I expect you can guess what was in them! And at the foot of the tree, leaning against the stem, which was most beautifully wrapped in red and green paper, were a Red Riding-hood doll in a scarlet cloak, and a green cart with a dapple-grey horse. And you know who they were for!

You cannot think how pretty it all looked, sparkling and shining in the firelight and candle-light. Bella and Billie thought the tree was lovely and so did Mr Peck. They all joined hands – Mrs Button and Mr Peck and Billie and Bella – and they danced round the Christmas tree, singing, 'Here we go round the Christmas tree, the Christmas tree, the Christmas tree. Here we go round the Christmas tree, on Christmas Day in the evening.'

Then there were sweets for everybody and

crackers to pull. Bella hugged the Red Riding-hood doll and Billie pulled the green cart with the grey horse round and round the room. And presently they sat by the fire and Mr Peck told a Christmas story and they sang 'While shepherds watched their flocks by night' before they went to bed.

Mr Peck stayed to have supper with Mrs Button after she had put Billie and Bella to bed. When it was time for him to go home, he looked at her with his eyes twinkling and he said, 'Thank you, Mrs Button, for a very pleasant evening. It was a handsome Christmas tree. I don't know that I ever saw one quite like it!'

And Mrs Button made him a little curtsey and her eyes twinkled too, and she said, 'Thank you, Mr Peck. I don't suppose you ever did. That was a *broom-tree*, you see!'

And as no doubt you have guessed, that is exactly what it was!